Templar Properties in France during and after the Order's Suppression (1307–1325)

Examining the administration of assets during the trial of the French Templars, as well as the settlement process that took place after the Order's dissolution, this book focuses on material aspects of the proceedings in France that have never been analysed in detail. These include the conflicts that accompanied the seizure of property, the actions of administrators, and the thefts and abuses that occurred at every stage of the process. The actions of Philip the Fair's sons to finalise the takeover of the Templars' property by the Hospitallers are also discussed. This book draws on documents that have not been used in previous research, including the report on the investigation conducted between 1322 and 1325 as part of the agreements concluded by Louis X and Philip V with the Hospitallers. This document is unknown to modern scholars and contains valuable information about the recovery of Templar property and the prosecution of abuses committed during this process.

This book adopts a new approach that departs from the dominant view that considers the Templar affair through the lens of the political aspirations of its most important participants, and this allows new insights into the circumstances and consequences of the Templar trial.

Of particular interest to scholars and students of the history of the Knights Templar, this book will also appeal to historians of the Knights Hospitaller, France under the last Capetians, and the papacy at the beginning of the 14th century.

Magdalena Satora is associate professor at the Cardinal Stefan Wyszynski University in Warsaw, Poland. She completed a doctorate in Medieval History at Nicolaus Copernicus University in Toruń in 2010, and she obtained habilitation in 2021 based on the work *Processus contra Templarios in Francia. Procès-verbaux de la procédure menée par la commission pontificale à Paris (1309–1311)*. Her research interests focus on the history of the Crusades, the Knights Templar, and late medieval France.

The Military Religious Orders: History, Sources, and Memory
Edited by Jochen Burgtorf and Nicholas Morton

The military religious orders were initially established in the twelfth century to care for and protect western pilgrims in the Holy Land. They later helped to defend the crusader states, participated in the Iberian Reconquista, and eventually played a significant role in warfare, charity, commerce, colonization, and cross-cultural encounters in Europe, the Mediterranean World, and even the New World. *The Military Religious Orders: History, Sources, and Memory* stimulate research on this fascinating phenomenon.

Templar Properties in France during and after the Order's Suppression (1307–1325)

Magdalena Satora

Routledge
Taylor & Francis Group
LONDON AND NEW YORK

First published 2027
by Routledge
4 Park Square, Milton Park, Abingdon, Oxon OX14 4RN

and by Routledge
605 Third Avenue, New York, NY 10158

Routledge is an imprint of the Taylor & Francis Group, an informa business

British Library Cataloguing-in-Publication Data
A catalogue record for this book is available from the British Library

ISBN: 9781041245148 (hbk)
ISBN: 9781041245155 (pbk)
ISBN: 9781003742241 (ebk)

DOI: 10.4324/9781003742241

Typeset in Times New Roman
by codeMantra

In memory of my Mum,
Mirosława Satora
(1953–2026)

Contents

Acknowledgements

This book is the result of a project funded by the National Science Centre in Poland (project number 2020/37/B/HS3/00329).

I would like to thank everyone who helped me with my research and writing of this book over the course of several years. In particular, I would like to thank Sławomir Jóźwiak, whose advice and comments have been invaluable to me over the years. My thanks also go to the staff at the Bibliothèque nationale de France, the Archives Nationales in Paris and the Archives départementales de la Haute-Garonne in Toulouse, among other institutions where I conducted my research, for their assistance. My thanks also go to the editor of this series, Jochen Burgtorf, for his help and valuable advice, and to Michael Grenwood and his team for preparing the book for publication. However, I am most grateful to my daughter, Julia, for her immense patience, and to Iwona and Wiola for their friendship and unwavering support.

Abbreviations

ADHG	Archives départementales de la Haute-Garonne
ADR	Archives départementales du département du Rhône et de la métropole de Lyon
ADTG	Archives départementales de Tarn-et-Garonne
ADV	Archives départementales de la Vienne
AN	Archives Nationales
BnF	Bibliothèque nationale de France
d. p.	denier parisis
d. t.	denier tournois
l.	livre
l. p.	livre parisis
l. t.	livre tournois
NAL	Nouvelles Acquisitions Latines
ob. t.	obol tournois
Reg. Clem. V	*Regestum Clementis papae V ex Vaticanis archetypis [...] edito, cura et studio monachorum ordinis sancti Benedicti,* vol. 1–9 (Rome 1885–1892)
s. p.	sol parisis
s. t.	sol tournois

Introduction

The trial and dissolution of the Knights Templar are among those events that, despite the passage of time and the efforts of many generations of historians, still arouse much controversy and provoke endless discussion. The reasons for the proceedings against the Order, which took place between 1307 and 1312, and the roles played by King Philip IV the Fair of France (1285–1314) and Pope Clement V (1305–1314) in them, are still considered mysteries that have not been fully explained. There is also much uncertainty surrounding the fate of the Templar properties, especially in the kingdom of France, where they had the most possessions and its ruler-initiated proceedings against the Order. Immediately after the arrest of the brothers in October 1307, all their houses were seized and then transferred to the administration of secular authorities. This included the Paris headquarters of the Order and its treasury, which stored money belonging to the monarch. This was because the French Templars had served as royal treasurers since the 12th century. At the turn of 1307 and 1308, the pope attempted to take control of the seized properties, resulting in a conflict with the French court. After several months of negotiations, during which theologians at the University of Paris were asked to clarify, among other things, issues relating to the seizure of properties belonging to an Order accused of heresy. An agreement was reached. During the meeting between Philip the Fair and Clement V in Poitiers in the summer of 1308, it was decided that the Templar properties would pass into the hands of Church commissioners, although the king's men would continue to participate unofficially in its administration. In 1312, when the Order was dissolved at the Council of Vienne, the pope also ruled that its properties should be transferred to the Hospitaller Order. This decision initiated a long and arduous process of settling accounts between the new owners and the king of France and his sons, who demanded the return of funds from the Parisian Temple treasury. However, to this day, it remains unclear what happened to the money and valuables stored in the Templars' treasury, what ultimately happened to the income collected from individual houses over several years, and what happened to their furnishings. Who exercised actual control over the assets throughout the proceedings also remains unanswered. Furthermore, the final financial outcome of the trial, the conclusion of the settlements between the Hospitallers and the French monarchy, and those who benefited from the Templar case have not yet been determined. Researchers have, of course, already taken an

DOI: 10.4324/9781003742241-1

interest in these issues, but they have not yet been thoroughly analysed. All these issues will be discussed in this book.

The first chapter will discuss the decisions made at the beginning of the trial by the king of France and the pope regarding the administration and future fate of the confiscated Templar property, as well as the negotiations that took place in this regard. Although these issues are well known, they require a fresh look and attention to certain aspects that have been overlooked by researchers to date. The second chapter will be devoted to an analysis of the practical aspects of managing the Order's assets at various stages of the proceedings. It will discuss, among other things, the various conflicts and abuses accompanying the actions taken in this regard, as well as the costs of the process affecting its final financial outcome. The issue of the use of money from the Templars' estates, which remains controversial to this day, will also be addressed. The third chapter will discuss the decisions concerning the Order's assets taken in connection with its dissolution during the Council of Vienne, as well as their consequences. The analysis will focus on the long-term settlements accompanying the transfer of the French Templars' properties to the Hospitallers and their final outcome.

0.1 Historiography

Issues relating to the Order's estates have been repeatedly raised by authors writing about the Templar trial in France and the roles played by Clement V and Philip the Fair.[1] This scholarship represents decisions relating to the management of seized properties and its subsequent fate through the prism of the policies pursued and the bilateral relations between the pope and the king. This lens significantly influences the conclusions presented in the works. The Templars' case is predominantly viewed as part of the confrontation between Philip the Fair and the papacy, and actions regarding properties are interpreted accordingly. Consequently, many of the theses proposed are based more on researchers' assumptions and intuition than on the actual content of the available sources, as will be discussed repeatedly throughout this book. These theses therefore require verification.

Discussions and decisions concerning the Templar properties were also the subject of interest for historians analysing the course of the Council of Vienne.[2] These events are well known, and their interpretation does not usually provoke much controversy. However, based on the available sources, the roles played by the most important participants in the negotiations conducted during the Council and the motives behind the decisions taken regarding the future of the Templar properties after the Order's dissolution should be revisited in a slightly different way than that seen in most works.[3]

Historiography has not devoted much attention to the practical management of the Order's seized possessions within the kingdom of France, from the time of their seizure until they were handed over to the Hospitallers after the Council of Vienne. Alain Demurger has addressed some of these themes in his works. In one article, he presents his reflections on the administration of the Order's estates in the county of Auxerre[4] in another, he discusses the decision-making process regarding the conversion of the pecuniary annuity granted by the Templars to the Savoy knight Otto de Grandson into a rent drawn from several commanderies, which reflected the involvement of the king of France and the pope in the administration of the seized estates at the time.[5] Elsewhere, Demurger examined the cost of maintaining and imprisoning the detained Templars, which was covered entirely by the revenues of the seized estates. He attempts to estimate the total expenditure on these purposes,[6] which is important for determining the financial outcome of the trial. However, these are only small snippets of the complex and multifaceted issue of the ongoing action on estates by representatives of the secular authorities and the Church.

One of my recent articles contains a more general summary devoted to the involvement of royal officials in matters relating to the Order's properties from a perspective that considers the effectiveness of the French state apparatus.[7] Nevertheless, the issues it discusses are by no means exhaustive of the entire subject matter. Interestingly, the treatment of estates by secular rulers and their representatives and various aspects of their administration in other countries have already been studied. The fate of the Templar properties in England[8] has been of greatest interest to historians to date, but work has also been devoted to the problem of the Aragonese estates.[9]

In the case of France, researchers have primarily focused on analysing and publishing individual documents produced at various stages of the proceedings. These include the inventories drawn up when the estates were seized, when their administrators were replaced, and when the Hospitallers took control of the houses. These documents not only form the basis for studies relating to the Templar trial but are also used to investigate various aspects of the Order's functioning, as reflected in the objects found in individual houses.[10] Also noteworthy in this context is the work of Auguste Pétel, who analysed and published an account of the income and expenses of a commandery, presented by its administrators.[11] This is the only study to provide insight into the functioning of a commandery under the control of king's officials. The document that forms part of it was used by researchers studying the everyday and economic life of the Templars.[12] Another example is the estimate of the income of the commandery of Épailly from 1308, related to the case of Otto de Grandson's rent, published by Demurger.[13]

Historians have also been interested in how the Hospitallers took over the French Templar estates. Joseph M. A. Delaville Le Roulx analysed it from the perspective of the history of the latter Order,[14] while the works of other researchers are dominated by regional approaches.[15] The most detailed study is an unpublished doctoral dissertation by Bernard de Gaulejac on the Hospitallers takeover of the Templar properties in south-west France. It is now held in the Archives départementales de la Haute-Garonne.[16] The author used sources that other researchers did not consult. It is therefore an extremely valuable work that deserves special attention. Publications devoted to the estates of the French Hospitallers in the decades following the 14th century are an important addition to research on this aspect of the Templar case. They enable us to evaluate the far-reaching effects of the transfer of estates.[17]

However, the issue of the settlements that accompanied the Hospitallers' takeover of the estates is almost completely ignored in historiography, particularly regarding the practical side of this process and the role played by the royal administration. Gaulejac has only addressed it in a regional context. Other scholars analysing the transfer of the French Templar estates and its circumstances have generally limited themselves to summarising the most important provisions of the three agreements signed by Philip the Fair and his two successors with the Hospitallers.[18] However, what is lacking is an analysis of the practical consequences of the agreements, which is essential for properly evaluating the entire process.

Finally, it should be noted that there is a substantial body of literature on the regional and local history of the Templar and Hospitaller Orders, which contains references to various events from the first and second decades of the 14th century relating to the trial and transfer of estates belonging to individual commanderies.[19] However, this information is usually fragmentary and does not allow any more general conclusions to be drawn.

This brief overview of works addressing various issues related to the material aspects of the proceedings against the Templars in the kingdom of France reveals an evident absence of comprehensive studies devoted to this multifaceted issue. Such studies should cover the decision-making processes concerning properties and the management of assets during the period when they remained under the control of secular and ecclesiastical authorities, as well as the settlements that took place after the Order's suppression. It is also necessary to consider not only the political factors influencing the actions taken but also the extremely important organisational conditions, which have so far been overlooked by researchers. Adopting such an approach will enable us to examine well-known sources from a different perspective, ask new questions, and explore materials that have not yet been utilised and are unfamiliar to contemporary historians.

0.2 Sources

The basis for the study of the material side of the Templar trial and its consequences are, on the one hand, sources relating to the decisions made by the French kings and popes involved in the proceedings against the Order and the subsequent settlement with the Hospitallers, and, on the other hand, documents that illustrate the wide-ranging effects of these decisions on a local scale, i.e., with regard to individual commanderies and their estates. In both the first and second cases, we have published documents that are well known to scholars, those that, despite available editions, have not previously attracted the interest of historians working on the Templar case, and unpublished documents, some of which have not been used in research on the trial to date.

Most of the important documents related to the decisions made by Philip the Fair and Clement V concerning the Templar estates, as well as the related negotiations, were published in the 19th and early 20th centuries. These documents are well-known to researchers. These include mainly papal bulls, royal orders, and correspondence exchanged between the pontiff and the monarch.[20] Many require reinterpretation or further clarification. This is also the case with the sources that form the basis of research into the proceedings of the Council of Vienne, i.e., the reports of the Aragonese envoys who participated in the deliberations and reported in detail to King James II (1291–1327),[21] as well as the subsequent actions of Pope John XXII (1322–1334) related to the settlement of the Hospitallers with the French crown.[22] Undoubtedly, however, the need for a thorough analysis and verification of the findings to date is most pertinent to the agreements made between the Hospitallers and Philip the Fair and his two sons, known primarily from the publications of Léopold Delisle.[23] They are among those documents related to the Templar case whose analysis has so far posed the greatest difficulties for researchers. This applies to their overall interpretation, the content of individual records, and even the sums agreed. Consequently, erroneous conclusions and over-interpretations that require clarification can be found in both older and more recent literature.

A separate group of sources comprises documents from the various stages of the proceedings and later settlements concerning individual commanderies. These documents have been published in various collections[24] or as appendices to works on the local and regional history of the Templars and the Hospitallers.[25] These also include the aforementioned inventories, minutes of the transfer of estates to the Hospitallers, and the administrator's records of the commandery of Payns, which are the basis for separate studies.

Among the published sources that have not so far piqued the interest of trial history researchers are documents related to the practical side of the proceedings. A good example of these are the royal letters included in the early 14th-century book of forms published by Charles-Victor Langlois.[26] These letters contain complaints addressed to the monarch concerning the activities of the administrators of the Templar estates during the period when they were under the control of the secular power. Their content has not yet been analysed in the context of the proceedings against the Order.[27] Researchers have rarely turned to other sources concerning the various conflicts that arose during the trial and the subsequent settlement period after the Order's suppression. Some of these, after protracted proceedings before various instances, found their way to the Parliament of Paris, whose judgements, published in the 19th century, are a valuable source for the study of this aspect of the Templar case.[28] The same is true of documents from the *Registres du Trésor des chartes* from the reigns of Louis X (1314–1316) and Philip V (1316–1322), as well as the records included in *Les journaux du Trésor de Charles IV*, which provide insight into royal officials' actions to recover the assets of the dissolved Order, and the final administration of Templar houses during the trial period.[29] These too await study.

However, a considerable number of documents concerning the practical side of the proceedings against the French Templars have not yet been published. While some have already been used by researchers but deserve further analysis, others remain unknown to contemporary historians. The most important collection of sources relating to the administration of the Order's estates and subsequent settlements is held at the Archives départementales de la Haute-Garonne (H, Fonds de Malte). It includes documents of a general nature, such as royal orders relating to the transfer of estates and the implementation of agreements with the Hospitallers, as well as documents relating to the affairs of individual commanderies. The latter include extensive collections of documents relating to long-standing arbitration and court proceedings concerning conflicts with estate administrators and the theft of the Templars' assets. Gaulejac appended a transcription of several dozen such sources to his dissertation.[30] However, later researchers have not made use of this resource or the documents themselves.

In addition to the material from the Archives départementales de la Haute-Garonne, Gaulejac also includes in his work a short extract from a source held today in the Archives départementales de Tarn-et-Garonne, of paramount importance for research into the material side of the Templar trial. It is an account of an investigation into outstanding debts and various misappropriations and abuses of the Order's properties, carried out by Renaud de Saint-Ouen on behalf of Charles IV (1322–1328) between 1323 and 1325.[31] The investigation covered the south of France and was most likely the final stage in implementing the provisions of Philip V's 1318 agreement with the Hospitallers. This comprehensive document provides valuable, unique information on not only the settlement process itself, which took place several years after the suppression of the Templars, but also on the organisation of the administration of the estates during the successive stages of the proceedings and the various types of abuses committed during and after the process. The numerous references to the latter issue deserve particular attention, as there are currently no other available sources with which to analyse it more closely. Gaulejac examined the report for his work but only considered it from a regional perspective. This meant that he overlooked many aspects that could be applied to the entire proceedings. No other researcher referred to this source again after him. Given the exceptional importance of the document for analysing the issues at hand, it will be published as an appendix to the work (Appendix).

Other hitherto unpublished sources relating to the Templar estates case are held in the Département des manuscrits of the Bibliothèque nationale de France and the Archies nationales. These include the maintenance and travel bills of the imprisoned Templar brothers, as well as other documents relating to settlements between the administrators of the estates and the prison guards. Demurger analysed these sources in an attempt to estimate the total expenditure on these matters.[32] However, these sources also primarily only contain information concerning the organisational aspects of the estates' administration and thus continue to merit attention. Thus far, however, researchers have not shown interest in the accounts of the Templar estates managers from the years immediately following the arrest of the brothers.[33] While these documents are less extensive and not as well preserved as the analogous accounts published by Pétel, they still allow us to analyse the actions of the royal official who managed the various houses.

The collection of the Bibliothèque nationale also contains the *Cartulaire général de l'Ordre du Temple* of the marquis of Albon, which is well known to researchers and contains transcriptions of documents relating to the history of the Order, including material from the period of the trial and the decades following its conclusion.[34] These include inventories of commanderies from 1313, some of which have not yet been published, as well as few orders from the reign of Louis X concerning settlements with the Hospitallers which have not yet been analysed by historians. In the Archives nationales, on the other hand, the attention of researchers dealing with the history of the French Templars is drawn to the extensive M (Ordres militaires et hospitaliers) and S (Biens des établissements religieux supprimés) series, which contain documents relating to individual commanderies. As these sources have been consulted and published many times, these collections were consulted in depth for the purposes of this work. Further research may reveal hitherto untapped sources on the management and transfer of estates, but it is likely that the results would supplement and provide more detail on general findings rather than change them.

0.3 Currency

In this book, sums related to various types of transactions, financial obligations, and estimated values of goods, acquisitions, and costs incurred in connection with the Templar case by various participants will be mentioned repeatedly. In the analysed sources, they are mostly given in livres tournois, and much less frequently in livres parisis, florins, or livres of Bordeaux. To aid the reader in understanding and comparing the amounts mentioned, they will be converted into livres tournois each time (given in brackets). This assumes that:

1 livre parisis = 1.25 livres tournois
1 livre tournois ≈ 1.5 florins
1 livre tournois = 1.25 livres of Bordeaux

In several cases, the sources only refer to "livres" without specifying the exact unit of account. It is also impossible to determine this based on the document's content and context. In such cases, the name of the unit is not specified in the text either. While this does disrupt the narrative somewhat, it does not significantly impact the conclusions presented in this book.

Another issue that complicates the analysis of the financial data cited in the context of the proceedings against the Templars is the fluctuating value of the French coin. Philip the Fair is known to have experienced significant financial difficulties during his reign, which he attempted to address by debasing the currency. This resulted in cyclical devaluations and subsequent attempts to restore the coin's value.[35] Unfortunately, we cannot determine the impact of this phenomenon on the figures contained in most of the analysed documents. Therefore, this aspect has not been included in the study. Nevertheless, the conclusions presented are sufficiently generalised that their credibility remains intact.

Notes

1 See, for example, E. Boutaric, 'Clément V, Philippe le Bel et les Templiers', *Revue des questions historiques*, 10 (1871), pp. 301–342 and 11 (1872), pp. 5–41; K. Schottmüller, *Der Untergang der Templer-Ordens*, vol. 1–2 (Berlin 1887); L. L. L. Lavocat, *Procès des frères et de l'ordre du Temple d'après des pièces inédites publiées par J. Michelet et des documents imprimés anciens et nouveaux* (Paris 1888); H. Prutz, *Entwicklung und Untergang des Tempelherrenordens: mit Benutzung bisher ungedruckter Materialien*

(Berlin 1888); J. Delaville le Roulx, 'La suppression des Templiers', *Revue des Questions historiques*, 68 (1890), pp. 29–61; C. V. Langlois, 'Le procès des Templiers', *Revue des Deux Mondes*, 61 (1891), pp. 382–421; C. V. Langlois, 'L'affaire des Templiers', *Journal des Savants* 6 (1908), pp. 417–435; G. Lizerand, *Clément V et Philippe le Bel* (Paris 1910), pp. 76–160, 25–340; J. Favier, *Philippe le Bel* (Paris 1978), pp. 426–480; S. Menache, *Clement V* (Cambridge 1998), pp. 205–246; M. Barber, *The Trial of the Templars* (2nd ed.) (Cambridge 2006); A. Demurger, *Les Templiers. Une chevalerie chrétienne au Moyen Âge* (Paris 2005), pp. 413–509; A. Demurger, *La persécution des templiers. Journal (1305–1314)* (Paris 2015).

2 E. Müller, *Das Konzil von Vienne 1311–1312. Seine Quellen und seine Geschichte* (Münster 1934); J. Lecler, *Histoire des conciles oecuméniques*, ed. G. Dumeige, vol. 8 *Vienne* (Paris 1964); L. Wetzel, *Le Concile de Vienne (1311–1312) et l'abolition de l'Ordre du Temple* (Paris 1993).

3 On the possible interpretation of the actions taken by participants in the diplomatic negotiations that accompanied the Council's deliberations, see M. Satora, *Sprawa templariuszy w dyplomacji zachodnioeuropejskiej (1307–1312)* (Poznań 2011), passim.

4 A. Demurger, 'Dal Tempio all'Ospedale. Il destino delle commende templari nella contea di Auxerre (secoli XIV)', in: *Acri 1291. La fine della presenza degli ordini militari in Terra Santa e i nuovi orientamenti nel XIV secolo*, ed. F. Tommasi (Perugia 1996), pp. 93–98.

5 A. Demurger, 'Othon de Grandson et les templiers d'Épailly', in: *Communicating the Middle Ages: Essays in Honour of Sophia Menache*, ed. I. Shagrir, B. Z. Kedar, M. Balard (London–New York 2018), pp. 39–49.

6 A. Demurger, *La persécution*, pp. 243–245.

7 M. Satora, 'Filip Piękny i majątki templariuszy – uwagi o działaniach francuskiego aparatu państwowego w sprawie zakonu (1307–1314)', *Saeculum Christianum*, 32 (2025), pp. 20–32.

8 C. Perkins, 'The Wealth of the Knights Templars in England and the Disposition of It after Their Dissolution', *The American Historical Review*, 15 (1910), no. 2, pp. 252–263; A. M. Leys, 'The Forfeiture of the Lands of the Templars in England', in: *Oxford Essays in Medieval History presented to Herbert Edward Salter*, ed. F. M. Powicke (Oxford 1934), pp. 155–163; J. S. Hamilton, 'Apocalypse Not: Edward II and the Suppression of the Templars', *Medieval Perspectives*, 12 (1997), pp. 90–100; J. S. Hamilton, 'King Edward II of England and the Templars', in: *The Debate on the Trial of the Templars (1307–1314)*, ed. J. Burgtorf, P. F. Crawford, H. J. Nicholson (Farnham 2010), pp. 215–224; P. Slavin, 'The Fate of the Former Templar Estates in England, 1308–1330', *Crusades*, 14 (2015), pp. 209–35; H. J. Nicholson, P. Slavin, "The Real Da Vinci Code': The Accounts of Templars' Estates in England and Wales during the Suppression of the Order', in: *Templars, Their Sources and Their Competitors, 1119–1314*, ed. K. Borchardt (Farnham 2016), pp. 233–246; J. M. Jefferson, 'Edward II and the Templar Lands in Lincolnshire', in: *L'économie templière en Occident. Patrimoines, commerce, finances: Actes du colloque international, Troyes, abbaye de Clairvaux, 24-26 octobre 2012*, ed. A. Baudin, G. Brunel, N. Dohrmann (Langres 2013), pp. 295–321; J. M. Jefferson, *The Templar Estates in Lincolnshire, 1185–1565: Agriculture and Economy* (Woodbridge 2020), pp. 41–64.

9 M. Vilar Bonet, *Els Béns del Temple a la Corona d'Aragó en suprimir – se l'orde (1300–1319)* (Barcelona 2000).

10 On the various lines of research on the inventories of French Templar houses, see J. Burgtorf, 'The Trial Inventories of the Templars' Houses in France: Select Aspects', in: *The Debate on the Trial of the Templars (1307–1314)*, ed. J. Burgtorf, P. F. Crawford, H. J. Nicholson (Farnham 2010), pp. 105–115. The author listed the most important editions and publications devoted to inventories from the territory of present-day France. This list is supplemented by later articles: J. M. Roger, 'L'inventaire de la maison du Temple de Bret (15 mai 1313)', *Revue historique du Centre-Ouest*, 10 (2011),

pp. 363–367; D. Carraz, 'Chartiers privés et autres documents familiaux conservés dans les archives templières. Le cas de quelques commanderies du Midi français', in: *Commilitones Christi. Miscellanea di studi per il Centro Italiano di Documentazione sull'Ordine del Tempio, MMXI–MMXVI*, ed. S. Sammarco (Rome 2016), pp. 184–185; J. Schenk, 'The Documentary Evidence for Templar Religion', in: *The Templars and Their Sources*, ed. K. Borchardt, K. Döring, P. Josserand, H. Nicholson (London–New York 2017), pp. 199–211; J. Picot, 'L'inventaire des biens de la commanderie du Temple de Monferrand en Basse Auvergne (vers 1308)', *Bibliothèque de l'École des chartes*, 174 (2018–2019), pp. 107–157.

11 A. Pétel, 'Templiers et Hospitaliers dans le diocèse de Troyes. Comptes de régie de la commanderie de Payns, 1307 – 1309', *Mémoires de la Société académique de l'Aube*, 71 (1907), pp. 283–372.

12 For example, J. Kreiser, 'Wirtschafts- und Finanzgebaren nordfranzösischer Templer-Häuser am Beispiel der Komturei Payns (Champagne)', in: *Erwerbspolitik und Wirtschaftsweise mittelalterlicher Orden und Klöster*, ed. K. Elm (Berlin 1992), pp. 115–123; M. Wilmart, 'Salariés, journaliers et artisans au service d'une exploitation agricole templière. La commanderie de Payns au début du XIVe siècle', in: *L'économie templière en Occident. Patrimoines, commerce, finances. Actes du colloque international (Troyes – abbaye de Clairvaux, 24–26 octobre 2012)*, ed. A. Baudin, G. Brunel, N. Dohrmann (Langres 2013), pp. 273–293.

13 A. Dmurger, 'La "prisée" de la maison templière d'Épailly en 1308', *Bulletin archéologique et historique du Chatillonais*, 1 (2019), pp. 32–48.

14 J. M. A. Delaville Le Roulx, *Les hospitaliers à Rhodes jusqu'à la mort de Philibert de Naillac (1310–1421)* (Paris 1913).

15 A. Du Bourg, *Histoire du Grand-Prieuré de Toulouse* (Toulouse 1883); J. Raybaud, *Histoire des grands prieurs et du prieuré de Saint-Gilles*, ed. N. César, vol. 1 (Nîmes 1904); M. Duval, 'La dévolution des biens du Temple aux Hospitaliers en Bretagne', in: *Actes du 97e Congrès national des Sociétés Savantes* (Nantes, 1972). *Assistance et assistés jusqu'au XVIe siècle* (Paris 1979), pp. 287–298; J. M. Roger, 'La prise de possession par l'Hôpital des maisons du Temple en Poitou et en Bretagne (mai 1313)', *Revue historique du Centre-Ouest*, 7 (2008), pp. 215–243; J. M. Roger, 'La dévolution à l'Hôpital des biens du Temple dans les bailliages de Troyes et de Chaumont', *Bulletin de la Société nationale des Antiquaires de France*, 2012 (2018), pp. 242–254.

16 B. de Gaulejac, *La liquidation des biens de l'ordre du Temple dans le Sud-Ouest de la France*, 1925 (unpublished thesis – ADHG, BH wms 731).

17 A. de Charmasse, *État des possessions des Templiers et des Hospitaliers en Maconnais, Charollais, Lyonnais, Forez et partie de la Bourgogne d'après une enquête de 1333* (Paris 1878); *L'Enquête pontificale de 1373 de 1373 sur l'Ordre des Hospitaliers de Saint-Jean de Jérusalem*, ed. A. M. Legras, vol. 1, *L'enquête dans le prieuré de France* (Paris 1987), pp. 93–96; J. M. Roger, 'Les maisons des Ordres du Temple et de l'Hôpital dans le bailliage de Chaumont au début du XIVe siècle, d'après l'enquête de 1333', *Cahiers Haut-Marnais*, 167 (1986), pp. 49–54; J. M. Roger, 'Les biens de l'Hôpital au bailliage de Troyes en 1333: la prisée de 1333, la déclaration de Coulours de 1338', *Mémoires de la Société académique du Département de l'Aube*, 135 (2011), pp. 243–298; J. M. Roger, 'La prisée des biens de l'Hôpital au bailliage de Chaumont en 1333', *Mémoires de la Société académique du Département de l'Aube*, 136 (2012), pp. 349–432; R. Favreau, 'L'enquête pontificale de 1373 sur l'ordre de l'Hôpital dans le grand prieuré d'Aquitaine', *Bibliothèque de l'École des chartes*, 164 (2006), pp. 447–538.

18 See, for example, the treatment of this topic in some more recent works: M. Barber, *The Trial* (2006), pp. 271–272; A. Luttrell, 'The Hospitallers and the Papacy, 1305–1314', in: *Forschungen zur Reichs, Papst- und Landesgeschichte: Peter Herde zum 65. Geburtstag*, ed. K. Borchardt, E. Bünz, vol. 2 (Stuttgart 1998), pp. 595–622; A. Luttrell, 'Observations on the Fall of the Temple', in: *Élites et ordres militaires au Moyen Âge: Rencontre autour d'Alain Demurger*, ed. P. Josserand, L. F. Oliveira, D. Carraz

(Madrid 2015), pp. 365–372; A. Demurger, *Les Hospitaliers: De Jérusalem à Rhodes, 1050–1317* (Paris 2013), pp. 456–458.

19 See, for example, E. Mannier, *Ordre de Malte. Les commanderies du Grand – Prieuré de France d'après les documents inédits conservés aux Archives nationales à Paris* (Paris 1872); A. Trudon des Ormes, *Étude sur les possessions de l'Ordre du Temple en Picardie* (Amiens 1892); A. Pétel, *La Commanderie de Payns et ses dépendances à Savières, à Saint-Mesmin, à Messon, et au Pavillon* (Paris 1905); A. Pétel, 'Templiers et Hospitaliers dans le diocèse de Troyes. Le Temple de Bonlieu et l'Hôpital d'Orient', *Mémoires de la Société académique d'agriculture, sciences et arts du département de l'Aube*, 73 (1909), pp. 257–358; 74 (1910), pp. 11–350; M. Miguet, *Templiers et Hospitaliers en Normandie* (Paris 1995); A. Soutou, *La commanderie de Sainte-Eulalie de Larzac* (Nîmes 1999); J. B. de Vaivre, *La commanderie d'Épailly et sa chapelle templière durant la période médiévale* (Paris 2005); V. Bessey, *Les commanderies de l'Hôpital en Picardie au temps des chevaliers de Rhodes, 1309–1522* (Millau 2005); P. Josserand, 'Les Templiers en Bretagne au Moyen Âge: mythes et réalités', *Annales de Bretagne et des Pays de l'Ouest,* 119 (2012), no. 4, pp. 7–33 and many others.

20 These sources have been published primarily in: P. Dupuy, *Histoire de la condamnation des Templiers* (Bruxelles 1713); E. Boutaric, 'Clément V'; *Livre de Guillaume le Maire*, ed. C. Port, Mélanges historiques, choix de documents, vol. 2 (Paris 1874); Reg. Clem. V, vols. 1–9; G. Lizerand, *Clément V*; *Vitae Paparum Avenionensium*, ed. E. Baluze, reed. G. Mollat, vol. 3 (Paris 1921).

21 *Papsttum und Untergang des Templerordens*, ed. H. Finke, vol. 2 (Müntzer 1907), nos. 125–148, pp. 230–306.

22 *Codice diplomatico del sacro militare ordine Gerosolimitano*, ed. S. Paoli, vol. 2 (Lucca 1737); *Lettres secrètes et curiales du Pape Jean XXII (1316–1334), relatives à la France*, ed. A. Coulon, S. Clémencet, vol. 1 (Paris 1906).

23 L. Delisle, *Mémoire sur les opérations financières des Templiers* (Paris 1889), no. 35–37, pp. 228–238. An English translation of the two treatises, based on a publication by Delisle, is also available in: *The Templars: Selected Sources*, trans. and annotated by M. Barber, K. Bate (Manchester 2002), nos. 78–79, pp. 323–328. However, it is not entirely accurate.

24 *Documents inédits pour servir à l'histoire du Poitou poubliés par la Société des antiquaires de l'Ouest* (Poitiers 1876); *Archives historiques de la Saintonge et de l'Aunis*, vol. 12, *Documents Relatifs à l'histoire de la Saintonge et de l'Aunis extraits des registres du Trésor des chartes*, ed. P. Guérin (Paris–Saintes 1884).

25 C. Métais, *Les Templiers en Eure-et-Loir, histoire et cartulaire* (Chartres 1902); A. Pétel, *La Commanderie*; A. Pétel, 'Templiers et Hospitaliers dans le diocèse de Troyes. Le Temple de Bonlieu', pp. 11–350; M. Miguet, *Templiers et Hospitaliers en Normandie*; J. Dubourg, 'La commanderie de Romestaing', *Revue de l'Agenais*, 130 (2003), pp. 127–144: J. B. de Vaivre, *La Commanderie*.

26 *Formulaires de lettres du XIIe, du XIIIe et du XIVe siècle*, ed. C. V. Langlois (Paris 1890); H. G. Schmidt, *Administrative Korrespondenz der französischen Könige um 1300. Edition des »Formelbuches« BNF ms. lat. 4763. Verwaltung – Gerichtsbarkeit – Kanzlei* (Göttingen 1997).

27 Karlheinz Dietz referred to one of the letters when analysing events relating to the fall of the Templars, but not to the proceedings themselves – 'Die Templer und das Turiner Grabtuch', in: *The Templars and Their Sources*, ed. K. Borchardt, K. Döring, P. Josserand, H. J. Nicholson (Farnham 2017), pp. 223–259.

28 *Les Olim, ou Registres des arrêts rendus par la Cour du Roi: sous les règnes de Saint Louis, de Philippe Le Hardi, de Philippe Le Bel, de Louis Le Hutin et de Philippe Le Long*, ed. A. A. Beugnot, vol. 2–3 (Paris 1847–1848); *Actes du Parlament de Paris,* ed. E. Boutaric, vol. 2, *1299–1328* (Paris 1867).

29 *Registres du Trésor des chartes*, ed. R. Fawtier, vol. 2.1, *Règnes de Louis X le Hutin et de Philippe V le Long* (Paris 1966); *Registres du Trésor des chartes*, ed. R. Fawtier, vol. 3.3,

Règne de Philippe de Valois (Paris 1979); *Les journaux du trésor de Charles IV le Bel*, ed. J. Viard (Paris 1917).

30 B. de Gaulejac, *La liquidation*, Pièces justificatives, nos. 1–39, pp. 90–176.

31 ADTG, H 317.

32 These documents mainly belong to the following collections: BnF, ms. fr. 20334; BnF, ms lat. 9800; BnF, Clairambault 1313; AN, K 37C; AN, K38.

33 AN, M1, no. 10; BnF, ms. lat. 9035, nos. 18–21.

34 On the scientific activities of the marquis of Albon, see D. Carraz, M. A. Chevalier, 'Le marquis d'Albon (1866–1912) et son Cartulaire général de l'ordre du Temple', *Hereditas Monasteriorum*, 1 (2012), pp. 107–128.

35 L. L. Borrelli de Serres, 'Les variations monétaires sous Philippe le Bel et les sources de leur histoire', *Gazette numismatique française*, 6 (1902), pp. 9–67; A. Dieudonné, 'Les variations monétaires sous Philippe le Bel', *Le Moyne Âge*, 9 (1905), pp. 217–257.

1 Decisions concerning the Templar properties (1307–1308)

1.1 Beginning of the proceedings

Founded in Jerusalem around 1120, the Order of the Knights Templar created a network of commanderies covering most of Europe during its nearly 200 years of existence. In France, the homeland of its founders and later of many of its members, there were several hundred Templar houses at the beginning of the 14th century. Researchers generally estimate that these accounted for two-thirds of all the Order's houses, but they disagree on the exact number. Most literature mentions 660 houses,[1] but some authors believe there were far fewer – around 300 or 400[2] – while others claim there were as many as 1,170.[3] This issue remains unresolved. The total value of the properties belonging to the French Templars, and the income they derived from it, is also unknown. No documents have survived and that would allow any conclusions to be drawn about the entire kingdom. However, we can certainly assume that the Order's assets in France were very large and played an important role in the functioning of local communities, as well as in the systems of production and trade in both cities, and the countryside.

In addition to their standard activities, which were carried out in commanderies scattered throughout the kingdom – primarily the collection of funds necessary to fulfil the Order's mission in the East – the French Templars also served successive rulers, playing an important role in their central administration. Since the time of Louis VII (1137–1180), the Templars had served as royal treasurers, with the monarch's treasury located in their Paris headquarters. However, in 1295, Philip the Fair decided to move it to the Louvre. He reversed this decision a few years later and, in 1303, the treasury returned to the Temple.[4] This cooperation undoubtedly testified to the French king's good relations with the Templars and his trust in the Order. This was further confirmed by *amortissement général* of all Templar properties in his kingdom, issued in April 1304,[5] and by additional privileges granted in October of that year.[6]

Despite all these clear signs of harmonious relations, when the king was informed of accusations of heresy levelled against the Order less than a year later, he took the allegations seriously. This sets in motion a sequence of well-known events leading to the arrest of the brothers and the initiation of inquisitorial proceedings against them. Almost immediately after hearing the revelations about the alleged crimes of the Templars, Philip the Fair decided to share his information

DOI: 10.4324/9781003742241-2

with the newly elected Pope Clement V. The opportunity arose during the pope's coronation, which took place in Lyon in November 1305.[7] During the meeting, the question of a new crusade was also raised, which proved to be of great importance for the subsequent decisions of the pope and the king of France regarding the Templars. From the outset of his pontificate, Clement V considered preparing a military expedition to the East to be his primary objective.[8] Philip the Fair agreed to lead the expedition, marking the start of their close collaboration.[9]

In addition to searching for leaders for the crusade, Clement V also made intensive efforts to develop the best possible plan for future action.[10] He knew that no major expedition could be undertaken without the involvement of the largest Military Orders. Despite having lost their lands in the East, these Orders still constituted the most significant Christian military forces, ready to fight the infidels. He therefore summoned the Grand Masters of the Templars and the Hospitallers for consultations.[11] Jacques de Molay and Foulques de Villaret were to present a plan for a future crusade and comment on the idea of reforming the Military Orders, a proposal first made at the Council of Lyon in 1274. This idea had repeatedly resurfaced since then in discussions at various levels of the Church hierarchy and in treatises on the reconquest of the Holy Land, many of which were written at the turn of the 13th and 14th centuries. The plan envisaged unifying the largest Orders, primarily the Templars and the Hospitallers. This would ensure better use of resources and streamline efforts to organise a future crusade. Many commentators believed that the Military Orders had strayed from their mission of conducting operations to defend the Christian faith and recover the lands lost in the East. Clement V decided to resume discussions on this subject and ultimately implement the reform project.[12]

The Grand Masters arrived for their meeting with the pope in the summer of 1307. Jacques de Molay presented Clement V with written opinions on both topics of interest, advocating the organisation of the *passagium generale* – a single great military expedition modelled on the First Crusade to the Holy Land[13] – and expressing strong opposition to the idea of merging the Military Orders.[14] From the pope's perspective, both statements were disappointing. According to Louis L. L. Lavocat, when Jacques de Molay opposed the plan to merge the Orders, Clement V was left with only two options: to reform the Templars or to suppress the Order.[15]

At the same time, the king of France reminded the pope of the accusations levelled against the Templars. Clement V informed the Grand Master of the accusations and, at his request and on the advice of the cardinals, decided to launch an investigation to verify their truth. In a letter dated 24 August 1307, he informed Philip the Fair of his decision and asked him to provide all the information he had on the alleged heresy.[16] He repeated this request in his 26 September correspondence.[17] However, the pope's planned actions had to be postponed due to his illness and the associated treatment. According to information contained in one of Clement V's letters, the delay was to last until at least mid-October.[18] Therefore, it seems that, soon after, the pope was ready to initiate an investigation into the allegations against the Templars, the outcome of which was impossible to predict. Furthermore, it was to be carried out with the knowledge and cooperation of the king of France. It is not known, however, what form the investigation was to take. Was the pope planning to arrest the brothers, as was the case with the inquisitorial procedure? Or was he considering a different type of investigation? In any case, a few weeks later, it transpired that the final decision on the matter had been made not by Clement V, but by Philip the Fair.

During the first half of September, the king convened a meeting with his closest advisers and Guillaume de Paris, the Grand Inquisitor of France. It was at this meeting that the decision was made to initiate inquisitorial proceedings against the Templars, most likely in response to the pope's letter in August, which was seen as a call to take concrete action. Philip the Fair, therefore, decided to arrest the members of the Order, perhaps even at the Inquisitor's request. The monarch's order in this matter is dated 14 September.[19] Consequently, on 13 October, a month later all the brothers residing in France were arrested. On the same day, all the Order's properties were also seized. The latter was standard practice under medieval French law, which was derived from Roman law. In criminal proceedings, the seizure of the defendant's properties served two purposes: firstly, it secured the properties in anticipation of possible subsequent confiscation; and secondly, it provided the means to support the prisoner. The person seizing the properties was obliged to ensure its proper and effective administration.[20] Similar solutions were used in inquisitorial proceedings. As early as 1198–1216, Innocent III (1198–1216) imposed on monarchs the obligation to seize the properties of those accused of heresy.[21] Therefore, the actions taken on the orders of the French king did not deviate from generally accepted principles.

Three days after the brothers were arrested, Philip informed the other monarchs of his decisions. In a letter dated 16 October and addressed to King James II of Aragon, he referred to the issue of the Templar properties, among other things. He wrote that if the Order were found innocent, its properties would be returned to it; otherwise, the king intended to transfer it to the Holy Land.[22] This was evidently the French court's official proposal for the further distribution of the Templar properties. To some extent, it reflected ideas that had emerged during the aforementioned discussion about unifying Military Orders. According to these ideas, if some of the Templar properties were taken away, it could be put to better use in the Holy Land than if it remained in their hands. From this perspective, Philip the Fair's idea seemed to coincide with Clement V's earlier plans to reform the Templars and the Hospitallers. However, it is not known whether the king had discussed this with the pope beforehand.

In any case, the arrest of the French brothers came as the biggest surprise to Clement V. Upon learning of it, the pope immediately interrupted his treatment, returned to Poitiers, and held an urgent meeting with the cardinals. He then wrote to Philip the Fair to express his outrage at the monarch's actions against the Templars without consulting him. Clement V considered the actions an insult to the Church and announced that he would send two cardinals to Paris to discuss the transfer of control over the proceedings to the Church with the king.[23]

Reading the papal letter, one might get the impression that the king of France's actions initiated open conflict with Clement V or were another episode in the loud and violent dispute previously waged with Boniface VIII (1294–1303) concerning the primacy of secular and spiritual authority.[24] This interpretation is all the more likely given that, in the following years, the monarch did not forget his deceased opponent, instead seeking to bring a posthumous trial against him for heresy.[25] Therefore, it is not difficult to imagine that the king of France also tried to impose his will on the new pope. When he encountered resistance, their relationship became similarly hostile, as it had been with Boniface VIII. Consequently, contemporary historiography tends to view the Templar case as a continuation of this political and ideological conflict. All actions and discussions concerning the Templar properties between the king and the pope during the proceedings are also viewed as part of this confrontation. Meanwhile, Clement V's indignation after the arrest of the French Templars and the letter he wrote in connection with this can be explained differently. According to an anonymous witness favourable to the Templars – who may have been a member of the Order – who wrote to the commander of Ascó shortly after the events in question, Clement V was outside Poitiers on the day the brothers were arrested. Upon learning of the arrest of several Templars present at the papal court, he immediately returned to the city and summoned the cardinals.[26] This suggests that, at that time, the pope had limited knowledge of the circumstances surrounding the arrests. News that the king's men had detained Templars who were, in a sense, guests of the pope could have understandably outraged him. As Hans Prutz pointed out at the end of the 19th century, he was apparently unaware of the role played by Guillaume de Paris in the decision to initiate proceedings.[27] This was most likely the result of a breakdown in communication between the French court and the papal curia, which was presumably caused by Clement V himself. In a letter dated late August, he wrote to Philip the Fair, asking him not to send his envoys in the first half of October, as he was due to undergo treatment.[28] The king and the Grand Inquisitor then acted without the pope's knowledge, causing a crisis. However, when the cardinals sent by Clement V arrived in Paris, they discovered the circumstances surrounding the order to arrest the Templars, which most likely calmed the situation. A few weeks later, on 22 November, the pope issued the bull *Pastoralis praeeminentiae*, ordering all Christian monarchs to follow Philip's example and arrest the Templars and seize their properties.[29] The matter was thus quickly resolved, as it turned out to be more of a misunderstanding than a deliberate act of defiance by the king of France against papal authority.

In the bull *Pastoralis praeeminentiae*, Clement V addressed the planned use of the Templar properties, among other things. He explained that the king of France had seized the Order's assets with the intention of transferring them to the Holy Land or returning them to the Templars if they were found innocent. Later in the document, the pope instructed rulers to draw up inventories in the presence of detained Templars and other witnesses when seizing their properties, and to ensure its best possible management. Thus, Clement V clearly accepted Philip the Fair's idea, repeating in his document what the king had previously written. It could even be speculated that it was the monarch's suggestion to transfer the seized properties to the Holy Land that prompted the pope to conduct an inquisitorial investigation, in accordance with the plan outlined by the king of France and Guillaume de Paris.

The implementation of this plan would bring Clement V closer to realising his greatest dream: the organisation of a new crusade.

From that moment on, the case of the Templars became a joint undertaking of Philip the Fair and the pope. However, it was undoubtedly the king of France who took action against the Order, despite having previously favoured and cooperated with it. Historians have long pondered the motives behind his decision. While opinions on this subject have changed over time,[30] vast majority of researchers cite financial issues as a possible motive. The most common explanation in this context is that Philip wanted to seize the Templars' assets to fill his empty treasury.[31] As is well known, the king of France struggled with serious financial problems throughout virtually his entire reign. Costly wars with the duchy of Aquitaine (1294–1303), and later with the county of Flanders (1297–1305) left the treasury empty, prompting Philip to seek various solutions, including debasing the currency, taking out loans, and confiscating the properties of Jews and Lombard merchants. These issues are well documented in the literature.[32] A slightly more detailed interpretation was presented by Ignacio de La Torre, who stated that Philip the Fair was primarily counting on seizing the silver in the Templars' treasury in order to use it to improve the corrupt currency.[33] Elsewhere, the same researcher agreed with the opinion expressed by Charles Guéry at the end of the 19th century, namely that the Templars became the target of the French king's attack because of their role as royal treasurers. As the financial balance was unfavourable to the monarch, he decided to dissolve the Order to avoid paying his debts. At the same time, by seizing the Templars' treasury, he was able to take over the deposits of others.[34] In the 1980s, Raymond Cazelles offered a different interpretation of Philip the Fair's situation. He proposed a theory that the attack on the Order was part of a broader process whereby the king took control of state finances and transferred them to increasingly influential representatives of the bourgeoisie.[35] Similar opinions were later presented by Sophia Menache and Demurger.[36]

All the above interpretations can be summarised by stating that Philip the Fair required the Templars' assets to achieve his domestic policy goals and meet the needs of his state. Meanwhile, in one of the earliest comments on the actions taken against the Templars, which was written in early November 1307, by the correspondent of James II of Aragon, Italian merchant Cristiano Spinola, a completely different issue was raised:

> [T]he pope and the king did this in order to have their money and because they wished to make one single house of the Hospital and the Temple and all the other brotherhoods, of which house the king intended and desired to make one of his sons the ruler.[37]

The author of these words clearly believed that Philip the Fair and Clement V were working towards the same goals. The idea of merging the Templars and the Hospitallers, transferring all the Templars' possessions to the new Order, and appointing the French king's son as its leader also features in later comments on the pope and king's intentions, primarily within Clement V's circle. Over time, people stopped talking about it, although English chroniclers returned to the subject after the dissolution of the Templars.[38] The idea is justifiable, given the pope's far-reaching plans and hopes for the crusade. If the Christians managed to regain the territories lost in the East, a leader would be needed for the newly created state. This ruler would need to have sufficient authority and be able to secure the necessary support from Europe. In the first decade of the 14th century, the only Western European monarch willing to commit himself and his family to regaining the Holy Land and organising a new crusade was the king of France.[39] Therefore, the proposal that his son should reign in the crusader state was understandable. In any case, this was a very distant prospect because, firstly, an effective, large-scale military expedition to the East had not yet been discussed at that stage of the crusade negotiations. Furthermore, this concept never appeared in any official documents or correspondence between Philip the Fair and Clement V, so if it was considered at all, it was only during initial bilateral talks and later ceased to be significant. Nevertheless, some researchers have identified it as one of the main motives for the French monarch's actions against the Templars.[40] Interestingly, none of these researchers mentioned the pope's intentions in this context, despite Cristiano Spinola mentioning them first in his commentary.

Against the backdrop of all the aforementioned assumptions regarding the reasons for Philip the Fair's attack on the Templars, which appears in both older and more recent literature, Jean Favier's opinion stands out. He repeatedly stated in his works that the king of France did not intend to seize the Order's properties.[41] However, this view is generally ignored by researchers analysing the possible causes of the Templars' downfall.

Despite discussions conducted by successive generations of historians, the question of Philip the Fair's actual intentions remains open. Based on the available sources, it is impossible to provide a definitive answer regarding the monarch's intentions concerning the Order's properties. While official royal statements always referred to the use of Templar goods for the needs of the Holy Land, considering the enormous financial challenges faced by Philip, as well as his previous actions towards Jews and Italian merchants, it is difficult to completely reject the assumption that he also hoped to derive some profit from this course of action. Regardless of whether the king of France intended to seize the Order's assets for his own use or to do exactly as he had declared in his official letters, it quickly became apparent that putting these ideas into practice would be very difficult. The pope stood in the way of their implementation.

Shortly after issuing the bull *Pastoralis praeeminentiae*, Clement V began to take control of the proceedings. In a letter dated 1 December, addressed to the king of France, he announced that Cardinals Bérenger Frédol and Étienne de Suisy would be sent back to Paris.[42] They arrived in the city before the end of the year. However, it transpired that they were facing difficulties in carrying out their mission. In a letter dated 24 December, Philip the Fair declared his willingness to hand over the imprisoned brothers to the cardinals. However, the king had other plans regarding the Order's seized properties. He promised only that it would be managed by trusted people appointed for this purpose, separately from his own possessions, so that it could be preserved in its entirety for the needs of the Holy Land.[43] Two conclusions can be drawn from his words regarding the planned decisions concerning the Templars and their possessions. First, at this stage, the monarch clearly did not anticipate the acquittal of the detained brothers, which is why he did not mention the return of their properties, only its alternative use. Philip the Fair took the same position in a letter dated 29 January 1308, addressed to James II of Aragon. As in his correspondence with Clement V, the king emphasised that the Order's properties were to be administered separately from royal properties and used for the needs of the Holy Land.[44] His view on this issue apparently differed from that set out by the pope in the bull *Pastoralis praeeminentiae*. Clement V still allowed for the possibility of a positive outcome to the Templar case. It is unclear whether this difference of opinion impacted on the negotiations taking place at the time.

The second issue raised in Philip the Fair's letter – the management of the Templars' goods and subsequent decisions relating to them – appears to have been of much greater importance to both sides. Not only did he want to maintain control over the assets during the proceedings, reflecting the aforementioned rules of procedure applicable in criminal and inquisitorial proceedings, but he also claimed the decisive vote on their disposal after the members of the Order were convicted. This was in line with the French practice of kings retaining the confiscated properties of heretics for themselves. Although, according to canon law, bishops were supposed to finance inquisitorial proceedings, it had become customary since the time of Louis IX (1226–1270) for French monarchs to pay for the activities of the tribunals and the maintenance of prisoners. This solution was even discussed at the councils in Toulouse in 1229, and Béziers in 1246, where the assembled clergy recognised the developing practice.[45] This differed from the rules in force in 13th-century Italy, for example, where the properties of a convicted heretic was divided between the bishop, the inquisitorial tribunal members, and the secular ruler. However, other solutions were adopted there regarding the financing of the proceedings. On the Iberian Peninsula, as in France, it was the king who retained all of the convicted person's properties.[46] Philip the Fair was therefore acting in accordance with accepted customs. However, what was new was the request made by Clement V in this matter, which deviated from established procedures. While the pope did have the right to claim the properties of an order enjoying the privilege of exemption, this clearly conflicted with French practice in similar situations. As no proceedings had ever been conducted against a large ecclesiastical institution before, there were no established solutions for such a situation. The matter therefore needed to be clarified. After the cardinals' visit to Paris, it continued to be the subject of discussion, and perhaps even conflict, between Philip and Clement V. Details of the case emerge from the account of Esquieu de Floyran, the prior of Montfaucon and one of the first accusers of the Templars. In the period following the arrest of the Templars, he stayed at the French court as a valet to Philip the Fair and, at the beginning of 1308, travelled with the monarch to Boulogne-sur-Mer for the wedding of his daughter Isabella to Edward II (1307–1327).[47] In a letter dated 29 January, addressed to the king of Aragon, Esquieu de Floyran wrote that the pope wanted to take over part of the Templar properties as it belonged to the clergy (*papa querat habere porsionem suam de bonis predistorum Templariorum tanquam personarum religiosarum*). Philip the Fair was advised against acceding to this, on the grounds that the Order had never been a religious community, but a heretical one, and the properties granted to it by the faithful had in fact been transferred to demons. As such, it should not be returned to the donors, but to secular rulers.[48] Reading these words, one gets the impression that the fate of the Templars had already been sealed and that, at that moment, the pope and the king were not so much arguing about the temporary management of the seized properties as much as they were about who should take it over once the proceedings were complete. Although both sides officially declared that the Order's assets should be used for the needs of the Holy Land, it was clear that neither Clement V nor Philip trusted the other and both wanted the final say. Esquieu de Floyran's words also suggest that the pope wanted to take over part of the properties himself, thereby departing from earlier agreements. The monarch may therefore have feared that the Templars' goods would not be used as he saw fit. Furthermore, Clement V had demanded immediate control over the seized properties shortly before, so the king may have seen the risk of losing influence over day-to-day decisions that guaranteed the financing of the huge undertaking that was the proceedings against the Order, in which the French state apparatus was involved. Conversely, Clement V may also have doubted Philip's sincerity, given his well-known financial difficulties. He may therefore have sought to secure at least part of the Templars' assets against the king of France's possible ambitions. However, the real intentions of both parties remain unknown.

In this situation, the king and the pope decided to discuss the issues related to the proceedings in person. To this end, at the turn of January and February, Philip the Fair set off from Boulogne-sur-Mer towards Poitiers.[49] However, he did not reach his destination and was back in Paris by the end of February.[50] According to one commentator, during this trip he learned that Clement V had suspended the activities of the French inquisitors. This was due to the retraction of incriminating testimony by some of the Templars.[51]

Henry Charles Lea suspected that the pope had suspended the proceedings because he feared that Philip the Fair would not fulfil the promises he had made regarding the Order's properties.[52] However, suspending the inquisitors' activities did not change the fact that the Templar houses remained under the control of the king's officials. The longer the impasse continued, in terms of both control over the seized properties and the continuation of the inquisitorial proceedings, the more time there was for potential abuses and the seizure of assets. Only the termination of the proceedings would mean the properties would have to be returned to the Templars. However, this was clearly not the pope's intention.

1.2 In the hands of university masters

It was not until the end of May 1308, several months after the pope's decision to suspend the work of the inquisitors, that Clement V and Philip the Fair finally met to discuss further action regarding the Templars. The period between these two events is generally regarded as a trial of strength between the two parties in the dispute over control of the detained Templars and their assets. Therefore, the actions taken by the monarch at that time appear to have been further attempts to persuade the pope to resume proceedings against the Templars and retain the Order's seized properties under royal administration. However, the available sources suggest that the situation was somewhat more complex and that the fate of the Order and its properties was decided not only by Philip the Fair and Clement V, but also by the masters of the University of Paris, who were asked to help resolve the doubts that had arisen.

Almost immediately after the king of France was informed of the pope's decision to suspend proceedings against the Templars in February 1308, he wrote a letter to the Masters of Theology at the Sorbonne in Paris, asking for consultation on issues related to the course of the proceedings and the Order's properties.[53] Researchers generally consider this move to be part of the French court's propaganda campaign against the pope's decisions.[54] This was modelled on the university's involvement in the dispute between the king of France and Pope Boniface VIII in 1303. At that time, the monarch invoked the authority of the Masters of Theology to support his position in the conflict between secular and spiritual power.[55] A comparison of the two situations may suggest that, in 1308, the king intended to follow the same procedure. However, a closer examination of the university masters' response, and an analysis of the discussions and decisions that took place over the following months, reveals that the Sorbonne theologians played a much more significant role this time than they had five years earlier.

The French court presented the most important accusations against the Order to the masters and scholars of the University of Paris immediately after the arrest of the Templars in October 1307. During a meeting at Notre-Dame Cathedral in Paris, king's officials and members of the Dominican Order presented the reasons for initiating proceedings against the Templars.[56] A few days later, during another meeting, this time at the Temple in Paris, Jacques de Molay and several dozen other brothers appeared before the university members and clergy. They all confessed to the crimes of which they were accused.[57] Four months after these events, Philip the Fair again addressed the Parisian Masters of Theology, asking them seven questions, five of which concerned procedural issues and the legal basis for the proceedings, while the remaining two were devoted to ambiguities related to maintaining control over the Templar properties and deciding their future fate. The king asked, among other things, whether a secular ruler could judge heretics and if the entire Order could be dissolved based on incriminating testimony from only some of the brothers. Regarding properties, he wanted to know if it could be confiscated by the secular ruler under whose jurisdiction it fell or if it should be handed over to the Church or transferred to the Holy Land, for which purpose it had been granted to the Order. If the latter solution was deemed appropriate, who should administer and dispose of the properties?[58]

Researchers analysing the content of the questions wondered what had motivated their specific wording. Paul F. Crawford concluded that they were phrased in such a way as to indicate to the masters the answers that Philip the Fair expected.[59] This suggests that when it came to properties, the king wanted it to be used for its original purpose of supporting the Holy Land, rather than being taken over by secular rulers or the Church.

Malcolm Barber, on the other hand, believed that the questions posed by the monarch were intended to portray the pope as someone who had neglected to defend the faith. Therefore, the king of France had to take matters into his own hands.[60] This suggests that the questions were formulated at the French court to serve the political goals of Philip the Fair rather than to present the Masters of Theology with genuine theological doubts. Nevertheless, the issues raised in the royal letter appear to have reflected actual ambiguities that had emerged during discussions at the papal court and possibly at the royal court in Paris at that time. The precedent-setting nature of the proceedings meant that the *modus operandi* had yet to be determined. This was certainly the case concerning the proceedings against a religious community in which only some members confessed to heresy and the doubts regarding the Templar properties. The conflict that had arisen shortly before between the French ruler and Clement V regarding the temporary seizure of the Order's estates, followed by their confiscation and subsequent distribution, had not yet been resolved. According to Esquieu de Floyran, both sides presented their arguments but did not have the opportunity to discuss the contentious issues, as the meeting between the pope and the king ultimately did not take place. Taking into account the situation in the papal curia at that time, where some cardinals, especially the Italians, were hostile towards Philip the Fair and suspicious of any cooperation between the king and the pope – including the matters regarding the Templars[61] – it is clear why a recognised authority, not directly involved in the proceedings and close to the papacy, was sought to find a solution to the existing problems. The University of Paris played precisely this role, especially in the field of theology, at the turn of the 13th and 14th centuries.[62]

The masters responded to the king's letter a few weeks later, on 25 March 1308. Regarding questions about properties, they stated that the estates should be used for the purpose they were granted for, i.e., the needs of the Holy Land. This position was identical to that initially proposed by Philip the Fair, ruling out the solution demanded by the pope, who wanted to take over part of the Order's properties as an ecclesiastical institution. As for their temporary administration, it was to be organised in such a way as to make the best possible use of the estates for their intended purpose.[63] On this issue, they gave a very ambiguous answer, leaving much room for discussion.

According to Menache, the reply of the Parisian masters proves the failure of royal propaganda.[64] Following this line of reasoning, it can be concluded that the monarch failed to convince the university's members of his arguments, including those based on the belief that the Order should be investigated again and subsequently dissolved, as it had been discredited and caused scandal among the faithful. However, in this case, the judgement of the Masters of Theology was in line with Philip the Fair's position. Nevertheless, the French court did not use these elements of the consultation for propaganda purposes, nor for the discussions held a few months later during the meeting between the king and the pope in Poitiers. This suggests that the purpose of the consultation was not merely to obtain leverage against Clement V. Philip turned to the university members to address the most significant concerns about the proceedings, and their reply formed the basis for subsequent actions and decisions by both the monarch and the pope. There are several arguments in favour of this.

First, preserved documents show that the key issues raised in the king's letter – namely, the participation of the secular ruler in the proceedings and the use of the Order's properties – were no longer under discussion between the pope and the French court. Regarding the Templar properties, there was no mention of Philip the Fair retaining control over it, nor of its takeover by secular rulers or the papacy after the proceedings had ended. This suggests that this issue must have been resolved, most likely by the university masters.

The role played by the university master's may also be confirmed by a statement made by Clement V in April 1308. We learn of this from Cardinal Bérenger Frédol's account to King James II of Majorca (1276–1311), which was summarised by an unknown correspondent in a letter dated 21 April, addressed to the Templar commanders in Gardeny and Ascó.[65] According to the cardinal, less than two months after the pope decided to suspend the French proceedings, his position changed. Bérenger Frédol reported that the fate of the Templars had already been sealed and that the Order would be dissolved. However, it had not yet been decided what would happen to its members and properties. The cardinal also recounted the details of a private consistory devoted to the Templars, which took place the week before Easter, on 14 April. According to his account, Clement V said at the time that the only remaining issue to be decided upon was the Order's properties. One of the French cardinals replied that the first thing to decide was the fate of the Templars themselves, and only then their properties. It suggests that the pope changed his mind about the Order without discussing the matter with the cardinals, whom he merely informed of his opinion. His decision must therefore have been influenced by something other than the discussion in the curia. From the anonymous letter quoted here, we also learn that information about the consultation of the Masters of Theology had already reached the papal court at that time, which allows us to link the two situations. Although Bérenger Frédol did not yet know the content of the answers given by the Parisian masters, this does not mean that the pope did not have such knowledge. As the issues concerning the possibility of further proceedings and the dissolution of the Order had been clearly resolved by the Masters of Theology, Clement V could make his own decisions on this basis. However, the masters' answer to the question concerning the administration of properties left room for discussion, which is why the pope spoke of the need to resolve this issue.

Finally, the last circumstance that speaks in favour of considering the March consultation crucial for subsequent events and decisions in the following months was the outcome of the negotiations in Poitiers in June 1308, particularly the content of the related documents. Regarding properties, Philip the Fair and Clement V only discussed how to administer the assets and who would make decisions about their use after the proceedings concluded. This was in line with the masters' decisions. Also noteworthy are excerpts from letters in which the monarch and the pope presented their proposals for resolving the aforementioned issues. In a letter about the matter of properties, the king of France wrote the following: "According to what God revealed to the pope and the king, the [Templar] properties could only be used for the needs of the Holy Land, in accordance with the intention of its donors."[66] Very similar words were also used in the papal reply.[67] Where did this divine inspiration come from? We can look for answers in the consultation of university masters. In response to a question about the Order's assets, the masters wrote that the Templars had received them "for the defense of the faith and for the needs of the Holy Land – that was the ultimate goal of the donors" and they should therefore continue to serve him.[68] This is likely to have been the starting point for the negotiations in Poitiers. Assuming that the masters had the decisive say in matters of properties, we can also presume that this applied to other issues related to the proceedings.

This demonstrates that the Parisian Masters of Theology decided the fate of the Order's assets and the Templars themselves. Their consultation enabled Clement V and Philip the Fair to overcome the impasse they had encountered at the beginning of 1308, providing the basis for the decisions made in Poitiers a few months later.

1.3 The decisions at Poitiers

In late spring of 1308, the king of France met with the pope. While the monarch was visiting Poitiers, where Clement V's court was residing at the time, important decisions were made regarding the proceedings against the Templars and their properties. The course of the official talks held at that time and the confidential correspondence exchanged on that occasion are well known, but since the arrangements made at that time were crucial for further action on the Templar properties, it is necessary to recall them. Some specific issues need to be looked at again and re-interpreted.

Upon his arrival in Poitiers with his suite, Philip the Fair was likely unaware of the details of the April consistory and that Clement V was prepared to resume proceedings against the Templars. This explains why, during the first public meeting on 29 May, one of the king's closest advisers, Guillaume de Plaisians, delivered a passionate speech reminiscent of the propaganda used during Philip's conflict with Boniface VIII. In it, he demanded that the pope take immediate action against the Order. We know the contents of the speech from two sources: an account by an Aragonese envoy who participated in the consistory, and a written draft.[69] A comparison of the two texts reveals that Guillaume de Plaisians' speech was much more confrontational than the written version, or at least as presented by James II's envoy, who was hostile towards the French monarch. According to the envoy's report, Guillaume de Plaisians openly attacked the pope and presented the French king as the leader in suppressing heresy and preventing the alleged crimes of the Templars. Despite his openly offensive attitude, however, he was said to have been very restrained in his comments on the Order's properties. According to the Aragonese account, Guillaume de Plaisians denied the allegations that the king of France wanted to enrich himself at the expense of the Templars. He pointed out that the monarch "perhaps" had the right to confiscate their properties but decided not to because he wanted it all to go to the Holy Land in accordance with his ancestors' intentions. For this reason, Philip the Fair entrusted their administration to other trusted persons, not his officials, and the income was to go to a separate fund, not the royal treasury.[70] This suggests that the French king had already renounced his claim to the properties granted to the heretical community, as Esquieu de Floyran had mentioned a few months earlier, and that the dispute over the right to control and potentially confiscate the goods of the French Templars had indeed been settled.

In response to Guillaume de Plaisians' speech at the same public consistory, Clement V stated that, although the king of France had ordered the arrest of the Templars without an explicit papal command, he had never suspected that greed was the reason behind this decision. In fact, he was convinced that Philip the Fair had acted out of faith, as demonstrated by his willingness to transfer the Templars' assets to the Church to support the Holy Land.[71] This suggests that the monarch may have already made declarations regarding the transfer of control of the goods to the pope. As Guillaume de Plaisians did not mention this solution in his speech, it is likely that an unofficial exchange of views on the matter has already taken place. However, it cannot be ruled out that Clement V's statement was his own interpretation of the words spoken by Guillaume de Plaisians intended to encourage Philip the Fair. Regardless of the pope's intentions, he did not publicly condemn the French monarch's possible mistakes regarding the Order's properties; in fact, he confirmed his honesty once again. It therefore seems that the tensions arising from this issue had somehow been defused, and even if not, both sides showed a willingness to reach an agreement.

Public declarations by Philip the Fair's representative and Clement V paved the way for further discussions about the Templar properties. However, these discussions could only take place once the issue of the brothers' trial and the future of the entire Order had been resolved. This was not an easy task. Guillaume de Plaisians' subsequent speech at the consistory on 14 June shows that formal and legal doubts continued to hinder progress. Nevertheless, on the same day, the pope announced an inquisitorial investigation, emphasising that he would not make any decisions until he had taken control of the detained members of the Order and its assets.[72]

Following Clement V's declaration, bilateral negotiations on the practical aspects of future proceedings began. These negotiations were conducted in writing, suggesting that they were secret. The pope probably expected resistance from at least some of the College of Cardinals, who were reluctant to cooperate closely with the French king on the matter of the Templars. This could have hindered the negotiations and the final decisions. This is confirmed by Clement V's own words in a letter he exchanged with Philip the Fair at that time concerning the revocation of the suspension of the French inquisitors in connection with their actions against the Templars. As the king was keen to reverse this decision, the pope promised that he would "do everything in his power to convince the cardinals."[73] Given this, it can be assumed that Clement V also preferred to consult the monarch directly on the issue of properties first and only present his decisions to the cardinals later.

The letters from Philip the Fair and Clement V discussing the administration of the Order's estates, which have survived to this day and were published by Edgard Boutaric, are undated. However, their content suggests that they were written between the consistory on 14 June and 27 June, when the monarch officially transferred control of both the Templar properties and the brothers who were held in royal prisons to the Church.[74]

It was Philip the Fair who first proposed further action regarding the Templars and their properties. The king declared his willingness to transfer control of the detained Templars to the Church, but as the Church would not be able to exercise this control independently, the Templars were to remain in royal prisons. The king devoted much more attention to the issue of properties. He presented a plan involving three parties to administer it: the pope, the French bishops, and the monarch. The bishops of individual dioceses were to take formal control of the properties. Direct administration, on the other hand, was to be handled by the bishops' administrators together with persons appointed by the king at the pope's request. These administrators were to report annually on their activities to the hierarchy and the French monarch. In turn, the pope was to appoint a general administrator to accept the final accounts. Once approved, the money would be transferred to the royal treasury, with an appropriate receipt issued each time. It could then only be paid out for the needs of the Holy Land, at the pope's discretion and with the consent of Philip the Fair or one of his successors. The king emphasised that this final safeguard was not due to a lack of trust in Clement V, but rather because of concerns about the intentions of future popes.[75] However, the proposed solutions suggested otherwise. Although the monarch no longer claimed the right to confiscate the Order's property, he still did not want to transfer it entirely to the Church. He wanted to retain influence over how the accumulated money was spent. Boutaric believed that, in practice, the latter solution meant that the king of France could take over all the funds. He could block any initiative to use the funds and thus never pay them to the Church, leaving him free to use them for his own purposes.[76] While it is unclear whether Philip's intentions were as far-reaching, his proposal demonstrates that he was certainly not willing to relinquish his involvement in the administration and subsequent distribution of the estates.

Clement V most likely recognised the potential danger of the French king becoming overly involved in the day-to-day management of the seized Templar properties because he disagreed with the solutions the king proposed. He made this clear in a letter in response to the monarch's proposal. According to the pope, the administrators of the estates were to be persons appointed by him and the bishops, separately for each diocese. Philip the Fair could only secretly suggest candidates he considered best suited to this role, who would be officially appointed by the pope or his appointees. A similar solution was to be applied in the case of commissioners, whose task would be to audit the administrators' accounts. Additionally, the pope would appoint persons responsible for the overall accounting of the income from the Templars' estates throughout the kingdom of France. The money collected would be placed under the king's control, and he would be obliged to issue receipts for it and ensure that it was spent only on aid for the Holy Land or on meeting the Templars' basic needs. However, the pope would have the final say on how it was used.[77]

Although Clement V excluded Philip the Fair from officially participating in the management of the Order's assets and decision-making regarding their future, he did not completely deprive him of influence over these issues. The solutions presented by the pope gave the king partial control over the management of the assets and the ability to block decisions on how the accumulated money was spent, especially since it was to be kept in his treasury. This compromise took into account the aspirations of both sides, guaranteeing joint involvement in decision-making processes concerning the assets. One can only wonder why the pope wanted to conceal the king's involvement in the further management of the estates. This was most likely related to the mood prevailing in the College of Cardinals, whose opposition he feared. However, it is also possible that he wanted to avoid similar demands from other monarchs who might also have wanted to retain influence over the Order's properties in their countries.

Some researchers believe that the adopted solutions granted the king complete control over the Templars' assets. This was to be guaranteed by the monarch to appoint people to manage the assets. These administrators were to make decisions regarding the management of the assets and take over the accumulated income.[78] This interpretation appears to be corroborated by a reference in Jean de Saint-Victor's chronicle to the agreements made in Poitiers. According to the author, the king was to retain control of all the assets until an agreement was reached with the pope regarding their future.[79] However, based on the aforementioned proposals presented by both Philip the Fair and Clement V, it is difficult to draw such a conclusion, since not only were the king's appointees to participate in the administration, but also representatives of the Holy See and French bishops. The involvement of the latter meant that managing the seized properties was no longer dependent solely on bilateral agreements between the king and the pope; it introduced an additional element of control over their commissioners' actions and decisions. Therefore, at this stage, there was certainly no question of Philip retaining the properties.

In his letter, Clement V also addressed the issue of what would happen to the detained brothers in the future. This issue does not appear to have raised much controversy or concern on the part of the pope, nor did it require the same level of detailed solutions as the administration of the Order's assets. Clement V agreed to Philip the Fair's proposal that the Templars should remain in royal prisons, stipulating only that Church commissioners appointed to conduct further investigations should have constant access to them.[80]

It seems that the papal project brought the discussion on key issues concerning further proceedings against the Templars to an end, with the king accepting the proposed solutions and agreeing to fulfil the set conditions. On 27 June, Philip the Fair issued an official letter committing himself to transferring control of the Order's assets to the Church. He emphasised that he had previously seized the assets to prevent their dispersal and that he did not intend to keep them for himself, but rather to return them to the Templars or transfer them to the Holy Land, depending on the outcome of the proceedings. However, now he was handing them over to administrators appointed by the pope and French bishops.[81] On the same day, the monarch also announced his decision to transfer the custody of the imprisoned Templars to Church commissioners.[82] The next day, hearings began for several dozen Templars brought to Poitiers at the pope's request.[83] This was followed by a public announcement of the decisions taken by Clement V, who, in the bull *Subit assidue* of 5 July, ordered that an inquisitorial investigation be resumed against individual members of the Order.[84]

Once the matter of the individuals had been resolved, the formal settlement of the properties issue could proceed. To this end, on 9 July, the king and the pope made written declarations stating that, in the event of the Order's dissolution, its properties would be allocated to the needs of the Holy Land. These provisions were also to apply to their successors.[85] On the same day, Clement V sent Philip the Fair a bull beginning with the words *Tibi, fili carissime*, in which he discussed the appointment of administrators of the properties and their subsequent settlements – issues that had already been raised during earlier negotiations. In accordance with the pope's wishes, the monarch could secretly appoint loyal individuals to participate in the management of the properties, as he saw fit. Clement V or the hierarchs appointed by him were to swear them in, just as they did their own administrators. The same applies to those responsible for auditing the administrators' accounts. Everyone involved in managing the estates had to submit regular reports, and those receiving money had to issue receipts. Annual financial summaries were to be prepared in two copies: one for the pope and one for the king. All funds collected were to be stored securely within the kingdom of France and used to meet the needs of the Holy Land. The final destination was to be decided exclusively by Clement V or his successors. These measures were to remain in force until the Templars' fate was sealed.[86] This was, therefore, a detailed elaboration of the papal proposals made during earlier negotiations.

The next step was for both sides to declare that no decisions concerning the Order's properties could harm the Church, the papacy, the king, or his subjects.[87] After that, Clement V officially announced his decision. On 12 July, he issued a bull addressed to Philip the Fair, explaining how the Order's French properties were to be administered and what was to happen to its income.[88] This did not contain any new decisions relating to those that had already been published. On the same day, Clement V also sent a letter to the French bishops instructing them to appoint administrators for the estates in individual dioceses. These administrators were to take an oath committing them to the honest management of the properties, and they were to submit regular reports on their activities. They were also to present annual accounts to the pope and the king of France.[89] However, the letter did not mention where the collected funds were to be allocated. It was not until May 1311 that Clement V sent the bishops more detailed instructions on the practical aspects of accounting. He explained how and by whom the financial reports were to be submitted. These were to be signed by the administrators of the estates, as well as the bishops. All these individuals were required to present their accounts in person to the king, the pope, or their envoys. If the administrators of the estates were found to be acting dishonestly, they would be given time to correct their mistakes;

if they failed to do so, both ecclesiastical and secular penalties would be applied. The pope also explained that the money collected was to be placed in a treasury controlled by the king of France and used to meet the needs of the Holy Land, in accordance with his own or his successors' decisions.[90]

Decisions concerning the administration of seized properties were supplemented by the bull *Ad omnium fere* dated 12 August 1308, in which the pope ordered all those in possession of Templar money or estates to hand it over to designated administrators under threat of excommunication.[91] The version of the document addressed to Christian prelates also requested assistance in apprehending the brothers still at large.[92] On the same day, Clement V issued the bull *Regnans in coelis*, announcing his decision to convene a Council to reach a final decision on the Templars. This was to be held in Vienne and was scheduled to open in October 1310.[93]

All of the above letters summarised and supplemented confidential negotiations and a decision-making process that lasted several weeks, during which the pope played a key role. Analysis of the sources shows that, after presenting his initial proposal, Philip the Fair took no further initiative and did not oppose Clement V's ideas; instead, he fulfilled the pope's conditions regarding the transfer of the Order's properties and members to the control of the Church. Clement V, on the other hand, acted in accordance with the cardinals' expectations: he first made an official decision to resume proceedings against the Order's members, and only then presented his plans regarding its properties. It therefore seems that, at the meeting in Poitiers, all the ambiguities that had arisen since the beginning of the proceedings were resolved, and the disputes and tensions between the king of France and the pope, as well as within the curia, were alleviated.

Having discussed matters relating to the proceedings against the Templars, Clement V and Philip the Fair proceeded to talk about the organisation of a military expedition to the East, which had been proposed by the Hospitallers at that time.[94] This was not yet a proper crusade, but rather actions that could be a prelude to one. It was agreed that funding for the expedition would come from the papal treasury and the French king, a decision announced during a consistory attended by the Grand Master of the Hospital.[95] The timing suggests that this issue was linked to decisions concerning the Templar properties. They provided the first opportunity from the beginning of Clement V's pontificate to gather the resources necessary for planning any serious military expedition to the East. Furthermore, during the negotiations, it was agreed that the money from the Order's houses was to be used for the needs of the Holy Land, without specifying that it could only be used for this purpose after the proceedings had been completed. On the contrary, the bull *Tibi, fili carissime* indicates that the solutions adopted concerned the period before the final resolution of the Order's case. This meant that the pope could proceed with the realisation of his dream of a crusade, counting on the involvement of Philip the Fair.

A report from the Aragonese envoys a few months later suggests that discussions may also have taken place in Poitiers regarding the use of the Templar properties after the trial. In a letter dated 10 March 1309, the envoys summarised for James II the words of one of the cardinals, who said that Philip the Fair wanted to transfer all the Order's possessions to his son as king of Jerusalem. This plan was primarily discussed in the early stages of the proceedings, as previously mentioned. The cardinal believed that such a solution would be unfair to the other princes and therefore advised the Aragonese ruler not to give the pope control over the Templar properties in his kingdom until a final decision had been reached.[96] However, this issue is not mentioned in any of the documents or correspondence from Poitiers, nor in the reports of the meeting between Philip the Fair and Clement V that have been preserved. Clearly, therefore, it did not preoccupy the interlocutors as much as other topics discussed.

Commenting on the March report of the Aragonese envoys, Demurger stated that Clement V had already decided to transfer the Templar properties to the Hospital by this point, although Philip the Fair was unaware of this.[97] However, the thesis is not corroborated by the surviving sources, and the earliest references to the pope's intentions in this matter date only to 1312, when they were discussed by the Council fathers gathered in Vienne.

Notes

1 This number of French houses was determined by Malcolm Barber based on E. Léonard, *Introduction au cartulaire manuscrit du Temple (1150–1317)* (Paris 1930), pp. 13–137; M. Barber, 'Supplying the Crusader States: The Role of the Templars', in: *The Horns of Hattin: proceedings of the second conference of the Society for the Study of the Crusades and the Latin East: Jerusalem and Haïfa, 2-6 July 1987*, ed. B. Z. Kedar (Jerusalem 1992), p. 319. Other researchers also accepted it – A. Demurger, *Chevaliers du Christ: Les ordres religieux-militaires au Moyen Âge (Xie-XVIe siècle)* (Paris 2002), p. 124; I. de La Torre, *Los Templarios y el Origen de la Banca* (Madrid 2004), p. 279.

2 According to Robert Fossier, two-thirds of the 610 houses, i.e. approximately 400, were located in the kingdom of France – R. Fossier, 'Les Hospitaliers et les Templiers au nord de la Seine et en Bourgogne (XIIe–XIVe siècles)', in: *Les ordres militaires: La vie rurale et le peuplement en Europe occidentale (XIIe–XVIIIe siècles)*, ed. C. Higounet (Toulouse 1986), p. 15. P. Josserand, in turn, estimated the number of French houses at approximately 300–350 – 'Les Templers en France: histoire et héritage', *Revue Historique*, 316 (2014), no. 1, p. 192.

3 L. Dailliez, *La France des Templiers* (Paris 1974), p. 29.

4 For further details on the organisation of the royal treasury before 1307, see L. L. Borrelli de Serres, *Recherches sur divers services publics du XII au XVIIe siècle*, vol. 3 (Paris 1909), pp. 5–31. See also E. Lalou, *Itinéraire de Philippe IV le Bel*, vol. 1 (Paris 2007), p. 139; A. Demurger, 'Trésor des Templiers, trésor du roi. Mise au point sur les opérations financières des templiers', *Pouvoir et Gestion*, 5 (1997), pp. 73–85.

5 *Monuments historiques: cartons des rois*, ed. J. Tardif (Paris 1866, repr. 1977), no. 1043, p. 364; H. de Curzon, *La maison de Temple de Paris. Histoire et description* (Paris 1888), *Documents annexes*, no. 4, pp. 305–307; H. Prutz, *Entwicklung*, no. 21, pp. 307–308.

6 H. C. Lea, *A History of the Inquisition in the Middle Ages*, vol. 3 (New York 1909), p. 252. On Philip the Fair's attitude towards the Templars before 1305, see also C. V. Langlois, 'Le procès', p. 396; G. Lizerand, *Clément V*, p. 82.

7 See, for example, L. L. L. Lavocat, *Procès*, pp. 125–126; A. Demurger, *La persécution*, pp. 26–28.

8 F. Heidelberger, *Kreuzzugsversuche um die Wende des 13. Jahrhunderts* (Berlin 1911), pp. 23–25; L. Thier, *Kreuzzugsbemühungen unter Papst Clemens V (1305–1314)* (Werl

1973), pp. 98–99; S. Schein, *Fideles Crucis. The Papacy, the West and the Recovery of the Holy Land 1274–1314* (Oxford 1991), p. 182; S. Menache, *Clement V*, p. 101.

9 For the most comprehensive study of the talks between the king and the pope in November 1305, see K. Wenck, 'Aus den Tagen der Zusammenkunft Papst Klemens' V und König Philipps des Schönen zu Lyon, November 1305 bis Januar 1306', *Zeitschrift für Kirchengeschichte* 27 (1906), pp. 189–202.

10 On Clement V's efforts to organise a crusade in the early years of his pontificate, see, for example, N. Housley, *The Avignon Papacy and the Crusades, 1305–1378* (Oxford 1986), pp. 12–13; S. Schein, *Fideles Crucis*, pp. 181–199.

11 Reg. Clem. V, vol. 1 (Rome 1885), no. 1033, pp. 190–191; *Papsttum*, vol. 2, no. 23, p. 36.

12 On the discussion on unifying Military Orders, see: G. Lizerand, *Clément V*, pp. 80–81; A. J. Forey, 'The Military Orders in the Crusading Proposals of the Late-Thirteenth and Early-Fourteenth Centuries', *Viator*, 38 (1980), pp. 320–323.

13 *Vitae*, vol. 3, no. 32, pp. 145–149. See also, for example, J. Delaville Le Roulx, *La France en Orient au XIVe siècle*, vol. 1 (Paris 1886), pp. 55–57; S. Schein, *Fideles Crucis*, pp. 200–202; A. Demurger, 'Les ordres militaires et la croisade au début du XIVe siècle: Quelques remarques sur les traités de croisade de Jacques de Molay et de Foulques de Villaret', in: *Dei gesta per Francos. Etudes sur les croisades dédiées à Jean Richard – Crusade Studies in Honour of Jean Richard*, ed. M. Balard, B. Z. Kedar, J. Riley-Smith (Aldershot 2001), pp. 117–128.

14 *Vitae*, vol. 3, no. 32, pp. 150–154; R. A. de Vertot, *Histoire des Chevaliers hospitaliers de S. Jean de Jérusalem, appellez depuis les Chevaliers de Rhodes, et aujourd'hui les Chevaliers de Malte*, vol. 1 (Paris 1726), *Preuves*, pp. 630–633; *Le dossier de l'affaire des Templiers*, ed. and trans. G. Lizerand (Paris 1923, repr. 1964, 1989); no. 1, pp. 2–15. See also, for example, J. Delaville Le Roulx, *La France*, p. 58; M. Barber, *The Trial* (2006), pp. 36–37; M. Satora, *Sprawa*, pp. 44–45.

15 L. L. L. Lavocat, *Procès*, p. 127.

16 P. Dupuy, *Histoire de la condamnation*, no. 42, pp. 188–189; *Vitae*, vol. 3, no. 19, p. 60; E. Boutaric, 'Clément V' (1871), pp. 324–325; L. L. L. Lavocat, *Procès*, pp. 126–127. The letter is extensively cited in: C. Mansuet Jeune, *Histoire critique et apologétique de l'Ordre des chevaliers du Temple de Jérusalem, dits Templiers*, vol. 2 (Paris 1789), p. 143. See also C. V. Langlois, 'Le procès', p. 397; A. Demurger, *La persécution*, pp. 38–40.

17 G. Lizerand, *Clément V*, Appendice, no. 6, p. 434; B. Barbiche, *Les actes pontificaux originaux des Archives nationales de Paris*, vol. 3 (Città del Vaticano 1982), no. 2318, p. 37.

18 E. Boutaric, 'Clément V' (1871), pp. 325–326.

19 E. Boutaric, 'Clément V' (1871), pp. 329–331; *Le dossier*, no. 2, pp. 16–24; G. Bordonove, *La Tragédie des Templiers* (3rd ed.) (Paris 2011), p. 127 (French translation).

20 P. Timbal, 'La confiscation dans le droit français des XIIIe et XIVe siècles', *Revue historique du droit français et étranger*, 21 (1943), pp. 44–50.

21 H. C. Lea, 'Confiscation for Heresy in the Middle Ages', *The English Historical Review*, 2 (1887), no. 6, p. 236.

22 *Papsttum*, vol. 2, no. 30, p. 47. See also M. Satora, *Sprawa*, pp. 96–97.

23 E. Boutaric, 'Clément V' (1871), pp. 332–335; B. Barbiche, *Les actes*, vol. 3, no. 2320, p. 38; *The Templars*, no. 68, pp. 249–250 (English translation). See also M. Satora, *Sprawa*, p. 112.

24 On the conflict between Philip the Fair and Boniface VIII, see P. Dupuy, *Histoire du differend d'entre le pape Boniface VIII et Philippes le Bel roy de France* (Paris 1655); G. Digard, *Philippe le Bel et le Saint-Siège de 1285 à 1304*, vol. 1–2 (Paris 1936); J. Favier, *Philippe le Bel*, pp. 250–288, 343–393; J. R. Strayer, *The Reign of Philip the Fair* (Princeton 1980), pp. 251–279; A. Paravicini Bagliani, *Boniface VIII. Un pape hérétique?* (Paris 2003), pp. 299–391.

25 On the French court's efforts to initiate an inquisitorial proceeding against the deceased pope, as well as its course, see *Boniface VIII en procès. Articles d'accusation et*

dépositions des témoins (1303–1311), ed. J. Coste (Rome 1995); G. Lizerand, *Clément V*, pp. 190–217; S. Menache, *Clement V*, pp. 191–199.

26 E. Boutaric, 'Clément V' (1871), pp. 332–335; B. Barbiche, *Les actes*, vol. 3, no. 2320, p. 38. See also M. Satora, *Sprawa*, pp. 112–115.

27 H. Prutz, *Entwicklung*, p. 155.

28 E. Boutaric, 'Clément V' (1871), pp. 325–326.

29 P. Dupuy, *Histoire de la condamnation*, no. 58, pp. 221–223; *Foedera, conventiones, literae et cuiuscunque generis acta publica inter reges Angliae et alios quosvis imperatores, reges ... ab anno 1101 ad nostra usque tempora*, ed. T. Rymer, vol. 2.1 (Hague 1739), pp. 30–32; *Memorias de D. Fernando IV de Castilla*, ed. A. Benavides, vol. 2 (Madrid 1860), pp. 619–621.

30 See, for example, a summary of discussions on this topic conducted between the late 19th century and the early 21st century in M. Barber, 'The Trial of the Templars Revisited', in: *The Military Orders*, vol. 2, *Welfare and Warfare*, ed. H. Nicholson (Aldershot 1998), pp. 329–342; M. Barber, *The Trial* (2006), pp. 295–301; M. Satora, *Sprawa*, pp. 56–57.

31 E. Mannier, *Ordre de Malte*, p. XVII; L. Niepce, *Le Grand-prieuré d'Auvergne: ordre des hospitaliers de Saint-Jean de Jérusalem* (Lyon 1883), p. 81; L. L. L. Lavocat, *Procès*, pp. 117–118; C. V. Langlois, 'Le procès', p. 395; H. C. Lea, *A History*, vol. 3, p. 255; L. L. Borrelli de Serres, *Recherches*, vol. 3, p. 38; J. Delaville Le Roulx, 'La suppression', pp. 51–52; J. M. A. Delaville Le Roulx, *Les hospitaliers à Rhodes jusqu'à la mort de Philibert de Naillac (1310–1421)* (Paris 1913), p. 34; J. R. Strayer, *The Reign*, p. 287; R. Cazelles, 'Les variations du prélèvement et de la répartition selon les équipes au pouvoir', in: *Genèse de l'État moderne*: *prélèvement* et *redistribution. Actes du colloque de Fontevraud, 1984*, ed. J. P. Genèt, M. Le Mené (Paris 1987), p. 203; A. Forey, *The Military Orders. From the Twelfth to Early Fourteenth Centuries* (Toronto and Buffalo 1992), pp. 35–37; N. Housley, *The Avignon Papacy*, p. 14; K. Elm, 'Der Templerprozeß (1307–1312)', in: *Macht und Recht. Große Prozesse in der Geschichte*, ed. A. Demandt (München 1990), p. 97; S. Schein, *Fideles Crucis*, pp. 242–243; M. Barber, *The Trial* (2006), pp. 52, 57, 288; G. Bordonove, *Philippe le Bel: Roi de fer* (2nd ed.) (Paris 2013), p. 296.

32 On the financial problems of Philip the Fair and the attempts to overcome them, see, for example, J. Favier, *Philippe le Bel*, pp. 137–205; J. R. Strayer, *The Reign*, pp. 148–155; M. Barber, *The Trial* (2006), pp. 44–53. For more information on coin debasement in the context of the Templars, see J. Piquet, *Des banquiers au Moyen Âge: les Templiers. Étude de leurs opérations financières* (Paris 1939), pp. 147–171; M. Barber, *The Trial* (2006), p. 52; I. de La Torre, 'The Monetary Fluctuations in Philip IV's Kingdom of France and Their Relevance to the Arrest of the Templars', in: *The Debate on the Trial of the Templars (1307–1314)*, ed. J. Burgtorf, P. F. Crawford, H. J. Nicholson (Farnham 2010), pp. 57–68. On the confiscation of the properties of Jews and Lombard merchants, see also S. Schwarzfuchs, 'The Expulsion of the Jews form France, 1306', *Jewish Quarterly Review*, 75 (1967), pp. 482–489; J. R. Strayer, 'Italian Bankers and Philip the Fair', *Explorations in Economic History*, 7 (1969), no. 1–2, pp. 113–121.

33 I. de La Torre, 'The Monetary Fluctuations', pp. 57–68.

34 C. Guéry, *La Commanderie de Saint-Etienne-de-Renneville (Eure) fondée par Richard d'Harcourt* (Évreux 1896), p. 59; I. de La Torre, 'The Templars' Banking Activities and Their Potential Connections to the Order's Demise', in: *The Templars. The Rise, Fall, and Legacy of a Military Religious Order*, ed. J. Burgtorf, S. Lotan, E. Mallorquí-Ruscalleda (London–New York 2021), pp. 179–187.

35 R. Cazelles, 'Les variations', pp. 203–207.

36 S. Menache, 'The Templar Order: A Failed Ideal?', *The Catholic Historical Review*, 79 (1993), pp. 16–20; A. Demurger, 'Trésor des Templiers', pp. 83–85.

37 *Papsttum*, vol. 2, no. 34, p. 51; J. N. Hillgarth, *Ramon Lull and Lullism in Fourteenth-Century France* (Oxford 1971), p. 93; S. Schein, *Fideles Crucis*, p. 241. Quoted from M. Barber, *The Trial* (2006), p. 85. See also M. Satora, *Sprawa*, pp. 182–183.

38 *Papsttum*, vol. 2, no. 75, p. 118 (comment from Spring 1308); *Papsttum*, vol. 2, no. 101, p. 183 (comment form March 1309); *Thomae Walsingham, quondam monachi S. Albani, Historia Anglicana*, ed. H. T. Riley, vol. 1 (London 1863), p. 127; *Adae Murimuth Continuatio Chronicarum. Robertus de Avesbury de Gestis Mirabilibus Regis Edwardi Tertii*, ed. E. Maunde Thomson (London 1889, repr. Cambridge 2012), pp. 16–17; *Chronicon Galfridi le Baker de Swynebroke*, ed. E. Maunde Thomson (Oxford 1889), p. 5. On the plan of merging the Military Orders and placing a monarch or royal son at the head of the new brotherhood, see also J. N. Hillgarth, *Ramon Lull*, pp. 93–94; A. J. Forey, 'The Military Orders in the Crusading Proposals', pp. 333–335.

39 On the stance adopted by individual Western European monarchs regarding the organisation of a new crusade in the early 14th century, see, for example, S. Schein, *Fideles Crucis*, pp. 182–199; M. Satora, *Sprawa*, pp. 46–49.

40 L. L. L. Lavocat, *Procès*, p. 185; J. N. Hillgarth, *Ramon Lull*, pp. 94–95; J. Favier, *Philippe le Bel*, pp. 476–477; A. J. Forey, 'The Military Orders in the Crusading Proposals', p. 337.

41 J. Favier, *Philippe le Bel*, p. 476; J. Favier, *Les papes d'Avignon* (Paris 2006), pp. 95–96.

42 P. Dupuy, *Histoire de la condamnation*, no. 59, pp. 223–224; *Vitae*, vol. 3, pp. 91–92; E. Boutaric, 'Clément V' (1871), pp. 336–337. On the content of the letter, see also M. Satora, *Sprawa*, pp. 116–117.

43 P. Dupuy, *Histoire de la condamnation*, no. 59, pp. 225–226; *Vitae*, vol. 3, pp. 92–94; L. L. L. Lavocat, *Procès*, pp. 163–164; G. Bordonove, *La Tragédie*, pp. 167–168 (French translation). See also C. Mansuet Jeune, *Histoire*, vol. 2, pp. 176–177. The letter is quoted extensively in A. Demurger, *La persécution*, p. 85.

44 *Acta Aragonensia: Quellen zur deutschen, italienischen, französischen, spanischen Kirchen- und Kulturgeschichte aus der diplomatischen Korrespondenz Jaymes II., 1291–1327*, ed. H. Finke, vol. 3 (Berlin 1908), no. 76, p. 174.

45 L. Tanon, *Histoire des tribunaux de l'inquisition en France* (Paris 1893), pp. 204–207.

46 L. Tanon, *Histoire des tribunaux*, pp. 534–538.

47 On Esquieu de Floyran's role in initiating proceedings against the Templars, see J. Clémens, 'La rumeur agenaise de l'enfermement templier au début du XIVe siècle', *Revue de l'Agenais*, 123 (1996), pp. 219–233 and 124 (1997), pp. 23–40; A. Demurger, *Les Templiers*, pp. 429–432; D. Bryson, 'Three "Traitors" of the Temple: Was Their Truth the Whole Truth?', in: *The Debate on the Trial of the Templars (1307–1314)*, ed. J. Burgtorf, P. F. Crawford, H. J. Nicholson (Farnham 2010), pp. 97–103; J. Clémens, A. Demurger, 'Esquieu de Floyran', in: *Prier et combattre: Dictionnaire européen des ordres militaires au Moyen Âge*, ed. N. Bériou, P. Josserand (Paris 2009), pp. 339–340; A. Demurger, *La persécution*, pp. 23–26.

48 *Papsttum*, vol. 2, no. 57, p. 84; C. V. Langlois, 'L'affaire', pp. 423–424 (French translation); *The Templars*, no. 70, pp. 256–257 (English translation). See also A. Pétel, 'Templiers et Hospitaliers dans le diocèse de Troyes. Le Temple de Bonlieu' (1909), p. 291; G. Lizerand, *Clément V*, p. 109; M. Satora, *Sprawa*, pp. 118–119.

49 *Acta Aragonensia*, vol. 3, no. 77, p. 176.

50 E. Lalou, *Itinéraire*, vol. 2, Paris 2007, pp. 305–306.

51 *Papsttum*, vol. 2, no. 75, p. 117. See also M. Satora, *Sprawa*, pp. 122–123.

52 H. C. Lea, *A History*, vol. 3, p. 279.

53 *Le dossier*, no. 5, pp. 56–63; G. Bordonove, *La Tragédie*, pp. 174–176 (French translation). See also G. Lizerand, *Clément V*, p. 112.

54 J. Delaville Le Roulx, 'La suppression', p. 11; M. Barber, *The Trial* (2006), p. 98; A. Demurger, *Les Templiers*, p. 445; P. F. Crawford, 'The University of Paris and the Trial of the Templars', in: *The Military Orders*, vol. 3, *History and Heritage*, ed. V. Mallia-Milanes (Aldershot 2008), p. 116; J. Théry-Astruc, 'The Flight of the Master of Lombardy (13 February 1308) and Clement V's Strategy in the Templar Affair: A Slap in the Pope's Face', *Rivista di Storia della Chiesa in Italia*, 70 (2016), no. 1, p. 42.

55 See S. Menache, 'A Propaganda Campaign in the Reign of Philip the Fair, 1302–1303', *French History*, 4 (1990), pp. 427–454.

56 'Excerpta e memoriali historiarum auctore Johanne Parisiensi, Sancti Vistoris Parisiensis canonico regulari' ed. L. Delisle, in: *Recueil des historiens des Gaules et de la France*, ed. M. Bouquet et al., vol. 21 (Paris 1855), p. 649. See also M. Barber, *The Trial* (2006), pp. 78–79; P. F. Crawford, 'The University', pp. 115–116; M. Satora, *Społeczny odbiór procesu i upadku zakonu templariuszy we Francji w pierwszej połowie XIV w.* (Malbork 2008), p. 58.

57 *Papsttum*, vol. 2, no. 32, p. 49; *Papsttum*, vol. 2, nos. 149–150, pp. 307–313; 'Excerpta e memoriali', p. 649. See also M. Satora, *Społeczny odbiór*, p. 59.

58 *Le dossier*, no. 5, pp. 60–62. See also G. Lizerand, *Clément V*, p. 112; M. Barber, *The Trial* (2006), pp. 98–99; P. F. Crawford, 'The University', pp. 117–118.

59 P. F. Crawford, 'The University', p. 118.

60 M. Barber, *The Trial* (2006), p. 100.

61 According to an Aragonese correspondent writing to the Templar commander of Lleida in the spring of 1308, even the cardinals appointed by Clement V were said to have expressed their opposition to his actions regarding the Order. During a consistory in December 1307, ten new cardinals threatened to resign, believing the pope to be too submissive to the king of France – the proceedings against the Templars being a clear example of this – *Papsttum*, vol. 2, no. 71, pp. 110–111. See also for example M. Barber, *The Trial* (2006), pp. 91–92; M. Satora, *Sprawa*, p. 73. For more on the position of the members of the College of Cardinals on the Templars, see M. Satora, 'The Role of the Cardinals in the Templars' Affair 1307–1308', *Ordines Militares. Colloquia Torunensia Historica. Yearbook for the Study of the Military Orders*, 16 (2011), pp. 93–103.

62 See S. Menache, 'La naissance d'une nouvelle source d'authorité: l'Université de Paris', *Revue Historique*, 268 (1982), pp. 305–327.

63 *Le dossier*, no. 5, pp. 62–71. G. Bordonove, *La Tragédie*, pp. 176–178 (French translation). See also L. L. L. Lavocat, *Procès*, p. 166; G. Lizerand, *Clément V*, p. 113; P. F. Crawford, 'The University', p. 119; M. Barber, *The Trial* (2006), pp. 100–101; M. Satora, *Społeczny odbiór*, p. 94.

64 S. Menache, 'Contemporary Attitudes Concerning the Templars' Affair: Propaganda's Fiasco?', *Journal of Medieval History*, 8 (1982), no. 2, pp. 141–142.

65 *Papsttum*, vol. 2, no. 78, pp. 122–123.

66 "secundum quod Deus inspiravit tam domino summo Pontifici quam regi, sic provideatur, quod dicta bona aliter non possint converti nisi in subsidium Terre sancte, secundum intentionem largitorum bonorum" – E. Boutaric, 'Clément V' (1872), p. 9.

67 "bona dicti ordinis non possint converti in totum vel in parte, nisi in subsidium Terre sancte, secundum intencionem largitorum bonorum ipsorum, et ita Deus summo Pontifici et regi inspiravit" – E. Boutaric, 'Clément V' (1872), p. 11.

68 "ad deffensionem fidei et subsidium Terre Sancte, et hoc fuerit finalis intencio dnacium illa bona [...] debent dicta bona ad dictum finem ordinari fideliter et servari" – *Le dossier*, no. 5, pp. 68–69.

69 Report of the Aragonese envoy – *Papsttum*, vol. 2, no. 88, pp. 140–150; C. V. Langlois, 'L'affaire', pp. 426–429; written version of the speech – *Le dossier*, pp. 110–124. Guillaume de Plaisians' speech has been analysed in detail many times. See, for example, G. Lizerand, *Clément V*, s. 122–124; M. Barber, *The Trial* (2006), pp. 107–111; M. Satora, 'Mowa Wilhelma de Plaisians o sprawie templariuszy jako przykład francuskiej propagandy politycznej początku XIV wieku', in: *Odkrywcy, princepsi, rozbójnicy*, ed. B. Śliwiński (Malbork 2007), pp. 217–232.

70 *Papsttum*, vol. 2, no. 88, pp. 142–143; C. V. Langlois, 'L'affaire', p. 427.

71 *Papsttum*, vol. 2, no. 88, pp.148–150; C. V. Langlois, 'L'affaire', p. 430. See also G. Lizerand, *Clément V*, p. 126.

72 See the draft of Guillaume de Plaisians' speech from 14 June – E. Boutaric, 'Notices et extraits de documents inédits relatifs à l'histoire de France sous Philippe le Bel', *Notices et extraits des manuscrits de la Bibliothèque Impériale*, 20 (1865), pt. 2, no. 29, pp. 182–186; *Le dossier*, pp. 124–136. See also the account of the consistory by the English envoy – L. Blancard, 'Documents relatifs au procès des Templiers en Angleterre', *Revue des sociétés savantes*, 4th. ser. 6 (1867), pp. 418–420. For more on the discussion that took place during the consistory, see also G. Lizerand, *Clément V*, pp. 126–128; M. Barber, *The Trial* (2006), pp. 112–115; M. Satora, *Społeczny odbiór*, pp. 63–66.

73 E. Boutaric, 'Clément V' (1872), p. 12. See also M. Satora, *Sprawa*, p. 140.

74 Barber rightly pointed out that, in a letter dated 27 June, the king of France mentioned transferring control over the Order's estates to commissioners appointed by the pope and French prelates, which was discussed during the written negotiations – *The Trial* (2006), p. 122. However, Demurger believes that the letters were written between 2 and 5 July, i.e. between the public consistory, which took place after the interrogation of several dozen Templars brought to Poitiers at the pope's request, and the issuance of the bull *Subit assidue*, in which Clement V presented his decision to resume proceedings against members of the Order – *La persécution*, p. 119. However, it is difficult to find arguments to support this thesis.

75 E. Boutaric, 'Clément V' (1872), pp. 8–9. See also G. Lizerand, *Clément V*, pp. 128–129; M. Barber, *The Trial* (2006), pp. 122–123; M. Satora, *Sprawa*, pp. 137–138.

76 E. Boutaric, 'Clément V' (1872), pp. 9–10.

77 P. Dupuy, *Histoire de la condamnation*, no. 56, p. 217; E. Boutaric, 'Clément V' (1872), pp. 10–11. See also M. Barber, *The Trial* (2006), pp. 123–124; M. Satora, *Sprawa*, pp. 138–139.

78 H. de Curzon, *La maison*, p. 201; L. L. L. Lavocat, *Procès*, p. 189; C. V. Langlois, 'Le procès', p. 418; G. Lizerand, *Clément V*, pp. 132–133; M. Barber, *The Trial* (2006), pp. 128, 137; B. Beaucage, 'La saisie des biens provençaux de l'ordre du Temple', in: *Normes et pouvoir à la fin du moyen âge: actes du Colloque « La recherche en études médiévales au Québec et en Ontario », 16-17 mai 1989, Montréal*, ed. M. C. Déprez-Masson (Montréal 1989), p. 94.

79 'Excerpta e memoriali', p. 649.

80 E. Boutaric, 'Clément V' (1872), p. 10.

81 G. Lizerand, *Clément V*, Appendice, no. 11, p. 442. See also H. Prutz, *Entwicklung*, p. 171; A. Demurger, *La persécution*, p. 111.

82 G. Lizerand, *Clément V*, Appendice, no. 10, pp. 440–441.

83 On this topic, see M. Barber, *The Trial* (2006), pp. 116–122; A. Demurger, *La persécution*, pp. 111–117.

84 P. Dupuy, *Histoire de la condamnation*, no. 70, pp. 267–271; *Livre*, pp. 234–239. See also M. Satora, *Społeczny odbiór*, p. 67.

85 Pope's letter – P. Dupuy, *Histoire de la condamnation*, no. 44, p. 190; *Vitae*, vol. 3, pp. 78–79; R. A. de Vertot, *Histoire*, vol. 1, *Preuves*, p. 639; B. Barbiche, *Les actes*, vol. 3, no. 2328, p. 40. King of France's letter – G. Lizerand, *Clément V*, Appendice, no. 12, p. 443.

86 G. Lizerand, *Clément V*, Appendice, no. 14, pp. 444–446; B. Barbiche, *Les actes*, vol. 3, no. 2329, p. 41.

87 King of France's letter dated 9 July – G. Lizerand, *Clément V*, Appendice, no. 13, p. 444. Pope's letter of 11 July – P. Dupuy, *Histoire de la condamnation*, no. 45, p. 190; *Vitae*, vol. 3, p. 79; B. Barbiche, *Les actes*, vol. 3, no. 2330, p. 41.

88 P. Dupuy, *Histoire de la condamnation*, no. 46, pp. 191–192; *Vitae*, vol. 3, pp. 79–81; B. Barbiche, *Les actes*, vol. 3, no. 2331, p. 41.

89 *Vitae*, vol. 3, p. 81; B. Barbiche, *Les actes*, vol. 3, no. 2332, p. 42.

90 Reg. Clem. V, vol. 6 (Rome 1887), no. 6816, pp. 132–133; B. Barbiche, *Les actes*, vol. 3, no. 2422, pp. 77–78. See also C. Mansuet Jeune, *Histoire*, vol. 2, p. 264.

91 P. Dupuy, *Histoire de la condamnation*, no. 71, pp. 272–275; Reg. Clem. V, vol. 3 (Rome 1885), no. 3400, pp. 281–283; *Livre*, pp. 267–269; B. Barbiche, *Les actes*, vol. 3, no. 2343, p. 46.
92 Reg. Clem. V, vol. 3, no. 3400, pp. 281–283; *Livre*, p. 268.
93 Reg. Clem. V, vol. 3, no. 3626; *Livre*, pp. 242–251.
94 On the Hospitallers' plan, see, for example, B. Z. Kedar, S. Schein, 'Un projet de "passage particulier" proposé par l'ordre de l'Hôpital, 1306–1307', Bibliothèque de l'Ecole des chartes, 137 (1979), pp. 211–226.
95 L. Blancard, 'Documents', p. 420.
96 *Papsttum*, vol. 2, no. 101, p. 183. See also A. J. Forey, 'The Military Orders in the Crusading Proposals', p. 335; A. Demurger, *La persécution*, p. 133.
97 A. Demurger, *La persécution*, p. 134.

2 Administration of the Templar properties (1307–1313)

2.1 In the hands of the king of France (1307–1308)

2.1.1 Disputes with vassals

On 14 September 1307, Philip the Fair issued an order concerning the arrest of French Templars, which also contained detailed instructions on the seizure of the Order's properties. On 13 October 1307, the king's men were to visit the Templars' houses, draw up inventories of their possessions, and organise their administration independently of the royal estates.[1] While the first part of the order was easily implemented, complications and conflicts quickly arose between Philip and his vassals regarding the management of the properties.

In the royal domain, it was the responsibility of the bailiffs, seneschals, and other officials appointed by the monarch to arrest the Templars and seize their properties.[2] The situation was slightly different in territories where Philip the Fair did not exercise direct authority, with the exception of Flanders, where the monarch entrusted this task to his official *vidame* of Amiens.[3] In the duchies of Brittany and Burgundy, the local princes carried out the operation, not the king's men.[4] A similar situation occurred in the county of Alençon, where Charles de Valois took control of the Templar houses.[5] In the south of France, the count of Armagnac and viscount of Lomagne (the latter being the brother of Clement V, Arnaud de Goth) not only seized the properties but began to profit from it almost immediately.[6]

Philip the Fair most likely considered this situation to be temporary and intended to take direct and complete control of all estates in the near future. In December 1307, he appointed general administrators for the entire kingdom[7] and then proceeded to implement his plan. A letter from early March 1308 concerning the transfer of properties into the duchy of Brittany has survived. In it, the king ordered that control of the confiscated Templar estates be handed over to the two knights he had sent for this purpose and that the accounts of the previous administration, along with all seized income, be transferred to the general administrators. According to the document, the second part of the order concerned all "bailiffs, judicial officials and territorial rulers" (*Baillivis & justiciariis nostris & aliis Dominis temporalibus*), who had the authority to seize the Templar properties throughout the kingdom.[8] However, the monarch's decision was met with resistance from at least some

DOI: 10.4324/9781003742241-3

of his vassals, who believed that it was their responsibility to manage the estates until the proceedings were concluded. In Brittany itself, the king's men, who did not arrive in Nantes until August 1308, were treated very badly and forced to leave the city, while the properties that had been taken were kept under the control of the duke.[9] We learn of these events from a note added almost 100 years later on the back of one of the documents concerning the case. However, the situation itself seems quite plausible. The only doubt that could be raised concerns the very late arrival of the monarch's envoys to the city. By August 1308, the meeting between Philip the Fair and Clement V in Poitiers had already taken place, and the process of taking control of the estates by representatives of the Church rather than the king had begun. However, this could have been the result of prolonged, consistent resistance by the duke of Brittany.

Philip the Fair's actions regarding the Templar properties also provoked opposition in Burgundy. Duke Hugues V (1306–1315) officially protested against the seizure of Templar properties under his jurisdiction by the king's officials.[10] Demurger believes that this protest was evidence of a lack of support for the French king's treatment of the Templars.[11] However, it is difficult to agree with this, since the dispute only concerned the administration of their properties and not the arrest of the Order's members, which was carried out without the slightest problem or resistance throughout the kingdom.

The reasons for the princes' opposition to the monarch's actions against the Templars are best understood through the discussion that took place in the first half of 1308, regarding the conduct of proceedings in the duchy of Aquitaine. This was part of a wider dispute between the kings of France and England regarding the duchy's status and the resulting feudal obligations under the 1303 peace treaty.[12] Edward II detained the Templar brothers and seized their properties, even though at the same time he refused to take the same action in his own kingdom.[13] However, he did not agree to hand over control of either to the French ruler. Philip the Fair repeatedly accused English officials in the duchy of Aquitaine of disobedience in this regard. Preserved documents show that this issue was first raised during talks held in Boulogne-sur-Mer at the wedding of Edward II and Isabella. It was revisited during a visit by the French embassy to the English court in spring 1308, and discussed again at a meeting in Poitiers attended by English envoys. During this discussion, Philip expressed the view that, as a monarch, he alone was obliged to act on matters of faith. Therefore, he believed that he alone had the right to detain members of the Order who enjoyed the privilege of exemption and to take control of its properties until the proceedings were completed. However, he did not question the prince's authority over the Templars' lands, which resulted from his territorial sovereignty. On the other hand, Edward II argued that matters relating to temporalities had always been the responsibility of princes and that the king of France had never before attempted to change this, so he should not do so now.[14] It can be assumed that the other vassals who opposed the transfer of control over the Order's estates to officials appointed by Philip the Fair held the same position. This was not an exceptional situation, as similar disputes were taking place in the kingdom of Aragon. There, too, some feudal lords opposed the seizure of the Templars' estates by the king's envoys following their arrest, arguing that this violated their rights. James II used arguments similar to those used by the king of France in his discussions with Edward II. He referred to the inquisitor's call to take action against the Order and, later, to the bull *Pastoralis praeeminentiae*, which was addressed exclusively to monarchs. Such explanations were not always effective. On many occasions, the king had to promise his vassals that their rights would be fully respected, and that the Order's properties would only be excluded from their control for the duration of the proceedings. However, it also happened that the seized properties remained in the hands of the nobles until the end of the trial.[15]

Philip the Fair also faced opposition from at least some of the princes and counts and was forced to leave the Order's estates in their hands. The dispute with Edward II was only resolved by the decisions made in Poitiers, which stipulated that the estates were to be placed under the control of the pope's envoys. This rendered the previous claims of the French king invalid. There was later another conflict concerning the administration of the Templars' estates in the duchy of Aquitaine, which had a slightly different dimension that will be discussed later.

In Burgundy, too, the king of France ultimately ceded control of the estates to Hugues V. In orders dated 22 May 1308, and 15 January 1309, Philip instructed the bailiffs of Sens and Mâcon to comply with the prince's demands and not to infringe upon his jurisdiction.[16] The prince's accounts from 1308 to 1309 show that some of the Templars' estates were indeed in the hands of his officials by that time.[17] Other Burgundian nobles also retained control over the Order's estates. In a letter dated July 1311, Clement V called on several of them to hand the estates over to the pope's administrators.[18] The situation was similar in the south of the kingdom. The count of Armagnac and the viscount of Lomagne handed control of their estates directly to the bishops rather than to the king's officials.[19]

All these examples, which come from various regions of France, suggest that Philip the Fair's officials were responsible for managing the Templars' estates within the royal domain. Outside of this area, however, this task was carried out by local feudal lords in at least some cases. This is also confirmed by later writings from the monarch and the pope. In January 1309, the former ordered the transfer of the Templars' estates to the control of Church envoys, addressing "princes, counts, barons, seneschals (…) and all others who have temporal power in the kingdom of France."[20] In a letter from the same period concerning the same issues, Clement V also mentioned "princes, counts, barons, etc." who had seized and controlled the Templar properties "in the name of the king or in their own name."[21]

This situation was clearly unforeseen by the king and made it much more difficult to maintain control over the Order's assets, creating opportunities for abuse. It also highlights the limitations of Philip the Fair's power: he was unable to impose his will on his vassals, as illustrated by the case of the duchy of Aquitaine. From the beginning of the proceedings, the monarch had to contend with not only the pope's opposition to his plans for the Templar properties but also the claims of princes and counts, further complicating the difficult task he had taken on.

2.1.2 *Administrators' responsibilities*

The royal instruction describing the procedure to be followed by the arrest of the Templars also contained guidelines on the actions to be taken with regard to the Order's properties.[22] Before arresting the brothers, the designated officials were to discreetly assess the value of each house's property. If they aroused any suspicions, they were to claim that they were gathering information to determine the amount of tithes due. The rest of the order concerned the arrest procedure. The king's envoys were to visit the Templars' houses alongside the persons designated to carry out the arrests, as well as witnesses chosen from among the most distinguished *prud'hommes* in the region. Their presence was intended to ensure the implementation of the planned procedures was fair and conscientious. The document then continued:

> They [the commissioners] will ensure that the vines and estates are cultivated and planted properly, and will entrust them to good, rich men of the region, together with the servants found in the houses, and in their presence this same day they will make inventories of all movable assets in each place, will append their seals.[23]

Preserved sources provide insight into the implementation of Philip's order. The first action taken after the brothers' arrest was to draw up an inventory of the seized properties. Only five of these documents have survived, listing goods belonging to Templar houses in Baugy, Bretteville-le-Rabet, Voismer, Courval, and Louvigny in Normandy.[24] These documents were published at the beginning of the 20th century by Delisle and are well known to historians. They all bear the same date – 13 October – and were prepared in the presence of numerous witnesses and brothers residing in the individual houses. The detained Templars' participation in their preparation was probably related to procedural requirements. The inventories were primarily compiled to guarantee the full return of property in the event of their owners being acquitted.[25] The presence of the detained Templars was therefore intended to ensure the greatest possible accuracy and fairness of the procedure. The importance of these documents is evidenced by the fact that they were used during an investigation into the assets of the Templars in the 1320s, ordered by King Charles IV.[26] Similar procedures were also used in other countries where brothers were arrested.[27]

Unfortunately, no inventories from outside Normandy have survived that would enable us to ascertain whether the same *modus operandi* was employed everywhere. While we have two additional documents listing household goods, one from Montferrand in Auvergne[28] and the other from Pézeans in Languedoc,[29] we cannot be certain of the dates or circumstances of their compilation. Both inventories have only survived in part, and neither contains information indicating the date of their creation. Jean Picot, who published the first document a few years ago, stated that it was created between October 1307 and March 1308. However, there is insufficient evidence to confirm this. If the inventory had been drawn up at the time of the arrest of the French Templars, it would have been dated 13 October 1307. However, it could also have been compiled during the change of administrator of the estates between 1308 and 1312, or in connection with their transfer to the Hospitallers after the Council of Vienne.[30] Furthermore, both the Montferrand and the Pézeans documents lack sections discussing procedural issues and listing witnesses to the inventory. Consequently, they offer no new insights into the process of creating inventories or subsequent activities related to the management of Templar properties.

In this context, it is worth noting the comment made by the chronicler Jean de Saint-Victor concerning the seizure of the Order's properties. He wrote that the king sent managers to the Templars' houses, who submitted inventories of estates and movable property to him and the pope.[31] No other surviving source mentions any such inventories being sent to Clement V in October 1307. Had this been the case, they would have been an extremely important tool for the pope when settling accounts with the secular administration. Transferring the inventories would also suggest close collaboration between the French court and the Holy See in managing properties at this early stage of the proceedings. However, this is not confirmed by other sources from that period.

In accordance with Philip the Fair's order, administrators had to be appointed to the houses after the inventories had been drawn up, to ensure their optimal functioning. Most information about their activities is provided by the accounts of income and expenses incurred by individual commanderies over the course of several months after the brothers' arrest. There are three such documents, drawn up by the administrators of the commanderies of Payns and Coulours near Troyes, and the commandery of Paluet in Auvergne. The first of these was published at the beginning of the 20th century by Pétel,[32] while the other two, which are held at the Bibliothèque nationale[33] and the Archives nationales,[34] have not attracted much interest from researchers to date. A significant obstacle to analysing the document concerning the commandery of Coulours is certainly its condition: the manuscript is damaged and illegible in many places. Nevertheless, it contains several interesting pieces of information, especially when compared with the accounts from Payns and Paluet.

The commandery of Coulours' list of income and expenses shows that the first administrator, Pierre Soier, who participated in drawing up the inventory after the brothers' arrest, held his position for only a few weeks. At the end of November, Nicholas (known only by his first name) was appointed as the new administrator and remained in this position for at least a year. This change was accompanied by the creation of another inventory, the contents of which are unknown.[35] In Normandy, the first administrators appointed after the seizure of the estates were local residents. Michel Miguet concluded that, given the random nature of their selection, they were also only intended to serve temporarily.[36] However, this was not the rule. The new administrator of the commandery of Sainte-Eulalie was not appointed until the end of January 1308.[37] The administrators of the commanderies of Payns and Paluet, on the other hand, remained in office from the moment of the Templars' arrest until September 1308 – 11 months in total.[38]

At the turn of 1308 and 1309, the first decisions were made regarding the establishment of an organised system for administering seized properties across the entire kingdom – specifically, the territory under the direct control of the monarch. On 22 December 1307, Philip the Fair appointed Guillaume de Gisors, archdeacon of Auge, Guillaume Pisdoe, provost of marchands, and Rénier Bourdon as general administrators and guardians of the Templar properties throughout the kingdom.[39] Another document, dated 27 February 1308, has been preserved in which the king instructs these same officials to administer the confiscated Templar properties.[40] The reason for the monarch's repetition of the order is unknown. A later settlement of accounts by the administrators shows that they had been performing their duties since December 1307.[41] Based on the available documents, it is difficult to determine the actual scope of their responsibilities at this stage of the proceedings. All that is known is that they appointed regional administrators.[42] However, it can be assumed that, in practice, they were involved in organising the entire system for managing the Order's properties and controlling all aspects of its operations.

We know a little more about the activities of the other administrators. Their financial reports reveal the actions they took and the decisions they made. As well as standard farm management activities, they transferred money to cover the costs of proceedings initiated, e.g., transport and possibly the maintenance of detained Templars.[43] However, it is not known who decided on the amounts to be paid. One of the later documents also mentions a loan granted by the administrators of the Order's estates to the bishop of Bayeux.[44] It can be assumed, however, that they did not act on their own initiative, but rather followed orders, most likely from the monarch. The administrators also acted as representatives of the commandery before various courts. The commandery of Coulours' accounts mention a four-day trip made by its administrator to Troyes to appear before the bailiff in a case against an unspecified person.[45] It follows that they were entrusted with tasks directly reflecting the aforementioned legal solutions derived from criminal and inquisitorial procedures, i.e., the efficient management of the defendant's property and the provision of funds for the prisoner's needs and maintenance.

Following the seizure of the Order's properties, steps were taken to recover all remaining assets in the hands of others. This included various types of movable property, as well as all financial obligations towards the Templars. According to the rule established by Boniface VIII's 1295 decree *Cum secundum leges*, all debts owed to a convicted heretic arising after the offence was committed were subject to confiscation and had to be repaid.[46] It is known that in such cases, French officials routinely sought both the property belonging to the detainee and any outstanding debts.[47] Shortly after the Templars were arrested, a public call was made for all items belonging to the Order to be handed over to royal officials. A document referring to such actions in the bailiwick of Sens reveals that a fisherman handed a chest of money received from a Templar to the local bailiff.[48] A letter from September 1308 mentions the appointment of a new administrator of the house in Payns and records that his duties included recovering all receivables and debts owed to local members of the Order.[49] In May 1309, the king also ordered administrators in Flanders to enforce the debt owed to the Templars by the inhabitants of Ypres.[50] Therefore, it seems that the activities carried out by royal officials at the very beginning of the proceedings were included in the administrators' duties, or that the cooperation between the two parties in this matter was regulated in some way. However, no surviving documents mention the activities of administrators in this field.

Analysis of the financial reports from the administrators of individual commanderies shows that such documents were prepared regularly. In all three cases, the reports were addressed to the regional royal administrator. The document from the administrator of Payns shows that his reports were prepared in triplicate.[51] One might wonder what the purpose of each copy was. recalls Jean de Saint-Victor's comment about the Templar houses' inventories submitted to the pope. While it cannot be ruled out that one copy of the documents relating to the seizure and administration of the Order's properties was submitted to Clement V, the surviving sources are silent on this subject.

The administrators presented their reports at various intervals and at different locations. Nicholas, the administrator of the commandery of Coulours, travelled to Paris in March 1308 for this purpose,[52] to Provins in July,[53] and to Coulommiers in the second half of August.[54] Meanwhile, the first administrator of the commandery of Payns took the documents to Coulommiers in September 1308,[55] while his successor presented his accounts in Paris.[56] It is reasonable to assume that the administrators took the documents to different locations depending on the whereabouts of the royal administrator of the Templars' estates in the bailiwicks of Troyes and Meaux, Jean Guérin, to whom they were submitted. It is known that their accounts were checked and often corrected or rejected. Information about such corrections can be found in the reports from Payns and Paluet.[57] These procedures enabled ongoing supervision of the administrators' activities.

It seems that during the first year after the arrest of the French Templars, when their estates in most of the kingdom remained under the control of the king's officials, attempts were made to develop a centrally managed system of administration, enabling control over the current activities of the administrators. Unfortunately, it is not known whether similar solutions were also introduced where the properties were seized by local princes and counts.

2.1.3 *Conflicts and complaints*

In the several months that the Templar estates were under the king's control, it is easy to imagine that their administrators encountered many unforeseen difficulties and were confronted with all sorts of conflicts. Many of these were initiated even before the arrest of the Order's members, while others were related to the day-to-day management of the estates. Some were probably resolved locally on an ongoing basis, while others led to lengthy litigation or were settled by the king. We know virtually nothing of the simplest ones, which did not require the involvement of higher authorities. The account of the commandery of Coulours' expenses only refers to a four-day journey made by the administrator to Troyes to appear before the bailiff in a case against an unspecified person.[58] However, we have no information about the subject of the dispute or how it was resolved.

For example, Philip the Fair's order on 12 May 1309 shows his involvement in settling matters initiated before the arrest of the Templars. In this order, he instructed the *vidame* of Amiens to settle a debt owed by the Order to the inhabitants of Ypres at the time of its arrest. The money to pay the debt was to come from the Templars' estates in Flanders.[59] It is likely that there were many more situations like this, with the former creditors of the Order turning to the monarch for help in recovering their money.

The proceedings concerning the dispute between the Templars and the Benedictines of the abbey of Saint-Benoît-sur-Loire regarding the lease payments for the Messon estate took a slightly different course. This dispute had begun several years before the trial. According to the 1303 agreement, as the Templars had stopped paying their dues, they were supposed to return the leased lands to the Benedictines. However, for some reason, they did not do so. After the royal administrators took control of the estates, the Benedictines demanded that the lease payments continue. However, the new administrator refused to pay the demanded amounts, prompting the landowners to complain to the general administrators. The latter carried out an investigation, questioning two imprisoned Templars, among other things, and then, in January 1311, ordered the administrator to either pay or return the property. The administrator probably opted for the former, as in 1313, the lands were transferred to the Hospitallers as part of the Templars' estate.[60]

We learn of a different kind of problem from a 14th-century book of forms containing a selection of royal orders, compiled by an unknown author. Published at the end of the 19th century by Langlois, it has so far attracted little interest from scholars working on the Templar trial. The text contains five documents related to the case of the Order. All were written in response to various complaints about the actions of estate administrators or other officials. Two of the letters refer to issues affecting tenants of estates. Since the Order's estates were not leased until after the Poitiers meeting, i.e., at the earliest in the second half of 1308, the orders relating to complaints concerning them were probably issued in 1309 or even 1310. Other documents concerning different issues may have been written as early as 1308.

The content of the royal orders makes it clear that the complaints and protests sent to the monarch were primarily financial in nature. For instance, one of the managers appointed by royal administrators to administer several Templar houses complained that he had not been paid for his work, including repairs to buildings under his authority.[61] In turn, the tenant of a house in Lagny-sur-Marne complained that the rent imposed on him was too high and had led him to ruin. His rent for the previous year – 100 l. t. – was to be paid by his brother, who had vouched for him. This would also have meant that he would have to sell his property, so he asked the monarch for help. The king granted his request, ordering the administrators to reduce the rent and postpone the payment date so that the brothers could fulfil their obligations.[62] The tenant of the Templar estates in Cordamble, Jean *Barbonel*, was in a much worse situation. He was accused by royal officials of mismanaging the estates and was thrown into prison as a result. They also seized goods belonging to him worth more than 500 l. p. (625 l. t.) and refused to provide a receipt. Jean *Barbonel* claimed that he had cultivated the land and vineyard properly and honestly, and that the charges against him were untrue, as was the investigation conducted in relation to him. The monarch ordered the provost of Paris to summon the estate administrators, both local and general (Guillaume de Gisors, Guillaume Pisdoe, and Rénier Bourdon) to verify the investigation and account for Jean *Barbonel*'s seized estates, granting and paying any reparations if he were found innocent.[63]

Complaints made by tenants to Philip the Fair also concerned the failure of administrators to comply with agreements made prior to the arrest of the Templars. For example, Pierre *Gridaine* claimed that two years before the proceedings against the Order began, he had made an agreement with the commander of Belle-Église regarding the trapping of animals. However, he alleged that the new administrators were not fulfilling the terms of this agreement. As he had done in other cases, the king ordered an investigation into the matter and, if justified, that the complainant's demands be met.[64] Unfortunately, it is not known whether this intervention brought a final resolution to the conflict. Evidence that this may not have been the case comes from another very similar case, which remained unresolved until 1319. We can reconstruct the latter's course in detail based on documents stored in the Archives départementales de la Haute-Garonne and the contents of the final royal ruling related to it, which was confirmed by the Parliament of Paris.[65] The case concerned three Italian merchants who leased the Brucafel and Montrond estates, which belonged to the Templar commandery of Douzens, for six years in 1305. Following the arrest of the brothers, the merchants were deprived of the right to continue using the estates and collecting the income due to them. They therefore lodged a complaint, demanding either a change of decision or compensation for their losses. The matter was referred by the king, who, in October 1309, ordered an investigation and, if necessary, payment of the sums due to the aggrieved parties. This confirms the course of action already evident in the documents. The order was sent to the seneschal of Carcassonne, who in turn, entrusted its execution to the *juge mage* and the new administrator of the Order's estates, who had been appointed by the bishop. One might question whether the new administrator was the right person to resolve the complaint concerning the actions of his predecessors, and whether he should instead have participated in the proceedings. However, it seems that, at that point in time, no procedures had yet been developed to resolve the conflicts that arose from such an unusual undertaking as the Templar trial, in legal and organisational terms. This is why the bailiff made this decision rather than another. In any case, the two commissioners who heard the merchants' and previous administrators' representatives' arguments were most likely unable to pass judgement, so the case was taken over by the general administrators. This seemingly simple conflict thus involved successive officials yet still did not lead to a resolution. The general administrators ordered another investigation, analysing the documents submitted by the parties and interviewing witnesses. The resulting verdict was intended as a compromise, but it did not satisfy the merchants' complaints. Consequently, in 1312, they decided to lodge an appeal, which went first to the general administrators and then to the *juge mage* of Carcassonne. The latter initiated new proceedings, which were hampered, however, by further requests and doubts put forward by the representative of the administrators of the estates. He argued that the merchants' appeal should have been addressed to the Holy See, as it formally exercised control over the Order's estates, rather than to royal officials. Ultimately, however, it was deemed that the administrators represented both the pope and the monarch and were thus entitled to participate in the proceedings. Following discussions and further preparations, 27 witnesses were heard in October 1313.[66] As a result of this investigation, the *juge mage* partially amended the earlier decisions. However, the surviving documents do not reveal what these changes concerned. In any case, the case was not concluded by this verdict. Furthermore, the Hospitallers, who had already taken over the Templar property belonging to the commandery of Douzens, became involved at this point. They appealed the verdict, arguing that although they had formally become the property's owners before the end of the proceedings, they had not participated in the proceedings at all. They took their appeal to the king, who entrusted the case to the Court of Appeal in Toulouse this time. Another complication arose there, as both the merchants and the former administrators of the estates considered the recent settlement to be a compromise and did not wish to challenge it. The Hospitaller representative, on the other hand, disagreed and decided to act only against the merchants, challenging only the provisions favourable to them. Consequently, the tribunal appeal annulled the previous judgements, concluding that they had been made by the wrong people. This resulted in yet another complaint to the king, this time from the tenants. Neither Philip the Fair nor his successor Louis X managed to resolve the issue before their deaths. It was not until 1319 that Philip V invalidated all previous settlements and announced that the matter would be resolved in the royal court. What happened next is unclear. However, it appears that the proceedings lasted for around ten years and are still ongoing. Throughout this time, successive administrators, other royal officials and witnesses who were questioned several times were involved, as well as the parties or their representatives. Undoubtedly, costs increased with each passing year and stage. This case illustrates the legal and organisational confusion that accompanied the transfer of formal control of the estates first to the Church, and then to the Hospitallers. Given the reason for the conflict – the administrators' lack of awareness of the ongoing relationship between the Templar houses and the local community when they took the estates out of the Templars' hands – one can guess that there were many more cases of this kind. However, most were probably resolved at an early stage without involving as many parties as in the case cited here.

Let us return to the book of forms of royal orders, which was mentioned earlier. Apart from the aforementioned disputes, which mainly concern property rights and financial settlements, another case of a completely different and rather unexpected nature is mentioned. One of the administrators complained to the king that the mayor of Amiens had tried to force him to resign from his post and accept a position as town clerk instead. In this case, there was no need for an inquiry; the king simply ordered the bailiff of Amiens to reprimand the mayor.[67] However, even such trivial matters could sometimes take an unexpected turn, complicating the administration of the Order's estates. Furthermore, they complicated the Templar case and made it very engaging from the point of view of the state apparatus.

2.2 Under the control of the Church (1308–1313)

2.2.1 Taking control of properties

Preparations for Church representatives to take control of the Templar estates had already begun at the meeting in Poitiers. On 12 July 1308, Clement V instructed the French bishops to appoint administrators of the Templar estates within their respective dioceses. These administrators were to swear an oath to perform their duties honestly and to present current accounts to the bishops. Once a year, they were to provide summaries in duplicate, one each for the pope and the king.[68] Meanwhile, Clement V had already made the first independent decisions regarding the Order's properties. These related to the annuity granted to Otto de Grandson by Jacques de Molay in 1297 and paid from the Order's treasury prior to the trial.[69] As it was no longer possible to fulfil this obligation given the circumstances, Clement V decided to grant Otto de Grandson the right to collect the revenues of the three Templar commanderies instead. The issue was discussed at a meeting between the pope and the king of France, as evidenced by a royal order issued on 30 July 1308. In the order, Philip instructed his officials to implement Clement V's decree, emphasising that he had been consulted.[70] On 17 August 1308, the pope confirmed the grant of the annuity but made one stipulation. If the income from the monastic houses exceeded the prescribed sum, it was to be placed in the hands of the bishops, who were to administer the Templar estates in their dioceses by order of the Holy See.[71] Clement V therefore assumed that, until the annuity was paid, the Order's seized properties would be under the control of the Church.

Philip the Fair issued the first documents enabling the de facto transfer of control of estates as early as the meeting at Poitiers. This is confirmed by references in the bulls *Faciens misericordiam* and *Regnans in coelis*, dated 12 August 1308. In these documents, Clement V wrote that the king of France had handed over control of the Templar estates to Church representatives.[72] However, Lavocat believed that these words were merely an attempt to mask papal weakness, rather than reflecting the real situation.[73] This is contradicted, however, by the content of the bull *Ad omnium fere*, which was addressed to Philip the Fair. In this document the pope omitted the instruction to transfer the fraudulently retained Templar estates to ecclesiastical administrators, as mentioned in copies sent to other recipients.[74] Therefore, the problem clearly did not concern the French monarch. This is also confirmed by a letter from Clement V to Edward II in early October 1308. In it, the pope accused the English sovereign of disposing of the Order's assets and cited the French king's decisions as an example to follow, as he had already handed over control of the assets to the Church and ordered his subjects to do the same as soon as possible.[75] Given this situation, it is difficult to imagine that Clement V was referring to events that had not actually taken place.

All these papal comments on the action taken by Philip the Fair and the declarations of the monarch himself contrast with source accounts of the position of other Western European rulers regarding the transfer of control of the Templar estates to representatives of the Church. In December 1308, presumably in response to a letter from Clement V in October, Edward II wrote that he had not yet made any decisions regarding the Templar estates.[76] However, in March 1309, James II's envoys to the papal court reported that the king of England had refused to hand over the estates until the proceedings against the Order had concluded. They advised James II to do the same.[77] The Aragonese monarch apparently decided to follow Edward II's example, as he too refused to hand over control of the estates. He wrote explicitly about this in letters to the pope in March 1310 and June 1311. In doing so, he invoked his regalian rights, maintaining that his ancestors had granted the estates to the Templars on condition that they defend the kingdom of Aragon's territory, and that these conditions precluded handing the estates over to someone else. At the same time, he declared that he would implement the papal decisions once the Templar case had been definitively resolved.[78] While other rulers did not oppose Clement V's decisions, they tried to safeguard their interests as best they could. For example, the King of Naples and Count of Provence, Robert (1309–1343) issued an official order directing that control of the Order's estates should be handed over to the pope's envoys. However, in a second letter, this time secret, he ordered his officials not to do so if this would deplete his revenues or restrict his rights in any way.[79] No documents have survived in France that show similar reservations expressed by Philip the Fair, either openly or in secret.

Available sources indicate that the process of transferring estates to French bishops began before the king of France had officially agreed to the arrangement. As early as 24 June 1308, Clement V's brother, the viscount of Lomagne, transferred the estates that had been under his control since the arrest of the Templars to the bishop of Lectoure, Guillaume des Bordes, another papal relative.[80] Further transfers occurred later, but their exact dates are unknown. What is known is that the bishops of Auch, Bazas, Bordeaux, and Carcassonne periodically administered the Order's estates independently.[81] However, certainly not all the bishops took control of the estates in their dioceses in 1308. Correspondence exchanged between the pope and the king at the end of 1308 and the beginning of 1309 shows that Clement V was only preparing to implement some of the decisions made at the Poitiers meeting at that time. This delay was probably due to the fact that the pope was on the move for several more months after his meeting with Philip the Fair, which hindered the normal work of his chancellery.[82] In a letter dated 27 December, Clement V asked the king to provide 20 copies of the documents required to take control of the estates in all French dioceses. The pope already had six copies of these documents, but this was insufficient for the entire kingdom.[83] In response to this request, on 15 January 1309, the king ordered his officials to hand over the estates to administrators appointed by Clement V or the French bishops.[84] While it is unclear whether this was the letter the pope was referring to, it was certainly an important step towards implementing the provisions of Poitiers throughout France.

On 5 January 1309, Clement V addressed the bishops, asking them to take charge of the estates in the dioceses under his authority. Having learned that Philip the Fair's orders concerning the transfer of estates had not yet been implemented everywhere, he asked them to appoint suitable people to take control of the Templar houses and organise their administration. These administrators were to be under the authority of general administrators appointed by the pope, whose names were indicated in the document. Following the example of earlier bulls, Clement V also stipulated that they were to swear an oath on the Gospel and be regularly accountable for their actions.[85] These orders were thus analogous to those already given by the pope to bishops at Poitiers. The only difference was that, at that time, there was still no question of implementing the monarch's orders in this regard.

On the same day, Clement V also granted the newly appointed general administrators of the kingdom of France an allowance to cover their travel expenses while carrying out their duties. These were to be paid from the revenues derived from the Templar estates.[86] At around the same time, the pope issued similar documents for other countries. Inquisitors and envoys sent to take control of the estates were also to be reimbursed for their travel expenses, but these costs were to be covered by the local clergy from their own resources.[87] A few months later, Philip drew attention to the problematic nature of this arrangement, as it did not guarantee uninterrupted funding for the missions. Clement V responded by assuring him that he had already sent people to various countries to take control of the Templar estates on his behalf and that he therefore hoped for speedy reimbursement from this source.[88] This shows that, in late 1308 and early 1309, the process of transferring the estates into the hands of the Church's representatives was sufficiently advanced in France for the pope to order that his envoys' expenses be paid from the revenues of the Templar houses to which they had access. In other countries, the transfer had either not yet started or had been completely blocked by the monarchs.

Early in 1309, Clement V sent out to the French bishops not only a letter urging them to take control of the Templar estates but also several other documents on a similar subject. Among these was the bull *Ad omnium fere*, in which Clement V ordered that all remaining estates in private hands be handed over to appointed administrators and that their contents be solemnly proclaimed in each diocese.[89] At the end of January, the pope also informed the king of France of his decision to appoint general administrators for his kingdom and of his plans for those unlawfully retaining Templar properties.[90] The process of the Holy See taking control of the estates and their management only began once all these documents had reached their addressees. This is estimated to have happened in spring 1309.

Correspondence between Clement V and Philip the Fair regarding the transfer of Templar properties reveals a collaborative relationship between the papacy and secular power. Although the king of France had previously claimed the right to seize the Order's estates, he now seemed to be implementing all the pope's decisions, at least according to official declarations. However, later sources show that this was accompanied by various problems and doubts. We learn most about this from a letter from Clement V to Philip at the beginning of May 1309, in response to the king's earlier correspondence. In it, the king outlined several questions that had arisen at the time regarding the Templar case within the French court and among the bishops. It is known that the latter gathered in Paris to discuss the details of the measures necessary to implement the pope's decisions in Poitiers and present the results of their deliberations to the king. Philip also expressed his concerns in writing about the orders issued by Clement V and his intentions.[91] He complained, among other things, that the delay in the proceedings against the Templars had led to rumours that the pope and the king were only interested in seizing the Order's properties and not in clarifying the matter. In response, Clement V said that these accusations were completely misplaced, as he had only used a small portion of the Templars' movable property to cover the travel expenses of Cardinals Bérenger Frédol and Étienne de Suisy.[92] In the spring of 1309, the pope had the opportunity to dispose of the Templars' possessions, which he took. Moreover, he apparently did so without making prior arrangements with Philip the Fair, who, according to the decisions of Poitiers, was responsible for ensuring that the estates were used for their intended purpose. Georges Lizerand believed that, in his letter, the king accused the pope of stealing the estates.[93] Of course, no such accusation is made in the cited correspondence, but Clement V apparently felt obliged to explain his decisions to the French sovereign.

Another accusation made by the monarch pertained to the wording used by the pope in his letters to the bishops. In a bull regarding the proceedings concerning the Order's properties, Clement V wrote that Philip "handed over the Templar properties to the pope and the Church." The king objected to this interpretation, emphasising that he never intended to hand over the properties, as it still belonged to the Templars. In Poitiers, they had only discussed its temporary administration. However, if people found out that he had the Templars "in his hands," it would cause a scandal. Therefore, he asked Clement V to correct this clearly in the documents sent to various recipients and instruct the inquisitors travelling to different countries in connection with the Order's case to announce this publicly. The pope promised to correct the documents.[94]

Both passages demonstrate the monarch's deep concern for conveying the right message about his actions. This can be seen as either part of a broad royal propaganda campaign aimed at concealing his true intentions or as the efforts of a ruler genuinely committed to suppressing heresy and furthering the cause of the crusades so as not to give the impression of having any other intentions. Interestingly, Philip the Fair mentioned a circumstance he had consistently omitted from his correspondence with Clement V: the seized properties could be returned to the Templars if they were acquitted. This discrepancy between the official message and the private arrangements between the king and the pope is notable. However, the pope did not object to this presentation of the case, suggesting an agreement between the two sides on this issue.

At the same time, when French bishops gradually took control of the Order's estates bacause of the decisions made in Poitiers, other events occurred, which cast doubt on Philip the Fair's honesty. In the summer of 1308, the management of some estates that had not yet been transferred to the bishops began to change. Houses previously managed by royal appointees began to be leased out. By the end of June 1308, a house in Ruetz in Champagne had been leased,[95] followed by a farm in Ambrief in July.[96] In other places, the equipment and animals belonging to the houses were sold first. Then, they were leased. This occurred in Bonlieu and Payns in Champagne, Bilbartaut near Paris, Sauce in the county of Auxerre, Courval, and likely other houses in Normandy.[97] A similar solution was probably used at the house of Saint-Eulalie in southern France. A receipt, issued on 3 October 1309, by the royal commissioner who was to collect the accounts of the administrators of the seneschalship of Rouergue in connection with his takeover of some of these house's furnishings, has been preserved. The document states that he had the right to dispose of movable property from the local Templar estates at his discretion.[98] While it can be assumed that this was the case prior to the leasing of the house, it is impossible to be certain, given that neither the receipt itself nor the accompanying authorisation issued by the regional administrator of the Templar estates a few months earlier mentions the purpose of the commissioner's mission or the orders under which he was acting.

Researchers usually assume that the money from the sale of movable property and lease payments went to the royal treasury, which was contrary to the provisions of Poitiers.[99] However, Pétel believes that this was the result of a compromise whereby the monarch could sell movable property and take money from several years of leases while waiving his claim to the entire estate.[100] The same researcher also believes that the sale of Templar properties by the king's officials signified recognition that the Order was effectively dissolved.[101] However, Demurger states that Philip the Fair decided to lease the Templars' houses immediately after the Poitiers meeting in order to obtain as much money as possible from the property sales and lease payments before transferring control of the properties to the Church.[102] The latter interpretation seems to be confirmed by the fact that, in September 1308, regional commissioner, Jean Guérin appointed a new administrator for the house in Payns. In the relevant document he stated that he was acting on behalf of the king without making any reference to the provisions of Poitiers.[103] This suggests that the royal officials continued to make decisions regarding the Order's properties, despite earlier provisions. Pétel considered this to be proof that Philip disregarded the pope's decisions and rights.[104] While this opinion contradicts the aforementioned thesis of the same researcher, who suggests that Clement V unofficially consented to the king of France's actions, the quoted fragment of the source fully justifies it. If Philip the Fair acted contrary to the agreements with the pope and his own declarations in autumn 1308, he would have been guilty of outright theft, to the detriment of the Holy See and the Church. This should have provoked some reaction from Clement V, but there is no mention of this in the papal documents from that period. On the other hand, if we were to accept Pétel's thesis concerning the compromise of Poitiers, it would mean that additional negotiations and agreements must have taken place during the meeting between the king and the pope, but the surviving sources are silent on this. However, another interpretation of these events is also possible, explaining both the decisions regarding the leasing of the estates and the appointment of a new administrator in Payns. Some guidance on this matter can be found in the words of Clement V himself. In the bull *Ad omnium fere*, dated August 1308, he wrote that he had decided to transfer the Order's movable property, together with certain estates, to meet the needs of the Holy Land.[105] In a letter dated May 1309, he admitted to using the Templars' movable property to cover the travel expenses of his envoys. These statements demonstrate that, at that stage of the proceedings, the pope permitted the sale of Templar house equipment and the subsequent allocation of the proceeds to other purposes, regardless of the outcome of the investigation. It is also known that, between 1309 and 1310, Clement V made decisions regarding the use of Templar assets in countries other than France. This was the case in Cyprus and Greece, where pope's envoys had already taken control of the Order's properties. In May 1309, the pope instructed the cathedral canons of Nicosia to give the Hospitallers the money he had previously given to the Templars. A few months later, he also transferred the income from the Templar properties seized by Amalric, Lord of Tyre, to the Order. All these funds were to be used for military activities aimed at conquering Rhodes. Furthermore, Clement V entrusted Foulques de Villaret with the administration of the Templars' possessions in Cyprus.[106] The following year, the pope ordered the Templar administrators in Morea (Peloponnese) to lend the Duke of Athens, Gautier de Brienne, all the income they had collected, as well as that which they were due to collect the following year, to fight the Greek schismatics.[107]

All of this suggests that a similar situation occurred in France. In Poitiers, there was talk of a crusade led by the Hospitallers and financed jointly by the pope and the king. As preparations began almost immediately, it was necessary to raise money quickly. Clement V therefore decided to transfer the Templars' movable property and some of their estates for this purpose. most of the Order's possessions were still under the control of Philip's officials at that stage, they were entrusted with selling the furnishings and leasing out the houses quickly, which would bring immediate profits. This is why the royal officials began work on this matter in June 1308, and continued the following year, by which time the process of taking control of the properties by French bishops and the Holy See's envoys was already underway. This would also explain the lack of opposition from Clement V, a point highlighted by Pétel. Pétel concludes that the sale of the movable property and the change in management of the houses took place with the consent, or even at the behest, of the pope's commissioners.[108] Such an agreement would also explain why Clement V was not more urgent in implementing the official decisions of Poitiers. Six months after the meeting with the king, the pope appointed envoys to administer the estates on his behalf, because at that time, the most important need was to urgently raise funds for the Hospitallers' expedition. This suggests that the money collected by the king's men did not go to the royal treasury, but rather to Clement V's coffers or directly to the Hospitallers. The way such transfers might have taken place will be discussed in a subsequent chapter.

The date at which the process of taking control of the French Templars' assets by bishops and papal administrators ended is unknown. From the surviving sources, we learn only that the latter encountered resistance from certain minor territorial rulers and hierarchs who refused to comply with the papal order to transfer the assets. The former mainly concerned the duchy of Burgundy, where, as late as 1311, Clement V called on certain feudal lords to hand their properties over to the Holy See's envoys.[109] The bishop of Lectoure's refusal to transfer control of the properties in his diocese to the papal administrators until 1311, after Clement V's intervention,[110] is an example of resistance on the part of the clergy. However, there are no sources indicating any difficulties experienced by the royal administration in the transfer of properties. The available documents also do not allow us to determine when the process of changing the management of the Templars' houses ended, nor whether this affected the entire kingdom or only some of the commanderies. It is also unclear how the efforts of Philip the Fair's officials to sell and lease the properties related to the Church's representatives took control of the Order's houses. It can only be assumed that the two processes complemented each other, although exactly how this worked is difficult to determine.

2.2.2 *Joint administration*

According to the bull *Tibi fili carissime* issued on 13 July 1309, Philip the Fair was permitted to appoint officials to administer the Templars' estates alongside representatives of the pope and bishops. These administrators were required to swear an oath to the prelates and act officially on behalf of Clement V, an opportunity which the monarch took advantage of. In a letter dated 6 April 1309, he informed the archbishops of Sens and Bordeaux that he had appointed Guillaume de Gisors, Guillaume Pisdoe, Rénier Bourdon, Arnaud Barrau, and Géraud de Sabanac as general administrators *pro securitate negocii.*[111] The first three had been performing this role since December 1307. Their appointment was confirmed by the archbishop of Narbonne in May 1309.[112] These administrators continued to perform their duties in 1311, when the king announced his choice of a new archbishop of Narbonne, as well as the bishops of Soissons and Bayeux.[113] However, only Guillaume de Gisors, Guillaume Pisdoe, and Rénier Bourdon were mentioned in the official documents drawn up during the financial settlements of the Templar guardians in the bailiwick of Senlis in 1310–1311. They were referred to as "co-administrators" of the Templars' estates in the kingdom of France (*adioins as curateurs donnes as biens du Temple du Raoyaume de France*[114]), appointed by the king with the pope's approval.[115] The same formula also appears in the decisions of the Parliament of Paris ten years later.[116] These same three commissioners were also responsible for the Order's possessions, which were held in the Paris treasury at the time of the Templars' arrest. In this capacity, they appeared before the papal commission investigating the entire Order in Paris in 1311.[117] The reason why some of the documents made no mention of Arnaud Barrau and Géraud de Sabanac is unclear. Perhaps the tasks entrusted to them related only to part of the kingdom or were not connected to the day-to-day management of the estates.

Documents issued by Clement V and Philip the Fair in Poitiers during the implementation of the decisions taken at that time show that the new solutions were to apply to the entire kingdom. This meant that the envoys of both the pope and the monarch gained influence over property administration, even in areas that had previously been under the control of local feudal lords. While this made it possible to create a coherent system of properties administration, it also caused problems. Implementing the provisions of Poitiers in the duchy of Aquitaine resulted in protests from Edward II and sparked a new conflict.

In November 1310, John of Hastings, the seneschal of Gascony and envoy of the English monarch, went to the pope to express his opposition to representatives of the king of France participating in the administration of the Templars' estates in the duchy of Aquitaine. Reiterating an argument from earlier Anglo-French discussions, he asserted that, as the territorial ruler, Edward II had the right to seize and confiscate the properties of heretics. John of Hastings also pointed out that the English monarch had transferred control of the Order's estates to church administrators on the condition that this would be done on the same terms as in other parts of the kingdom of France. This meant that Edward II's powers would be identical to those of Philip the Fair. John of Hastings therefore, demanded that the king of France recall his men, and that Edward II be permitted to appoint his own administrators to join the papal commissioners.[118] We also have a report from the same seneschal, addressed to the English monarch and dating from around the same period.[119] This report shows that the seneschal's concerns about Philip's involvement in the administration of the Templars' estates were more far-reaching than previously thought. He believed that the king of France could take money from the seized commanderies for himself and gain access to many fortified houses in the event of an armed conflict with Edward II.[120] Although these reservations were not presented to the pope, they reveal a different aspect of the Templar case and its consequences to the financial and procedural problems analysed so far. It would be extremely interesting to find out whether the issues raised by the seneschal were also considered at the French court and in the papal curia. Unfortunately, however, no such sources have survived.

Clement V responded to the claims made by Edward II's representative in a letter to Philip the Fair dated 9 November 1310. In it, he asked the king to comply with the requests of the English ruler by revoking all decisions that could harm his interests and ordering administrators to act in such a way as not to harm them in the future.[121] The manner of implementation of these recommendations, the French monarch's attitude towards them, and whether the role of royal administrators in the duchy of Aquitaine was restricted in any way in the following years are all unknown. What is known is that the issue of the Templars' estates was raised again in the tripartite negotiations.

During the Council of Vienne, where discussions were held on possible solutions to the Franco-English conflicts concerning Aquitaine, the pope suggested transferring the Templar seized properties in the duchy to Edward II.[122] It is unclear whether Clement V was referring to John of Hastings' proposal to exchange administrators or if he intended to transfer complete control of the Order's estates to the English ruler, as had been done in other parts of his kingdom. In any case, subsequent documents suggest that Philip agreed to the pope's proposal[123] thereby losing influence over the future of the Templars' estates in the duchy of Aquitaine.

Little is known about how cooperation between papal and royal administrators worked in practice. Documents concerning the accounts of prison guards in the bailiwick of Senlis from 1310 to 1312 reveal that all financial orders came from administrators appointed by the king.[124] These orders were carried out by Rénier de Creil and Pierre de Senlis, who had served as regional administrators of properties and collectors of dues from the Templar houses in the bailiwick of

Senlis since March 1308.[125] Therefore, it appears that, at the local level, day-to-day settlements took place without the participation of papal or episcopal commissioners. Furthermore, documents relating to the dispute over the rights to the Clarois farm show that Rénier de Creil was also involved in other decisions relating to the management of the estates. On this occasion, the complaint lodged by the heirs of the property's owner, who had leased it to the Templars, was directed against the administrators of the Order's properties, and above all against Rénier de Creil. He was accused of making it difficult for the new owners to take control of the property. At the beginning of 1312, the Parliament of Paris ordered him to transfer the property to the complainants.[126] This would corroborate an earlier thesis put forward by some researchers, which states that French officials retained full control over the properties even after the meeting in Poitiers and the formal transfer of management to Church administrators. However, other preserved sources suggest that this was not always the case.

Interesting information on certain aspects of joint properties administration can be found in documents related to the case of Italian merchants who, after the arrest of the Templars, lost the right to use the property they had leased from them.[127] Initially, the tenants' complaints were directed at the royal administrators. After 1309, however, an administrator appointed by the bishop became involved in the proceedings. Together with the *juge mage* of Carcassonne, he was tasked with settling the dispute between the former administrators and the tenants. However, in 1312, the next stage of the proceedings saw the administrators of both the pope and the monarch appear as parties to the conflict. Documents have been preserved in which they agreed to have the case re-examined by the *juge mage*. The first document was signed by the general and diocesan administrators on behalf of the Holy See, and the second by those appointed by the pope at the king's request.[128] Therefore, although the complaint initially concerned a period when the Templars' estates were managed solely by royal administrators, the Holy See became involved in the proceedings at a later date.

A similar situation arose during proceedings relating to a dispute between tenants of the Cours and Peyremale estates and papal administrators. The tenants complained that the administrators were hindering their harvests and their right to hunt and were charging them for their visits. In turn, the latter accused the tenants of neglecting vine cultivation, failing to distribute customary alms, and preventing the faithful from using the chapel. In 1312, the case was referred to the *juge mage* of Carcassonne, with both papal and royal administrators involved,[129] as in the case of the proceedings concerning Italian merchants. Documents relating to these proceedings also reveal that, for a period at least, it was the pope's administrators who were directly involved in management, hence the complaints against them. Therefore, it appears that an identical model of administration was not introduced throughout the country following the implementation of Clement V's decision in Poitiers. In different regions, the involvement of commissioners appointed by the pope, bishops, and the king in decision-making on current matters related to the functioning of houses and farms varied. In any case, they all participated in it for at least some time.

The final document discussed here also shows that, even when the pope's administrators were in charge of managing the estates, the new management method for the properties was maintained or changed, i.e., they were leased out. This solution was most likely introduced throughout the country, as evidenced by documents concerning the subsequent transfer of control of the estates to the Hospitallers, among other things. Preserved records from 1313 show that there were tenants in the houses in Ansigny, Cenan, and La Lande-de-Parthenay in Poitou at the time of the transfer.[130] Renaud de Saint-Ouen's report also mentions tenants several times.[131]

According to the instructions of Clement V, administrators were required to submit two copies of their annual accounts: one for the king and one for the pope.[132] It is unclear how this process worked in practice. However, a letter from Clement V to one of the general administrators, dated August 1312, indicates that the financial reports were sent to the auditors appointed by the pope and king, who checked them.[133] However, no further information on this subject has been found. Later sources only mention five accounts prepared by the general administrators during their involvement in managing the estates. These accounts were used to draw up a final summary of their activities. These were then stored in the royal treasury.[134] It can be assumed that these were the documents that the administrators were required to submit to the king and the pope annually. If so, the general administrators' accounts would have been prepared regularly, as planned by Clement V. However, these are only assumptions.

Although preserved sources indicate that the provisions of Poitiers were gradually implemented in France, and administrators appointed by the Holy See, bishops and the monarch cooperated on matters related to the administration of properties, not everything went as the pope and the king would have wished. In November 1309, Philip sent a letter to Clement V, which most likely referred to abuses relating to the management of the Order's properties. While the document itself has not survived, we can infer its contents based on a later papal commentary. Clement V referred to Philip's letter during a meeting with his envoys who had delivered it. According to their account, the pope expressed his dissatisfaction, stating that he was aware of the Templar properties being wasted and destroyed (*sciebat quod omnia erdebantur et dissipabantur)*, as he had predicted during the talks in Poitiers.[135] Barber believed that Clement V was referring to thefts allegedly committed by Philip the Fair.[136] However, the available sources provide no evidence that the king of France used the Order's assets for his own purposes, as was the case in other countries. In 1308, for example, Edward II ordered that supplies for troops going to Scotland be gathered from Templar lands and that wool stored in Templar houses be handed over to pay the king's debts.[137] A similar situation occurred in Aragon, where money and valuable items found in the Templars' houses went straight to the royal treasury. James II then distributed these items generously to his family and other orders. The monarch also used the income seized from the commanderies to reward his subjects.[138] In France, no documents containing any instructions from Philip the Fair regarding the transfer of the Order's assets for purposes unrelated to the proceedings have survived. Therefore, Clement V's statement may have referred not to the king's actions, but to those of others involved in the administration of the Templar properties at that time, who committed numerous abuses, as discussed in subsequent chapters.[139]

We know that, at the end of December 1309, the pope replied to the monarch's letter, also referring to issues related to the Order's properties. However, the content of this reply is unknown.[140] It is unclear whether any measures were planned to counteract dishonest practices, or if any changes were made to how the properties were managed. Therefore, it can be assumed that the solutions introduced in the first few months after the Poitiers meeting remained in place until the Templar properties were transferred to the Hospitallers in 1313.

2.2.3 What happened to the Templars' money?

The question posed in the title has puzzled researchers for hundreds of years. It was already mentioned in one of the earlier chapters in the context of the sale of movable property belonging to the Order and the leasing of their houses after the meeting in Poitiers. Now, we will examine this issue from a broader perspective and attempt to answer the question of what happened to all the proceeds from the Templars' estates, which were collected over almost five years while the proceedings were ongoing.

The prevailing view among historians is that the Templars' financial resources ended up entirely in the hands of Philip the Fair. Literature most often states that the monarch seized all the money and valuables in the Templars' Paris headquarters at the time of the brothers' arrest[141] and that all income from the Order's confiscated properties went to his treasury.[142] However, bothclaims are mere speculation and are not confirmed by any surviving sources. The surviving documents provide clues that allow us to paint a different picture of the situation.

In accordance with Clement V's wishes, as expressed at the end of the Poitiers talks and in subsequent official documents, the Templars' money and current income from their estates were to be collected in a safe place within the kingdom of France and handed over to the pope for use in the Holy Land.[143] Notably, there was no mention of their possible return to the Templars, as was the case with their seized properties, nor of their transfer to potential successors. In this situation, two possibilities arose: either the Order's money was collected by Philip the Fair's men and handed over to the pope, as set out in the documents and in accordance with Clement V's will; or the king kept it for himself, thus failing to comply with the provisions of Poitiers.

Had the king of France decided to seize the Templars' money, it would certainly have triggered an open conflict with Clement V, much more serious than at the beginning of the proceedings. However, the preserved sources, and above all the correspondence exchanged between the two parties after the Poitiers meeting, show no signs of disputes on this subject. Furthermore, such large sums, which were probably kept in the Order's treasury and collected as ongoing income from individual commanderies and, later, as fees from tenants, must have affected the king's financial situation, at least temporarily. However, this did not happen.

To grasp the scale of the sums involved, it is helpful to review what we know about the Templars' financial resources and income. Unfortunately, we have very little information on this subject, and what we do have is fragmentary. Nevertheless, researchers have repeatedly attempted to estimate the size of the Order's income. Initially, these estimates were based on imagination alone; later, they were mainly based on the number of tithes paid by the Order.[144] It is known that, in 1294, the French Templars paid 6,000 l. t., suggesting that their income amounted to 60,000 l. t. However, at the beginning of the 20th century, Léon-Louis Borrelli de Serres dismissed such estimates as misguided and inaccurate.[145] Equally dubious is the proposal put forward by the contemporary researcher Ignacio de La Torre. Using data from the British Isles on the income of local Templar commanderies at the start of the 14th century as a basis, he estimated the average income of a house to be 232 l. t. He then multiplied this sum by the estimated number of houses in France (i.e., 660) and converted the final result of his calculations into the amount of silver. He concluded that the French Templars had accumulated approximately 61,612 kg of silver over 16 years – roughly from the time they left the Holy Land until their arrest in October 1307. This suggests that their treasury could have contained around 100,000 kg of silver at that time.[146] These are very far-reaching estimates which should be described as purely theoretical. Demurger considered them "arbitrary and hazardous."[147] Unfortunately, we have no other estimates at our disposal.

We cannot say much more about the income derived from the Templars' estates during the trial. We only have isolated examples of estimated sums, as well as details of the fees paid by some tenants in the first dozen or so years of the 14th century. For example, the surviving documents tell us that the Templar estates in Brucafel and Montrond, which belonged to the commandery of Douzens, were leased in 1305 for 1050 l. t. per year.[148] In 1308, Clement V and Philip the Fair exchanged the annuity that Otto de Grandson received from the Templar treasury for the right to collect an income of 2000 l. t. from three Burgundian houses: Thors, Épailly, and Coulours. However, it transpired that the income from the Épailly house, estimated at 2,194 l. 3 d. t. in November 1308,[149] was sufficient to repay this obligation. Another example can be found in the calculations concerning the commandery of Montricoux, Occitania, whose income amounted to 1100 l. t. per year after 1312.[150] In 1315, as part of repaying their debts to Italian bankers, the Hospitallers transferred the income from 17 houses and their associated farms in Auvergne to them. These were expected to bring in 3000 l. t. per year. They also transferred several dozen other houses located in various regions, whose income was estimated at 4000 l. t.[151] These sums differ considerably. We also have information about some of the lease payments from the period when the Templars' estates were under the control of the king's and the Church's administrators. A summary of these is presented in Table 2.1 below.

Based on this rather random data, we can assume that the annual income of the French Templar houses amounted to several tens of thousands of livres. However, it was not the same every year, as the final amount paid by tenants was also affected by their expenses and unforeseen circumstances.[152] Nevertheless, if this is added to the cash in the Order's treasury, the total sum certainly had a significant impact on the monarch's finances, which researchers estimate to be

Table 2.1 Rent paid for the lease of Templar houses in France between 1308 and 1312[153]

	1308	*1309*	*1310*	*1311*	*1312*
Ambrief	124 l. p.				
Ballan (part of the estate)		200 l.			
Laon, Ardon			124 l. p.		
Bonlieu	200 l. t.	200 l. t.	200 l. t.	200 l. t.	200 l. t.
Magnac					104 l. t.
Puybonnieux		300 l. t.	300 l. t.		300 l. t.
Bellechassagne, Foulventour, La Bussière-Rapy		430 l. t.			
Foulventour, La Bussière-Rapy				300 l. t.	233 l. 6 s. 8 d. t.
Mons, Bonnefare, Chaumont				390 l. t.	
Chaumont					33 l. 6 s. 8 d. t.
Le Palais		160 l. t.	160 l. t.	160 l. t.	63 l. 6 s. 8 d. t.
Bilbartaut		9 l.			

worth 400,000–600,000 l. t. per year.[154] Favier and Barber believed that seizing the Templars' houses in 1307 brought the king immediate profit, allowing him to temporarily replenish his coffers.[155] However, Borrelli de Serres, who carefully analysed the financial documents from the reign of Philip the Fair, concluded that none of them mentions any money from the Templars' treasury going into the royal coffers. What is more, shortly after seizing the Order's assets, the king was forced to borrow large sums from Lombard bankers[156] and once again lowered the value of the coin.[157] The monarch repeated this latter measure several times during the proceedings against the Order, while attempting to strengthen the currency in the meantime. However, the chronology of these changes is not connected to events relating to the Templars.[158] Instead, it can be linked to the cyclical financial assistance provided by Clement V, who was aware of the French king's financial difficulties. At the beginning of his pontificate, the pope granted Philip annates for three consecutive years to help improve the value of the coin.[159] He also granted him income from tithes for the same period to fund the war in Flanders.[160] Notably, Clement V also supported the French monarch following the seizure of the Order's properties, granting him additional tithes in 1310 and 1312, to bolster the royal treasury.[161] If the king had taken the Templars' money against the pope's will, it can be assumed that the latter would not have transferred further income to him. However, Clement V clearly recognised the unabated difficulties faced by Philip, as he explicitly stated during a meeting with the monarch's envoys in December 1309. He said that the lack of money in the royal treasury was due to the wars that had been fought, and that, since these wars had now ended, the monarch's financial situation could improve in the future. During the same conversation, the pope also mentioned the squandering of the French Templars' assets, but did not comment on the possible seizure of the Order's money by the king.[162] This statement paints a picture that is also confirmed by the comments of the Aragonese envoys to the papal court, who criticised the French king and closely followed his actions relating to the Templar properties. In a report dated April 1309 addressed to James II, they stated that France had "never had a monarch so poor and so little respected."[163] Clearly, therefore, even these outside observers did not see any improvement in Philip the Fair's financial situation while the Order's properties remained under his control.

Therefore, it appears that the Templars' money did not enter the royal treasury and that the monarch still required the pope's support in the form of further tithes. If it was not Philip the Fair who took the cash from the Parisian Temple and the income from the French houses, then, in accordance with the agreements made in Poitiers, it should have gone to Clement V. Even in this case, the inflow of such large sums should have left a trace in the sources and noticeably impacted the pope's capabilities and decisions, particularly regarding the organisation of the planned crusade for which the funds were intended. This impact should have been all the more noticeable given that the pope and his curia were also struggling with financial difficulties. In 1308–1309, the official papal income amounted to around 70,000 florins, or less than 47,000 l. t.[164] In February 1309, envoys of James II reported that, according to cardinals close to Clement V, his coffers were empty due to expenses incurred for the Hospitallers' expedition.[165] In November of the same year, the pope himself described his financial situation in a similar manner in a letter to the king of Aragon, mentioning the enormous sums allocated to aid the Hospitallers and to finance the war against Venice that was being waged at the time.[166] The Templars' money would therefore also have provided significant assistance to Clement V.

We have two source documents that provide insight into the transfer of funds collected from Templar houses during the trial. Both have been known to historians since at least the late 19th century, yet researchers studying the Templars rarely refer to them. The first is an excerpt from the *compte du domaine* of the seneschalship of Carcassonne for the year 1310. According to the document, Enguerrand de Marigny travelled to Carcassonne, collected the income from the confiscated properties of the Jews and the Templars, and transported it personally to Avignon. Unfortunately, the source from which this information originates has not survived to the present day. However, it was quoted in the monumental *Histoire de Languedoc* by Claude Devic and Joseph Vaissète.[167] Since its publication, researchers have repeatedly referred to the excerpt in various contexts, and no one has questioned its authenticity.[168] There is therefore no reason to doubt it. Historians analysing the proceedings against the Order also drew attention to it but considered the information it contained to be misleading and inaccurate. Antoine Du Bourg and, a hundred years later, André Soutou stated that, although the source mentions Enguerrand de Marigny's trip to Avignon, he actually took the money from the Templars' houses to the king, not the pope.[169] However, this account is corroborated by the findings of Favier, who traced Enguerrand de Marigny's travels in detail. These show that the royal chamberlain was in Avignon in August 1310, as evidenced by the bulls issued to him by the pope on 7, 16 and 17 August, as well as a letter from Clement V dated 23 August, which was handed to him during his stay.[170] The researcher's findings also reveal that Enguerrand de Marigny most likely visited the pope in August 1309, March 1311, and August 1313.[171] Each visit was accompanied by various expressions of favour from Clement V towards Enguerrand de Marigny, his relatives, and his friends.[172] While not all of these visits necessarily involved the transfer of money from the Templars' estates to the pope, there is a cyclical pattern to them that suggests this may have occurred. However, as there are no other sources to confirm this, such assumptions remain in the realm of conjecture.

The second source to consider when analysing the possible fate of the Templars' money concerns the finances of Clement V in the final years of his pontificate. These are the minutes of an investigation conducted at the behest of Pope John XXII between 1318 and 1322, which concerned the sums allocated by Clement V at the end of his pontificate in 1312–1314. The documents from these proceedings contain the records of testimonies from cardinals and other members of the pope's immediate entourage, among other things, and were published in their entirety by Franz Ehrle in 1889.[173] John XXII was primarily interested in the money that Clement V had given to his nephew prior to his death, so that it could be used for the needs of the planned crusade. As this objective was not realised, the new pope sought to recover all the funds to use for the needs of the Holy Land.

The testimonies of the questioned witnesses and various documents by John XXII, which are included in the case files, contain information about the sums of money available to Clement V towards the end of his life. According to calculations from August 1311, we learn from these documents that the total income to the papal treasury amounted to 1,300,000 florins (almost 870,000 l. t.). However, the treasurer who testified was unable to say when all the payments were made.[174] The income and expenditure balance sheet drawn up in January 1313 totalled 987,000 florins (658,000 l. t.).[175] This time, the minutes noted that this sum had been collected over a period of approximately three and a half years, i.e., from around the second half of 1309 onwards. A few months later, in the summer of 1313, Clement V told one of the cardinals that he had collected approximately 1,040,000 florins (690,000 l. t.) during his entire pontificate. In addition to cash, the pope also possessed many other valuables, which were kept in chests in a designated room.[176] In June 1312, shortly after the end of the Council of Vienne, Clement V decided how to distribute his funds in the event of his death. His bequests totalled 814,080 florins (approximately 543,000 l. t.).[177] As Peter D. Partner observed, the document containing the decisions on this matter was not formally a "last will" or "testament," but a "disposition in the event of death" (*donatio mortis causa*).[178] This may suggest that the solution adopted was unique. Initially, Clement V emphasised his commitment to the crusade and stated that, although it was not possible to organise a new expedition to the East at that time, he wanted to secure funds for future activities. Therefore, he decided to give 300,000 florins (200,000 l. t.) to his nephew, viscount of Lomagne, Bertrand de Goth, so that he or one of his relatives could participate in the *passagium generale* with 500 knights. The pope decided to give the rest of the money (314,080 florins, or approximately 210,000 l. t.) to members of his family and people from his immediate circle, as well as to finance various "pious works" (*pia opera*) (200,000 florins, or approximately 133,000 l. t.). These provisions were supplemented by a new disposition on 9 April 1314, in which Clement V decided to leave his successor 70,000 florins (approximately 47,000 l. t.) and deposits in Paris and Montpellier totalling no more than 15,821 florins (approximately 10,547 l. t.).[179] The latter amount was indicated by one of the treasurers who testified, referring to three deposits held at the beginning of 1314 in Paris, Montpellier, and at the castle of Duras.[180] According to the witnesses, the pope ordered everyone involved in drafting both documents to keep them strictly confidential until his death.

The sums mentioned during the proceedings demonstrate the vast wealth that Clement V accumulated in a relatively short period of time. Researchers analysing his financial situation wonder where such large sums came from. The prevailing opinion is that the pope collected them in a "secret" treasury and accumulated them as part of an unofficial, "parallel" system of clergy taxation (*secreta servitia*), which was intended to provide him with additional income.[181] In fact, a register belonging to Jean de Lescapon,[182] one of the officials involved in keeping the accounts of Clement V's treasury (referred to as *secundus thesaurarius* or "second treasurer"), which was found in 1336, mentions "secret" income related to this practice. This was the title of one of the 16 sections included in his records.[183] Another one was labelled "Gifts" (*dona data domino*), but nothing is known about the others. Apart from the "secret services," it follows that money also flowed into the papal coffers from other sources, most of which we do not know. Among these sources could have been sums from the estates of the French Templars. Of course, neither Clement V's financial documents nor the witness statements given during the proceedings conducted by John XXII mention this, but the information they contain about the enormous wealth accumulated by the pope in less than four years (from 1309 to 1313), that is, during the period when the Order's assets remained under the joint control of ecclesiastical and royal administrators, suggests that this was indeed the case.

Assuming that the Order's financial resources and income did indeed go to Clement V's treasury, their fate would have been as follows: According to the decisions made in Poitiers, these funds were to be used for the crusade and could only be allocated by the pope. This is why they were added to his personal coffers (*camera*) rather than going to the official curial treasury (*thesaurus*).[184] This division of Clement V's financial resources is evident in documents relating to the organisation of the Hospitallers' military expedition of 1308–1309. At the time, the pope emphasised that the funds for its organisation were to come *de nostra camera* and *de thesauro nostrae camerae*, and not from tithes or other church revenues.[185] Thus, he indicated the existence of a separate fund from which he intended to finance the expedition. After 1309, he collected money in it to give to the organisers of the new crusade, which was referred to as the *passagium generale*, once binding decisions on its preparations had been made. However, after the Council of Vienne ended, he realised that it would not happen soon and that he might not live to see it due to his health, so he decided to distribute the accumulated funds. It was then that he donated 300,000 florins (200,000 l. t.) to support the crusade. As entrusting them to one of his family members could have drawn criticism from those around him and perhaps also prompted protest from Philip the Fair, who was involved in implementing the provisions of Poitiers, he ordered all witnesses to keep their decisions secret. This was most likely the case, as John XXII only learned of his predecessor's bequest after his death.[186] His decision to initiate proceedings to determine the exact content of Clement V's order and to recover the unused money suggests that the deceased pope did not dispose of his private funds, and that his decisions of 1312 and 1314 were not part of his personal will. Otherwise, John XXII would have had no grounds to interfere in his predecessor's family affairs. According to the decisions made in Poitiers, Clement V and his successors were to oversee the proper expenditure of the Templars' estate funds. This suggests that funds from French Templar houses were indeed involved.

The investigation also revealed that, between June 1312 and April 1314, the deceased pope had decided to allocate part of the money he had lent to the French and English monarchs to the crusade.[187] According to the official findings, the kings received 100,000 and 160,000 florins (approximately 67,000 and 107,000 l. t., respectively).[188] Edward II is known to have repaid most of his debt to Bertrand de Goth.[189] However, the viscount was unable to recover any money from the loan taken out by the king of France.[190]

John XXII wanted to take over all the funds donated by his predecessor for the crusade. However, Bertrand de Goth opposed this, arguing that Clement V had intended to allocate the funds to the *passagium generale* and not to a smaller expedition as the new pope had proposed.[191] Ultimately, it was agreed that the viscount would pay 150,000 florins (100,000 l. t.) into John XXII's treasury, bringing the investigation to an end. At the same time, the pope confirmed the remaining decisions of his predecessor, as set out in documents from 1312 to 1314.[192] This confirms once again that Clement V did not dispose of his own money in them.

This information suggests that only some of the Templars' money, which had probably been going to the papal treasury (*camera*) since mid-1309, was allocated to the crusade by Clement V. According to Clement V's wishes, a total of 430,000 florins (approximately 287,000 l. t.) was to be used for this purpose. However, it is unclear how much the kings of France and England paid towards their obligations, or what happened to the remaining sums in the hands of the pope's nephew. It can be assumed that much of the money given by Clement V to his entourage and pious causes also came from funds collected from the houses of the French Templars, but nothing can be said for certain on this subject.

There are still some doubts regarding the financing of the Hospitallers' 1309 expedition. This has already been mentioned in the context of the sale of the Templar properties and its leasing after the meeting in Poitiers. However, Philip the Fair's financial involvement in the expedition remains unclear. This issue seems to be closely related to the previous one.

In August 1308, the pope announced that the king of France was to give the Hospitallers 100,000 florins (approximately 67,000 l. t.).[193] Menache rightly pointed out that this was "wishful thinking"[194] given the emptiness of the monarch's treasury. Nevertheless, in late September 1308, Clement V asked Philip the Fair to pay the Order the agreed-upon sum.[195] In early February 1309, when appointing a legate to represent him during the expedition, Clement V wrote that the king of France was generously contributing to its financing.[196] However, problems arose because the king believed that Foulques de Villaret was not sufficiently informing him about the expedition's preparations and that the French Hospitallers' participation in the venture was too small.[197] The pope justified the Grand Master while praising the monarch's involvement in the expedition's preparations.[198] On 27 October 1309, Clement V again asked Philip for financial assistance. He pointed out the risk of the entire undertaking failing and mentioned that, in addition to the money he had promised earlier, he had lent the Hospitallers another 50,000 florins (approximately 33,000 l. t.) from his treasury.[199] This is the last known letter concerning the financing of the expedition by the king of France. Shortly before, Foulques de Villaret had set sail eastward with a small fleet.[200]

Researchers analysing this correspondence generally conclude that it reflects Philip the Fair's desire to dominate the crusade movement and expand his political influence. Initially, the monarch wanted to take full control of the planned crusade. When he failed, he did not give the Hospitallers the promised money.[201] This interpretation is supported by Elisabeth A. R. Brown's findings that there is no trace of payments linked to this issue in the French crown's financial documents.[202] However, later correspondence between Clement V and Philip makes no mention of the king breaking his word on this matter. Furthermore, the pope's February 1309 letter and subsequent praise of the monarch's involvement in organising the expedition suggest that Philip did indeed become involved in the preparations carried out by the Hospitallers. This seemingly contradictory information can be explained by revisiting the events that followed the meeting in Poitiers. Let us recall that Clement V allocated the Order's movable property and some of its real estate to the Holy Land. Soon after, the process of selling equipment and leasing some of the houses began. This quickly generated profits that could be used immediately. Perhaps this money was intended as Philip the Fair's contribution to the planned crusade. This would explain why the ruler declared such a large sum despite his disastrous financial situation and why there are no traces in the royal financial documents of payments from his treasury or income from the sale of Templar properties and lease fees. In this case, the king's role would be to reorganise the management of the Order's assets as quickly as possible and collect the expected 100,000 florins (approximately 66,000 l. t.), not to reach his own coffers. Another possibility was transferring the financial resources and valuables from the Order's houses, as well as the income accumulated between the seizure of the properties and the formal takeover by the Church commissioners, to the pope. It is difficult to identify any other source from which Philip could have transferred such a large sum of money at that time without leaving traces in the documents.

Assuming these assumptions are true, one might ask why the pope sent a letter to the king on 27 October, asking for money for the Hospitallers. This can be explained by delays in implementing the Poitiers plan, the need to allocate larger sums to the ongoing expedition, or Philip's continued resistance to transferring funds to the Order due to his reservations about the French Hospitallers' insufficient involvement in the undertaking. It is reasonable to assume that Philip did not want to give money belonging to the French Templars to leaders of the Hospital who were not directly connected to France. Such an attitude, focused on prioritising the French Hospitallers, was not unusual at the time. James II, seeking to achieve his own political goals related to the Reconquista, decided to take similar action. He forbade the Hospitallers from taking horses and money out of the country, arguing that their resources should be used for local needs.[203] Therefore, it seems that neither monarch was willing to sacrifice their own interests or those of their subjects for crusading plans.

Therefore, it seems that Clement V and Philip the Fair sought to implement the provisions of Poitiers, which allowed for Templar funds to be used to organise a military expedition to the East. The monarch fulfilled his obligation to collect and transfer funds to the pope, who had the right to dispose of them at his discretion. Some of the funds probably ended up in the hands of the Hospitallers. After Clement V's death, another portion had the opportunity to fund a new expedition, but it ultimately did not take place. The rest was transferred for unrelated purposes. Despite the efforts of both sides, the initial goal was not achieved.

2.3 Thefts and negligence

According to Demurger, the Templars' estates were seized by Philip the Fair's officials so swiftly and effectively in October 1307 that major losses in the form of misappropriation, which occurred in other countries, were avoided.[204] However, surviving documents paint a completely different picture of the situation. They reveal that the process of seizing and managing the Templar properties were rife with abuse and theft. These abuses were committed by those appointed to carry out the procedures accompanying the arrest of the Templars and the seizure of their houses, as well as by those responsible for the subsequent administration of the seized properties: local territorial rulers and the surrounding population. Dishonesty occurred during both the period when the king and his vassals exercised control over the properties and the period when it was taken over by representatives of the Church. We have no documents from the time of the trial in which Philip the Fair mentions this issue. All we know is that the king and the pope exchanged letters on the matter towards the end of 1309, but the details of their correspondence are unknown.[205] While it is clear that both parties were aware of the scale of the abuses, there is no evidence in the surviving sources of any decisions or actions taken by either party to limit the losses. Therefore, it is most likely that no solutions were introduced by the end of the proceedings that would have enabled real control over the activities of those directly managing the estates or the elimination of abuses. This, in turn, created a sense of impunity and encouraged further dishonesty.

Information on various types of misappropriation and neglect primarily comes from documents created after the trial, during subsequent investigations aimed at locating and recovering the Order's misappropriated assets. The most comprehensive of these is the aforementioned account on the investigation conducted by Renaud de Saint-Ouen, which provides information that has not yet been analysed by researchers. This document was produced more than a decade after the dissolution of the Templars and the distribution of their properties. Despite the passage of time, the commissioners obtained information about many irregularities. A summary of these reveals the scale of the phenomenon and the complexity of its consequences. Other sources merely supplement the picture emerging from this document.

According to surviving records, valuable items and animals began to disappear from Templar houses even before the members of the Order were arrested. Some brothers, having learned of the planned arrests, hid the items or took them with them when they fled. Jean de Châlons, a servant who appeared before the cardinals in Poitiers in 1308, testified that the commander of France, Gérard de Villiers, had fled with 50 horses. He then took 18 galleys with other high-ranking Templars and set sail.[206] This was not an isolated incident. The Italian chronicler Ptolemy of Lucca wrote that some Aragonese Templars also attempted to escape by sea with "immense treasures," but their plans were thwarted by the wind.[207] However, in the case of Gérard de Villiers, Demurger noted that many of the captured Templars, who knew about the escape of such an important dignitary of the Order, attributed various actions and offences to him. This is why their accounts are not very reliable.[208]

Jean de Châlons also informed the cardinals of the treasure belonging to Hugues de Pairaud, a visitor to France,[209] which was supposedly taken by one of the fleeing knights, Hugues de Chalon.[210] Unfortunately, his account does not specify what he meant by "treasure." However, it probably refers to items described in detail in one of the 1320 documents from the *Chambre des Comptes*. This document reveals that, before the proceedings against the Order began, Hugues de Pairaud entrusted a chest containing gold and silver coins to the commander of Dormelles and Beauvoir, Pierre Gaudes. Expecting to be arrested, the latter went to nearby Moret and gave the chest to a fisherman named Étienne Petot for safekeeping. Upon hearing a public call for the return of the Templars' assets, the fisherman handed the chest over to the bailiff of Sens. Several years later, the money found its way into the royal treasury.[211]

A similar situation is described in Renaud de Saint-Ouen's report. The commissioner noted that the knight Pierre de Castillon was in possession of a horse that he had received from the Templar brother, Gérard de Lavergne.[212] While there were certainly more such cases, given the circumstances they probably only involved minor components of the Templars' assets and did not significantly reduce the total value of the seized properties.

Much more serious irregularities occurred when territorial rulers seized the Order's properties. Some of them took land, household furnishings, and money belonging to the Order. An example of this occurred in Burgundy, where the Viscount of Vesoul, Jean de Faucogney, seized the Templar grange in Amancey and took all its furnishings. He only handed it over to the papal administrator in Burgundy in 1311, together with 40 l. t. as compensation for the stolen furniture.[213] Also in 1311, the pope called on other Burgundian nobles to settle their accounts and hand over control of the Templars' estates to his envoy.[214] This suggests that they had not done so despite three years having passed since the decisions in Poitiers. However, some decisions had to wait a few more years. The Viscount of Besançon, Hugues de Chalon-Arlay, only ordered the return of the seized properties in his 1312 will.[215]

Similar situations also occurred in the south of France. Renaud de Saint-Ouen's investigation revealed that, following the Templars' arrest in 1307, the count of Armagnac seized money and movable property from the house of Ayguetinte, totalling over 400 l. t. He only returned them after they were taken over by the Hospitallers.[216] In turn, the viscount of Lomagne took over the income from the Templar houses in Bordeaux and Arcins for several years. After the brothers were arrested, he seized the property belonging to the commandery of Gimbrède. However, in 1308, he handed it over to the bishop of Lectoure.[217]

Information is also available regarding abuses that took place in Flanders. Filip Hooghe cited the example of the actions of the castellan of Saint-Omer, who seized income from various confiscated properties and handed some of it over to lord Philippe d'Ypres. Lord of Watten, François de Haveskercke, is said to have acted similarly, seizing several lands belonging to the Templars in the castellany of Cassel.[218]

These various cases of appropriation show how freely local rulers seized the Templar properties and disposed of them at will. This reflects their attitude towards the Order as well as their perception of the inquisitorial procedure as an opportunity to enrich themselves at the accused's expense, since the accused were unlikely to return to reclaim their property. It also demonstrates the difficulty of controlling the actions of vassals by their superior, the king of France.

The situation surrounding the arrest of the Order's members was also exploited by neighbours, who tried to enrich themselves at its expense in various ways. A prime example of this was the actions taken by the chapter of Carcassonne, which seized a Templar-owned plot of land in Brucafel almost immediately after the brothers were arrested and ordered the construction of a mill and a canal on it. Over the next few years, it is likely that no one claimed the land that had been appropriated. Preserved sources indicate that the Hospitallers only began a legal battle for the return of the property and compensation for their losses after they took over the property belonging to the commandery of Douzens. The proceedings, which began in 1313, were prolonged because the chapter's representative raised various formal objections. Among other things, he questioned the administrative affiliation of the disputed lands and the authority of the commander of Douzens at the time to represent the Hospitaller Order. The case was further complicated by the fact that it also concerned the king, who was owed fees for a mill built by the chapter. The *juge mage* of Carcassonne ruled in favour of the Hospitallers. However, in 1314, the chapter's representative refused to accept the ruling and announced that he would appeal to the monarch. A year later, he obstructed the proceedings again by refusing to recognise the secular court's jurisdiction to settle the dispute between the two ecclesiastical institutions. He requested the intervention of Bérenger d'Auvergne, the papal commissioner supervising the transfer of the Templar properties. However, when the commissioner agreed to take up the case, the seneschal of Carcassonne objected, arguing that it was already being examined by a secular court. The Hospitallers protested this time, probably expecting greater favour from the papal commissioner. Ultimately, however, the chapter also questioned his competence, and its representative appealed directly to the pope.[219] In 1315, he appealed against the excommunication imposed on those who had unlawfully detained Templar properties.[220] The Pontiff's response and the final resolution of the conflict are unknown. It is also unclear how the secular authorities involved in the case responded to the chapters and the Hospitallers' conclusions, or how the issue of the mill fees owed to the king was resolved. In any case, the course of the proceedings once again demonstrates the complexity of cases involving the unlawful seizure of Templar properties and how individuals and institutions exploited the legal confusion surrounding the trial and its aftermath.

Renaud de Saint-Ouen's report also contains information about various types of theft and misappropriation of the Order's properties that took place after the brothers were arrested. We learn from the report that the knight Bernard de Durfort, Lord of Flamarens, cut down a Templar forest from the commandery of Gimbrède. This brought him a profit of 200 l. 5 s. t.[221] In turn, a certain P. de *Spahone* seized the territory of *Alito*. Two investigations were conducted in this case during the trial: one by the administrator of the Templar estates at the time, Davin de Roaix, and the other by order of the king. However, it appears that neither was completed, or that neither resulted in a decision to return the seized lands. Renaud de Saint-Ouen's report states that it was not until 1323 that the seneschal of Toulouse took any action in this matter.[222]

There are also documented cases of the theft of individual items and animals. Renaud of Saint-Ouen's account most often refers to the seizure of "movable property" (*bonis mobilibus*) from one of the Templar houses.[223] In only two cases do we learn exactly what was stolen – one document mentions a metal vessel (*olla metali*),[224] another mentions clothes (*linthamina et vestes linee*).[225] Despite the passage of time, the commissioners managed to uncover these crimes and find the perpetrators. This shows that the local community was well aware of the situation and was still willing to inform the king's envoys about dishonest neighbours more than a decade later.

However, not all reports of theft turned out to be true. In 1316, the king ordered the bailiff of Sens to investigate a complaint from a tenant of the Templar estate in Fontenay-près-Chablis. The tenant claimed that, after the arrest of the Templars, Guiot Beline and Étienne Tartier had cut down 25 arpents of forest belonging to the house and caused him damage. Although the estate administrators initially found them guilty and ordered them to pay compensation to the tenant, the bailiff ultimately acquitted both men.[226] It therefore appears that, on this occasion, it was the informant who was seeking to enrich himself dishonestly.

Another opportunity for abuse of various kinds arose when the French bishops took control of the Templars' assets. Preserved documents show that some of those entrusted by Clement V with managing the assets in the months following the meeting in Poitiers treated them as a convenient source of income. Renaud de Saint-Ouen revealed several such cases during his investigation. These included the archbishop of Auch, Armanieu II d'Armagnac, who took control of the Ayguetinte estate from his relative, the count of Armagnac, and collected income from it for the next four years[227] and the bishop of Lectoure, who, in 1308, appointed his administrator of the commandery of Gimbrède and ordered him to pay half its income to the bishop. It was not until 1311 that proper administrators gained access to these estates.[228]

There were also some high-ranking clergymen who were not satisfied with merely drawing temporary income from the Order's estates; they went much further. The most surprising case in this regard is that of the papal chamberlain, Cardinal Bertrand des Bordes, and bishop of Bazas, Guillaume V Arnaud de La Mothe. Renaud de Saint-Ouen's investigation revealed that they took advantage of the fact that the bishop was holding the commander of the province of Provence, Bernard de Roche, prisoner in order to enrich themselves and their relatives. They not only took his silver tableware and the money he had with him in prison, which was worth about 1000 l. t., but also forced him to certify forged grants of Templar property in Agenais. These documents were backdated to the summer of 1307 – before the arrest of the Order's members – and bore Bernard de Roche's seal. Through this scheme, the cardinal acquired the right to collect income from several Templar houses, totalling 400 l. t. per year. He or his brother Pierre des Bordes, who was also involved in the fraud, exercised this right for at least five years.[229] All of this information was reported to the commissioners by Raymond de *Borda*, a former notary of Pierre des Bordes. The case becomes even more astonishing when we consult the papal registers. It turns out that Clement V confirmed this grant in 1311. The document in question, dated 1 April, states that Bertrand des Bordes was granted lifetime income from several Templar houses in Agenais and some estates belonging to the commandery of Gimbrède in return for his services to the Order and the Church. It also includes a relevant letter from Bernard de Roche, dated 8 July 1307.[230] This raises the question of whether the pope was aware of how the document he had confirmed had come into being, or if the cardinal had deceived him too. In any case, this situation sheds a very negative light on both the hierarchs who committed fraud and Clement V, who was either unaware of the dishonest actions of the clergy in his immediate circle or was complicit in them.

The papal registers from 1311 contain another document confirming the grant to Pierre des Bordes of the Templars of Agenais. A letter dated 1 July reveals that Bertrand de Trèbes, the commander of Agen and Gimbrède, who was imprisoned in the bishop of Bazas's prison alongside the commander of Provence,[231] in agreement with the latter, granted the cardinal's brother ownership of half of the mills in Roques near Astaffort.[232] However, Renaud de Saint-Ouen's account makes no mention of this grant or its consequences. Furthermore, the document issued by Clement V differs from the previous one in that it includes confirmation of the grant by Grand Master Jacques de Molay in June 1307. If it also turns out to be forged, then the forgers must also have had access to the Grand Master's seal, which seems much less likely than in the case of the commander of Provence, who was imprisoned in the south of France. It therefore seems that such a grant did indeed take place before the Templars' arrest and that only one document is false.

But let us return to Renaud de Saint-Ouen's findings. The commissioners were informed that Pierre des Bordes had not only collected income from the Order's estates but had also taken control of the commandery of Gimbrède's forest and appropriated a horse and various items from the local house.[233] As a result of the commissioners' actions, he paid at least some of the money owed. It is not known whether this brought the proceedings against him to an end.

It is also said that one of bishop of Bazas' relatives received a forged grant from Bernard de Roche while he was in prison. A copy of this document was found among those collected during the royal commissioners' investigation. This document granted knight Gautier de La Mothe the right to income from Templar properties in the diocese of Agen, worth 100 l. t. per year. It was established that he had been collecting this income from the moment the members of the Order were arrested until Renaud de Saint-Ouen, and his companions discovered the fraud.[234]

Bishop of Bazas himself committed yet another abuse. In the second half of 1308 (after Clement V's decisions in Poitiers) or at the beginning of 1309, he seized control of the Templar houses in Cours and Romestaing. He then consistently refused to hand them over to the pope's commissioner. Only at the express order of Clement V, issued on 28 January 1310, and promising that all sums due to the bishop for his several months of service as administrator would be paid, did he do so.[235] However, the submitted accounts revealed that the sum in question was an enormous 1312 l. 10 s. of Bordeaux (1050 l. t.). Despite repeated reminders, the new administrator, Gérard de Bussy, did not comply with the papal order and did not pay the requested sum. The Cardinal Chamberlain intervened and ordered the payment again, even if it meant using the income from other commanderies. Other administrators, however, did not agree to such transactions, claiming that they were awaiting instructions from the pope himself. In 1312, bishop of Bazas complained to Clement V that he had only received 120 l. of Bordeaux (96 l. t.), a tiny fraction of the sum demanded. The pope ordered the administrators to pay under threat of excommunication.[236] This led to a serious conflict between the Church representatives involved in managing the properties. Once again, we must ask what Clement V's intentions were: did he believe in the legitimacy of bishop of Bazas's demands, even though other administrators of the Order's properties considered them excessive, or did he consciously agree to such abuse? The available sources provide no clues in this regard. However, the pope's exceptional favour towards the Cardinal Chamberlain and bishop of Bazas' subsequent actions in matters related to the Templar properties may suggest an agreement between the Head of the Church and these two hierarchs.

Apart from the obvious thefts and various types of misappropriation mentioned so far, the arrest and trial of the Templars also provided an opportunity to default on financial obligations to the Order. However, one might question whether the blame for these omissions should lie solely with the debtors or whether they were at least partly due to the circumstances and the administrators' failure to take appropriate action. The sudden arrest of the brothers, the protracted proceedings, and the subsequent changes in administrators certainly created numerous legal and organisational issues and uncertainties. Furthermore, no documents have survived that suggest any measures were taken during the proceedings to settle the debts owed to the Order, apart from public calls for the return of the Templar property in autumn 1307. The matter was further complicated by the fact that most of the properties were leased out later on. In practice, this meant that it was unclear, at least for some time, whether and to whom the earlier debts should be repaid. This obstacle probably only disappeared after the proceedings were completed and the process of actively recovering the Templars' lost assets began, involving the royal administration. All available sources referring to outstanding debts owed to the Order date from this period.

In 1315, Louis X referred to loans owed to the Templars prior to October 1307, instructing that the debtors be prosecuted.[237] This was not an easy task, as Renaud de Saint-Ouen and his companions were still collecting outstanding amounts in the 1320s. Their report details several such cases. The most challenging case involved the count of Périgord, who borrowed 285 l. 4 s. 5 d. t. from his brother Gérard Lavigne in 1297. The count did not repay the debt until his death in 1311, and it was only settled after the Parliament of Paris ruled on the matter in 1323.[238] It is also known that the same Templar lent money to several other individuals over several years prior to the trial, who also failed to fulfil their obligations, or only did so partially. According to the commissioners' findings, the total amount of their debts was 133 l. ob. t.[239] The unpaid loans granted by the commanders of La Bussière-Rapy and Montricoux[240] were slightly lower, but the report shows that the commissioners managed to recover only a small part of these sums during the investigation.

Other sources tell us that Count of Hainaut, Guillaume I (1304–1337), for example, had not repaid the debt he incurred with the Templar procurator-general Jean de Fouilloy[241] in 1325, which amounted to 333 l. 6 s. 8 d. p. (416 l. 13 s. 4 d. t.)[242] Milon, the abbot of the Benedictine monastery in Dijon, borrowed 500 florins (approximately 333 l. t.) from Hugues de Pairaud but consistently refused to repay them. Consequently, at the end of 1325, Charles IV ordered that the money be recovered from the guarantors of the loan.[243] The debt owed by Gilles and Jean de Compiègne was significantly higher. It amounted to 4,050 l. t., which was only paid in full after royal officials auctioned the heirs' land in 1319.[244] In this case, however, it is unclear whether the debt was a loan or related to another matter. The unpaid debts also originated from the period after the brothers' arrest. According to the *Journaux du Trésor*, shortly after the Order's properties were seized, its administrators lent 1,800 l. t. to the bishop of Bayeux. This sum was only recovered from his heirs in 1324.[245]

Following the arrest of the Templars, issues emerged regarding the repayment of other obligations owed to the Order. For example, the inhabitants of Ayguetinte in Occitania, stopped fulfilling their obligations to the local commandery a year after the trial began. These obligations consisted of delivering a fixed amount of grain each year. When this was reported to Renaud de Saint-Ouen or one of his deputies, the debtors had to pay the outstanding sum of 9 l. t.[246] This was not an isolated case. During the investigation, similar debts owed to the commanderies of Bordères[247] and Montricoux[248] were also settled, as were outstanding fees for the use of meadows and pastures belonging to other houses.[249]

In Burgundy, Countess Mahaut d'Artois stopped paying the rent due to the Templars of Salins after initiating proceedings against the Order. Her treasurer reported arrears in this matter as early as July 1308.[250] The matter was ultimately settled in 1311 with the papal administrator of the Templar estates in the duchy, at a cost of 406 l. t. for the years 1308–1309.[251]

Those obliged to pay their debts due to various court proceedings also failed to do so. Examining the court records in Montsaunès revealed 28 such cases. The debtors repaid a total of 13 l. 5 s. 6 d. t.,[252] while in Montricoux, 16 cases were found and 6 l. 3 d. t. was recovered.[253] In other places nine persons were required to repay a total of 5 l. 11 s. 8 d. t.[254] While these sums were relatively small, the significant number of cases that the commissioners had to address is noteworthy. Additionally, there were cases of unpaid debts related to proceedings that were already pending at the time of the trial.[255] This demonstrates the scale of the problem. If several dozen cases were revealed in only three towns, there must have been many more throughout the kingdom. Each one required an individual investigation and various measures leading to debt enforcement.

A similar problem arose concerning the execution of certain testamentary dispositions in favour of the Templars. Some heirs took advantage of the situation by failing to transfer money bequeathed for the Holy Land in their relatives' will. Renaud de Saint-Ouen's report details several dozen such cases, which were uncovered during an investigation in the seneschalships of Beaucaire and Toulouse.[256] Once again, questions arise as to the scale of the financial losses incurred throughout France and the measures required to enforce all the obligations. Unfortunately, we are unable to estimate this, even approximately.

Those directly involved in the procedures surrounding the seizure and subsequent administration of properties also played a significant role in depleting the Templars' assets. While some researchers have written that royal officials participated in the plundering of properties and neglected their proper management,[257] unfortunately, this issue has not yet been analysed in depth. However, it is reasonable to assume that officials of kings, princes and counts also took advantage of the opportunity to enrich themselves, as did the aforementioned territorial lords. Various types of abuse had already occurred during earlier inquisitorial proceedings, which were accompanied by the confiscation of the accused's property. For example, in 1304, it was discovered that royal administrators involved in managing the properties of heretics in southern France had dishonestly seized a castle and numerous lands and movable property, among other things.[258] In the case of the

Templars, however, the scale of the proceedings was different, as was the number of officials involved. The trial of a church institution and subsequent changes of administrators made uncovering abuses and negligence by officials much more difficult than in other similar cases.

In the months following the brothers' arrest, while the Order's properties were under the control of the king's officials, audits of the accounts submitted by the administrators revealed some irregularities. One example of this occurred in September 1308, when the administrator of the estates in the bailiwick of Auvergne examined the documents presented by the administrators of the commandery of Paluet. It transpired that both the inventory and the statement of receipts were incomplete. The inventory omitted a large proportion of the house's and chapel's furnishings, while the statement of receipts omitted part of the income. Following the investigation, it was decided that the administrators would not be paid.[259]

Unfortunately, it is not known whether equally detailed inspections were carried out in later periods. The next documents to mention abuses by administrators date back to the reign of Louis X. In the aforementioned order of August 1315, the monarch referred to people who had dishonestly enriched themselves while compiling inventories and carrying out administrative duties. He also listed abuses committed by collectors of various types of dues related to the Order's properties, as well as unreliable tenants. The latter's negligence and destruction rendered some of the property unusable. The king ordered that all stolen items be recovered and that those responsible be punished.[260] It therefore appears that the scale of the problem was significant and affected the entire kingdom, and that the monarch was fully aware of this.

The accuracy of Louis X's diagnosis of the situation presented in his order is confirmed by the accounts of Renaud de Saint-Ouen's investigation and other documents from that period. The commissioner's report details several dozen cases of abuse by administrators and collectors. Despite the passage of time, some of them did not present accounts of their activities and, as a result, did not pay the amounts due.[261] Others submitted the relevant documents but avoided paying the money.[262] During the investigation, debts dating back to the years immediately following the arrest of the Templars were uncovered.[263] In some cases, the submitted documents omitted certain amounts collected for various debts.[264] Renaud de Saint-Ouen recovered documents drawn up by the envoys of the former administrators of the Order's estates. These documents contained information about debts that had been repaid but not settled by those administrators.[265] The report also noted the case of Durand *Payrola*, who reported unpaid lease payments despite having previously received them. The tenants sued him for this. It is not known how the case ended.[266] However, tenants did not always fulfil their obligations, which testified to their dishonesty and the ineffectiveness of the collectors and supervisors of the estates. In this respect, the debts could relate to fees for one year[267] or even several consecutive years.[268] However, Renaud de Saint-Ouen's report makes no mention of any damage allegedly caused by the tenants. Therefore, it is most likely that Charles IV's order to the commissioners did not include the enforcement of obligations in this regard.

As well as inaccuracies in settlements and the avoidance of debt repayment, the administrators, supervisors, and tenants of estates were also guilty of various types of misappropriation. Guillaume de Caumont, for example, was appointed by Philip the Fair to administer the Templars' estates in Agenais. However, he misappropriated two mills and two fiefdoms belonging to the commandery of Cours. Even after the dissolution of the Order, he refused to return the property to the Hospitallers, despite receiving appropriate confirmation from successive monarchs. He only did so in 1326, following another intervention by the seneschal of Agen.[269] Renaud de Saint-Ouen's account also mentions a certain *magister Andus* de Rochefort, who collected income from the village of Plagne, belonging to the commandery of Montsaunès, for five years.[270] This suggests that he must have misappropriated it at the beginning of the proceedings. However, the circumstances are unknown. Similar situations occurred later in the proceedings when control of the properties was transferred to bishops, who then passed it on to tenants. The administrator of the commandery of Gimbrède, who was appointed by the bishop of Lectoure, transferred half of the income for 1308 (100 l. t.) to his principal and kept the other half for himself.[271] This administrator and his brother took part of the Templar house's furnishings, worth an additional 100 l. t.,[272] and the custodians and later tenants of the house in Ruetz did the same. They took the movable property belonging to it, which was later valued at 553 l. 3 s. t. The next tenant, who took over the property between 1308 and 1309, filed a complaint in this case. However, it is not known whether any action was taken at that time to recover the lost property or money. The surviving documents show that an investigation into the matter was conducted during the final settlements with the tenants in 1314. As a result, the estimated amount was ordered to be returned, but the entire process was not concluded until five years later, when the debt was enforced against the heirs of the dishonest tenants.[273]

The examples of abuse and theft listed here, traces of which can be found in preserved sources, were certainly only the tip of the iceberg. Given that the available documents from the investigations and executions date from at least several years after the trial of the Templars and are fragmentary, it is reasonable to assume that the actual scale of abuse throughout the kingdom was enormous. It can therefore be concluded that the abuses significantly reduced the Order's assets and the sums collected on an ongoing basis in the royal treasury and transferred to the pope. Therefore, it is impossible to disagree with Clement V's words from late 1309, quoted in an earlier chapter, regarding the widespread squandering of French Templar properties.

2.4 Process and properties administration costs

According to accepted customs and established legal procedures, all expenses related to the proceedings against the Templars were to be financed from the income of their houses. Unfortunately, we do not have any records of the costs incurred for the entire kingdom of France, or even for any of its regions, so we are unable to even approximately determine the extent to which the expenses depleted the sums collected during the proceedings, which, according to the papal decision in Poitiers, were to be allocated to the crusade fund. We can therefore only attempt to make very cautious estimates of the costs incurred based on rather random, detailed data.

As it is impossible to make reliable calculations and draw up a final financial balance sheet for the process, let us look at the issue of the expenses incurred in connection with it from a different perspective and consider to what extent they reduced the standard income of the French Templars, and, consequently, how much they depleted the funds that could have been allocated annually to organising a new crusade, compared to the situation before the brothers' arrest. From this point of view, we can divide the trial costs into two categories for separate analysis:

1 The brothers' maintenance and travel expenses, which at least partially coincided with the Order's standard operating costs, were paid from the commandery's income, regardless of the proceedings (even before the trial, the Templars' food, clothing, and travel expenses were covered by the commandery). Therefore, it can be assumed that the commanderies' income was not significantly reduced compared to before the trial, and it may even have been higher.
2 Expenses related to ongoing investigations, i.e., salaries and travel expenses of people involved in the investigation, costs of producing documents and administering seized properties, and others. They did not translate in any way into expenses incurred in connection with the standard functioning of the Order before the trial and therefore depleted the income from the French Templars' estates in their entirety over a period of five years.

2.4.1 Maintenance and travel of prisoners

Information on the costs of maintaining and transporting the French Templars from their arrest until the dissolution of the Order at the Council of Vienne comes primarily from various types of bills and receipts issued at different stages of the process. At that time, the brothers were imprisoned throughout the kingdom. Most of them were transported to various places of detention or interrogation, depending on the stage of the proceedings and the needs of the moment. While investigations conducted by inquisitors in individual dioceses did not require long journeys, appearing before the papal commission deliberating in Paris or the cardinals in Poitiers often meant travelling several hundred kilometres and undertaking a journey lasting several days. Their travels also included transfers to other prisons. We do not know why these transfers occurred or how often they happened. Additionally, they travelled to councils, during which the brothers received the verdicts of the inquisitorial tribunals.

The Templar guards held in prisons and transported to other locations were given specific sums of money to cover their food and other basic needs. The earliest accounts of these costs currently available date from the first months after their arrest. The commandery of Paluet's statements of expenses incurred during the first year of the trial mentions a sum of 6 l. t. paid for the needs of three Templars transported to Riom at the beginning of the proceedings.[274] Unfortunately, it is unclear whether this money was intended for the journey itself or for a period of detention in the local prison. The commandery of Coulours' accounts provide equally limited information about the period after the Templars' arrest. We learn from them that the local administrator transferred 20 l. for the Templars' journey from Troyes to Paris.[275] It is likely that the brothers went there for interrogation. Unfortunately, there is no record of how many there were or how long they stayed in the city. We also do not know what basis was used to calculate the amounts paid. No documents from this stage of the proceedings survive,mention the applicable rates for prisoners.

Much more information about the sums transferred for the maintenance of individual brothers can be found in the records of the transfer of prisoners to various places of confinement in the Paris region at the beginning of 1308.[276] Within a period of about a dozen days, from 25 January to 11 February, 28 groups of Templars left the Parisian Temple and were transported to prisons outside the city, while others were transferred to the Temple to replace them. The document details the costs of each journey, indicating the sums allocated for prisoners' maintenance and guards' remuneration. The accounts show that these sums were intended to cover the transfer itself and a total of 25–30 days' imprisonment for the brothers. This information was analysed in detail by Demurger.[277] Based on data from several selected accounts, he calculated that the daily rate allocated for the maintenance of one transported Templar was, on average, 2 s. 5 d. p. (approximately 3 s. 4 d. t.)[278] He assumed that all the amounts indicated for the brothers' needs were for a period of 25 days. However, the information contained in the individual accounts shows that, in most cases, the amounts given were for 30 days.[279] Therefore, the average daily rate was slightly lower than Demurger indicated, amounting to 2 s. p. (2 s. 10 d. t.) However, similar calculations performed on all accounts reveal that expenses allocated to the Templars varied. In most cases, the total cost per prisoner was 2 s. p. (2 s. 10 d. t.) per day,[280] but in some cases it was 1 s. 4 d. p. (1 s. 8 d. t.)[281] and in one case, 2 s. 6 d. p. (approximately 3 s. 7 d. t.)[282] One might wonder whether these differences were related to the status of those being transported; for example, knights might possibly be provided with better conditions than servants. However, if we examine the composition of the groups more closely, no pattern emerges. Attempting to calculate the average rate is further complicated by the account for the journey of one of the Order's dignitaries, Hugues de Pairaud, to Rochefort-en-Yvelines, which shows that his expenses totalled 20 l. p. (25 l. t.), equivalent to 6 s. 8 d. p. (8 s. 4 d. t.) per day.[283] We are dealing with quite varied amounts here, and the document contains no clues that would explain these discrepancies. They probably did not result from differences in the rates allocated for the brothers' basic needs, but rather from fluctuating travel costs depending on factors such as journey length and mode of transport (e.g., cart or horseback). Later accounts of prisoners' travel expenses provide a little more insight into this issue. We have two such documents from early 1311, created in connection with the participation of Templars imprisoned in the bailiwick of Senlis in proceedings conducted by the papal commission in Paris.[284] The expenses listed included funds for the Templars' basic needs (2 s. p. [2 s. 10 d. t.] per day per prisoner), the cost of hiring carriages and horses, hay[285] for the carriages and feed for the horses, accommodation in Paris (6 or 8 d. p. per day), and the servant's wages to accompany the brothers during their stay. One of the accounts also lists other Templar expenses exceeding the standard amounts allocated to them: 20 s. p. (25 s. t.). Therefore, the basic maintenance rate for the brothers could have been 2 s. p. (2 s. 10 d. t.), as indicated in the early 1308 accounts. However, another preserved source relating to the Paris proceedings refers to a different amount. The minutes of the papal commission's investigation in Paris refer to the sums paid to the brothers who came to the city to participate in the proceedings. In April 1310, the Templars complained to the commissioners that the money they received was insufficient, given the high cost of staying in Paris. The document shows that the brothers were paid 1 s. p. (1 s. 3 d. p.) per day[286] and that their weekly expenses for accommodation and food amounted to at least 7 s. 4 d. p. (9 s. 1 d. t.) This included accommodation costs (3 d. p. per day), food and candles (4 d. p. [5 d. t.] per day), bedding (2 s. 6 d. p. [approximately 3 s. 1 d. t.] per week), laundry (18 d. p. [approximately 1 s. 10 d. t.] every two weeks), travel within Paris (16 d. p. [1 s. 8 d. t.] each), and shackling (2 s. p. [2 s. 6 d. t.] for each shackling and unshackling).[287] There are clear differences between the daily rate and the costs included in this amount, and the sums indicated in the accounts. The latter shows that the costs of accommodation, travel, and shackling were not covered by the money paid for the Templars' maintenance, but by other means. Furthermore, the daily rate received was twice that presented in the letter from the brothers to the commissioners, written a few months earlier. Why the change? This can be explained by the timing of the two summaries. In April 1310, most Templars had not yet heard the verdicts of the inquisitorial proceedings and had come to Paris of their own accord to defend the Order. By contrast, the brothers who appeared before the commission in early 1311 had mostly already been absolved and were testifying to the Templars' guilt.[288] According to the bishop of Paris's instructions, after the inquisitorial trials were over, prisoners who had been absolved were to be treated better.[289] This may have affected the funds allocated for their travel. The presence of a servant to assist the brothers during their stay in Paris, which did not occur before 1311, may also suggest this situation. Furthermore, improvements to their travel and accommodation conditions may have incentivised the Templars to make incriminating statements against the Order.

Unfortunately, the information cited here regarding the brothers' travel expenses does not allow us to draw any general conclusions. Although the documents mention the same rate (2 s. p. [2 s. 6 d. t.]) for the prisoners' basic needs in several cases, the accounts show that "basic needs" were not always interpreted in the same way. Estimates are also complicated by the travel costs included in the accounts. These vary greatly, making it impossible to identify any consistent patterns in the amounts paid to transferred prisoners.

In addition to the Templars' travel accounts, we have documents detailing the sums paid for the maintenance of brothers imprisoned in the bailiwick of Senlis between 1310 and 1312. These are mainly receipts for money received by the guards from time to time, as well as several other documents concerning the financing of the prisoners' additional needs. Demurger calculated that 123 sources of this kind have been preserved in three collections at the Bibliothèque nationale and two at the Archives nationales.[290] Five additional documents, which were not considered by the researcher, are included in other Bibliothèque nationale collections,[291] bringing the total to 128. These documents cover the period from January 1310 to April 1312 and refer to 12 prisons in which a total of 135 Templar prisoners were held.[292] There are also two similar receipts from the archdiocese of Sens from 1310 to 1311.[293] Unfortunately, these only provide the total amounts paid to the Templar guards, without breaking down the costs of maintaining the prisoners and paying the guards' salaries. From the perspective of the issues discussed here, they are therefore useless.

According to documents from the bailiwick of Senlis, the daily rate per Templar was 12 d. p. (15 d. t.) or 16 d. p. (20 d. t.),[294] depending on whether he had been absolved during the inquisitorial proceedings. This was noted in the accounts. In addition, the Templars were provided with clothing, bedding, and necessary equipment from time to time. Preserved receipts mention the following amounts: 10 s. 8 d. p. (13 s. 4 d. t.) for the servant, and 16 s. p. (1 l. t.) for the chaplain, paid twice a year, which gives a total of 21 s. 4 d. p. (26 s. 8 d. t.) and 32 s. p. (2 l. t.) per year, respectively.[295] We also have an order from the general administrators of the Templar estates, dated February 1311 and addressed to the administrator of the bailiwick of Senlis, which indicates that, in addition to the daily food allowance, the following sums were to be allocated to the prisoners of Senlis: 60 s. p. (75 s. t.) per year for a knight, chaplain, or provincial commander, and 40 s. p. (50 s. t.) per year for a sergeant. These sums were to be paid in three instalments on fixed dates.[296] It can be assumed that any money remaining after the cost of clothing had been deducted was spent on additional irregular expenses, such as fees for sewing and delivering clothes[297] or remuneration for the doctor treating the brothers,[298] and perhaps also on travel costs. Another item in the accounts was remuneration for priests who visited the absolved Templars. This ranged from 4 to 10 s. p. (5 to 12 s. 6 d. t.) per month.[299] Therefore, the cost of maintaining a single prisoner appears to have been influenced by several different factors, making it difficult to determine a standard rate.

Using information from the accounts of the bailiwick of Senlis, Demurger tried to calculate the total annual cost of keeping the Templars imprisoned in the kingdom of France. In his calculations, he considered only some of the variables affecting the sums paid. First, he calculated the annual cost of feeding one prisoner, taking into account the two rates that appeared in the documents. He then multiplied this figure by 2000, assuming this was the number of prisoners, and added 35% to cover the estimated costs of clothing, equipment, and the salaries of guards and priests who visited the Templars.[300] This calculation gave results of 49,275 l. p. (61,593 l. 15 s. t.) and 65,699 l. p. (82,123 l. 15 s. t.), respectively, based on daily rates of 12 d. p. (16 d. t.) and 16 d. p. (20 d. t.)These are wide-ranging estimates based on partially uncertain data. We do not know if the same rates applied across the whole of the kingdom of France or how many brothers were imprisoned at any stage of the proceedings. Although we have several sources of information that may provide clues on this matter, none of them are specific enough to answer the question of how many Templars were imprisoned. Demurger probably based his estimates on Clement V's statement from early 1308. During a private consistory, the pope complained that, due to the escape of a Templar who was a papal *cubicularius* and had been imprisoned in Poitiers,[301] secular rulers would be reluctant to hand over control of the remaining Templars, who he claimed numbered 2000.[302] However, it is unclear how accurate this figure was, or if it referred to all Templars or only those detained in the kingdom of France. The context suggests that the pope was referring to all members of the Order. This seems to be confirmed by a statement made by Guillaume le Maire, bishop of Angers, a few years later. In his commentary on the Templars' case, addressed to participants at the Council of Vienne, he stated that the Order's guilt had been confirmed by 2000 witnesses.[303] It can be assumed that he meant all of the witnesses, not just those from the kingdom of France. While the majority of Templars interrogated in other countries denied the charges against them, incriminating testimony was also provided by individuals outside the Order. This suggests that the French Templars constituted only a part of the total number of witnesses. Some light on this issue is shed by information provided by Philip the Fair in a letter to James II dated 29 January 1308. Reporting on the course of the proceedings, the French monarch wrote that more than 600 Templars had already confessed to the charges against them.[304] As the interrogations had been ongoing for several months by that time, it is reasonable to assume that most of the imprisoned Templars had already testified. These assumptions seem to be confirmed by Demurger's own findings, which suggest that the surviving French trial documents contain information about 1126 Templars who participated in various stages of the trial.[305] However, as not all documents from the proceedings have survived, it is likely that there were more prisoners than this. The last mention of the number of Templars comes from a letter from Clement V to Philip the Fair in early November 1311. In it, the pope warned the French ruler that between 1500 and 2000 Templars had gathered near Lyon, intending to play an active role in defending the Order at the Council of Vienne.[306] While it is possible that Clement V exaggerated the number of arrivals out of fear, it probably did not exceed the total number of brothers who were able to move around independently at that time, i.e., those who had been absolved in the inquisitorial trials. However, it is still unclear whether only French Templars attended the Council of Vienne or if there were also Templars from other countries present. Taking all this information and the associated reservations into account, it can be estimated that more than 1126, but certainly fewer than 2000 French Templars took part in the proceedings.[307]

Bearing this in mind, let us return to Demurger's calculations. Let us assume that the cost of imprisoning Templars was the same throughout the kingdom. However, it is known that these costs varied over time, partly due to the different treatment of brothers who obtained absolution in inquisitorial proceedings. This should be taken into account when making estimates. The problem is that the inquisitorial trials ended at different times in different dioceses, making it impossible to perform calculations for the entire country. This leads us to conclude that it is impossible to estimate, even approximately, the total cost of maintaining the imprisoned brothers. We can only speculate that they amounted to several tens of thousands of livres tournois per year. However, considering earlier estimates regarding the number of Templars in French prisons, these costs were probably lower than those calculated by Demurger. Additionally, the issue of guards' salaries must be considered. These were included in the researcher's calculations as part of the prisoners' maintenance costs. For the purposes of the estimates proposed in this work, however, they have been excluded from this category, meaning the final sums should be reduced further. Therefore, we can speak of an amount of several tens of thousands of livres, but probably less than 50,000.

In addition to information about expenses for the imprisoned brothers, the accounts of the administrator of the commandery of Payns also mention the costs of maintaining a Templar sister. The financial summary details the costs of food, clothing, and shoes for the sister, who remained in the Templar house following the arrest of the male members of the Order.[308] The list of costs also includes the servant's remuneration (13 s. t. and a shirt).[309] It can be assumed that these sums were similar to those allocated for the same purpose prior to the trial. However, the situation changed after the decision was made to lease the house in Payns in spring 1309. The accounts show that the sister was sent away with 10 s. t.[310] There is no information on how the issue of the sister's maintenance was resolved at a later date. Therefore, we do not know whether the expenses for this purpose remained at the same level or changed.

Preserved sources indicate that Templar donats also received money during the trial. For example, in 1309, Eblon de Craisseron, who was connected to the house in La Bussière-Rapy, received 10 l. t. for this purpose.[311] Two years later, seven donats and chaplains (the exact number is unknown) were paid a total of 91 l. 18 s. t.[312] These two pieces of information are insufficient to determine how these expenses related to the commandery's standard operating costs, let alone the total cost of payments to the donats. However, alongside the references to the maintenance of the sister, they demonstrate that expenses relating to the maintenance of imprisoned brothers should not be the only ones considered when making final estimates.

All the costs listed here add up to a total amount of several tens of thousands of livres tournois. While it is impossible to specify the exact amount, one might question whether it was actually lower than the standard cost of maintaining the brothers prior to the trial. It is known that the rates paid for prisoners' needs were usually minimal. If the brothers' complaints to the papal commissioners in 1310 are to be believed, these rates were not even sufficient to cover the basic needs that had probably been provided to members of the Order beforehand. We also have information on the amounts allocated for the maintenance of the absolved brothers who were living in houses taken over by the Hospitallers after the trial. This shows that, in 1319, Templars staying in Picardy commanderies were paid 2 s. 6 d. t. per day for basic necessities, and approximately 6 l. t. per year for clothing.[313] This is considerably more than they received during the trial. Therefore, it can be assumed that the total cost of maintaining the imprisoned Templars during the several years of proceedings did not exceed the standard expenses incurred for this purpose prior to the brothers' arrest.

2.4.2 Other costs of the proceedings

In addition to the Templars' maintenance and travel expenses, the list of expenses related to the proceedings included the salaries and travel expenses of those involved in various procedural matters and prisoner custody, as well as sums allocated for materials necessary for preparing documents and other occasional needs.

The proceedings lasted several years, involved over 1000 defendants detained and imprisoned in various parts of the kingdom of France, and required the involvement of a large number of people. These included royal officials involved in the arrest of the Templars, prison guards, commissioners who interrogated the Templars, scribes who accompanied them, and various papal and royal envoys who participated in the negotiations and implementation of Clement V's decisions. All of these individuals were rewarded for their work and received money for travel and, in some cases, food while performing their duties. Sources from various stages of the process mention these payments.

The first bills related to the proceedings concerned the actions taken on the day of the brothers' arrest. The commandery of Payns' statement of expenses included 60 s. t. for food and other expenses incurred by those who detained the Templars.[314] Interestingly, over 40-armed men arrived at the Order's house on that day. The accounts of the commandery of Coulours, in turn, indicate the cost of food for those who took part in the activities surrounding the brothers' arrest, although their role is unclear.[315] However, it seems that, in this case too, it was the armed men who were to take the Templars to prison, as expenses relating to the preparation of the house inventory made on this occasion were included in a separate item. Unfortunately, due to damage to the manuscript, the amount allocated for this purpose is illegible.

The commandery of Paluet's accounts included slightly different expenses. The accounts state that the administrator of the house paid 84 l. t. to a group of foot and horse guards who transported three Templars to Riom.[316] This is a substantial sum, particularly given the number of Templars escorted to prison, but the source provides clear evidence of the amount. However, this sum is all the more puzzling given that it exceeds the cost of detaining the Templars in the entire bailiwick of Bourges several times over, as indicated in a later document. The local bailiff's accounts show that the costs amounted to 29 l. 6 s. 8 d. p. (37 l. 11 s. t.).[317] Therefore, it can be assumed that this sum not only covered the remuneration paid to those involved in the arrest of the Templars and their transfer to prison, but also the costs of preparing documents related to these procedures. There may also have been expenses incurred by renting the carts used to transport the detainees. However, this remains speculative. Assuming that the cost of arresting the brothers in each of the 25 bailiwicks and seneschalships in the kingdom of France amounted to several dozen livres, the total expenditure would be estimated at up to 1000 l. t. However, if such large sums were also paid to guards transporting the brothers to prison in other places, as in Paluet, the total amount could have been much higher.

After the Templars were imprisoned, the guards took over their custody. Additional personnel were hired to transport the prisoners to interrogations or other prisons. The aforementioned settlement of the operation to transfer some of the prisoners from the Parisian Temple to other locations at the beginning of 1308 provides detailed information on their remuneration.[318] According to the summary contained within, guards supervising Templars at the Order's headquarters were paid different rates depending on how long they performed this function. Those who guarded prisoners for 110 days were to receive 100 s. p. (125 s. t.), equivalent to less than 11 d. p. (approximately 14 d. t.) per day. Those who stayed for 100 days were to be paid 4 l. p. (5 l. t.), or less than 10 d. p. (approximately 12 d. t.) per day. The lowest remuneration was intended for guards who performed their duties for 90 days. They were to receive 70 s. p. (approximately 87 s. t.), i.e., slightly over 9 d. p. (approximately 11 d. t.) per day. Guards who supervised Templars held in other Parisian prisons were paid 10 d. p. (12 d. t.) per day. The remuneration of the guards who supervised the Grand Master was recorded separately. Their commander, who was also referred to as the guard of the 24 Templars in the Bois de Vincennes, was to receive 6 s. p. per day (7 s. 6 d. t.), and the four squares were to receive 5 s. p. per day (6 s. 3 d. t.). Meanwhile, the five sergeants guarding the prisoners in Bois de Vincennes were granted 2 s. p. per day (2 s. p. 6 d. t.).

The remuneration for the guards who participated in the brothers' transfer was determined slightly differently. A sergeant on horseback was to receive 4 s. p. (5 s. t.) per day, and a sergeant-at-arms was to receive 7 s. p. (less than 9 s. t.) per day. For sergeants on foot, the rate depended on where they were transporting the Templars. Those taking the brothers to another Parisian prison or the immediate vicinity, i.e., approximately 8 km (2 *lieues*) from the city were to receive 2 s. p. (2 s. 6 d. t.) per day. Those travelling further afield were to receive 20 d. p. (25 d. t.) per day.

Demurger calculated that the total remuneration paid to all the people mentioned in the document was 323 l. 10 s. p. (404 l. 5 s. t.),[319] but the total sum given in the list exceeds 534 l. 2 s. p. (667 l. 12 s. t).[320] Taking into account only the guards involved in transporting the Templars, the final sum is over 271 l. 10 s. p. (339 l. 7 s. t.). The reason for this discrepancy is unclear. In any case, it demonstrates that the salaries of those responsible for supervising the Templars represented a substantial financial burden for the organisers of the proceedings at that time and, consequently, for the Templar commanderies. Considering that the amounts given refer only to the first few months of the proceedings and to the Paris region only, it is reasonable to assume that, on a kingdom-wide scale, they were many times higher. However, this primarily applies to the first stage of the process, when the brothers were transported to the locations where interrogations were taking place.

We also know how much was paid to prison guards in the bailiwick of Senlis between 1310 and 1312. Accounts from this period show that the daily rate for guarding a group of 7–12 Templars ranged from 3 to 6 s. p. (3 s. 9 d. to 7 s. 6 d. t.), regardless of how many guards were assigned to the task.[321] Some accounts specify the amounts paid to the guard and his assistants. These show that the guards usually received 3 s. t., while the servants received 12 d. t. per day.[322] However, there were cases where the rate was 2 s. t. and 12 d. t.[323] or 4 s. t. and 16 d. t.[324] It is unclear what caused these variations. Perhaps they depended on the guards' negotiating skills or on the importance of the person in question. Based on the information contained in the sources, it is not possible to say for sure.

Demurger took into account the salaries paid to the guards at the bailiwick of Senlis when trying to calculate the total cost of imprisoning the Templars. However, he did not account for the differences in rates paid to some guards and servants in his estimates.[325] While this did not affect his calculations, as he took the total salary costs into account, it is important if we want to draw general conclusions about the sums paid to guards. Due to the discrepancies in salaries and the lack of information regarding the reasons for them, it is impossible to determine standard amounts applicable to all individuals involved in guarding the Templars, whether in the bailiwick of Senlis or elsewhere in the kingdom. It can be noted, however, that the rates paid in 1310–1312 did not differ greatly from those paid to guards and their assistants according to the list from early 1308. Thus, over the course of several years, there were no major changes in this regard, nor were identical amounts established for all guards.

The travel expenses of the brothers staying in Senlis prisons, who participated in the Paris proceedings at the beginning of 1311, also included the wages of guards and servants. These accounts show that at least five people were involved in each of the brothers' journeys. The January accounts list the amounts paid to two mounted guards (4 s. p. [5 s. t.] per day), three mounted servants who participated in the journey (3 s. p. [less than 4 s. t.] per day), and one servant who assisted the Templars during their stay in Paris (12 d. p. [15 d. t.] per day).[326] One might wonder whether the servant who remained with the brothers in the city was one of those who took part in the journey. If not, he would have been the sixth person to participate in the trip and receive remuneration for doing so.

Similar expenses appear in the second bill from the same period. This time, two sergeants on horseback and three servants also took part in the journey.[327] They were to receive the same remuneration as in the first case. However, one servant remained in Paris with the four brothers, who were to receive 18 d. p. (approximately 22 s. t.) per day, and two sergeants on horseback, who were to transport the Templars around the city and receive 4 s. p. (5 s. t.) per day. It follows that the situation of the brothers had already changed at that time, and that at this stage of the proceedings additional servants were hired to assist them. This, of course, increased the overall cost of the Templars' journey, but we are unable to assess the scale of this increase.

In addition to the usual expenses associated with guarding imprisoned members of the Order, other costs occasionally arose. These included sums paid in connection with the search for fugitives. For instance, the bailiff of Bourges recorded in his accounts the sum of 26 s. 8 d. p. (33 s. 4 d. t.), paid to the men who pursued brother Adam de Valencourt.[328] It is known that several dozen Templars escaped at the time of the arrest,[329] and that others left prison during the proceedings.[330] Therefore, the total cost of searching for them must have been many times higher, although it certainly did not constitute a significant sum on the list of all the trial's costs.

In addition to the prison guards, those involved in the proceedings against the Templars included inquisitors and commissioners who investigated the entire

Order. There are no records of the remuneration of the former, nor of the amounts allocated to them for expenses incurred while travelling within the kingdom of France. It is reasonable to assume that the funds for this purpose were derived from the income collected from the Templars' properties, as was the case in other countries where Church commissioners took control of the estates.[331] However, the precise amounts remain unknown. The only information we have is the amounts granted by Clement V to envoys in other countries who were tasked with investigating members of the Order. They received four florins (3 l. 4 s. t.) per day, regardless of their destination. It could be assumed that the same rate applied in the kingdom of France. However, it is not known whether the pope appointed a special representative to deal with the French proceedings, as was the case in other countries. An investigation into individual members of the Order has already been conducted there and did not require any further supervision. In Poitiers, Clement V reversed his decision to suspend the activities of the inquisitors so that they could participate in further trials held in individual dioceses and conducted by specially appointed commissions.[332] While their members certainly received remuneration, the amount is unknown.

There is much more that can be said about the costs of the commission that investigated the entire Order in Paris between 1309 and 1311. Papal letters indicate that the three bishops on the commission were to receive 12 florins (8 l. t.) per day,[333] two of the other commissioners were to receive 5 florins (3 l. 6 s. 8 d. t.)[334] each, and one was to receive 3 florins (2 l. t.).[335] The salaries of one bishop and one archdeacon are unknown, but, following Demurger, we can assume that they did not differ from the rates granted to other members of the commission of the same rank, amounting to 12 and 5 florins (8 l. t. and 3 l. 6 s. 8 d. t.) respectively. In his work, this researcher presented a detailed list of the attendance of all commission members during subsequent meetings,[336] enabling us to calculate the total amount paid to them. After adding up all the amounts, we find that the total is 7394 florins (4929 l. 7 s. t.). It would probably be necessary to add the remuneration of the notaries involved in the proceedings to this amount. However, we do not know the amount of this remuneration. Nevertheless, based on the sum of the payments to the commissioners alone, it can be concluded that the Paris proceedings were very costly compared to other expenses related to the French trial.

Another cost incurred during the proceedings against the Templars was the money paid to envoys travelling between the papal court and the courts of Western European monarchs. In the aforementioned letter to Philip the Fair in May 1309, Clement V wrote about using movable property from Templar houses to cover the travel expenses of Cardinals Bérenger Frédol and Étienne de Suisy to the French court in connection with the Order's case.[337] Royal envoys who travelled to discuss issues related to the proceedings with the pope also received money from the Order's assets. A document from spring 1309 shows that Guillaume de Plaisians travelled to Toulouse to discuss the Templar case with Clement V. Half of the costs of his 46-day journey, totalling 189 l. 3 s. t., were to be covered by the Order's assets.[338] While we have no other documents of this type, we can assume that Guillaume de Plaisians' settlement reflects the practice adopted for the purposes of the proceedings. The situation was similar in other countries. In Aragon, for example, James II ordered the urgent collection of dues from the Templars' leased estates in 1312 to cover the travel expenses of envoys negotiating the future of the Order's properties.[339] In Portugal, in turn, such expenses were included in the settlement with the Grand Master of the newly formed Order of Christ, which took over the properties of the local Templars.[340]

In addition to the costs associated with the activities of those involved in the proceedings, there were other expenses too. These included the sums spent on parchment and ink for writing the brothers' interrogation reports and the many other documents created for the trial. While these sums were not large individually, they could constitute a considerable expense on the scale of the entire proceedings. We also have a document mentioning another, less obvious cost of the proceedings. One of the prison guards' accounts from Senlis in November 1310 lists expenses for equipping and securing the places where the brothers were held. Among the purchases were locks and materials needed to install bars on the windows. The remuneration for the worker who was to install them was also included. The total cost was 40 s. 4 d. p. (50 s. 5 d. t.)[341] It is reasonable to assume that this was not an isolated case, particularly given that the Templars were held in smaller places of confinement rather than royal prisons. The bill for the brothers' trip to Paris in 1311 also mentions the cost of putting them in chains, amounting to 12 d. p. (15 d. t.)[342] This expense is also referenced in a letter written by the Templars during the papal commission proceedings. They stated that a sum of 2 s. p. (2 s. 6 d. t.) had to be paid for shackling and unshackling.[343] According to their account, they had to cover these costs themselves from the money they received for maintenance. However, this was an exceptional situation, as their participation in the work of the papal commission was voluntary. At other times during the proceedings, such expenses were probably covered by different funds.

Finally, it is worth mentioning a brief reference in the source material that appears to contradict the findings presented thus far. As mentioned at the start of this chapter, the agreement between Clement V and Philip the Fair, as well as the established practice of inquisitorial proceedings at the time, indicated that all costs associated with the proceedings were to be covered by the income generated from the Templars' properties. However, papal documents from December 1308 mention the payment of 51 s. 8 d. burd. (41 s. 4 d. t.) from the curia's treasury to Jean de *Truleria* for expenses incurred in preparing a document concerning "Templar matters."[344] The wording of this document and the time period to which it refers suggest that this expense was related to the ongoing trial. If so, some of the costs would have been covered by sources other than the Order's assets. Nevertheless, it was probably a minor expense, and Clement V did not yet have the Templars' money at his disposal at the end of 1308, so he chose to cover it from his own funds. Unfortunately, there are no other sources that would clarify this matter.

This very fragmentary information on the amounts allocated for the remuneration and travel expenses of those involved in the proceedings, as well as for other minor expenses, does not allow any general calculations to be made. However, it gives an idea of the order of magnitude of the total sums spent on this aspect of the proceedings. Taking into account primarily the sums paid to the guards and commissioners conducting the Paris proceedings, it is reasonable to assume that the total annual expenditure for these purposes did not exceed several thousand livres. The irregular costs of necessary materials and additional work relating to prisoner care or the preparation of places of confinement only increased this sum slightly.

2.4.3 Properties administration costs

The procedures relating to the seizure and subsequent management of the Order's properties required the involvement of a large number of people. This, of course, meant that they had to be paid. The properties administration costs also included travel expenses incurred by the administrators in connection with their duties, as well as the preparation of various documents. To these should be added the costs of court proceedings, both during the trial and long after its conclusion. Some of these disputes had been ongoing since the time of the Templars and should be considered part of the "standard" functioning of religious houses rather than a consequence of the proceedings against the Templars and the seizure of their properties. However, others related to decisions and actions taken by royal and later Church administrators should be considered a consequence of the trial. Consequently, the expenses they generated should be included in the costs of the proceedings.

Information about the salaries of administrators can be found in the expense accounts of the commanderies of Payns and Paluet. The first document reveals that Jean de Hulles, who served as administrator from the arrest of the Templars on 14 September 1307, until 14 September 1308, (i.e., for 11 months), received 17 l. 19 s. t.[345] The remuneration of his successor, Thomas de Savières, amounted to 10 l. t.,[346] but it is difficult to determine the period to which this sum relates. The accounts he presented covered income and expenditure for nine months, from 14 September 1308 to 29 June 1309. However, they also show that on 6 April 1309, the house he managed was leased out.[347] This would certainly have significantly reduced the scope of his duties if he continued to perform them at all. Therefore, it is difficult to say whether the two administrators were paid the same salary or whether the rates differed. Even in the case of a single house, it is difficult to draw any conclusions on this issue. Based on the income and expenditure information contained in the accounts, we can conclude the extent to which the administrators' salaries burdened the commandery's finances. Pétel calculated that the income for the 11 months when Jean de Hulles was administrator amounted to 30 l. t.,[348] meaning that his remuneration accounted for over one-third of the final amount accumulated during that period. This is, of course, a significant amount. The situation was slightly different when Thomas de Savières held this position. The commandery's income at that time was 60 l. t., meaning his remuneration accounted for one-sixth of this sum.

The accounts of the commandery of Paluet's record that two administrators and an unspecified number of companions, who performed their duties from the arrest of the Templars in September 1307 until the beginning of September 1308 (i.e., for ten and a half months), expected 50 l. t. in remuneration. The difference between income and expenditure in this case was 40 l. 3 s. 3 d. t.,[349] which would not have been enough to pay the administrators. Ultimately, however, they did not receive the expected sum due to significant discrepancies in the presented accounts and inventory.

Both examples demonstrate that the administrators' salaries placed a significant financial burden on the commandery. Of course, it is not known how much was paid to people performing this function in different parts of the kingdom or what factors influenced this amount. However, bearing these uncertainties in mind, it seems that, during the period when the houses of the Order were under royal administration, the cost of the administrators' salaries significantly reduced the income of the individual houses. Furthermore, regional administrators were responsible for the day-to-day management of the estates and were also paid salaries. In the second half of 1308, at least some royal officials were given an additional task: the sale of equipment from the houses, which were then to be leased out. Jean Guérin is an example of this. From autumn 1308, he was involved in selling the furnishings of the house in Payns.[350] He probably received additional payment for this task. However, the surviving sources do not provide any information on the amount of his remuneration. Nor is there any mention of the remuneration of other regional supervisors.

Accounts of individual houses also include references to travel expenses and other costs incurred by administrators. Unfortunately, the vast majority of these are rather enigmatic. For instance, the summary of expenses for the commandery of Coulours reveals that the inventory of goods following the arrest of the Order's members cost a total of 24 s. t., of which 4 s. t. was paid to the clerk who compiled the document, and the remainder was spent on food and wine for all those who witnessed the proceedings.[351] Further information contained in the source is fragmentary due to its poor condition. The next expenses mentioned in the document were related to preparing three copies of the settlement and the administrator's trip to submit the documents to the regional supervisor. However, the amounts paid in connection with this are unknown. We only know that the administrator was accompanied on his journey by a servant and a scribe. Only half of the costs of their presence were covered by the commandery's income[352]; the administrator must have paid for the rest himself. The servants also took part in other trips for which their wages are included in the document. When the administrator travelled with one servant, the servant received 18 d. t. per day; when the administrator travelled with two servants, each servant received 12 d. t. per day. The document also stated that one-third of their other travel expenses would be covered.[353] The amount the administrator received for his expenses is also known. When travelling, he received 10 s. t. per day.[354] Another section mentions the cost of the wine he drank and the white bread he ate during his stay at the house he managed.[355] It is unclear whether these meals were exceptional or if other administrators received similar provisions. The commandery of Payns' accounts do not include such costs. They only mention expenses for preparing documents and the administrator's travel costs. The cost of parchment, ink, and the scribe's salary for preparing three copies of the administrator's accounts totalled 40 s. t.[356] Elsewhere, 60 s. t. is mentioned as having been spent on parchment and preparing two copies of documents.[357] Either way, these were not large sums of money. The administrators' travels from Payns generated slightly higher costs. Jean de Hulles' six-day trip to Coulommiers cost 28 s. t.,[358] while his successor travelled much further, accompanying the scribe all the way to Paris. Their eight-day journey cost 4 l. t.[359]

It seems that the additional expenses relating to the management of the Templars' assets at the start of the process were an individual matter, with no identifiable pattern. Nevertheless, these costs undoubtedly increased the already high expenses associated with administering the assets at this stage of the proceedings.

The situation changed after the Poitiers meeting and the decision to alter the management of the estates. Leasing at least some of the houses significantly reduced administration costs. The administrators' salaries, as well as their travel and subsistence expenses, were removed from the list of related expenses. However, supervisors and collectors were still employed, and inventories and accounts were still drawn up. At the same time, as a result of Clement V's decisions in Poitiers, bishops, their commissioners, and, later, envoys of the Holy See were temporarily involved in the administration of Templar properties. It is known that some of the houses taken over by the bishops in 1308 were not immediately leased out. They continued to be managed by persons appointed by the bishops. Furthermore, the prelates themselves also derived income from this source. There is a case on record of the bishop of Bazas demanding 1312 l. 10 s. burd. (1050 l. t.) in remuneration, claiming that this sum covered the costs he had incurred.[360] However, it is unclear what these costs were as they are not mentioned in any document relating to this matter. However, this was most likely an exceptional situation and should be classified as one of the abuses that occurred at that time. It is hard to believe that other administrators would expect payments significantly higher than the income generated by the assets under their control. Unfortunately, we have no documents that would enable us to provide further information on the costs of managing the Templar properties during the transition period between the meeting in Poitiers and the takeover of management by the pope's envoys.

In January 1309, Clement V appointed general administrators for the kingdom of France and set the amounts allocated to them for travel expenses. They were to receive 40 s. p. (60 s. t.) per day while away from home carrying out their duties.[361] However, we know nothing about the amounts received by the local administrators and collectors of dues from the Templars' estates appointed by them. The total remuneration for those involved in managing the estates was certainly much lower during this period than after the arrest, when the estates remained under the control of the royal officials, and probably during the period when they were temporarily supervised by bishops.

In addition to the administrative costs mentioned so far, there were also occasional expenses relating to arbitration and court proceedings concerning administrators' decisions and actions. Some of these proceedings lasted several years or even a decade and involved many people, meaning the associated expenses increased over time. However, we are unable to estimate these costs, even in individual cases.

The fragmentary information presented here on the costs of administering the estates at various stages of the process shows that, although they were initially very high due to the need to involve many people and the probable lack of detailed top-down regulations on remuneration, the sums spent on this purpose most likely decreased significantly after several months, when the vast majority of the estates had been leased and the pope's envoys had taken control of the entire operation. Although the solutions adopted after the Poitiers meeting, whereby the houses' furnishings were sold and transferred to the tenants, reduced the value of individual estates and thus limited their future income in the long term, they initially brought quick and relatively large profits. At that stage, this was probably the main goal of Philip the Fair and Clement V.

Can we therefore draw any conclusions about the final financial outcome of the Templar case, and whether the proceedings were "profitable" from the perspective of the pope and the king of France, who declared that the funds from the Order's assets were to be used for this purpose? Assuming that the expenses for the maintenance and travel of the imprisoned Templars were lower than, or roughly equal to, the standard costs incurred for these purposes prior to the trial, the remaining costs of the proceedings and the management of the seized assets must be considered. As we do not know the total amount, based on the fragmentary information available, we can only speculate that they amounted to several tens of thousands of livres in total. This is certainly a substantial sum to be deducted from the income from the Order's properties. Unfortunately, it is impossible to estimate what percentage of the total amount collected from individual houses was spent on the trial, but it can certainly be said that if proceedings against the Templars had not been initiated and a decision had been made to reform the Order in some way, it would most likely have brought greater financial benefits than the actions actually taken, resulting in several years of investigations and a rather unstable system of managing the seized properties. In addition to the expenses incurred in this connection, one should consider the abuses and thefts mentioned in an earlier chapter, which accompanied such operations and significantly reduced the value of the French Templar properties and income. The only clear financial benefit of initiating the inquisitorial procedure and implementing the associated solutions regarding the property of the accused was the swift and unconditional seizure of vast estates and the opportunity to amass substantial funds in a relatively short period. However, it seems that the pope and the king were satisfied with this situation.

Notes

1 *Le dossier*, no. 2, pp. 22–24.
2 See, for example, Philip the Fair's order addressed to the bailiff of Rouen – *Le dossier*, pp. 16–29. For more on the persons involved in the arrest of the Order's members and the seizure of their properties, see also A. Demurger, *La persécution*, pp. 46–50.
3 F. Hooghe, 'The Trial of the Templars in the County of Flanders (1307–1312)', in: *The Debate on the Trial of the Templars (1307–1314)*, ed. J. Burgtorf, P. F. Crawford, H. J. Nicholson (Farnham 2010), pp. 291–293; A. Rayniers, 'Le procès des templiers dans l'espace belge actuel au début du XIVe siècle (1307–1312)', *Le Moyen Age*, 129 (2023), no. 3, pp. 759–764.
4 P. Josserand, 'Les Templiers en Bretagne, no. 4, p. 14; A. Demurger, *La persécution*, pp. 50–51.
5 L. Delisle, *Études sur la condition de la classe agricole et l'état de l'agriculture en Normandie au moyen-âge* (Paris 1903), no. 16, p. 727.
6 Appendix, fols. 10r, 18r; B. de Gaulejac, *La liquidation*, p. 19.
7 E. Lalou, *Itinéraire*, vol. 1, p. 301.
8 P. H. Morice, *Mémoires pour servir de preuves à l'histoire ecclésiastique et civile de Bretagne*, vol. 1 (Paris 1742), cols. 1216–1217.
9 P. H. Morice, *Mémoires*, cols. 1216–1217. See also P. Josserand, 'Les Templiers en Bretagne', pp. 14–15 (The author gives 3 March as the date of the royal letter, although the document bears the date 6 March).
10 E. Petit, *Histoire des ducs de Bourgogne de la race capétienne, avec des documents inédits et des pièces justificatives*, vol. 7 (Dijon 1901), Pièces justificatives, no. 6191, p. 467.
11 A. Demurger, 'Dal Tempio all'Ospedale', p. 96.
12 On the Anglo-French conflicts concerning the duchy of Aquitaine and subsequent attempts to resolve them, see M. Gavrilovitch, *Étude sur le traité de Paris de 1259 entre Louis IX, roi de France & Henri III, roi d'Angleterre* (Paris 1899), pp. 18–38 and 95–104; C. Johnson, 'The Homage for Guienne in 1304', *English Historical Review*, 23 (1908), pp. 728–729; Y. Renouard, 'Les papes et le conflit franco – anglais en Aquitaine de 1259 à 1337', *Mélanges d'archéologie et d'histoire*, 51 (1934), no. 1, pp. 258–292; P. Chaplais, 'Règlement des conflits internationaux franco – anglais au XIVe siècle (1293–1337)', *Le Moyen Âge*, 57 (1951), pp. 269–302; P. Chaplais, 'La souveraineté du roi de France et le pouvoir législatif en Guyenne au début du XIVe siècle', *Le Moyen Âge*, 69 (1963), pp. 449–469; E. Lalou, 'Les négotiations diplomatiques avec l'Angleterre sous le règne de Philippe le Bel', in: *La « France anglaise » au Moyen-Âge: Colloque des historiens médiévistes français et britanniques. Actes du IIIe congrès national des sociétés savantes (Poitiers 1986). Section d'histoire médiévale et de philologie*, vol. 1 (Paris 1988), pp. 325–355.
13 On Edward II's position regarding the charges against the Templars at the beginning of the proceedings, as well as the related diplomatic activities, see M. Barber, *The Trial* (2006), pp. 217–219; H. J. Nicholson, *The Knights Templar on Trial. The Trial of the Templars in the British Isles 1308–1311* (Stroud 2009), pp. 24, 45–46; M. Satora, *Sprawa*, pp. 236–238, 248–249.
14 *Lettres de rois, reines et autres personnages des cours de France et d'Angleterre depuis Louis VII jusqu'à Henri IV tirées des archives de Londres*, ed. J. J. Champillon-Figeac, vol. 1 (Paris 1839), no. 29, p. 59; *Gascon Register A (1318–1319). Edited from British Museum Cottonian M.S. Julius E.i.*, ed. G. P. Cuttino, vol. 2 (London 1975), p. 368; E. A. R. Brown, 'The Political Repercussions of Family Ties in the Early Fourteenth Century: The Marriage of Edward II of England and Isabelle of France', *Speculum*, 63 (1988), no. 3, pp. 587–588 and 594–595. See also M. Satora, *Sprawa*, pp. 102–106.

15 A. Forey, *The Fall of the Templars in the Crown of Aragon* (Aldershot 2001), pp. 115–116; J. M. Sans i Travé, *La fi dels templers Catalans* (Lleida 2008), pp. 336–337.
16 E. Petit, *Histoire*, Pièces justificatives, no. 6191, p. 467; E. Petit, *Histoire*, Pièces justificatives, no. 6255, p. 475; E. Lalou, *Itinéraire*, vol. 2, p. 345. See also J. Richard, *Les ducs de Bourgogne et la formation du Duché du XI au XIV siècle* (Dijon 1954), p. 380; A. Demurger, 'Dal Tempio all'Ospedale', p. 96.
17 J. Richard, *Les ducs*, p. 381.
18 Reg. Clem. V, vol. 6, no. 7034, pp. 2013–214.
19 Appendix, fol. 18r.
20 P. Dupuy, *Histoire de la condamnation*, no. 75, p. 280; *Vitae*, vol. 3, no. 29, p. 141; *Lettres de rois*, vol. 1, no. 18, p. 28; *Livre*, p. 241; *Gascon Register*, vol. 1, no. 40, p. 225.
21 *Livre*, pp. 232–233.
22 C. Mansuet Jeune, *Histoire*, vol. 2, pp. 150–151; *Le dossier*, no. 2, pp. 22–25; E. Boutaric, 'Clément V' (1871), pp. 330–331; *The Templars*, no. 67, p. 247 (English translation); G. Bordonove, *La Tragédie*, p. 127 (French translation). Guillaume de Paris conveyed identical instructions to the inquisitors – C. Mansuet Jeune, *Histoire*, pp. 151–152; L. L. L. Lavocat, *Procès*, p. 132.
23 Quoted from *The Templars*, no. 67, p. 247.
24 L. Delisle, *Études*, no. 16, pp. 721–723; *Le dossier*, no. 4, pp. 46–55 (**Baugy**); L. Delisle, *Études*, no. 16, pp. 723–724 (**Bretteville-le-Rabet**); L. Delisle, *Études*, no. 16, p. 725 (**Voismer**); L. Delisle, *Études*, no. 16, pp. 726–727 (**Courval**); L. Delisle, *Études*, no. 16, pp. 727–728 (**Louvigny**).
25 P. Timbal, 'La confiscation', p. 49.
26 Appendix, fols. 11r, 12r., 18r.
27 B. Beaucage, 'La saisie', p. 88.
28 J. Picot, 'L'inventaire', pp. 107–157.
29 The document is stored in the Archives départementales des Bouches-du-Rhône, 56 H 2777. See D. Carraz, 'Chartiers privés', pp. 167–192.
30 To support his thesis, Jean Picot cited examples of inventories created in early 1308, but most of these come from the county of Provence, where the Templars were arrested later than in France. The only inventory from the kingdom of France is that of the commandery of Sainte-Eulalie in Larzac, drawn up in January 1308, in connection with a change of property managers, not the arrest of the brothers. Picot also stated that the Montferrand document must have been drawn up before Philip the Fair convened the estates general in March 1308 – J. Picot, 'L'inventaire', pp. 116–118. However, it is difficult to find a connection between these two events.
31 'Excerpta e memoriali', p. 649.
32 A. Pétel, 'Templiers et Hospitaliers dans le diocèse de Troyes. Comptes', pp. 283–372.
33 Financial report by the administrator of the commandery of Coulours – BnF, ms. lat. 9035, nos.18–21.
34 Financial report by the administrator of the commandery of Paluet – AN, M1, no. 10.
35 BnF, ms. lat. 9035, no. 18.
36 M. Miguet, *Templiers et Hospitaliers en Normandie*, p. 49.
37 A. Higounet-Nadal, 'L'inventaire des biens de la commanderie des templiers de Sainte-Eulalie du Larzac en 1308', *Annales du Midi*, 68 (1956), pp. 257–262.
38 AN, M1, no. 10; A. Pétel, 'Templiers et Hospitaliers dans le diocèse de Troyes. Comptes', p. 325.
39 E. Lalou, *Itinéraire*, vol. 1, p. 301.
40 *Monuments historiques*, no. 1060, p. 366.
41 *Inventaire d'anciens comptes royaux*, ed. R. Mignon, C. V. Langlois (Paris 1899), p. 265.
42 See, for example, AN, S 4952, dos. 13, no. 4.
43 AN, M1, no. 10; BnF, ms. lat. 9035, no. 18.

44 *Les journaux du trésor de Charles IV*, no. 6415, col. 1069.
45 BnF, ms. lat. 9035, no. 20.
46 V. Lavenia, 'Confisca dei beni', in: *Dizionario storico dell'Inquisizione*, ed. A. Prosperi, V. Lavenia, J. Tedeschi, vol. 1 (Pisa 2010), p. 375.
47 See examples of such activities in: H. C. Lea, 'Confiscation', pp. 248–249.
48 C. V. Langlois, 'Registres perdus des archives de la Chambre des comptes de Paris', *Notices et extraits des manuscrits de la Bibliothèque nationale*, 40 (1917), p. 258; J. B. de Vaivre, *La Commanderie*, Annexe, no. 31, pp. 188–189. See also M. Satora, 'Filip Piękny', pp. 26–27.
49 A. Pétel, 'Templiers et Hospitaliers dans le diocèse de Troyes. Comptes', p. 348.
50 J. J. Lambin, 'Les Templiers d'Ypres', *Messager des sciences et des arts de la Belgique*, 2 (1934), pp. 195–196; A. Rayniers, 'Le procès', p. 764.
51 A. Rayniers, 'Le procès', p. 342.
52 BnF, ms. lat. 9035, no. 20.
53 BnF, ms. lat. 9035, no. 21.
54 BnF, ms. lat. 9035, no. 21.
55 A. Pétel, 'Templiers et Hospitaliers dans le diocèse de Troyes. Comptes', p. 342.
56 A. Pétel, 'Templiers et Hospitaliers dans le diocèse de Troyes. Comptes', p. 372.
57 AN, M1, no. 10; A. Pétel, 'Templiers et Hospitaliers dans le diocèse de Troyes. Comptes', pp. 321, 327, 338.
58 BnF, ms. lat. 9035, no. 20.
59 L. A. Warnkönig, A. E. M. Gheldolf, *Histoire de la Flandre et de ses institutions civiles et politiques, jusqu'à l'année 1305*, vol. 5 (Bruxelles 1864), no. 66, pp. 446–447; F. Hooghe, 'The Trial', p. 295.
60 A. Pétel, *La Commanderie de Payns et ses dépendances à Savières, à Saint-Mesmin, à Messon, et au Pavillon* (Paris 1905), pp. 28–30.
61 *Formulaires*, no. 8, p. 17; H. G. Schmidt, 'Administrative Korrespondenz', no. 410, p. 457.
62 *Formulaires*, no. 5, p. 15; H. G. Schmidt, 'Administrative Korrespondenz', no. 224, pp. 334–335. Quoted also in K. Dietz, 'Die Templer', pp. 348–349.
63 *Formulaires*, no. 7, p. 16; H. G. Schmidt, 'Administrative Korrespondenz', no. 375, p. 435.
64 *Formulaires*, no. 4, p. 15.
65 ADHG, H 125–126; *Actes*, vol. 2, no. 5692, p. 271; *Les Olim*, vol. 3.2 (Paris 1848), pp. 1336–1339. See also B. de Gaulejac, *La liquidation*, pp. 22–23; M. Satora, 'Filip Piękny', pp. 28–29.
66 The extensive witness interview records (ADHG, H 126) have survived in fairly good condition. They are undoubtedly a valuable, albeit little-known, source of information on the economic history of southwestern France.
67 *Formulaires*, no. 6, p. 16; H. G. Schmidt, 'Administrative Korrespondenz', no. 335, p. 408.
68 *Vitae*, vol. 3, p. 81.
69 On Otto de Grandson's relationship with the Templar Order and Jacques de Molay, see, for example A. Forey, 'Otto of Grandson and the Holy Land, Cyprus and Armenia', *Crusades*, 16 (2017), pp. 79–93; A. Demurger, 'Othon de Grandson', pp. 39–43.
70 *Registres*, vol. 1, *Régne de Philippe le Bel* (Paris 1958), no. 406, pp. 64–65; Reg. Clem. V, vol. 4 (Rome 1886), no. 4404, p. 213. For more on the circumstances of Clement V's decision concerning Otto de Grandson's annuity and its effects, see A. Demurger, 'Othon de Grandson', pp. 43–49.
71 Reg. Clem. V, vol. 3, no. 2938, p. 138. See also J. B. de Vaivre, *La Commanderie*, Annexe. no. 34, pp. 197–198; A. Demurger, 'Othon de Grandson', pp. 44–45.
72 Reg. Clem. V, vol. 3, no. 3402, pp. 284–285; *Livre*, pp. 245, 252.
73 L. L. L. Lavocat, *Procès*, p. 200.
74 See *Vitae*, vol. 3, pp. 108–111.
75 *Foedera*, vol. 1.4, p. 130. See also C. Mansuet Jeune, *Histoire*, vol. 2, pp. 202–203.

76 *Foedera*, vol. 1.4, p. 134.
77 *Papsttum*, vol. 2, no. 101, pp. 182–184. See also J. M. Sans i Travé, *El Procés dels Templers catalans. Entre el turment i la glòria* (Lleida 1991), p. 153; M. Satora, *Sprawa*, p. 208.
78 On that topic, see A. Forey, *The Fall*, pp. 125–126; M. Satora, *Sprawa*, pp. 209–210.
79 B. Beaucage, 'La saisie', p. 95.
80 B. de Gaulejac, *La liquidation*, p. 18 (The author gave this date based on an excerpt from Renaud de Saint-Ouen's report, which is now only legible in small fragments).
81 Appendix, fols. 10r, 18r; Reg. Clem. V, vol. 5 (Rome 1887), no. 5282, pp. 56–57; *Actes*, no. 5692, p. 271.
82 D. M. Bryson, 'Clement V and the Road to Avignon, 1304–1309', in: *On the Margins of Crusading: The Military Orders, the Papacy and the Christian World*, ed. H. Nicholson (Farnham 2011), pp. 69–71. On the delays in the production of documents related to the Templar case, see M. Satora, *Sprawa*, pp. 79, 152–153.
83 G. Lizerand, *Clément V*, Appendice, no. 18, p. 450; B. Barbiche, *Les actes*, vol. 3, no. 2356, p. 51. See also M. Satora, *Sprawa*, pp. 151–152.
84 P. Dupuy, *Histoire de la condamnation*, no. 75, p. 280; *Vitae*, vol. 3, no. 29, p. 141; *Lettres de rois*, vol. 1, no. 18, pp. 28–29; *Livre*, pp. 241–242; *Gascon Register*, vol. 1, no. 40, pp. 225–226. See also H. Prutz, *Entwicklung*, p. 179; A. Pétel, 'Templiers et Hospitaliers dans le diocèse de Troyes. Comptes', pp. 311–312; M. Barber, *The Trial* (2006), pp. 137–138.
85 Reg. Clem. V, vol. 4, no. 5011, pp. 433–435; *Livre*, pp. 232–234.
86 Reg. Clem. V, vol. 4, no. 5018, p. 439.
87 Reg. Clem. V, vol. 4, no. 5013, p. 436; Reg. Clem. V, vol. 4, nos. 5099–5100, pp. 477–480. For more on the solutions used in England, see W. E. Lunt, *Financial Relations of the Papacy with England to 1327* (Cambridge 1939), pp. 560–562.
88 *Papsttum*, vol. 2, no. 106, pp. 199–200.
89 Reg. Clem. V, vol. 3, no. 3401, pp. 283–284; *Livre*, pp. 241, 267–269; B. Barbiche, *Les actes*, vol. 3, no. 2344, p. 46.
90 On 27 January 1309, Clement V sent an envoy to Philip the Fair to inform him of the two issues – *Vitae*, vol. 3, no. 19, p. 115.
91 Apart from the property issue, the king and the prelates raised various doubts about the proceedings against the Order's members. On this subject, see M. Barber, *The Trial* (2006), pp. 131–132; M. Satora, *Sprawa*, pp. 155–158.
92 *Papsttum*, vol. 2, no. 106, p. 191. B. Barbiche, *Les actes*, vol. 3, no. 2368, p. 56.
93 G. Lizerand, *Clément V*, p. 145.
94 *Papsttum*, vol. 2, no. 106, pp. 195–196, 199.
95 *Registres*, vol. 2.1, no. 2764, pp. 532.
96 AN, S 4952, dos. 13, no. 4.
97 All these houses were most likely leased in 1309: **Bonlieu** on 23 March 1309 – A. Pétel, 'Templiers et Hospitaliers dans le diocèse de Troyes. Le Temple de Bonlieu' (1910), no. 37, pp. 341–346; M. Barber, *The Trial* (2006), p. 138 (Barber mistakenly wrote that the house was leased at Easter); **Payns,** 6 April 1309 – A. Pétel, 'Templiers et Hospitaliers dans le diocèse de Troyes. Comptes', p. 364; **Bilbartaut** in 1308 or 1309 – E. Mannier, *Ordre de Malte*, p. 204; **Sauce** in 1309 (?) – A. Demurger, 'Dal Tempio all'Ospedale', pp. 95–96; A. Demurger, *Les Templiers*, p. 469; **Courval** at the end of 1309 – M. Miguet, *Templiers et Hospitaliers en Normandie*, pp. 44–50.
98 ADHG, H. 123, no. 1; B. de Gaulejac, *La liquidation*, Pièces justificatives, no. 1, pp. 90–91.
99 M. Miguet, *Templiers et Hospitaliers en Normandie*, p. 46; M. Barber, *The Trial* (2006), p. 138.
100 A. Pétel, 'Templiers et Hospitaliers dans le diocèse de Troyes. Le Temple de Bonlieu' (1909), p. 293.

101 A. Pétel, 'Templiers et Hospitaliers dans le diocèse de Troyes. Comptes', p. 291.
102 A. Demurger, *Les Templiers*, p. 468; A. Demurger, *Les Hospitaliers*, pp. 451–452; A. Demurger, *La persécution*, p. 132.
103 A. Pétel, 'Templiers et Hospitaliers dans le diocèse de Troyes. Comptes', pp. 348–349.
104 A. Pétel, 'Templiers et Hospitaliers dans le diocèse de Troyes. Comptes', p. 308.
105 P. Dupuy, *Histoire de la condamnation*, no. 71, pp. 273–274; Reg. Clem. V, vol. 3, no. 3400, p. 282; *Livre*, p. 268.
106 *Cartulaire général de l'Ordre des Hospitaliers de S. Jean de Jérusalem 1100–1310*, ed. J. Delaville le Roulx, vol. 4 (Paris 1906), no. 4882, pp. 224–226; *Bullarium Cyprium*, vol. 2, *Papal Letters Concerning Cyprus, 1261–1314*, ed. C. Schabel (Nicosia 2010), nos. 50–51, pp. 366–368; *Bullarium Cyprium*, nos. 73–75, pp. 385–394. See also J. Riley-Smith, *The Knights Hospitaller in the Levant, c. 1070–1309* (Basingstoke 2012), p. 223.
107 Reg. Clem. V, vol. 4, no. 5768, p. 235; *Acta Clementis PP. V.*, ed. F. M. Delorme, A. L. Tautu (Vatican 1955), no. 42, p. 74. See also H. C. Lea, *A History*, vol. 3, p. 334.
108 A. Pétel, 'Templiers et Hospitaliers dans le diocèse de Troyes. Le Temple de Bonlieu' (1909), p. 294.
109 See Section 2.3.
110 See Section 2.3.
111 ADHG, H 125, fol. 38v.
112 ADHG, H 125, fol. 39v.
113 ADHG, H 127 fol. 17 r; E. Lalou, *Itinéraire*, vol. 2, p. 368.
114 BnF, ms. lat. 9800, no. 13.
115 BnF, ms. fr. 20334, no. 58; BnF, Clairambault 1313, no. 36.
116 In 1319, Arnaud Barrau was described in this way – *Les Olim*, vol. 3.2, p. 1337.
117 *Le Procès des Templiers*, ed. J. Michelet, vol. 2 (Paris 1851), p. 218; *Processus contra Templarios in Francia. Procès-verbaux de la procédure menée par la commission pontificale à Paris (1309–1311)*, ed. M. Satora, vol. 1 (Leiden 2020), p. 910. See also L. L. L. Lavocat, *Procès*, pp. 352–353.
118 P. Dupuy, *Histoire de la condamnation*, no. 78, pp. 311–312; *Vitae*, vol. 3, pp. 143–144; *Lettres de rois*, vol. 2 (Paris 1847), no. 17, pp. 27–28; *Gascon Register*, vol. 1, no. 38, pp. 223–224. See also C. Mansuet Jeune, *Histoire*, vol. 2, pp. 256–257.
119 Étienne Baluze dates this document to 1310 (*Vitae*, vol. 3, p. 144), while George P. Cuttino dates it to 1311 (*Gascon Register*, vol. 1, no. 331, p. 691). However, neither of these dates can be confirmed.
120 *Vitae*, vol. 3, p. 144; *Gascon Register*, vol. 1, no. 331, pp. 691–692.
121 P. Dupuy, *Histoire de la condamnation*, no. 77, pp. 310–311; *Vitae*, vol. 3, pp. 142–143; *Lettres de rois*, vol. 2, no. 26, pp. 37–38; *Gascon Register*, vol. 1, no. 39, pp. 224–225. See also C. Mansuet Jeune, *Histoire*, vol. 2, p. 257.
122 J. R. Carter Jr., 'Gascon Archival Materials in a British Museum Manuscript', *Manuscripta*, 16 (1972), nos. 3, 76, p. 154; E. A. R. Brown, 'The Political Repercussions', p. 586, n. 32.
123 J. R. Carter Jr., 'Gascon Archival Materials', no. 49, p. 152; E. A. R. Brown, 'The Political Repercussions', p. 586, n. 32. See also M. Satora, *Sprawa*, p. 111.
124 BnF, ms. fr. 20334, no. 58; BnF, Clairambault 1313, no. 36; BnF, ms. lat. 9800, no. 13.
125 AN, S 4952, dos. 13, no. 4.
126 *Actes*, no. 3932, p. 89; *Les Olim*, vol. 3.1, pp. 640–641.
127 See Section 2.1.3.
128 ADHG, H 125, fols. 1v-4v.
129 ADHG, H 127. See also B. de Gaulejac, *La liquidation*, p. 23.
130 *Documents inédits*, no. 25, pp. 94–95; J. M. Roger, 'La prise de possession', p. 240.
131 Appendix, fols. 1r., 2r., 4r. etc.

132 Reg. Clem. V, vol. 6, no. 6816, pp. 132–133; G. Lizerand, *Clément V*, Appendice, no. 14, pp. 445–446.
133 Reg. Clem. V, vol. 7 (Rome 1887), no. 8336, p. 176.
134 *Inventaire d'anciens comptes*, p. 265.
135 E. Boutaric, 'Clément V' (1872), s. 26; *Monumenta Germaniae Historica: Constitutiones et Acta Publica Imperatorum et Regum*, vol. 4.1, ed. J. Schwalm (Hannover 1906), no. 514, p. 470.
136 M. Barber, *The Trial* (2006), p. 138.
137 C. Perkins, 'The Wealth', pp. 256–257; A. M. Leys, 'The Forfeiture', pp. 160–161; J. S. Hamilton, 'Apocalypse', p. 91; J. S. Hamilton, 'King Edward', p. 219, n. 28; H. J. Nicholson, *The Knights*, pp. 78–79; J. M. Jefferson, 'Edward II', p. 316.
138 M. Vilar Bonet, *Els Béns*, pp. 85–94; A. Forey, *The Fall*, pp. 139–142; J. M. Sans i Travé, *La fi*, pp. 346, 356–364.
139 For a possible interpretation of the pope's words, see also M. Satora, *Sprawa*, pp. 160–161.
140 G. Lizerand, *Clément V*, Appendice, no. 25, pp. 463–464. On that topic see also M. Satora, *Sprawa*, p. 161.
141 E. Mannier, *Ordre de Malte*, pp. XVII–XVIII; C. V. Langlois, 'Le procès', p. 418; J. M. A. Delaville Le Roulx, *Les hospitaliers*, p. 34; G. Bordonove, *La Tragédie*, p. 339; R. Pernoud, *Les Templiers* (11th ed.) (Paris 2018), p. 89.
142 G. Bordonove, *La Tragédie*, p. 339; A. Luttrell, 'Observations', p. 369.
143 See Section 1.3, which discusses the contents of the bull of 9 July 1308 and the letter to the French bishops of 12 May 1311.
144 See examples of estimates of the Templars' income in: K. Schottmüller, *Der Untergang*, vol. 1, pp. 62–63; H. C. Lea, *A History*, vol. 3, pp. 250–251.
145 L. L. Borrelli de Serres, *Recherches*, vol. 3, pp. 32–33.
146 I. de La Torre, *Los Templarios*, p. 279.
147 A. Demurger, 'Les ordres religieux-militaires et l'argent: sources et pratiques', in: *The Templars and Their Sources*, ed. K. Borchardt, K. Döring, P. Josserand, H. J. Nicholson (Farnham 2017), p. 177.
148 ADHG, H 125, fol. 46r.
149 *Registres*, vol. 1, no. 406, p. 65; A. Demurger, 'La "prisée"'. See also A. Demurger, 'Othon de Grandson', pp. 44–45; A. Demurger, 'Les ordres religieux-militaires', p. 182.
150 Appendix, fol. 9r.
151 *Registres*, vol. 2.1, no. 277–278, pp. 60–61.
152 See examples of tenant settlements that include amounts reducing their charges in Renaud de Saint-Ouen's report – Appendix, fol. 4v.
153 AN, S 4952, dos. 13, no. 4 (**Ambrief**); ADV, 3 H 1/138 (**Ballan**); AN, K 37, no. 39 (**Laon** and **Ardon**); A. Pétel, 'Templiers et Hospitaliers dans le diocèse de Troyes. Le Temple de Bonlieu' (1910), no. 37, p. 342 (**Bonlieu**); Appendix, fol. 4v (**Magnac, Puybonnieux, Bellechassagne, Foulventour, La Bussière-Rapy, Mons, Bonnefare, Chaumont, Le Palais**); E. Mannier, *Ordre de Malte*, p. 204 (**Bilbartaut**).
154 E. A. R. Brown, 'Royal Salvation and Needs of State in Early-Fourteenth-Century France', in: E. A. R. Brown, *The Monarchy of Capetian France and Royal Ceremonial* (Aldershot 1991), IV, p. 29; B. Causse, *Eglise, finance, et royauté: la floraison des décimes dans la France au Moyen Age*, vol. 1 (Lille-Paris 1988), p. 245; S. Menache, *Clement V*, p. 93.
155 J. Favier, *Philippe le Bel*, pp. 437–438; M. Barber, *The Trial* (2006), p. 85.
156 L. L. Borrelli de Serres, *Recherches*, vol. 3, pp. 38–39.
157 J. Piquet, *Des banquiers*, p. 188; R. Pernoud, *Les Templiers*, p. 89.
158 L. L. Borrelli de Serres, *Recherches*, vol. 3, pp. 33–34, n. 7; G. Lizerand, *Clément V*, pp. 344–345. On the chronology of monetary changes during the reign of Philip the Fair, see also A. Dieudonné, 'Les variations', pp. 238–148 *passim.*

159 C. Samaran, G. Mollat, *La Fiscalité pontificale en France au XIVe siècle: période d'Avignon et grand schisme d'Occident* (Paris 1905), pp. 23–24; S. Menache, *Clement V*, pp. 92–93.
160 K. Wenck, 'Aus den Tagen', pp. 200–202; G. Lizerand, *Clément V*, p. 56.
161 L. Bourgain, 'Contribution du clergé à l'impôt sous la monarchie française', *Revue des questions historiques*, 48 (1890), p. 70; S. Menache, *Clement V*, p. 93. On the tithes granted to Philip the Fair, see also J. R. Strayer, *The Reign*, p. 153; B. Causse, *Eglise*, vol. 1, p. 255.
162 E. Boutaric, 'Clément V' (1872), p. 26; *Monumenta Germaniae Historica*, no. 514, pp. 469–470 (the document is incorrectly dated 24 December 1310). See also E. A. R. Brown, *Customary Aids and Royal Finance in Capetian France: The Marriage Aid of Philip the Fair* (Cambridge 1992), p. 33; S. Menache, *Clement V*, p. 97.
163 *Acta Aragonenisa*, vol. 1 (Berlin 1908), no. 179, p. 263.
164 B. Guillemain, *Les recettes et les dépenses de la Chambre apostolique pour la quatrième année du pontificat de Clément V (1308–1309): introitus et exitus 75* (Rome 1978), p. XXXI; F. P. Caselli, 'L'evoluzione della contabilità camerale nel periodo Avignonese', in: *Aux origines de l'État moderne. Le fonctionnement administratif de la papauté d'Avignon. Actes de la table ronde d'Avignon (23–24 janvier 1988)* (Rome 1990), p. 416.
165 V. Salavert y Roca, *Cerdeña y la expansión mediterránea de la corona de Aragón 1297–1314*, vol. 2 (Madrid 1956), no. 332, p. 414. See also N. Housley, 'Pope Clement V and the crusades of 1309–10', *Journal of Medieval History*, 8 (1982), p. 33.
166 *Acta Aragonensia*, vol. 3, pp. 207–208. On the conflict with Venice, see, for example, N. Housley, 'Pope Clement V', pp. 36–37.
167 C. Devic, J. Vaissète, *Histoire générale de Languedoc*, vol. 9 (Toulouse 1885), p. 325.
168 See, for example, *Cartulaire et archives des communes de l'ancien diocèse et de l'arrondissement administratif de Carcassonne*, ed. A. Mahul, vol. 5 (Paris 1857), pp. 341–342; J. Favier, *Un conseiller de Philippe le Bel: Enguerran de Marigny* (Paris 1963), p. 607; *Histoire de Carcassonne* (2nd ed.), ed. J. Guilaine, D. Fabre (Toulouse 1990), p. 100.
169 A. Du Bourg, 'Prise de possession par les Hospitaliers de la Maison du Temple de Toulouse', *Mémoires de la Société archéologique du Midi de la France*, 11 (1874/1879), p. 174; A. Soutou, *La commanderie*, p. 21.
170 J. Favier, *Un conseiller*, p. 646.
171 J. Favier, *Un conseiller*, pp. 791, 794–795.
172 J. Favier, *Un conseiller*, pp. 648–649.
173 'Der Nachlass Clemens V und der in Betreff desselben von Johann XXII (1318–1321) geführte Process', ed. F. Ehrle, *Archiv fur Literatur und Kirchengeschichte des Mittelalters*, 5 (1889), pp. 1–166. For more on the process, see also L. Guérard, 'La succession de Clément V et le procès de Bertrand de Got, vicomte de Lomagne (1318–1321)', *Revue de Gascogne*, 32 (1891), pp. 5–20.
174 'Der Nachlass', pp. 86–87, 88–89, 146.
175 'Der Nachlass', pp. 71, 146.
176 'Der Nachlass', pp. 44–46.
177 'Der Nachlass', pp. 15–26; E. Berchon, 'Histoire du pape Clément V', *Actes de l'Académie nationale des Sciences, Belles Lettres et Arts de Bordeaux*, 3th series, 56 (1894), Pièces justificatives, no. 1, pp. 141–156 (French translation of the document).
178 P. D. Partner, '*Camera Papae*: Problems of Papal Finance in the Later Middle Ages', *The Journal of Ecclesiastical History*, 4 (1953), no. 1, p. 56.
179 'Der Nachlass', pp. 26–31; E. Berchon, 'Histoire', Pièces justificatives, no. 2, pp. 156–161.
180 'Der Nachlass', p. 65.
181 F. Baethgen, 'Neue Beiträge zur Geschichte des päpstlichen Finanzwesens um die Wende des 13. Jahrhunderts', *Quellen und Forschungen aus Italienischen Biblioteken*

und Archiven, 24 (1932–1933), pp. 138–139; P. D. Partner, '*Camera Papae*', pp. 57–59; B. Guillemain, *Les recettes*, pp. XXXIII–XXXIV; F. P. Caselli, 'L'espansione delle fonti finanziare della Chiesa nel XIV secolo', *Archivio della Società romana di storia patria*, 110 (1987), p. 66. On the "secret services" see also W. E. Lunt, *Financial Relations*, pp. 479–481.

182 On the role played by Jean de Lescapon at the papal court, see F. Baix, 'Notes sur les clercs de la Chambre apostolique (XIIIe–XIVe siècles)', *Bulletin de l'Institut historique belge de Rome*, 27 (1952), pp. 26–28; B. Guillemain, *Les recettes*, p. 18, n. 81.

183 F. Baethgen, 'Neue Beiträge', Beilagen, no. 2, p. 148.

184 A reference to the existence of two treasuries referred to as *thesaurus ecclesie romane* and *camera romane ecclesie* appears in one of the documents in which Clement V distributed the collected money – 'Der Nachlass', p. 29. See also P. D. Partner, '*Camera Papae*', p. 56.

185 Reg. Clem. V, vol. 4, no. 3753, p. 30; *Registrum Simonis de Gandavo: diocesis Saresbiriensis, AD 1297–1315*, ed. C. T. Flower, M. C. Burdett Dawes, vol. 1 (Oxford 1914), p. 306.

186 'Der Nachlass', pp. 5–6.

187 'Der Nachlass', p. 29. It is known that, in October 1313, Clement V granted Edward II a loan "as a private person" (*tanquam personae privatae*). For more on this loan, see Y. Renouard, 'Édouard II et Clément V d'après les Rôles gascons', *Annales du Midi*, 67 (1955), pp. 133–140.

188 'Der Nachlass', pp. 6, 91. The amount of the loan to Edward II was confirmed by one of the witnesses – 'Der Nachlass', pp. 44–45. However, the publisher of the documents incorrectly calculated that Clement V lent the monarchs a total of 320,000 florins ('Der Nachlass', p. 135). Subsequently, other researchers cited incorrect amounts in their works – G. Lizerand, *Clément V*, pp. 366–367; P. D. Partner, '*Camera Papae*', p. 56; J. Favier, *Un conseiller*, p. 616; J. Favier, *Philippe le Bel*, p. 500; F. P. Caselli, 'L'espansione', p. 66; S. Menache, *Clement V*, p. 51.

189 'Der Nachlass', pp. 48, 57.

190 'Der Nachlass', pp. 96–97.

191 'Der Nachlass', p. 91. On John XXII's efforts to organise the crusade, see, for example, G. Dürrholder, *Die Kreuzzugspolitik unter Papst Johann XXII (1316–1334)* (Strasbourg 1913).

192 'Der Nachlass', p. 103.

193 *Papsttum*, vol. 2, no. 92, pp. 157–158. See also N. Housley, 'Pope Clement V', p. 31; A. Luttrell, 'The Hospitallers and the Papacy', p. 603.

194 S. Menache, *Clement V*, p. 108; S. Menache, 'When Ideology Met Reality: Clement V and the Crusade', in: *La Papauté et les Croisades / The Papacy and the Crusades*, ed. M. Balard (Franham 2011), p. 112.

195 Reg. Clem. V, vol. 3, no. 2986, pp. 151–153; B. Barbiche, *Les actes*, vol. 3, no. 2350, p. 49. See also G. Lizerand, *Clément V*, p. 302; A. Luttrell, 'The Hospitallers and the Papacy', p. 605.

196 Reg. Clem. V, vol. 4, no. 3753, p. 30.

197 *Cartulaire général*, vol. 4, no. 4831, pp. 198–199; S. Schein, 'Philip IV and the Crusade: A Reconsideration', in: *Crusade and Settlement. Papers Read at the First Conference of the Society for the Study of Crusades and the Latin East and Presented to R.C. Smail*, ed. P. W. Edbury (Cardiff 1985), p. 123; S. Schein, *Fideles Crucis*, p. 227; A. Luttrell, 'The Hospitallers and the Papacy', pp. 606–607; A. Demurger, *Les Hospitaliers*, p. 474.

198 *Codice diplomatico*, vol. 2, no. 20, p. 22; *Vitae*, vol. 3, no. 19, pp. 120–121; B. Barbiche, *Les actes*, vol. 3, no. 2369, p. 56. See also G. Lizerand, *Clément V*, p. 304; A. Luttrell, 'The Hospitallers and the Papacy', p. 609.

199 *Vitae*, vol. 3, no. 19, pp. 105–108; *Cartulaire général*, vol. 4, no. 4884, pp. 227–228. See also A. Luttrell, 'The Hospitallers and the Papacy', p. 609; S. Menache, 'The

Hospitallers during Clement V's Pontificate: The Spoiled Sons of the Papacy?', in: *The Military Orders*, vol. 2, *Welfare and Warfare*, ed. H. Nicholson (Aldershot 1998), p. 157.
200 On the course of the expedition, see, for example, S. Schein, *Fideles Crucis*, p. 230; S. Menache, *Clement V*, p. 110.
201 J. N. Hillgarth, *Ramon Lull*, p. 83; A. J. Forey, 'The Military Orders in the Crusading Proposals', p. 342; C. Tyerman, 'Sed nichil fecit? The Last Capetians and the Recovery of the Holy Land', in: *War and Government in the Middle Ages*, ed. J. Gillingham, J. C. Holt (Cambridge 1984), p. 170; A. Luttrell, 'The Hospitallers and the Papacy', p. 609.
202 A. Luttrell, 'The Hospitallers and the Papacy', p. 609, n. 80.
203 L. Thier, *Kreuzzugsbemühungen*, pp. 87–88; A. Luttrell, 'The Hospitallers and the Papacy', p. 604; A. Demurger, *Les Hospitaliers*, pp. 473–473. For more on James II's policies regarding the crusade and the Hospitallers' expedition, see N. Housley, 'Pope Clement V', pp. 32–34.
204 A. Demurger, *Les Templiers*, p. 469.
205 See Section 2.2.2.
206 Alan Forey believes that Jean de Châlons could have met the commander of France before news of his possible arrest reached the Order's members, and that Gérard de Villiers was merely carrying out his regular duties of transporting horses to the East – A. Forey, 'Fugitives during the Templar Trial', in: *The Templars. The Rise, Fall, and Legacy of a Military Religious Order*, ed. J. Burgtorf, S. Lotan, E. Mallorquí-Ruscalleda (London–New York 2021), pp. 200–201. In this case, there could be no question of the loss of part of the Order's properties, only its relocation. For other references to the escape of Gérard de Villiers, see A. Demurger, *Le peuple templier, 1307–1312. Catalogue prosopographique des templiers présents ou (et) cités dans les procès–verbaux des interrogatoires faits dans le royaume de France entre 1307 et 1312* (Paris 2019), pp. 476–477.
207 Tholomeus von Lucca, *Historia ecclesiastica nova nebst Fortsetzungen bis 1329*, ed. O. Clavout, L. Schmugge, Monumenta Germaniae Historica, Scriptores, vol. 39 (Hannover 2009), p. 661. See also E. Bellomo, 'Colliding Perceptions: Italian Views of the Templar Trial from Contemporary Authors to Angelo Fumagalli's Delle antichità longobardico-milanesi (1792)', in: *The Templars. The Rise, Fall, and Legacy of a Military Religious Order*, ed. J. Burgtorf, S. Lotan, E. Mallorquí-Ruscalleda (London–New York 2021), p. 278.
208 E. Bellomo, 'Colliding Perceptions', p. 477.
209 *Papsttum*, vol. 2, no. 155, p. 339; A. Demurger, *Le peuple*, p. 230.
210 For more on the escape of Hugues de Chalon, see A. Demurger, *Le peuple*, p. 92.
211 C. V. Langlois, *Registres*, p. 258; J. B. de Vaivre, *La Commanderie*, Annexe, no. 31, pp. 188–189. See also M. Bompaire, 'Trésor des Templiers et trésor des Juifs au XIVe siècle', *Bulletin de la Société française de numismatique*, 53 (1998), no. 7, pp. 185–186; A. Demurger, *La persécution*, pp. 281–282.
212 Appendix, fol. 9r.
213 BnF, NAL 57, fols. 278–279 (The original document can be found in the Archives départementales du Doubs, B 433); J. Finot, *Les sires de Faucogney, vicomtes de Vesoul: notices et documents* (Paris 1886), p. 129; J. Courtieu, A. M. Courtieu, *Sources parisiennes relatives à l'histoire de la Franche-Comté, incluant le catalogue des manuscrits relatifs à la Franche-Comté qui sont conservés dans les bibliothèques publiques de Paris, par Ulysse Robert, 1878* (Besançon 2001), p. 47.
214 Reg. Clem. V, vol. 6, no. 7034, pp. 2013–2014.
215 BnF, ms. fr. 4628, fol. 148r.
216 Appendix, fol. 18r; ADHG, H 288, no. 1, fol. 1v. See also B. de Gaulejac, *La liquidation*, p. 19.
217 Appendix, fol. 10r; B. de Gaulejac, *La liquidation*, pp. 18–19.
218 F. Hooghe, *The Trial*, p. 293.

219 ADHG, H 128; H 129. See also B. de Gaulejac, *La liquidation*, pp. 45–46; M. Satora, 'Filip Piękny', p. 29.
220 A. Du Bourg, *Histoire*, p. 589.
221 Appendix, fol. 18r. See also B. de Gaulejac, *La liquidation*, p. 20.
222 Appendix, fol. 8r.
223 Appendix, fols. 3r, 11r, 17r.
224 Appendix, fol. 4v.
225 Appendix, fol. 16r.
226 *Registres*, vol. 2.1, no. 3563, p. 748.
227 Appendix, fol. 18r. See also B. de Gaulejac, *La liquidation*, p. 19.
228 Appendix, fol. 4r. See also B. de Gaulejac, *La liquidation*, pp. 18–19.
229 Appendix, fol 18r. See also B. de Gaulejac, *La liquidation*, p. 19.
230 Reg. Clem. V, vol. 6, no. 7602, pp. 458–463.
231 A. Demurger, *Le peuple*, p. 443.
232 Reg. Clem. V, vol. 6, no. 7183, pp. 280–288.
233 Appendix, fols. 1r, 10r, 11r.
234 Appendix, fol. 18v.
235 Reg. Clem. V, vol. 5, no. 5282, pp. 56–57. On the case of bishop of Bazas, see also B. de Gaulejac, *La liquidation*, p. 21.
236 Reg. Clem. V, vol. 7, no. 8336, pp. 176 (dated 6 August 1312).
237 ADHG, H Malte, Douzens 3, pièce 17; BnF, NAL 69, fols. 86–89; B. de Gaulejac, *La liquidation*, Pièces justificatives, no. 16, pp. 134–136.
238 Appendix, fols. 6r, 13r.
239 Appendix, fol. 3r.
240 Appendix, fol. 16r.
241 A. Demurger, *Le peuple*, pp. 176–177.
242 *Les journaux du trésor de Charles IV*, no. 7474, col. 1229.
243 *Registres*, vol. 3.3, no. 7411, p. 208.
244 *Registres*, vol. 2.1, no. 2826, pp. 547–548.
245 *Les journaux du trésor de Charles IV*, no. 6415, col. 1069.
246 Appendix, fol. 5r.
247 Appendix, fol. 2r.
248 Appendix, fol. 3r.
249 Appendix, fol. 4r.
250 BnF, ms. fr. 8551, pp. 9–10, 31 (The original documents can be found in the Archives départementales du Doubs, B 431); J. P. Redoutey, 'Philippe le Bel et la Frenche-Comté', in: *Provinces et États dans la France de l'Est: Le rattachement de la Franche-Comté à la France. Espaces régionaux et espaces nationaux. Colloque de Besançon, 3 et 4 oct. 1977*, ed. R. Fiéter, F. Lassus (Paris 1979), p. 216.
251 BnF, ms. fr. 8551, p. 31 (The original document is held in the Archives départementales du Doubs, B 431); J. P. Redoutey, 'Philippe le Bel', p. 216.
252 Appendix, fol. 5r.
253 Appendix, fol. 5r.
254 Appendix, fol. 5r.
255 Appendix, fol. 4v.
256 Appendix, fols. 4r, 10r, 4v.
257 E. Mannier, *Ordre de Malte*, p. XVIII; G. Bordonove, *La Tragédie*, p. 338; M. Miguet, *Templiers et Hospitaliers de Bure: histoire et rayonnement d'une commanderie bourguignonne* (Langres 2012), p. 43, n. 58 (his comment referred to the administrators of the commandery of Payns); A. Luttrell, 'Observations', p. 369.
258 H. C. Lea, 'Confiscation', pp. 250–251.
259 AN, M1, no. 10.

260 ADHG, H Malte, Douzens 3, pièce 17; BnF, NAL 69, fols. 86–89; B. de Gaulejac, *La liquidation*, Pièces justificatives, no. 16, pp. 134–136.
261 *Les journaux du trésor de Charles IV*, no. 8242, col. 1343; *Les journaux du trésor de Charles IV*, no. 8725, col. 1414. The procurator of the heirs of Raymond Dupuy, referred to in *Les journaux du trésor* as *commissarius supper bonis Templariorum senescallie Caturcensis*, presented the account on 11 October 1325 – *Les journaux du trésor de Charles IV*, no. 8687, col. 1409. Renaud de Saint-Ouen's report mentions Raymond Dupuy, *receptor*, who failed to fulfil his obligation to settle his accounts and was therefore subject to enforcement proceedings – Appendix, fol. 11r. This is probably the same person.
262 E.g. Appendix, fols. 4r, 4v, and others.
263 Appendix, fol. 17r.
264 E. g. Appendix, fols. 2r, 16r-17r.
265 Appendix, fols. 16r, 18r.
266 Appendix, fols. 16r, 18r.
267 Appendix, fols. 2r, 16r.
268 Appendix, fols. 17r, 4v.
269 A. Du Bourg, *Histoire*, pp. 397–398 (The author gives the date 1330); B. de Gaulejac, *La liquidation*, pp. 20, 85; J. Dubourg, 'La commanderie', no. 2, p. 140.
270 Appendix, fol. 2r.
271 Appendix, fol. 4r.
272 Appendix, fol. 17r.
273 *Registres*, vol. 2.1, no. 2764, pp. 531–532.
274 AN, M1, no. 10.
275 BnF, ms. lat. 9035, no. 18.
276 AN, J 413, no. 28.
277 A. Demurger, *La persécution*, pp. 52–53; 89–93.
278 A. Demurger, *La persécution*, p. 92.
279 The bills themselves do not specify the number of days to which they refer. However, as the daily pay rates for the guards are given at the start of the document and the total amount they were to receive for their work is detailed in the individual bills, it is possible to calculate the time period to which the accounts refer. Nevertheless, the document does not specify whether the amounts allocated to the Templars refer to the same period in each case. Nevertheless, I accept this assumption following Demurger.
280 This was the case for eight of the 14 groups for which the daily rate per prisoner could be calculated. These included a group of 16 brothers who travelled to Dammartin on 31 January, a group of six brothers who travelled to Saint-Maur-des-Fossés on 5 February, and a group of six brothers who were transferred to Chaillot (?) on 11 February, etc. – AN, J 413, no. 28.
281 This was the case for five groups, including a group of eight brothers who travelled to Saint-Denis on 31 January and a group of six brothers who travelled to Thiers-sur-Thève on the same day, etc. – AN, J 413, no. 28.
282 This was the case for eight Templars, who travelled to Crépy-en-Valois on 11 February – AN, J 413, no. 28.
283 AN, J 413, no. 28.
284 BnF, Clairambault 1313, no. 37; BnF, ms. fr. 20334, no. 57. See a detailed analysis of both documents in: A. Demurger, *La persécution*, pp. 251–254.
285 Demurger translated the word *feure*, which appears in the documents, as "blacksmith" (fr. ferreur) – *La persécution*, pp. 252, 254. However, the text suggests that it refers to *feurre*, meaning hay for carriages.
286 The source does not specify whether it was livres parisis or livres tournois. However, it is known that the former coin was used in Paris, a fact also mentioned in the brothers'

accounts of their trip to the city, during which they participated in the proceedings before the papal commission.

287 *Le Procès*, vol. 1 (Paris 1841), p. 151; *Processus*, vol. 1, p. 229; M. Barber, *The Trial* (2006), p. 154; A. Demurger, *La persécution*, pp. 192–193.

288 On the proceedings before the papal commission in Paris, see, for example, M. Barber, *The Trial* (2006), pp. 139–201; A. Demurger, *La persécution*, pp. 151–232, 247–262; *Processus*, vol. 1, pp. 6–18 (editor's commentary).

289 *Le dossier*, no. 9, pp. 142–145. See also A. Forey, 'Templars after the Trial. Further Evidence', *Revue Mabillon*, 23 (2012), pp. 89–90.

290 BnF, ms. fr. 20334 (69 documents); BnF, ms lat. 9800 (12 documents); BnF, Clairambault 1313 (40 documents); AN, K 37C, no. 40 ter; AN, K 38, no. 8/2 – A. Demurger, *La persécution*, p. 235, n. 8.

291 BnF, ms. lat. 17062, no. 85; BnF, ms. fr. 10430, no. 425, fol. 66; BnF ms. fr. 25993, nos. 156–157; BnF, Clairambault 34, no. 1, p. 2509.

292 Demurger mentions 11 prisons in which a total of 122 prisoners were detained (A. Demurger, *La persécution*, p. 236). A further 13 Templars should be included from the prison in Creil – BnF, Clairambault 34, no. 1, p. 2509.

293 BnF, Clairambault 8, no. 39, p. 425; BnF, ms. fr. 26627 (Pièces originales 143), Aunoy 85.

294 See table in: A. Demurger, *La persécution*, p. 245.

295 BnF, ms. fr. 20334, nos. 7, 24, 36, 70, 75; BnF, ms. lat. 17062, no. 85.

296 BnF, Clairambault 1313, no. 36. See also A. Demurger, *La persécution*, pp. 238–239.

297 BnF, Clairambault 1313, nos. 39, 46; BnF, ms. lat. 17062, no. 85; BnF, ms. fr. 20334, no. 62.

298 BnF, ms. fr. 20334, no. 62.

299 In January 1311, the priest in Crépy-en-Valois received 32 s. p. for eight months (BnF, ms. lat. 9800, no. 14); in Luzarches (BnF, Clairambault 1313, nos. 12, 25, 30, 39) and in Senlis (BnF, ms. fr. 20334, nos. 59, 67; BnF, Clairambault 1313, nos. 35, 41) 6 s. p. per month; 6 s. p. per month in Asnières at the beginning of 1311 (BnF, Clairambault 1313, no. 38), later 10 per month (BnF, ms. fr. 20334, no. 16); and 8 s. p. per month in Villiers-Saint-Paul – BnF, Clairambault 1313, nos. 27, 34, 43 and others.

300 A. Demurger, *La persécution*, pp. 243–245.

301 Giacomo da Montecucco, the commander of Lombardy and papal *cubicularius*, fled on 13 February 1308. For more on the circumstances surrounding his escape, see, for example, E. Bellomo, *The Templar Order in North-West Italy (1142–c. 1330)* (Leiden 2008), pp. 204–206; J. Théry-Astruc, 'The Flight', pp. 35–44.

302 *Papsttum*, vol. 2, no. 74, p. 114. See also G. Lizerand, *Clément V*, p. 120; M. Barber, *The Trial* (2006), p. 95.

303 *Livre*, p. 288.

304 *Acta Aragonensia*, vol. 3, no. 76, pp. 174–175.

305 A. Demurger, *Le peuple*, p. XXVI.

306 G. Lizerand, *Clément V*, Appendice, no. 30, p. 472; B. Barbiche, *Les actes*, vol. 3, no. 2424, pp. 78–79. See also J. Lecler, *Histoire*, p. 64; A. Demurger, *La persécution*, p. 269.

307 In recent years, Helen Nicholson has estimated the total number of members of the Order during the trial at 1,700 – H. J. Nicholson, 'Review of Alain Demurger, Le peuple templier, 1307–1312…', *Speculum*, 97 (2022), no. 1, p. 169. However, this differs from the figures given in the sources cited here.

308 While the document does not specify the exact amount allocated for the sister's food, it does list the costs of clothing and footwear, totalling 33 s. 10 d. t. – A. Pétel, 'Templiers et Hospitaliers dans le diocèse de Troyes. Comptes', pp. 338, 367, 369.

309 A. Pétel, 'Templiers et Hospitaliers dans le diocèse de Troyes. Comptes', p. 333.

310 A. Pétel, 'Templiers et Hospitaliers dans le diocèse de Troyes. Comptes', p. 370.

311 Appendix, fol. 4v.

312 Appendix, fol. 4v.

313 V. Bessey, *Les commanderies*, no. 2, pp. 316, 319; A. Demurger, *La persécution*, pp. 274–275.
314 A. Pétel, 'Templiers et Hospitaliers dans le diocèse de Troyes. Comptes', p. 371.
315 BnF, ms. lat. 9035, no. 18.
316 AN, M1, no. 10.
317 *Les journaux du trésor de Charles IV*, no. 2860, cols. 498–499.
318 AN, J 413, no. 28.
319 A. Demurger, *La persécution*, p. 92.
320 In one bill, the total amount allocated for guards and Templar expenses was provided, so it is not possible to specify the remuneration amount.
321 For instance, Guillaume de Glatigny was paid 5 s. t. per day for himself and one servant, and the same rate later applied to two guards and a servant – BnF, ms. lat. 9800, no. 6; BnF, Clairambault 1313, no. 10. The same was true for Simon de Saint-Péravy, who received 5 s. t. regardless of whether he was assisted by one or two servants – BnF, Clairambault 1313, no. 33; BnF, ms. fr. 20334, no. 44.
322 BnF, ms. fr. 20334, nos. 43, 59; BnF, Clairambault 1313, nos. 25, 29, 48.
323 BnF, ms. lat. 9800, no. 12.
324 BnF, ms. fr. 20334, no. 9.
325 A. Demurger, *La persécution*, pp. 244–245.
326 BnF, Clairambault 1313, no. 37.
327 BnF, ms. fr. 20334, no. 57. Although we do not know the date of the bill, we do know that the four Templars concerned appeared before the papal commission at the end of February 1311 – *Le Procès*, vol. 1, p. 619; *Processus*, vol. 1, p. 682.
328 *Les journaux du trésor de Charles IV*, no. 2860, col. 499. Adam de Valencourt was in the Empire at the time of the arrest of the French Templars, but later fled. He was interrogated by the bishop of Paris in 1309. He must therefore have been detained at an earlier point – A. Demurger, *Le peuple*, p. 456.
329 On this topic, see A. Demurger, *La persécution*, pp. 54–58; A. Forey, 'Fugitives'.
330 See, for example, the letter regarding the payment of wages to the Templar guards in Plailly, despite the fact that some of prisoners escaped – BnF, ms. lat. 9800, no. 18.
331 See, for example, Clement V's letter to Philip the Fair from May 1309, which discusses financing travel allowances for inquisitors in countries other than France – *Papsttum*, vol. 2, no. 106, p. 200. See also the papal decisions to grant money to envoys travelling to Cyprus and Greece, where Templar properties had come under the control of the Church – Reg. Clem. V, vol. 6, nos. 7599–7600, p. 458. In countries where the Order's properties remained in the hands of secular rulers, the local hierarchs were to bear the envoys' expenses. See, for example, the decisions concerning envoys travelling to Aragon and Castile – Reg. Clem. V, vol. 4, no. 5013, p. 436; Reg. Clem. V, vol. 6, no. 6715, pp. 103–104.
332 On the establishment and activities of diocesan commissions conducting investigations into individual members of the Order, see A. Demurger, *La persécution*, pp. 131–149.
333 Reg. Clem. V, vol. 3, no. 3523, p. 318; Reg. Clem. V, nos. 3529, 3531, p. 319. On the remuneration of members of the papal commission, see also A. Demurger, *La persécution*, p. 174.
334 Reg. Clem. V, vol. 3, no. 3517, p. 317; Reg. Clem. V, no. 3527, p. 318.
335 Reg. Clem. V, vol. 3, no. 3523, p. 318.
336 A. Demurger, *La persécution*, p. 175.
337 *Papsttum*, vol. 2, no. 106, pp. 191–192. See also G. Lizerand, *Clément V*, p. 144.
338 *Les journaux du trésor de Philippe IV le Bel*, ed. J. Viard (Paris 1940), no. 5991, col. 883.
339 A. Forey, *The Fall*, p. 123.
340 *Monumenta Henricina*, ed. A. J. Dias Dinis, vol. 1 (Coimbra 1960), no. 68, p. 129. See also C. Porro, 'Reassessing the Dissolution of the Templars: King Denis and Theirs Suppression in Portugal', in: *The Debate on the Trial of the Templars (1307–1314)*, ed. J. Burgtorf, P. F. Crawford, H. J. Nicholson (Farnham 2010), p. 173.

341 BnF, Clairambault 1313, no. 24.
342 BnF, Clairambault 1313, no. 37.
343 *Le Procès*, vol. 1, p. 151; *Processus*, vol. 1, p. 229.
344 B. Guillemain, *Les recettes*, no. 318, p. 30.
345 A. Pétel, 'Templiers et Hospitaliers dans le diocèse de Troyes. Comptes', p. 342.
346 A. Pétel, 'Templiers et Hospitaliers dans le diocèse de Troyes. Comptes', p. 372.
347 A. Pétel, 'Templiers et Hospitaliers dans le diocèse de Troyes. Comptes', pp. 348, 364.
348 A. Pétel, 'Templiers et Hospitaliers dans le diocèse de Troyes. Comptes', p. 294.
349 AN, M1, no. 10.
350 See, for example, A. Pétel, 'Templiers et Hospitaliers dans le diocèse de Troyes. Comptes', pp. 355–356 and others.
351 BnF, ms. lat. 9035, no. 18.
352 BnF, ms. lat. 9035, no. 21.
353 BnF, ms. lat. 9035, no. 21.
354 BnF, ms. lat. 9035, no. 21.
355 BnF, ms. lat. 9035, no. 20.
356 A. Pétel, 'Templiers et Hospitaliers dans le diocèse de Troyes. Comptes', p. 342.
357 A. Pétel, 'Templiers et Hospitaliers dans le diocèse de Troyes. Comptes', p. 372.
358 A. Pétel, 'Templiers et Hospitaliers dans le diocèse de Troyes. Comptes', p. 342.
359 A. Pétel, 'Templiers et Hospitaliers dans le diocèse de Troyes. Comptes', p. 372.
360 Reg. Clem. V, vol. 7, no. 8336, pp. 176. On the case of bishop of Bazas, see Section 2.3.
361 Reg. Clem. V, vol. 5, no. 5018, p. 439.

3 The Council of Vienne and further decisions (1311–1325)

3.1 Council discussions and papal decisions (1311–1312)

Four years after proceedings against the Templars began in the kingdom of France, a Council convened in Vienne in October 1311 to decide on the outcome of the case. The Council fathers were also to discuss organising a new crusade. From Clement V's perspective, this was to be a crucial moment in his pontificate, as he hoped to return Christians to the Holy Land. The conclusion of the Templar trial would have created an opportunity to achieve the main objective of the proceedings, namely the transfer of the Order's assets for the purposes of the crusade. Both goals seemed within reach. However, the reality turned out to be much more complicated.

While the course of the deliberations and discussions of the Council fathers concerning the Templar case and the subsequent fate of the Templar properties is known, the motives behind Clement V's final decisions on both issues, as well as the roles played by the various participants, remain unclear. Furthermore, some of the threads concerning the activities of Philip the Fair's representatives at the Vienne assembly require further investigation and reinterpretation.

Although there was no mention in 1308 of the Council participants taking part in deciding the disposition of the Order's possessions after its eventual dissolution, the pope decided to put the issue up for discussion. Its participants turned out to be not only the Council fathers, but also representatives of monarchs with a special interest in the future fate of the Templar estates. From the outset of the deliberations in Vienne, envoys of James II of Aragon were present, actively seeking to secure their principal's interests and meticulously reporting on the discussions' progress. Their reports, published at the beginning of the 20th century by Heinrich Finke, remain the most important source of information about the negotiations that took place outside official meetings and the opinions expressed by the most influential hierarchs in the pope's entourage.[1] They are all the more interesting because the main task set for the envoys by the king of Aragon was to secure a favourable settlement of the Templar estates. Consequently, most of the conversations they had with the hierarchs attending the Council concerned this very issue.

Interestingly, during the first few months of the Council, only a small delegation representing the king of France was present in Vienne. Guillaume de Plaisians

DOI: 10.4324/9781003742241-4

arrived in the town with a chaplain and two scribes.[2] He was known to have repeatedly represented Philip the Fair in his dealings with the pope on matters concerning the wider affairs of the Church. However, the most important discussions regarding the Templars and the crusade had previously taken place with the monarch.[3] Furthermore, the Aragonese reports contain no information about any activity by Guillaume de Plaisians. This suggests that the French ruler was not significantly involved in the ongoing discussions at that stage and did not intend to exert any influence. This was not to change until spring 1312.

The Aragonese envoys, however, had been asking the pope from the very beginning of the Council about the fate of the Templar properties. They first discussed the matter with Clement V at the beginning of November. At that time, the pope was reluctant to discuss the matter, merely stating that no secular ruler could claim the Order's estates as they belonged to the Church. He added that, at that point, the issue was not the Templar properties, but the future of the Order itself.[4] Initially, the pope asked the Council fathers whether the brothers should be granted the right of defence. While many participants in the discussion were in favour of this solution, Clement V himself strongly opposed it.[5] The discussions were discontinued.

James II's envoys also sought the views of the other prelates on the Templar estates. They repeatedly asked Cardinal Bérenger Frédol about the behind-the-scenes discussions. During one conversation in early November, he advised them that the Aragonese monarch should under no circumstances agree to transfer the estates to the Church, but rather to another order. This was the only way he could retain his rights to them.[6] The bishop of Valencia, Rajmundo de Pont (1288–1312), also attended the meeting. He told the envoys that, in his opinion, the goods would not be given to the king of France or any other secular ruler, as they could be used to fight each other. He predicted that neither the bishops nor the Hospitallers would take control of them, but rather a new Military Order would receive them.[7] This seems to reflect the various ideas discussed by the clergy gathered in Vienne. It also alludes to concerns raised two years earlier by John of Hastings in a letter to Edward II. He suggested that if the king of France had access to the Templar houses in Gascony, he could use them to fight the English. It appears, therefore, that this view was shared by some clerics. The bishop of Valencia's words also show that no serious discussion had yet taken place regarding the disposition of Templar properties, nor had any concrete plans been made. This suggests that the pope had not yet shared his opinion on the subject with the prelates either.

A few weeks later, the situation changed when Clement V initiated the first discussions on the Order's estates. In December 1311, the Aragonese wrote that the pope wanted to know the Council fathers' opinion on the matter.[8] He had already discussed it with the cardinals much earlier. During a conversation with the Aragonese envoys in October 1311, Bérenger Frédol recalled that it had been discussed at a consistory two years earlier. At the time, he himself pointed out that the Templar possessions in Aragonese territory had not been granted for use in the Holy Land, but rather for the defence of the Church and the kingdom's borders.[9]

Other clerics also had the opportunity to comment on this in writing. Guillaume le Maire responded to the papal call for opinions on matters to be dealt with by the

Council. Regarding the matter of the Templar possessions, he wrote only that they should remain at the disposal of the Holy See, and that no secular ruler had the right to take anything from them.[10] This rather enigmatic statement did not contribute much to the debates of the time.

Much more specific was the mention of the future of the Templar properties contained in a crusade memorandum addressed to the Council fathers, written by one of Philip the Fair's closest advisors, Guillaume de Nogaret. Addressing the issue of financing a future expedition, he stated that the Order's movables and income from its estates should be used for organising the expedition and meeting subsequent needs in the Holy Land. However, this sum would be reduced by the costs of holding services in Templar churches, maintaining brothers in prison or elsewhere doing penance, and the expenses of collectors raising funds from the Order's estates. However, before an expedition took place, the money collected on an ongoing basis was to be temporarily transferred to the king of France.[11] This proposal was analogous to the arrangements adopted during the trial. Significantly, Guillaume de Nogaret completely sidestepped the issue of the Templar immovable property. If one considers his memorandum an expression of Philip the Fair's intentions, it suggests that prior to the Council of Vienne, the king had no expectations regarding this issue and that it was not discussed between the French court and the pope.

However, among Guillaume de Nogaret's documents held in the *Trésor des chartes*, there was another letter concerning the future of the Templar estates. It set out arguments in favour of transferring these estates to an existing Order rather than a newly created one.[12] Unfortunately, the author and date of composition are unknown. It is reasonable to assume, however, that it was in Guillaume de Nogaret's archives because such a concept was in line with his position or considered favourable by the French court. This opinion was most likely written down during the Council, when the disposition of the estates was discussed, including their transfer to another Order. Nevertheless, the intended recipient and purpose of this document remain unclear.

Other participants in the Council only commented on the Templar properties during the official discussion initiated by Clement V. In letters dated 12 and 27 December, James II's ambassadors wrote that the pope intended to hand over the estates to the Hospitallers. However, most of the Council fathers favoured the establishment of a new Order in the East. Some wanted the estates to go to the bishops, who would use them for the needs of the Holy Land or according to the donors' wishes. A third group agreed with the pope's position. Clement V announced that the assets would not be handed over to the new Order or any of the existing national Orders, but would instead be given to the Hospitallers, as they would be the only ones capable of protecting themselves from attacks by secular rulers.[13] From the Holy See's perspective, this was certainly an extremely important argument, reflecting the situation and aspirations of the time, and it seems that it determined the outcome.

Over the next few months, issues related to the Templars were not discussed during the official sessions of the Council. However, the Aragonese suspected that it was the subject of unofficial talks between the pope and the envoys of the king of France in February 1312. In the middle of that month, a delegation from Philip the Fair arrived in Vienne. It consisted of the king's brother, Louis d'Evreux, the counts of Boulogne and Saint-Pol, Enguerrand de Marigny and Guillaume de Plaisians. They stayed in the city for 12 days and, according to reports from James II's envoys, discussed with Clement V and five of his closest cardinals how to end the proceedings against the Order.[14] The talks were secret, and the Aragonese only discovered that an agreement had been reached between the participants on matters concerning the king of France's visit to Vienne. James II's envoys suspected that this agreement concerned the Templars. Some researchers share this opinion.[15] However, there are doubts about this. Firstly, following the departure of the French envoys, Cardinal Bérenger Frédol – who had participated in the secret meetings and would usually provide the Aragonese with detailed information on matters of interest to their principal – informed them that it was not yet known whether the Order would be abolished. He also did not provide them with any new information regarding the distribution of the Templar properties.[16] This suggests that these issues were not discussed during the pope's meetings with Philip's envoys at Vienne. Secondly, the composition of the delegation that arrived in Vienne suggests that its purpose was not to conduct serious negotiations, particularly regarding matters concerning the Church. An analysis of nearly 200 embassies from the reign of Philip the Fair, departing from the Paris court in various directions, showed that delegations including so many envoys, such as the monarch's brothers and other members of his council, were usually representative in nature or took part in peace negotiations after wars had ended.[17] Moreover, in the early stages of the proceedings, the king and the pope negotiated directly, primarily in writing. Therefore, it is unlikely that, at the crucial moment preceding the final decision, the monarch would have decided to abandon this established practice. Perhaps the members of the royal council came to the pope to discuss the planned announcement of the start of preparations for a new crusade, Philip the Fair's involvement in it, and other general matters. Thirdly, after the envoys returned to Mâcon, where the king was staying at the time, he sent a letter to Clement V regarding the Templar trial, which may also indicate a lack of binding agreements on this matter. In his letter of 2 March, Philip referred to the continued existence of the Order and the distribution of its properties. He asked the pope to dissolve the Order and declared his willingness to comply with Clement V's decision to transfer the Templars' goods to the Hospitallers or a newly created Order. He emphasised only that the goods should be used for the needs of the Holy Land.[18] Joseph Lecler rightly pointed out that the letter makes no mention of envoys being sent or talks being held.[19] The monarch's comments refer directly to official discussions that had taken place shortly beforehand, involving the Council fathers. The idea of dissolving the Order, rather than condemning it, was a response to the lack of agreement on granting the brothers the opportunity to defend themselves. The concepts mentioned in the letter regarding the further use of the Templar properties also referred directly to the content of the December talks with the prelates. Therefore, it seems that the French envoys who returned from Vienne simply informed the monarch of the difficulties encountered in resolving the matter, rather than reporting on their own negotiations and agreements with the pope.

Researchers have also considered the true meaning of Philip the Fair's letter. Konrad Schottmüller, followed by Favier and Barber, described the king's request to dissolve the Order as an "ultimatum" to Clement V.[20] However, it is difficult to discern any threat in the letter. The significant aspect of the king's words seems to be his suggestion to dissolve the Order rather than pass judgement on its guilt. This idea appears for the first time in the monarch's correspondence with the pope,[21] and seems to refer to the course of the Council discussions. A second key element of the letter is Philip's consent to dispose of the Templar properties according to Clement V's wishes,[22] which confirmed the lack of an idea on how to resolve this matter on the part of the king, as appeared from Guillaume de Nogaret's proposal. Therefore, if the French court had proposed the idea of transferring all the properties to a new Order headed by Philip the Fair's son in any earlier negotiations with the pope, this was no longer an option at this stage.

Clement V replied to the king's letter on 8 March. He merely stated that, should the Order be dissolved, its assets would be used to support the Holy Land while safeguarding the rights of the king and his subjects.[23] This response further confirms that no serious negotiations regarding the distribution of the Templars' goods took place between the pope and Philip the Fair at that time. Furthermore, the pope's letter was similar to the answer he gave shortly afterwards to James II's envoys who had inquired about the matter of properties. He assured them that, although the fate of the Order had not yet been decided, all the rights of secular rulers would be preserved in the event of its dissolution.[24] Therefore, it appears that, at that stage, Clement V attempted to remove secular rulers from the decision-making process regarding the Order's properties, making it clear to them that the final decision rested with him or the Council.

Around the same time, Enguerrand de Marigny arrived in Vienne for the second time. While the exact date of his visit is unknown, it is reasonable to assume that he brought with him the king's letter of 2 March and took Clement V's reply of 8 March. The report of the Aragonese envoys merely states that, during his time in the city, he engaged in lengthy discussions with the pope. However, the envoys did not know what they were about. They suspected that the subject of the discussions was the Templars and, more specifically, the Order's properties. This was supported by the fact that, shortly afterwards, Clement V summoned the Hospitaller priors from France and Provence, with whom he also held talks of an unknown nature.[25] Lizerand and Favier shared the Aragonese's opinion.[26] Nevertheless, if Clement V had wanted to discuss the significant matter of transferring the Templars' goods to the Hospitallers, it seems likely that he would have summoned the Grand Master's representative, rather than the priors of France and Provence. With the latter, he could discuss matters concerning the French Templar properties and related obligations. Later sources tell us that the question of the future settlement between the Hospitallers and the king of France had already been discussed at the Council of Vienne.[27] This issue may well have been the subject of the pope's discussions with the priors, and Clement V may have discussed it with Enguerrand de Marigny.

The chamberlain's visit most likely finalised the preparations for the arrival of Philip the Fair in Vienne. The king arrived in the city with his brothers and a large suite on 20 March.[28] A few days later, Clement V resumed the Council's discussion on how to proceed with the Order. However, this time, the most important question he posed to the prelates did not concern the manner of further proceedings or the issue of granting the brothers the right of defence. Instead, it concerned the possibility of the pope dissolving the Order by his provision.[29] The assembled clergy responded as Clement V had expected, recognising his right to determine the future of the religious community. Consequently, on 3 April, during a solemn public consistory, the pope announced the Order's dissolution.[30]

In the papal bull *Vox in excelso*, which concerned the dissolution of the Templars, Clement V referred to their properties several times. Although the trials did not provide sufficient grounds to condemn the Order as heretical and the Council fathers expressed conflicting opinions on how to proceed, he decided to dissolve the Order by apostolic provision to avoid the complete squandering and destruction of its properties.[31] However, researchers analysing the document usually omit this passage and do not consider it when evaluating the reasons for the papal decision. Instead, they primarily focus on the influence of Philip the Fair and his arrival in Vienne on Clement V's actions. According to this interpretation, the pope ended the proceedings against the prelates' wishes out of fear of the French monarch.[32] However, Clement V explicitly stated his intentions and goals in ending the Templar case. From the beginning of the proceedings, the pope declared his intention to conclude them as quickly as possible, a goal that remained his motivation throughout the Council. The arrival of Philip the Fair only served to hasten the final decision, which was necessary to begin implementing and announcing the plans for the crusade. Consequently, on 3 April, immediately after announcing the provisions contained in the bull *Vox in excelso*, Clement V declared that the king of France and his brothers and sons were participating in the new military expedition to the East. It was to take place within six years. The pope also announced a six-year tithe to be levied on the entire Church for this purpose.[33]

In this situation, a final decision on the Order's properties still needs to be made. The Aragonese envoys reported that Clement V intended to announce his decision on the matter during the next public session, scheduled for four days later.[34] However, this proved impossible, as the pope encountered further resistance from the Council fathers. In a letter dated 15 April, the Aragonese provided an update on the discussions surrounding the matter. Many participants, including French clergy, opposed the transfer of properties to the Hospitallers, favouring the creation of a new Order instead. The envoys also reported that Clement V and Philip the Fair had both tried to persuade the Council fathers to change their minds. They only succeeded in persuading a few French prelates.[35] Thus, the monarch accepted the papal decision regarding the Templar properties and actively supported Clement V's efforts to have it accepted by the entire Council. Interestingly, he did so despite the fact that the majority of his own Council opposed the idea of transferring the properties to the Hospitallers. According to the Aragonese envoys, only Charles de Valois and Enguerrand de Marigny supported this solution.[36] Favier even believed that the royal chamberlain was one of the concept's authors, as evidenced by his activity during the Council and later in England, where he tried to convince Edward II to accept and implement the papal decision regarding the Templar properties.[37] Interpreting Enguerrand de Marigny's role in this way would suggest that the French court imposed a solution that suited them on the pope and the entire Council. However, the Aragonese accounts of earlier discussions about the properties, as well as the correspondence between Philip the Fair and Clement V in March, contradict this assumption. On the other hand, Barber expressed the opinion that it was Enguerrand de Marigny who convinced Philip to accept a solution involving the transfer of properties to the Hospitallers. The researcher described this as an "acceptable compromise."[38] While it is possible that this was the case, the surviving sources do not allow us to say this with certainty.

In a later report, dated 22 April, James II's envoys wrote again about the efforts made by the king and the pope to persuade the mainly French and Italian clergy to support Clement V's idea. Once again, the success was only partial. The impatient pope announced that, although he very much wanted the Council fathers' consent to transfer the Templars' goods to the Hospitallers, he would make his own decision if he did not receive it.[39] This is indeed what happened. Cardinal Bérenger Frédol also informed the Aragonese envoys that Clement V and Philip the Fair had agreed to exempt the Iberian Peninsula from the general provisions relating to the Templar properties.[40] All of these decisions were reflected in the bull *Ad providam*, which was issued on 2 May 1312. In it, the pope emphasised that only the Holy See had the right to decide the fate of the Templars' goods and that the final decision had been preceded by debates with prelates. Consequently, all estates and movable properties belonging to the Order at the time of the brothers' arrest, together with the rights attached to them, were to be transferred to the Hospital. Finally, the pope ordered anyone in possession of Templar properties to transfer it to the new owners, under threat of excommunication and revocation of all Church grants.[41]

It turns out that during the Council of Vienne, as had been the case a few years earlier in Poitiers, it was Clement V who played the leading role in the decision-making process concerning the Templar properties. The English chronicler Walter of Guisborough even stated that the Council did not deserve to be called such, because the pope made all the decisions himself.[42] By dissolving the Order and transferring its assets to the Hospitallers, Clement V was able to raise funds for a crusade, while also achieving his initial intention to merge the two Orders. Some commentators – primarily Italian chroniclers who were consistently critical of the actions of the French king and the pope – claimed that both Clement V and Philip the Fair had been bribed by the Hospitallers or had taken Templar money for themselves.[43] Such comments are, of course, not surprising. The pope's determination to achieve his desired outcomes, coupled with his generosity towards the Hospitallers, may have led outside observers to suspect hidden motives behind the decision to transfer the assets. From a research perspective, however, all these comments must be treated with great caution and primarily viewed as reflections of rumours circulating in various circles.

The bull *Ad providam* was supplemented by other documents concerning the implementation of its provisions and related matters regarding the subsequent use of the properties. The first of these, issued on 2 May, saw Clement V appoint three commissioners for each diocese to supervise the transfer of the properties to the Hospitallers on his behalf.[44] Four days later, the pope announced the contents of the bull *Considerantes dudum*, which addressed the future of the Order's members. He stated that all Templars who had reconciled with the Church were to be provided with maintenance from the income of the former Templar properties. They were to reside in the former houses of the Templars or other Orders.[45] Thus, Clement V imposed a significant burden on the new owners of the properties. Moreover, during the Council, there was discussion about the need to reform the Hospital and extend control over its activities, particularly its finances. This was reflected in subsequent papal decisions. On 29 May 1312, Clement V prohibited the Hospitallers from disposing of any of their properties without the Holy See's consent. This applied to both their existing possessions and the goods taken over from the Templars.[46] This prohibition placed significant restrictions on the Order's independence. In December 1312, the pope went even further. By virtue of the bull *Licet dudum*, he temporarily suspended all the Hospitallers' privileges except the privilege of exemption.[47] In another document, *Dudum in generali Concilio*, dated 31 December 1312, Clement V set out plans to reform the Order. He ordered an assessment of the value of their properties and annual income to determine how many armed men the Hospitallers should maintain in the East. The pope believed that more brothers should be involved in military activities and that their estates should bear a greater burden of the costs. This was intended to prevent the Hospitallers from engaging in unnecessary activities and amassing excessive wealth. To implement this plan, Clement V intended to enlist the help of prelates and secular rulers to oversee the Order's finances. They would all receive statements detailing the expected income and planned expenses of the individual houses. The pope also announced a review of all the Hospitallers' privileges and expressed his willingness to revoke them (except for the privilege of exemption) if they caused any conflicts with other clergy. This was intended as a prelude to a deeper reform covering all areas of the Order's functioning.[48] Therefore, the prospect of acquiring the Templars' wealth was linked to a significant reduction in the Hospitallers' autonomy from prelates and secular rulers. However, given what had happened to the Templars, it seems that the Hospitallers had no real opportunity to protest. They therefore had to accept the grant, which allowed them to continue their activities in the East and strengthen their presence in the Mediterranean, despite the inconveniences associated with the planned reform.

In some respects, the Council was also disappointing for Clement V, as the pope realised that the new crusade had been postponed for so long that he might not live to see his plan come to fruition. For this reason, almost immediately after leaving Vienne, he drew up a document in which he transferred money, probably from the Templars' estates, originally intended for the crusade, to his nephew and allocated the funds for other purposes.[49]

In addition to attempting to reform the Hospital, Clement V was forced to make decisions to enable the implementation of the provisions of the bull *Ad providam*.

To this end, on 16 May, he ordered all administrators, both ecclesiastical and those appointed by secular rulers, to transfer the Templar properties to the Hospitallers within one month of receiving the order.[50] On the same day, the pope sent separate letters to monarchs – including Philip the Fair – as well as to bishops, asking them to assist in the transfer of all properties to the Hospitallers.[51] These documents were intended to officially initiate the process of transferring the former Templar houses. A few months later, doubts emerged regarding their content. They did not take into account reservations about preserving the existing rights of lay people resulting from the Templars' previous commitments. Consequently, on 13 January 1313, Clement V issued a bull correcting the drafting error in the earlier documents. In it, he confirmed all rights related to the Order's properties.[52] All that remained was to await the response of the secular rulers who were involved in managing the Templar properties or having full control over it. Their cooperation was essential for implementing the decisions made in Vienne.

3.2 Settlements between the Hospitallers and Philip the Fair (1312–1314)

3.2.1 The agreement of March 1313 and the king of France's doubts

In the months following the end of the Council, no significant decisions were made regarding the practical aspects of transferring the French Templar properties. However, it is likely that the pope held talks with Enguerrand de Marigny, who was staying at the curia from late April to early June 1312, regarding this matter. According to Favier, the chamberlain was responsible for ensuring that Clement V would not change his mind about the Templar properties.[53] Unfortunately, no accounts from this period have survived that would allow us to reconstruct the content of these discussions. Nevertheless, it cannot be ruled out that the final settlement after several years of administering the French Templar properties, or the details of transferring the goods, were agreed upon. This would certainly have required the agreement of both parties. During Enguerrand de Marigny's stay, Clement V sent Philip the Fair the aforementioned letter requesting assistance in transferring the properties to the Hospitallers. The king replied a little over three months later. In a letter dated 24 August 1312, Philip agreed to the transfer on the condition that all rights to the properties belonging to him or his subjects were preserved.[54] This condition is not surprising, especially given the error made by the scribe, which was corrected by the pope himself a few months later. With Philip's formal consent, direct talks could begin between the Hospitallers and the king regarding the terms of the properties' takeover. On 17 October 1312, Grand Master Foulques de Villaret appointed representatives to oversee the transfer, and these talks began. The delegation was led by Albrecht von Schwarzburg, Visitor of the Hospital in the West, and one of his seven companions was Leonard de Tibertis, Prieur of Venice.[55] Leonard de Tibertis travelled to France to negotiate an agreement on the financial terms of the Templar properties' takeover with the king.

The agreement that formed the basis for subsequent settlements between the French Crown and the Hospitallers was signed on 21 March 1313.[56] Like many sources concerning the trial of the Templars, it has been misread and misinterpreted for hundreds of years, both in terms of its overall significance and the content of individual provisions. It therefore requires detailed re-examination.

The document states that the Hospitallers reached an agreement with the French king regarding the sums owed to him by the Templars in their former role as royal treasurers. Meanwhile, in July 1312, James II's envoy to the papal curia reported that Philip the Fair had demanded reimbursement for the costs of the proceedings against the Order.[57] This was not true, yet this version was repeated by subsequent researchers, who often mentioned the costs of administering the properties.[58] In reality, the trial-related expenses were covered on an ongoing basis by the Templars' commanderies' income, which was not questioned before or after the event, so no additional settlement was required. The same was true of the costs of administering the estates. Earlier documents made no mention of money from the treasury or the final settlement of the royal treasurer, whose duties ceased at the time of his arrest. This issue was not raised during the meeting in Poitiers, nor in any correspondence between the king and the pope, nor in any financial documents or orders issued by the monarch. Therefore, it can be assumed that this issue had not been resolved prior to that. If this were the case, it would mean that some of the money owed to the French crown either remained in the Parisian Temple or ended up in the papal treasury, where the Templars' other financial resources were kept during the trial. However, other theories have been put forward by researchers on this subject. For example, Langlois and Régine Pernoud claimed that Philip's men destroyed the treasury records in 1307 to prevent an unfavourable settlement for the monarch.[59] According to Charles Tranchant, the king falsely claimed that the Templars had embezzled funds belonging to him.[60] In turn, Delisle and Georges Bordonove wrote that the accounting records relating to deposits and loans taken out by the royal family had been falsified.[61] All of these claims are based on the assumption that Philip's financial balance sheet in October 1307 was negative, and that the king attempted to defraud the Hospitallers. While these assumptions are tempting for those seeking evidence of dishonesty on the part of the French court in the Templars' case, they are not supported by the sources.

Researchers also have doubts about the amount that the Hospitallers were supposed to repay to the king of France. The document states that the monarch was owed 200,000 l. t. Anthony Luttrell claimed that Philip the Fair refused to present any documents proving the extent of the debt.[62] In another text, the same researcher wrote that the sum included not only funds from the treasury, but also the costs of managing the Templars' estates.[63] However, neither this source nor any other documents confirm these claims.

Some authors argue that the indicated amount was unrealistic given the king's poor financial situation. In fact, it was Philip the Fair who owed money to the Order, not the other way around.[64] In this context, researchers mention the sums entering and leaving the royal treasury, as well as the various extraordinary loans that the monarch was said to have taken out from the Templars. Older literature most often mentions 500,000 l. t., which the king was supposed to allocate to his sister's dowry.[65] However, Schottmüller emphasised that this loan is not confirmed by any sources and that references to it may be the result of a mistake relating to the Templars' role as royal treasurers.[66] Borrelli de Serres held a similar view, observing that the dowry sum was undoubtedly excessive compared to sums granted to other French princesses at the time. He also mentions the dowry of Philip's daughter Isabella, said to be 18,000 l. t.[67] According to some authors, the monarch also borrowed this amount from the Templars.[68] This information originates from 14th-century English chronicles and, as Brown has pointed out, it is not corroborated by any French or English royal documents.[69]

In the context of the alleged loans made by the king of France from the Templar treasury, a passage from the *Chronicle of Amadi* is sometimes cited, which describes a dispute between the Order's treasurer, Jean de Tour, and the Grand Master, Jacques de Molay. This dispute was caused by the treasurer's independent financial decisions. According to the chronicler, he lent Philip the Fair 400,000 florins (approximately 267,000 l. t.) without the Grand Master's consent, prompting a violent reaction from his superior.[70] However, no surviving accounts from the Templar treasury or royal documents allow this story to be verified.[71] The majority of researchers are sceptical about its veracity, citing other reasons for doubt as well.[72]

Although the references to loans mentioned here seem dubious, another document suggests that the royal family did indeed owe money to the Templars. The 1316 agreement between the Hospitallers and Louis X stated that Philip the Fair and his relatives had not repaid loans taken out prior to the arrest of the Templar brothers.[73] However, the document does not specify the amount of these liabilities. Consequently, it remains unclear whether the sum of 200,000 l. t. specified in the 1313 agreement is accurate or if it should be substantially reduced.

Langlois took a slightly different approach to the issue of Philip the Fair's loans from the Templars. He argued that the monarch did not have to repay them because canon law prohibited the repayment of debts to heretics.[74] It is known that, according to the rulings of Boniface VIII, this was not true, but in any case, they did not apply to the Templars because the Order had not been declared heretical. The question of the settlement of the debts incurred therefore remained open, as evidenced by the provisions of the agreement of 1316.

Returning to the amount demanded by Philip the Fair, unfortunately, we do not have any financial documents that would allow us to verify it in any way. However, Borrelli de Serres's comments shed some light on this issue. He explained that the sum indicated by the royal officials did not equal the deposits in the Parisian Temple but corresponded to the summary of expected revenues and receivables of the royal treasury for a period that had not previously been settled. This period began at the time of the previous settlement on St. John's Day in 1307 and ended with the arrest of the Templars. The author also provided examples of comparable balance sheets from the early 1290s, covering the period from late June to late October. These showed that the Templars owed the king 165,000 l. p. and 102,000 l. p. respectively (206,250 l. t. and 127,500 l. t.).[75] This suggests that the calculations of Philip's officials may have been accurate. Unfortunately, apart from these assumptions, we cannot say anything more on the subject.

If the amount specified in the agreement did not correspond to the actual calculations, at least some of this money could be seen as a ransom demanded by the king of France from the Hospitallers, or as his "spoil." Regardless of whether the monarch's demands were fully justifyed, or whether the amount given exceeded the value of the debt, they do not appear to have caused much controversy. Neither the Hospitallers nor Clement V, who had most likely been aware of them since his meeting with the king in Vienne,[76] protested them. The aforementioned report of the Aragonese envoy from July 1312 also shows that the amount demanded by Philip was known to the papal entourage, who apparently did not discuss it much either. Apart from a brief comment by James II's envoy, there is no other mention of this in the sources. This suggests that the French king's claims were considered justified, or at least that Clement V considered them to be so and presented them as such to the curia.

In addition to detailing the sum owed by the Hospitallers to the monarch, the agreement sets out key terms for repaying the debt. These conditions are often overlooked by researchers, but they were extremely important from the point of view of the Order and affected the actual amount of its liability. Firstly, the agreement stated that the sum of 200,000 l. t. was to be reduced by the value of all goods taken from the Templars' estates by the king's men since their seizure, provided these goods had brought the king any benefit. According to Luttrell, this meant that the Hospitallers renounced all movable property seized after the arrest of the French Templars by Philip the Fair and his officials, as well as the income derived from the estates during the proceedings.[77] However, the money collected from the Templars' commanderies was accounted for on an ongoing basis with the participation of the pope's commissioners. Furthermore, there is no mention of it ever going to the Hospitallers in any document of Clement V or during any negotiations. Therefore, it could not have been the subject of an official agreement between the king of France and the Order. Borrelli de Serres, who also mistakenly assumed that this provision referred to income from seized properties, rightly pointed out that the total amount was certainly much higher than 200,000 l. t.,[78] which would render the terms of the agreement – that the debt would be reduced by sums previously collected from the Templar properties – completely meaningless. Therefore, the above provision must have primarily concerned either movable property that had fallen into the hands of the king's officials and not been returned, or immovable property that the king used for his own purposes. Examples of the former could include the cross-mentioned in Philip's will, which belonged to the Templars.[79] However, this is only speculation, as the document does not indicate how or when it came into the monarch's possession. The agreement probably included the Order's headquarters in Paris, which Philip continued to use as a treasury throughout the proceedings.[80] It is possible that there were more cases like this, and that the provision in the treaty reducing the Hospitallers' obligation referred to these.

The above solution demonstrates that both parties to the agreement were aware that the king benefited from certain Templar assets, and that the monarch himself did not evade responsibility in this regard. While we cannot assess the fairness of the accounts that Philip's officials were to present, they certainly influenced the final amount owed by the Order.

The second condition concerned the enforcement of debts owed to the Templars. It was agreed that debts known to or easily discoverable by the king's officials would be credited towards the Hospitallers' payments. This meant that Philip was willing to instruct his officials to recover unpaid debts, thereby relieving the Order of this responsibility. While this provision was beneficial to the Hospitallers in that they did not have to seek repayment of at least some of the debts owed to the Templars themselves or collect such a large sum from other sources as provided for in the agreement, it complicated and prolonged the settlement process considerably in the following years, generating further costs. Nevertheless, it appears that the Hospitallers had no better alternative at that stage, and the solution adopted should be viewed as an act of goodwill by the French court.

The remaining amount after deductions was to be repaid in six instalments over three years. The first instalment was due on All Saints' Day, just over seven months after the agreement was signed. It was therefore assumed that, within this timeframe, it would be possible to compile an inventory of the Templars' goods seized by the king's men, and to recover or at least estimate the amount of debt owed to the Templars, which could then be credited to the Hospitallers. The latter also needed time to gather the remaining sum. This was, therefore, a fairly short deadline for fulfilling all obligations. Perhaps Philip's officials already had preliminary calculations. Otherwise, it would be difficult to imagine how all the provisions could be implemented.

Repaying the sum specified in the agreement would ensure that the Hospitallers would be exempt from any financial claims by the French monarchy. The settlement process was expected to be relatively straightforward. Another success for the Order was certainly the fact that, shortly afterwards, the process of transferring the French Templar properties to them began.

However, events occurred in the spring of 1312 that could have hindered or even halted the efforts to take over the properties. Shortly after the agreement between the king and the Hospitallers was signed, Albrecht von Schwarzburg arrived in France. As well as supervising the transfer of properties, he was also tasked with introducing necessary changes to the Order's functioning and representing the Grand Master in his dealings with the pope and secular rulers.[81] Philip the Fair considered this intervention in the affairs of the French Hospitallers to be too far-reaching, and he openly objected to it. Lizerand and Barber concluded that the king's reaction was aimed at preventing the Order from effectively taking over the Templar properties.[82] However, when it came to the Hospitallers' operations in France, it seems that the monarch consistently maintained the position he had presented several years earlier during discussions on financing the Order's military expedition, which culminated in the conquest of Rhodes. At that time, he had defended the independence and importance of the French Hospitallers, refusing to contribute money to a venture in which they were insufficiently represented. Now, he did not want a dignitary from Rhodes to decide the fate of the Templars' assets in his kingdom. Nor did he want the new acquisitions to contribute more to the Order's central treasury than assets from other countries did. Considering the repeated reluctance of other monarchs to hand over control of the Templars' possessions to the pope and the Hospitallers, the French king's attitude is hardly surprising.

Philip expressed his dissatisfaction with the actions taken by Albrecht von Schwarzburg in his correspondence with the pope. In response, in a letter dated 8 June 1313, Clement V explained that the Grand Master's representative had come to France only to request overdue *responsiones* from the French Hospitallers, which were urgently needed by the brothers in the East. Without these sums, efforts to recover the Holy Land were hindered. Albrecht von Schwarzburg also intended to present gifts to the king and his son Louis before departing.[83]

This explanation apparently satisfied Philip, as within three months he ordered his officials to follow Albrecht von Schwarzburg's instructions to the French Hospitallers regarding their obligations to the French crown.[84] The monarch no longer questioned his role and apparently saw no obstacles to continuing the process of transferring the Templar properties to new owners, which had begun a few months earlier.

3.2.2 Transfer of Templar properties to the Hospitallers

The agreement of 21 March 1313 was implemented almost immediately. Just seven days after it was signed, Philip the Fair issued an order to transfer all properties belonging to the Templars in France to the Hospital. This was formally confirmed by the Parliament of Paris on the same day.[85] The document was supplemented by further instructions concerning various aspects of the process of taking over the properties. On 11 May, the king addressed judicial officers, informing them of the 28 March decision and ordering them to support the Hospitallers' efforts to recover their property and protect the Order from abuse.[86]

Philip's orders were supplemented by instructions from the general administrators regarding the details of transferring control of the estates. In a letter dated 5 May, the administrators ordered local officials to ensure that their agents and tenants provided the necessary assistance to the Hospitallers, including welcoming them into the Templars' houses, providing them with food, handing over all necessary documents, and the money needed to repair damaged properties and buildings.[87] This entitled the new owners to take over part of the income from the period when their predecessors' estates were under the control of the king's and pope's commissioners. Depending on the condition of the properties and their associated farms, these sums could be quite substantial. For example, the minutes of the transfer of the house of Valcanville to the Hospitallers in May 1313 noted that the buildings and mills were severely damaged and in need of extensive repairs,[88] which would have required significant financial investment. In this situation, the financial support provided to the Order was undoubtedly crucial to the redevelopment of the Templars' houses. This solution was likely not the sole initiative of Philip the Fair and the administrators of the estates, but rather an agreement made in advance with the pope. Perhaps it was one of the topics discussed by the French king's envoys at the Council of Vienne.

News of the king's agreement with the Hospitallers and royal consent to the transfer of French possessions was communicated to Clement V immediately. As early as 27 March, the envoy of Philip the Fair reached Avignon and conveyed the news to the pope. The following day, the pope expressed his satisfaction with the French king's decision to Albrecht von Schwarzburg, contrasting it with the attitudes displayed by other monarchs who were openly opposed to the implementation of the papal decision of Vienne.[89]

The royal administration quickly began distributing and implementing the order to transfer the estates. On 20 April, Louis, Count of Champagne, issued letters ordering the transfer of properties to the Hospitallers in accordance with Philip the Fair's will.[90] A few days later, the bailiff of Amiens gave a similar order to his subordinate provosts.[91] Meanwhile, the Hospitallers were permitted to publicly announce the monarch's decision.[92]

Around April and May, the order reached the bailiffs and seneschals. Jean Raybaud provided a detailed description of the information flow process in the Priory of Saint-Gilles. An analysis of the documents shows that the Hospitallers played an active role in the process. Leonard de Tibertis delivered Philip the Fair's letters and the Parliament's *arrêt* to six local seneschals. Then, he appointed a special representative to oversee the process of taking over properties in the area on behalf of the Grand Master. This representative was Raymond d'Olargues, the lieutenant of the Prior of Saint-Gilles. He was to be accompanied by two other brothers. In early May, the three of them went to the seneschal of Beaucaire and Nîmes, who solemnly handed over control of the Templars' houses to Raymond d'Olargues. This was symbolised by placing a gold ring on his finger.[93] It is conceivable that the Hospitallers undertook similar actions throughout the kingdom. As a result, the process of actual takeover of the estates by their new owners began shortly thereafter. Information about its course is derived from various types of reports concerning the implementation of royal orders in different parts of the country,[94] as well as inventories compiled on this occasion.[95] These documents show that the transfer was completed by the end of July at the latest. All documents refer to dates in May and June. However, it is possible that the takeover process was not completed everywhere within these two months because, in an order issued in mid-July, Philip the Fair demanded its completion before the Feast of Saint Mary Magdalene, 22 July.[96] This deadline appears to have been binding for officials throughout the kingdom, as reflected in the final settlement of the general administrators, which was drawn up at the king's request.[97] Of course, this does not mean that the new owners took control of all components of the estates they received at that time. In an order dated 15 September 1313, the general administrators once again instructed the local officials to transfer all real estate and land under their control to the Hospitallers, along with the relevant documentation.[98] The rest of the document shows that the delays were related to properties that had previously been leased. This is why the order specified measures are to be taken to enable the new owners to take full control of the estates. Despite these problems, which were most likely mainly formal, available sources indicate that the Hospitallers officially took possession of the Templars' properties throughout the kingdom in spring 1313.[99] This was in stark contrast to the situation in most other countries, whose rulers had not yet agreed to the transfer. Only in Cyprus did the new owners officially take over the properties at the end of 1313. Elsewhere, the process of taking over the properties began much later and lasted much longer. On 15 July 1313, the pope wrote to the king of Sicily, asking him to transfer the Templar properties to the new owners. He also criticised the king's reluctance to do so, contrasting it with the thoroughness with which the king of France had transferred all the properties located in his territories to the Hospitallers.[100] However, Clement V's appeal apparently had no effect, as in September 1317 and again in December 1319, John XXII repeated his calls on the same matter. Despite these interventions, however, the Hospitallers failed to take over all the local estates.[101] In England, after the Council of Vienne, Edward II continued to reward his allies with grants of Templar properties and appropriated their furnishings.[102] On 1 August 1313, he officially prohibited the Hospitaller prior from taking over the properties of the dissolved Order in his kingdom, claiming that executing the papal order would be detrimental to the crown, even if it came to pass. However, he changed his mind at the end of November of the same year, and it was only then that the transfer began in England, a process that was to last for the next dozen or so years.[103] In early December 1313, the count of Provence consented to the Hospitallers taking over the Templars' estates.[104] Later still, decisions were made in the German states and Polish lands. There, the process began in 1314, but some princes delayed the transfer of properties for many years.[105] On the Iberian Peninsula, too, the rulers retained control over the Templar properties for several years after the process began. This situation was due to the provisions of the bull *Ad providam*, which stated that the fate of the properties was to be decided by subsequent arrangements.[106]

Therefore, it seems that Philip the Fair's position on implementing the decisions made at the Council of Vienne differed from that of other monarchs, most of whom were reluctant to relinquish control of the Order's properties. Nevertheless, researchers are generally sceptical of the French king's intentions. Many also believe that transferring the French Templars' properties was difficult and not completed by 1313. Barber stated that the French Hospitallers had a much greater problem with the takeover of the estates than other countries did.[107] Lea, on the other hand, believed that Philip retained control of the Templar properties and income until his death.[108] Schottmüller and Demurger expressed the opinion that Philip and his officials created obstacles to delay the transfer of properties to the Hospitallers for as long as possible.[109] Demurger went even further in one of his works, writing that some properties remained in the king's hands and never reached its new owners.[110] Jocelyn N. Hillgarth and Sylvia Schein expressed a similar opinion.[111] This view aligns with Tranchant's perspective from the 1880s, which posited that some properties were not transferred to the Hospitallers despite receipts being issued for it.[112]

Some of these claims do not refer to any specific source material. Others are based on references to individual commanderies that may be misinterpreted without in-depth analysis and consideration of the broader context. This is the case with the commandery of Toulouse, often cited as an example of the difficulties faced by the French Hospitallers. The literature repeatedly states that the commandery did not pass into the hands of its new owners until 1326.[113] However, this is a misunderstanding, clarified by a careful reading of the sources.

The protocol for the transfer of property in Toulouse to the Hospitallers is dated 8 May 1313.[114] Renaud de Saint-Ouen's report mentions settlements related to the acquisition of local estates in the same year.[115] However, the new owners quickly transferred part of the property in Toulouse and Larramet to Raymond de Soubrian on a life lease, as evidenced by the 18 December 1313 agreement signed by Albrecht von Schwarzburg.[116] Later sources indicate that a similar agreement was made with Bernard de Roquenégade for the property in Vaour belonging to the same commandery.[117] Eleven years later, in the spring of 1324, the Hospitallers decided to regain full control of the house and their other properties there. They asked the king to intervene, justifying their desire to terminate the agreement by pointing out that it contradicted the papal ban on selling assets formerly belonging to the Templars, which had been issued in 1313.[118] As a result, Charles IV's officials temporarily seized the property. A little later, in May 1325, they reached a settlement in which the Hospitallers took full control of all the claimed property. In return, Raymond de Soubrian was to receive one-third of the income from the house in Toulouse, and Rémi Barbeau, who had represented him during the dispute, was granted the right to continue occupying one of the rooms.[119] As a result of this agreement, in July 1326, the house in Toulouse returned to the hands of the Hospitallers.[120] This final decision was not related to the prolonged transfer of the Templar properties but rather to the decisions of the new owners, who, immediately after taking over the house, decided to lease it.

A similar situation occurred in the case of at least a dozen other French houses, which, shortly after being taken over by the Hospitallers, were temporarily transferred to the Genoese merchant Antonio Pessagno as part of a debt repayment agreement.[121] The Order had apparently been unable to settle its debts for a long time, as the properties remained in the hands of the creditor until 1350. Jean-Marc Roger believed that the Hospitallers only took them over from the Templars at this time.[122] However, this is not true, even though the Order did not collect income from at least some of these properties for several decades.

Demurger, in turn, after analysing documents concerning the administration and takeover of Templar properties by the Hospitallers in the county of Auxerre, came to the conclusion that the local estates most likely did not pass into the hands of their new owners until 1316. This assumption was based on the count of Auxerre's confirmation of ownership of all the Hospitaller houses, including those previously belonging to the Templars, issued in January of that year.[123] However, the researcher did not mention that the document also refers to *amortissement*, which seems crucial for its proper interpretation. The *amortissement* issue was not always directly related to the actual takeover of Templar properties by the Hospitallers. This concerned, among others, the commandery of Montmorency, for which the payments due by the right of *amortissement* were made only a few years after its acquisition, i.e., in 1318.[124] Another example is a document issued by Charles de Valois in May 1323, in which the count confirmed the Hospitallers' ownership of properties in the Chartres area and released them from all obligations relating to these properties, which had been transferred much earlier. However, the Order had to pay 670 l. t. for this privilege.[125] Such delays in settling obligations relating to the

Hospitallers' acquisition of properties were probably due to the Order's financial difficulties at that time. At the same time, it is known that the Hospitallers took over the Templar houses in the county of Auxerre around the same time as in other parts of the country. As early as 1314, the commandery of Saulcy was headed by a new commander.[126]

However, not all French Templar houses and estates fell into the hands of the Hospitallers. One example is the house in Montricoux, which the Templar accuser Esquieu de Floyran leased in 1312.[127] This was not his only acquisition from that time period. Surviving documents show that, in June of 1313, Philip the Fair ordered the sale of some of the property belonging to the commandery of Lacapelle-Livron to pay Esquieu de Floyran an annuity.[128] This was likely compensation for his role in exposing the Order's crimes. Before reporting the Templars to the king of France, Esquieu de Floyran met with James II of Aragon. James II did not believe the reports of Templar heresy but promised that, should they prove true, Esquieu de Floyran would be paid 3000 l. and an annuity of 1000 l.[129] A similar promise was likely made to him by the king of France as well. Philip used the Templar estates to carry out the arrangement, suggesting that the pope knew about the matter and had to agree to it. However, the Hospitallers opposed him. Just a few months after part of the commandery of Lacapelle-Livron's property was sold, a representative of the Order claimed compensation for it.[130] His complaint went to the king, but the outcome is unknown. The case of the house of Montricoux was more complex. It remained in the hands of Esquieu de Floyran for almost a decade. However, since he failed to properly account for his income, it was taken from him in 1322.[131] Around the same time, the Hospitallers claimed it. According to the report by Renaud de Saint-Ouen, the estate in Montricoux came under the control of Alphonse of Spain, the king's lieutenant in Languedoc, at the will of the Order and the king.[132] This indicates that the estate was the subject of dispute and, until the dispute was resolved, it was to be managed by the royal official. According to available documents, the house was still in his possession in 1325, as were other estates in the area that were once owned by the Templars and were also the subject of dispute proceedings.[133] The dispute was likely resolved before 1332, as a document from that year states that the Hospitallers exchanged the Montricoux estates for lands in Douzens and Goyran.[134]

Another exception was the Paris headquarters of the Templars. As previously mentioned, it continued to house the royal treasury after the arrest of the Order's members.[135] This remained the case after 1313, even though other houses had already been transferred to the Hospitallers.[136] Presumably because of its importance to the monarch, it was considered one of his acquisitions, which, under the agreement of March 1313, were to remain with him, while reducing the debt of the Hospitallers. This situation continued until 1317, when the former house of the Templars was transferred to the widow of the king's deceased brother, Clementia of Hungary, by decision of Philip V, in exchange for the palace in Vincennes, which had previously been granted to her by her husband. However, the document stated that, if he could not dispose of the Templar house, the king was to transfer the Hôtel de Nesle to the queen instead.[137] This suggests that the king's right to the former headquarters of the Order was being challenged at the time. It can be assumed that the Hospitallers claimed it. This version of events is confirmed by the later involvement of Pope John XXII in the matter. In a letter dated 17 November 1319, the pope asked Philip V to transfer the Parisian house of the Templars to the Hospitallers.[138] He repeated his appeal in April 1320.[139] This most likely resulted in some kind of agreement, as the royal treasury – part of which was still stored in the Templar house – was moved to the Louvre in its entirety later that same year.[140] However, this did not mark the end of the matter, as the house remained in Queen Clementia's possession until her death in 1328. It was only then that it was handed over to the Hospitallers.[141]

The fate of the Templars' estates in Montricoux and Paris seems to confirm the view that the French court obstructed the transfer of properties belonging to the dissolved Order or even prevented it entirely. However, in both cases, we are dealing with exceptional situations that can be explained by the circumstances at the time. Consequently, they cannot be regarded as representative of the monarch's policy, which generally permitted the transfer of properties to new owners in spring 1313.

The preserved records of the Templar houses being taken over by the Hospitallers, along with the inventories drawn up at the time, provide insight into how the transfer was carried out. The procedure for transferring control over individual properties was generally similar: a royal official arrived at the site together with an envoy of the Hospitallers and several or a dozen or so witnesses and handed over the keys to the entrance and all buildings to the new owner.[142] The next step was to draw up an inventory of all the assets. In southern France, in Larramet and Larmont, these inventories were recorded during the official transfer of properties and included in the protocols.[143] The situation was similar in Toulouse.[144] However, the record of the transfer of the house in Lectoure only mentions that the Hospitaller representative drew up an inventory.[145] In contrast, the document concerning the transfer of the house in Fleurance on the same date completely omits this issue.[146] Inventories were also drawn up in Poitou at the time of transfer, as evidenced by the dates of the preserved documents and the persons mentioned within them. The inventories from Ansigny, Bret, Cenan, and La Lande-de-Parthenay were drawn up by the same notary who was involved in the transfer of all three houses to the Hospitallers.[147] In preparing them, it is known that account was taken not only of information gathered on the spot, but also of the accounts of the estate's tenants at the time. At Ansigny, account was also taken of the previous regional administrator of Poitou.[148] The Sours inventory, which detailed not only the house's furnishings but also its income, was drawn up entirely based on the main tenant's (*major firmarius*) accounts. He took an oath on the Gospel before the document was written down to confirm his honesty.[149] In contrast, the inventory at Fleurance was drawn up by an envoy of the new owners. At Joigny, the furnishings of the chapel were listed by the new commander of the Hospitallers. He was accompanied by his confreres and envoys of the prevost of Saint-Florentin.[150]

Thus, it appears that there was no single, detailed procedure for the transfer of estates applied throughout the country. In fact, the procedure only differed slightly, which did not affect the final outcome or the documents produced. All the available property transfer protocols show that local officials followed the instructions of the king and general administrators to some extent. They make no mention of any conflicts or obstacles in the implementation of the transfer; on the contrary, they prove that the whole process went smoothly. However, not all scholars have interpreted them in this way. Tranchant, who published the minutes of the transfer of estates in the Poitou area at the end of the 19th century, concluded that because only some of the houses in the region were included in the document, the others did not come into the hands of the Hospitallers. This was reportedly due to the malice of Philip the Fair, who had not consented to the transfer of all the estates.[151] This is a far-fetched assumption that is not supported by other sources. Referring to this issue, Roger expressed his conviction that, in addition to the existing protocol, others were most probably created that did not survive to the present day.[152] This is the simplest and most obvious explanation. Due to the large number of houses, the handover process may have been managed by different people or staggered over time, resulting in separate documents.

Researchers have not raised any concerns regarding the inventories created in connection with the transfer. These inventories demonstrate the care taken by those involved in the procedures to document the components of the transferred estates as accurately as possible. In this context, Jochen Burgtorf has drawn attention to the composition of the group of witnesses involved in drawing up the inventory of the house of Toulouse. This included a merchant and a "master of the arts." Given the rich furnishings of the chapel, their presence was probably linked to a desire to estimate the value of the items being inventoried as precisely as possible.[153] This demonstrates that both parties involved in the process were committed to conducting it fairly and honestly, at least on a formal level. Of course, this applies only to the few surviving documents. However, apart from the cases of the houses in Paris and Montricoux mentioned earlier, we have no other documents that directly contradict such a transfer.

When the estates were taken over, the Hospitallers also dealt with the initial formalities relating to the acquired rights. For instance, the minutes of the handover of the house in Valcanville state that the inhabitants took an oath of allegiance to the new landowner.[154] However, most of the issues dealt with concerned the lease of houses and the property belonging to them. This was the case at La Caillebotière in Brittany, for example, where the Hospitaller envoy Jean de Châlons officially agreed that the previous tenant Fraval should continue to derive income from the farm. The royal sergeants involved in the procedure then informed Fraval that he could lodge a formal protest with the local bailiff if he had any objections to the solutions adopted.[155] A few days later, in Lanouée, the procedure was similar, except that Jean de Châlons asked the tenant himself whether he had any objections to the transfer of the estate.[156] However, the presence of tenants apparently caused some complications or doubts, because in September 1313, the general administrators issued new instructions on how to deal with cases where Templar estates remained in their hands. This stipulated that the new owners were to receive a lease from the overseers. However, all dues for the earlier period, including the last incomplete year, were to be collected by the royal collectors.[157] This order was not always obeyed, and in some cases the Hospitallers took over the money from the tenants. Renaud de Saint-Ouen's report mentions several such cases. The commissioners' findings show that brother Jean de Montboucher collected 10 l. t. from the lease of the commandery of Magnac's estate for the year 1312, but did not hand the money over to the king's officials.[158] Meanwhile, brother Jean de *Affariis* collected 20 l. t. from the Plagne estate, which had been wrongfully seized by *Andus* de Rochefort for five years. The commissioner stressed that this had already occurred following an agreement between the Order and the king (it is unfortunately not known which king), meaning that the Hospitallers had to return the entire sum.[159] Even more money was seized by the commanders of La Villedieu, Castelsarrasin, and Toulouse, who received 100 l. t. from Davin de Roaix in 1313. They too had to hand over the entire amount.[160] It is difficult to say whether such situations were the result of a misunderstanding that the general administrators were supposed to clear up in their September order, or whether the Hospitallers were deliberately abusing their position. It is also impossible to assess the scale of this problem.

At the time of taking over the property, the Hospitallers also exercised their rights, granted in the royal order, to finance necessary repairs from the income of individual houses. On 8 June 1313, Raymond d'Olargues ordered the new commanders to ask the collectors or tenants of the estates to give them the money they needed.[161] Renaud de Saint-Ouen's report notes that the tenant of the houses of Foulventour and La Bussière-Rapy in southern France actually transferred 33 l. t. to the Hospitallers.[162] While this was probably not an isolated case, it is difficult to determine how widespread this practice was, or to what extent such financial transfers enabled the restoration of farms to a usable condition.

Following the formal takeover of the Templars' properties by their new owners, the process of recovering individual assets and the various receivables associated with them began. From the Hospitallers' perspective, this was an extremely challenging process, requiring significant commitment at central and local levels. As early as December 1312, Clement V asked Philip the Fair for assistance with this process.[163] The monarch and his administration attempted to facilitate this in various ways from the outset, although organised and systematic action had not yet been established at this stage.

On 11 May 1313, the king ordered judicial officers to permit the Hospitallers to take possession of all properties previously belonging to the Templars, including any that had been illegally appropriated.[164] Philip later issued more detailed orders and became personally involved in resolving certain issues. In a letter dated 20 June, Philip the Fair informed the seneschal of Carcassonne that he had taken the Order under his protection and therefore requested that the official show him favour when settling disputes relating to the former Templar estates.[165] This letter was probably in reference to proceedings that had been initiated shortly beforehand concerning a dispute between the Hospitallers and the chapter of Carcassonne over lands that had been illegally seized after the arrest of the Templars.[166] A few months later, the king intervened in the case once more. After the chapter appealed against one of the *juge mage*'s decisions concerning the proceedings, the king instructed the seneschal of Carcassonne to deal with the case quickly, disregarding the defendants' protests.[167] Further orders indicated an awareness of the difficulties involved in recovering the Templar estates. In August, the king again ordered judicial officers to ensure that all Templar properties unlawfully seized after their arrest was transferred to the Hospitallers.[168] At the same time, Philip directed that officials grant the new owners a deferment on debts relating to the estates they had taken over, and that they settle cases involving the Hospitallers as quickly as possible. They were also to ensure that the Templar estates were not used for any purpose other than the Holy Land.[169] This final instruction suggests that the Hospitallers were taking action that did not align with the monarch's intentions regarding the transfer of the estates. However, the details of these improper practices and how the king's officials would have counteracted them remain unknown.

The monarch also enlisted the help of his administration to recover money owed to the Templars. On 20 August, he ordered the seneschals and other judicial officers to implement Albrecht von Schwarzburg's order. Albrecht had recently ordered the commanders of the Hospitaller houses in France to repay 20,000 l. p. (25,000 l. t.) to the king from the debts owed to the Templars rather than taking it from their estates' income.[170] In November, Philip the Fair had already explicitly ordered the sergeants of the seneschal of Carcassonne to ensure that all debts to which their predecessors were entitled were transferred to the Order.[171]

As we lack the necessary resources, we cannot assess how the royal orders were implemented or what assistance the royal administration provided in the process of taking over former Templar properties. It is possible that the royal administration supported the Hospitallers in the same way as the bailiff of Rouen, who issued them with a document, most probably in 1313, containing a detailed list of all the estates and annuities formerly belonging to the Templars of the commandery of Saint-Etienne-de-Renneville.[172] This letter was addressed to the new owners and could have formed the basis for claims against debtors and individuals who had taken possession of some assets.

Regardless of the involvement of the royal administration in the process of recovering properties, a representative of the pope also participated. While still in Vienne, Clement V appointed Bérenger d'Auvergne as his special envoy to oversee the Hospitallers' effective acquisition of properties in individual countries.[173] On 23 April 1314, Philip the Fair issued a letter of safe conduct for him.[174] In July of that year, at the Order's request, the papal commissioner ordered parish priests in the diocese of Carcassonne and the province of Narbonne to publish excommunication sentences for those who had not yet returned Templar properties to the Hospitallers or summoned them to appear before him and explain why they had failed to do so.[175] A few months later, on 23 January 1315, he officially ordered all clergy and laypeople who were still in possession of Templar property for whatever reason to hand it over to the new owners.[176] A month later, he appointed regional commissioners to assist him in enforcing this order.[177] Thus, more and more people became involved in the process of recovering the assets of the dissolved Order.

The Hospitallers needed help in taking actual control of the properties granted to them, not only because some of it remained in the hands of unauthorised persons, but also because of misappropriation attempts that had already occurred during the transfer. For example, the prior of the monastery of Saint-Sépulcre in Sambrières tried to seize some of the property belonging to the commandery in Troyes through fraud. He asked the king to confirm his rights to the property by providing false information (*falsitate suggesta et eritate tacita*). He then used the letter he received from Philip the Fair to dispute the Hospitallers' right to take over the former property of the Templars. The Order lodged a complaint, however, and in July 1314, the monarch ordered the bailiffs of Chaumont, Troyes and Sens to settle the dispute. An investigation was conducted, which was decided in favour of the complainants. The prior of Saint-Sépulcre appealed against the decision in Parliament of Paris, acting against both the Hospitallers and the officials who had issued the judgement. The final decision is unknown, but it is known that, without waiting for it, the prior filed another complaint with the bailiff of Sens. In response, the Hospitallers appealed to the king again, who ordered the new proceedings to be suspended.[178] What happened next is unknown. However, this was certainly not the only attempt to exploit the confusion surrounding the transition period, during which the new owners were just getting acquainted with the actual state of their properties and were gathering the relevant documents.

When the estates were transferred to the Hospitallers in 1313, the process of settling with the previous administrators, tenants, and collectors also began. Unfortunately, there are no documents that mention the practical side of this procedure. However, we can assume that it was organised similarly to the earlier settlements, which were presented annually to controllers appointed by the king and the pope. The only information we have from the available sources is that, in December 1312, Clement V permitted Philip the Fair to appoint two officials to audit the accounts of the Templar administrators alongside his envoys.[179] Later documents, however, show that the previous general administrators, acting on behalf of the king – namely Guillaume de Gisors, Guillaume Pisdoe, and Rénier Bourdon – were involved in these procedures.[180] Presumably, therefore, the pope also delegated this task to the general administrators he himself had appointed. However, there is no mention of them in the surviving sources.

From the outset, the settlement process was accompanied by various problems and misunderstandings. Some administrators wanted to hand over their accounts to the Hospitallers, even though the Order was not entitled to accept them. Bernard Rasseur de Narbonne refused to hand over the house in Douzens to the new owners because they refused to accept the documents he presented.[181] Arnaud IV de Canteloup, the archbishop of Bordeaux, who had controlled the Templar estates in his diocese for some time, claimed as late as the early 1320s that he had submitted his report to the Hospitallers.[182] Many administrators and collectors did not submit accounts at all. Gillon Barillat, the provost of Coulommiers who administered the commandery of Coulommiers, did not submit any documents, and after his death his heirs relinquished the inheritance to avoid paying their dues to the sovereign.[183] Similar cases can be found in later documents concerning the actions of royal commissioners enforcing old debts related to the Templar cause. These referred to cases carried out several, or even a dozen years after the proceedings against the Order had concluded. They refer to administrators and collectors who, for various reasons, failed to account for their actions during the trial period, and this was later charged to their heirs.[184]

In addition to checking the documentation, the settlement controllers (formerly the general administrators) were also responsible for enforcing the resulting claims. An example of such action can be seen in the proceedings carried out at their behest against tenants who had misappropriated movable property from a house in Ruetz. The auditors' envoy and the former administrator of the property conducted an investigation, which confirmed the allegations. Based on this, the amount owed by the tenants was established by deducting from the value of the stolen equipment the amounts they had spent on repairs that the farm required.[185] There were certainly many such situations requiring additional findings and explanations. If any irregularities were found, or if the manager or tenant declared expenses for necessary farm repairs, this would have required verification each time. This made the settlement process lengthy and required the involvement of more people than the papal and royal auditors.

Due to the numerous obstacles of this nature, it was extremely challenging, if not impossible at that stage, to compile a comprehensive summary of the financial outcomes of the management of the Templar estates by royal and ecclesiastical administrators over several years. Later documents published in *Inventaire des anciens comptes royaux* by Robert Mignon reveal that the former general administrators, Guillaume Pisdoe and Rénier Bourdon, did not prepare a final report until September 1325. This was based on the five annual accounts submitted earlier and had been substantially revised and supplemented. It is also known that, at that time, the accounts of administrators from across the kingdom were kept in the royal treasury in separate books for each bailiwick and seneschalship. However, it is unclear whether these were annual reports or were filed at the end of the proceedings. The list of collected financial documents also mentions an inventory of the Parisian Temple, as well as a separate account most probably based on this inventory. Unfortunately, neither of these sources has survived to the present day, so we know virtually nothing about their contents. The reference to the summary drawn up by the general administrators only indicates that the final figure was 1494 l. 16 s. 7 d. p. (1868 l. 9 d. t.).[186] This is a surprisingly low amount for the administration of Templar houses throughout the kingdom over five years. Therefore, it is probably not the total amount collected from the Order's estates over several years, minus the administrative costs. However, if we assume that income from the estates was sent to Avignon on an ongoing basis and that part of the income for the final year was transferred to the Hospitallers for necessary repairs to buildings and equipment, this figure becomes entirely plausible. Any other explanation is difficult to substantiate.

Apart from the final financial outcome of the proceedings, the condition of the Templars' movable property remains largely unknown. It is known that some of this property was sold before the houses were leased out. Researchers have also written about organised theft of the properties. Du Bourg stated that, immediately after the Templars' house in Toulouse was seized, the king's men took all the money and valuables stored there.[187] Several other works mention that Philip the Fair seized all the cash from the Paris treasury of the Templars, as well as the furnishings of their houses and chapels.[188] Of course, it is well known that the scale of abuse and theft was enormous. This has been discussed in earlier chapters. However, the surviving documents do not indicate that these actions were inspired by the monarch and organised from above. Furthermore, inventories compiled at various stages of the process and following its completion demonstrate that misappropriation did not occur universally. For example, the inventory of the commandery of Sainte-Eulalie from January 1308 included chalices and a precious cross that were part of the chapel's furnishings.[189] A similar list from Payns, dating to September 1308, also mentions silver objects and liturgical books.[190] All nine of the 1313 inventories currently at our disposal also mention various types of valuables. These include silver and gilded chalices, as well as ivory and crystal objects[191] and liturgical books.[192] The chapel in Joigny also contained a reliquary holding a fragment of Saint Margaret's arm.[193] In turn, the inventory from Toulouse lists two crosses, each containing two fragments of the True Cross: one gilded and decorated with 45 coloured stones,[194] and the other made of silver and decorated with 17 stones.[195] Although the inventory from the Parisian Temple has not survived, other sources tell us that, in 1311 – almost four years after the Templar properties were seized by the king's officials – there were still valuable reliquaries and other items. These items are mentioned in the minutes of the proceedings conducted by the papal commission in Paris at that time. Wishing to verify information provided by a witness regarding a mysterious head worshipped by the Order's members, the commission asked the administrators of the Templar treasury in Paris to find the object in question. Guillaume Pisdoe, Guillaume de Gisors, and Rénier Bourdon found a silver-plated reliquary and showed it to the commissioners.[196]

According to the inventories, some of the houses contained items that predated the proceedings and belonged to the previous occupants. In Bret, for example, a Templar mantle was discovered that must have been there since at least 1307.[197] In Larmont, meanwhile, an altar cushion bearing the Templar symbol was found,[198] and in Toulouse, an altar cloth bearing a red cross.[199] This shows that even those items of equipment that were not needed by the administrators, tenants, or new owners were not removed from these houses within a few years. Furthermore, comparing the 1313 inventories with those from 1308 reveals that the furnishings of the various houses were generally quite similar. This suggests that there was no systematic plundering, as some researchers have suggested, and that at least some of the houses retained their furnishings virtually intact. Therefore, the outcome of several years of managing the Templars' houses was not entirely negative, and the Hospitallers did not simply take over empty, ruined buildings, as one might assume from some literature on the subject.

3.2.3 ***The Hospitallers' new obligations***

In the order concerning the transfer of Templar properties to the Hospitallers, dated 28 March 1313, Philip the Fair emphasised that the new owners were to be responsible for financing the brothers' imprisonment and the inquisitorial proceedings against them.[200] This stipulation was a logical consequence of acquiring control of the properties, and it would become one of the foundations for subsequent settlements.

It seems that when the transfer of the Templar properties was completed, the Hospitallers actually fulfilled their obligation. The 1314 accounts of the Order's treasurer in Toulouse provide interesting information on this subject. These accounts cover the period from 13 March to 25 July of that year – four and a half months – and contain a detailed list of expenses related to the maintenance of eight imprisoned Templars. Unfortunately, the document is significantly damaged, making part of the text impossible to read.[201] Despite this, the document enables us to reconstruct the financial activity of the Hospitallers in southern France after they acquired the Templar properties.

The accounts indicate that 9 or 18 d. t. per day was paid for the prisoners' meals.[202] It is unclear what this amount depended on. It is possible that the lower rate applied to sergeants and the higher rate to knights and chaplains.[203] However, it cannot be ruled out that 9 d. t. was allocated for brothers who had not been absolved and 18 d. t. for those who had, as was done in the bailiwick of Senlis in 1310. Unfortunately, the source text does not provide any information on this subject. Significantly, both amounts were lower than those recorded in the bailiwick of Senlis accounts (15 or 20 d. t.). Given their financial difficulties, it can be assumed that the Hospitallers wanted to reduce the costs of maintaining the Templars. However, it is also possible that different amounts were paid for the maintenance of prisoners in different parts of the country. Unfortunately, we have no sources that would allow us to solve this mystery. No other accounts from this period have survived for comparison purposes, nor are there any documents indicating whether the Hospitallers decided independently on the rates of payment for prisoners at that stage, or whether someone else made this decision. The question, therefore, remains unanswered.

In addition to the amounts allocated for the daily maintenance of former Templars, there were other expenses. The accounts specified the sums paid for clothing, additional allowances, and other necessities. However, due to damage to the manuscript, the total amount of these payments is unknown. Only the total amount allocated for these purposes can be indicated. This equated to 12 l. 1 s. 6 d. t.[204] Without knowing the details, it is difficult to compare this with the amounts spent on similar purposes as specified in the accounts of the bailiwick of Senlis.

The accounts of the Hospitaller treasurer also reveal how much the Templar guards were paid. The document mentions a rate of 18 d. t. per day paid to four people, which amounts to 6 s. t.[205] However, it is difficult to compare these rates with the salaries of the guards from the bailiwick of Senlis because different amounts were paid to the guards and their servants there, whereas here there is no such division. Nevertheless, this sum was closer to the wages of servants in the bailiwick of Senlis than to those of the guards. As with the previous rates, it can be assumed that these amounts were reduced in relation to the Hospitallers' difficult financial situation.

In addition to the standard costs of imprisoning the Templars, the Hospitallers also covered expenses related to the ongoing inquisitorial proceedings. The Order's treasurer included in his accounts the sums paid in connection with the Templars' participation in the council of Carcassonne, where they were probably sentenced.[206] The document listed the costs of paying the guards who transported the brothers and accompanied them during their stay in the city, as well as the cost of renting the carriages used to transport the seven prisoners.[207] Unfortunately, it is not possible to specify the amount of individual expenses or the total cost of this journey.

The total amount allocated for the Templars' maintenance and travel during the period covered by the settlement was 231 l. 5 s. 8 d. t., which was slightly over 10% of the total revenue indicated in the document: 2180 l. 16 s. 10 d. t.[208] Unfortunately, it is impossible to use this information to assess the proportions for the whole year, or to determine how this amount compared to other costs incurred by the Hospitallers at that time. It is also unclear for how long the Order paid sums relating to the Templars' imprisonment in Toulouse. Following the conclusion of the inquisition proceedings, the circumstances of at least some of the Templars undoubtedly changed. However, it is not known when this happened or what exactly happened to the brothers.

Even after the proceedings against the Order had concluded, the Hospitallers were still obliged to pay for the maintenance of the former Templars, regardless of their individual situation. Some of the brothers who were absolved and released from prison were required to remain in the houses that had been taken over by the new owners. They were also granted pensions.[209] Those remaining in prison were also to be supported from the income of the former Templar estates.[210] It is unclear who decided on the amounts allocated to both groups. Papal documents concerning France suggest that bishops were responsible for dealing with this matter.[211] However, a letter from John XXII has also been preserved, which suggests that the monarch was involved in this issue. The pope explained to Philip V why he had refused to confirm the pension (5 s. p. per day [6 s. 3 d. t] and 6 l. p. [7. l. 5 s. t.] per year for clothing) granted to a certain Templar by Philip the Fair.[212] It is difficult to say why the king made this decision, or whether it was an isolated incident or within his remit at some point. In this context, one of the remarks made by a Templar during the proceedings before the papal commission in Paris in 1310 comes to mind. Pierre de Bologne explained to the commissioners why some of the brothers had made incriminating statements against the Order, suggesting that some had been promised substantial lifetime pensions in return.[213] If this were the case, determining the amount of such pensions would most likely have been the monarch's or his officials' responsibility. However, as there are no sources to confirm Pierre de Bologne's words, this is merely supposition.

Apart from the aforementioned letter from John XXII, other sources from the time of his pontificate clearly show that the issue of providing for the former Templars was already exclusively a matter for the Church. There were various ambiguities and doubts associated with this issue. Guillaume Mollat cited the example of questions posed by bishops to the pope regarding the obligation to pay for the food and other needs of brothers imprisoned in the archdiocese of Sens but originating from the province of Narbonne. It was agreed that the money for their maintenance should come from their home province, not the province where they were imprisoned.[214]

Another unknown factor is the pension amount of the French Templars. The only information on this subject from the first years after the end of the trial that we currently have is the aforementioned reference to an individual rate set by Philip the Fair. Therefore, it is unclear whether general or regional decisions were made at that stage or if different pensions were set for different Templars. By way of comparison, in the British Isles, the amounts were the same for all members of the Order, whereas elsewhere they varied according to rank. In Aragon, some brothers were even able to negotiate their pensions.[215] However, we do know that the cost of supporting the former Templars was such a burden to the indebted Hospitallers that, in December 1318, the pope ordered it to be reduced. To this end, he appointed special commissioners to operate in individual dioceses.[216] Six months later, the lists of income and financial burdens of the commanderies of Picardy recorded that the former Templars living there received 17 s. 6 d. t. per week and 6 l. 5 s. t. for clothing per year.[217] It is possible that these were already reduced rates, but this cannot be confirmed. When compared with the sums allocated for the brothers' maintenance in the bailiwick of Senlis accounts from 1311 – 11 s. 8 d. t. per week for food and other necessities, and a maximum of 2 l. t. per year for clothing – it becomes clear that the total cost of maintaining the former Templars was much higher during the trial, amounting to several tens of thousands of livres per year. Even after the rates were reduced, this was undoubtedly a substantial sum for the French Hospitallers.

In addition to the costs of maintaining the brothers living in the former Templar houses, the Hospitallers also covered the maintenance costs of members of the Order serving prison sentences. However, in this case, we have no information about the applicable rates or the number of prisoners. The only thing we can be sure of is that there were fewer and fewer Templars serving prison sentences over time, and thus the associated costs decreased. The same was true of the brothers who remained at liberty. Some abandoned the monastic life a few years before the end of the proceedings, while others simply died.[218] Some former Templars also refused to transfer to other Orders as expected under the provisions of the bull *Considerantes dudum*, choosing instead to live a secular life. In such situations, they lost their allowances.[219] Conversely, there are also cases of brothers who were captured after the proceedings had ended,[220] as well as those who returned from captivity in the East several years after the Order's dissolution.[221] However, such situations were certainly rare.

Former Templar houses taken over by the Hospitallers also housed Templar sisters. The 1319 expense reports of the commanderies of Picardy refer to the allowances they received. The amount depended on their social status. For example, a sister from a wealthy family received 12 s. 6 d. t. per week and 100 s. t. per year for clothing, whereas a sister of lower origin received 15 l. t. per year for all expenses. In two other houses, the pension was 10 s. t. per week and 75 s. t. per year for clothing.[222] Of course, these individual details do not allow us to draw any general conclusions. We do not know how many sisters were staying in the Templars' houses before the brothers were arrested, nor how many remained there afterwards. However, the costs associated with their presence were probably not too burdensome for the Hospitallers. It can be assumed, though, that the indebted Order tried to limit these costs, as it did with the sums paid to former brothers.

3.3 Further settlements and the recovery of property (1315–1325)

3.3.1 Louis X's decisions and the new agreement (1316)

After Philip the Fair's death, his sons and successors continued to settle accounts with the Hospitallers. Their actions and decisions in this matter have not yet been analysed in depth. Nevertheless, literature contains some far-reaching opinions on their motives. Some researchers believe that they attempted to seize as much of the former Templar properties as possible and extract the largest sums of money from their successors as they could, imitating their father's actions or perhaps going even further.[223] These claims require verification.

Louis X, who ascended the throne in November 1314, made several important decisions during his brief reign concerning the transfer of Templar properties and settlements with the Hospitallers. One of his first decisions regarding this matter was to honour Philip the Fair's wish to transfer some of the money owed to him by the Order under the terms of the agreement of 1313 to Charles, Count of La Marche. On the eve of his death, the late king ordered that 140,000 l. t. of the Hospitallers' debt be transferred to his younger son, having previously spent the dowry money he had received for his wife Blanche, daughter of Mahaut d'Artois.[224] After Louis X confirmed this decision, Charles immediately set about enforcing the debt. He took advantage of the fact that the efforts to calculate the Hospitallers' debt, involving the king's men, had not yet been completed at that time. As the Order was unable to estimate the total sum seized by Philip the Fair's officials after the arrest of the Templars, Louis X's envoys regained access to some of the property. Charles took this opportunity to order them to confiscate some of the Hospitallers' income and equipment. Leonard de Tibertis complained about these actions to the king, who, in June 1315, decided to return everything that had been taken from the Hospitallers despite his brother's protests.[225] The monarch ordered that all money not yet transferred to the count be returned to the Order. He promised the Hospitallers that he would pay the outstanding sum from other sources.[226] This does not mean that Louis X renounced repayment of the Hospitallers' debt, but it was to be repaid exactly as stipulated in the 1313 agreement. This undoubtedly demonstrates the king's favour towards the Order, even in a dispute involving his brother, and contradicts researchers' claims that Philip the Fair's successors had dishonest intentions.

Louis X's subsequent decisions regarding the recovery of Templar properties and funds still in the possession of unauthorised people also demonstrate his commitment to supporting the Hospitallers in matters relating to the transfer of assets. On 12 June 1315, Louis X confirmed the powers of the papal commissioner Bérenger d'Auvergne and his companion Bertrand Castelli to supervise the transfer of properties to the Hospitallers. He instructed them to compel all Templar debtors and those who had unlawfully seized Templar properties to return it.[227] On 26 July,

Louis X issued a further order addressed to all judicial officers, instructing them to assist the papal envoys in recovering the Templar properties and transferring them to its new owners.[228] Therefore, at this stage, the responsibility for locating and seizing the property destined for the Hospitallers primarily rested with the papal envoys, while the royal officials were merely to support them. It is easy to see, however, that the latter's role was crucial in practice, as they were the ones who could take action against debtors and usurpers locally. Without their participation, the papal commissioners' mission would have been very difficult, if not impossible, to carry out.

Subsequent orders by Louis X clarified and supplemented the scope of tasks entrusted to Bérenger d'Auvergne and Bertrand Castelli. On 26 August 1315, the king ordered them to prosecute anyone who had participated in the seizure of Templar properties, and, on that occasion, had taken possession of any movable or immovable property. They were also to prosecute those who had not repaid debts incurred with the Templars before their arrest, as well as dishonest tenants and collectors who had contributed to the depletion of the Order's properties. The order applied to the entire kingdom.[229] In a subsequent letter, the monarch added that, in cases where someone refused to return goods in their possession despite intervention, searches could be conducted and coercion used.[230] Any recovered components of unlawfully acquired Templar property were to be given to the Hospitallers.[231] In the order of 26 August, the king also instructed tenants who had damaged or misused the properties to restore it to its original condition.[232] This decision supplemented earlier solutions, whereby the Hospitallers could receive funds for essential repairs from the income collected by designated collectors from the houses of the Templars. Unfortunately, it is unclear how these solutions were intended to work or to what extent. In any case, the solutions were certainly beneficial to the Hospitallers, demonstrating the monarchs' awareness of the problems the new owners encountered when taking over the estates.

Unfortunately, we have no sources that would allow us to trace how Louis X's decisions were implemented or what effect they had. Until the king's death, i.e., within about a year of the orders being issued, we can only guess that no serious investigations were carried out and that few, if any, goods were recovered. No documents have survived that testify to Bérenger d'Auvergne's actions at that time, nor any that confirm the monarch's July 1315 order to judicial officers reached its recipients. However, we know that proceedings concerning the financial settlements of former tenants were underway at that time, overseen by Guillaume de Gisors, Guillaume Pisdoe and Rénier Bourdon. Evidence of this comes from an order dated 4 January 1315, which concerns the enforcement of a debt from dishonest tenants of a house in Ruetz. This was the result of a previous investigation.[233]

Regardless of the French ruler's decision and the possible actions of his officials, the Hospitallers themselves attempted to resolve property issues and recover all the money owed to them. In February 1315, the Grand Master instructed Pierre de Chaudeyrac, his newly appointed lieutenant in the Priory of Navarre, to compile a list of all Templar properties in the dioceses of Rodez, Mende, Carcassonne and Albi, in order to claim the seized and unrecovered assets.[234] The Order's representatives were also involved in various negotiations and proceedings relating to unlawful appropriation of properties and ongoing conflicts dating back to the time of the Templars. In some cases, they resolved disputes concerning the properties and money of their predecessors amicably. In others, they sought help from local authorities or resorted to court rulings. One example of successful negotiations conducted by the Hospitallers regarding property issues was the case of the l'Échillais estate in the diocese of Saintonge. Geoffroi Goumar received the estate as a fief from his cousin Aimery Goumar and then joined the Templar Order, transferring his lands to them. Aimery refused to remove the feudal encumbrances to which he was entitled until the properties were taken over by the Hospitallers, and the new owners could not agree to this. Ultimately, however, both parties reached an agreement: in June 1316, the Order sold the estate back to Aimery for 1000 l. t.[235] This transaction was confirmed by the king in October 1317.[236] However, it is unclear whether the pope, who had previously prohibited the Hospitallers from disposing of their properties, also gave his consent. There is no source information on this subject. It is reasonable to suspect that the Order sought the consent of the pope for the transaction beforehand, which would have further complicated the already difficult process of taking over all the properties belonging to their predecessors.

Taking over the Templars' property of Sainte-Vaubourg in Normandy proved to be a much more complicated process. In this case, intervention from the king's officials was necessary. Preserved documents show that one local official prevented them from using the Templars' former meadow, while others made it difficult to collect rent from Rouen residents. There was also a problem with gaps in the documentation taken over after the dissolution of the Order. It can be assumed that the Hospitallers encountered such obstacles on various occasions. The mayor of Rouen demanded that the new owners provide proof of the annuity grant, but they were unable to do so. Consequently, the Hospitallers lodged a complaint with Pierre de Hangest, the bailiff of Rouen, who, at the beginning of 1315, ordered the local viscount to assist the Order in enforcing all its rights. He pointed out that the city authorities should not require the Hospitallers to present documents confirming grants made to their predecessors, since this was often impossible.[237] In many cases, these were privileges granted so long ago that appropriate confirmation would have been difficult to find. Nevertheless, this intervention did not resolve the issue of the rent, as other local officials continued to make similar demands of the Hospitallers. In 1319, the bailiff of Rouen provided them with *vidimus* of confirmation of all grants made to the Templars in Normandy by John Lackland in 1199.[238] This was probably intended to finally clarify all formal doubts. Also dating from 1319 is Philip V's order allowing the Hospitallers to use and sell part of the forest belonging to the commandery of Sainte-Vaubourg, as it had been under the Templars.[239] It seems, therefore, that even such a minor matter had to be dealt with by the monarch himself.

Miguet primarily viewed the documents related to this issue as evidence of local officials' intentional obstruction of the Hospitallers' takeover of the Templar properties.[240] While this interpretation of the events is justified, it does not consider all aspects of the matter. Alternatively, it could be seen as an example of royal officials helping the Order to overcome the formal difficulties it faced, thus fulfilling Philip the Fair's order of August 1313, which was later repeated by Louis X and probably also by Philip V.

There were also disputes so difficult to resolve that they had to be dealt with by the Parliament of Paris. On 5 April 1315, for example, it issued an *arrêt* concerning the conflict between the Hospitallers and the chapter of Péronne over prebends transferred to the Templars in the 12th century. Following the arrest of the Order's members, control over them was temporarily transferred to the king's officials. After the trial, the bailiff of Vermandois ordered their transfer to the Hospitallers, a decision that the chapter protested against on the grounds that the previous grant had been cancelled at the time of the Templars' dissolution. The Parliament ordered that the transfer of income to the Hospitallers be suspended, instead remaining in the hands of the king until the case was finally resolved.[241] Once again, the Hospitaller Order was in dispute with other clergy, who were using the Templars' trial as an opportunity to gain financial benefits or reduce their own obligations. The outcome of the dispute is unknown, but, considering the course of similar proceedings mentioned in earlier chapters, it is likely that it was not resolved quickly. Similar conflicts between the Hospitallers and the chapters of Saint-Quentin and Noyon did not end until 1321.[242]

Despite the extent to which the state apparatus was involved in recovering all the Templars' assets, and the concessions made by Philip the Fair and Louis X, it soon became clear that the Hospitallers' financial situation did not allow them to repay their debts to the monarch under the 1313 agreement. Consequently, discussions were held regarding new solutions, resulting in an agreement being reached on 14 February 1316.[243] According to Luttrell, the real reason for signing the agreement was the absence of many of the documents necessary for the final settlement, which complicated and prolonged the negotiations between the Hospitallers and the French court.[244] However, this hypothesis is not supported by the available sources.

The introduction to the signed agreement outlines the Hospitallers' financial obligations at that time. Firstly, it references a sum of 200,000 l. t., which was the subject of an agreement made three years earlier. This suggests that it had not yet been repaid. However, it is unclear whether the Order had repaid any of the debt or was unable to make any payment. Secondly, the Hospitallers undertook to pay Louis X the sum of 60,000 l. t. for expenses relating to the Templar brothers, their properties and protection of their interests. Therefore, contrary to the belief of some researchers,[245] this was not a matter of the costs of the trial, but rather of financing the maintenance of former Templar members who were still in royal prisons, as well as covering the expenses related to various proceedings accompanying the takeover of their properties and the enforcement of debts owed to them. The document notes that these costs exceeded the income from the houses taken over by the Hospitallers at the time, demonstrating the difficult situation of the Order. Conversely, it would be unreasonable to expect the king alone to cover such high costs, given that he had already involved the state apparatus in helping the Hospitallers to recover all Templar properties.

The next part of the agreement set out a new method for settling debts owed to the monarch. Firstly, the Hospitallers renounced one of the points of the agreement with Philip the Fair, which stipulated that all Templar assets seized by the king's men during the proceedings, and which had benefited the king, were to reduce the Order's liability arising from the Parisian treasury settlement. Under the new agreement, all property that had fallen into the hands of royal officials during the proceedings was to go to Louis X. This provision suggests that the relevant calculations had not yet been completed at that time. The adopted solution thus made it easier for both parties to finalise the settlement.

According to the second point, the Hospitallers waived the repayment of all loans taken out by Philip the Fair, his wife, Louis X, and his brothers from the Templars before their arrest. As previously mentioned, the total value of these loans is unknown. The only puzzling fact is that they were not mentioned in the 1313 agreement. This most likely means that, at that time, it was planned to resolve this issue in the same way as other debts. However, it was subsequently decided to include them in the general settlements, probably to simplify the process.

The next point stipulated that the Hospitallers would give the king two-thirds of the sums returned by the former administrators of the Templar estates after they had presented their final accounts. As the administrators were still in the process of submitting documents, which would then be verified by representatives of the pope and the monarch, the amount of money to be paid to the royal treasury was still unknown. However, since the income of Templar houses was accounted for annually during the settlement process, at this stage it could only be money collected in the incomplete final year or sums not settled by the administrators in previous years for some reason. Furthermore, it is known that the income from the previous year reduced the sums transferred to the Hospitallers when they took over the Templar houses in 1313. Therefore, the decision did not concern very large sums of money.

The fourth point concerned debts owed to the Templars that had been incurred prior to the brothers' arrest. The monarch was to take over two-thirds of all outstanding financial obligations, as well as the same proportion of assets remaining under the control of people outside the Order. However, if any of the debtors were found to be insolvent, the Hospitallers would not be held responsible for their debts. However, if any property or money owed to the Templars fell into the hands of the Hospitallers – as is known to have happened – they were obliged to transfer the appropriate sums to the king.

Another provision stipulated that two-thirds of all outstanding lease payments for Templar properties, from the time of the brothers' arrest until the properties were transferred to the Hospitallers, should be paid to the king. As with previous decisions, this required investigations to determine the amount of unpaid liabilities, followed by their enforcement. However, these issues were not mentioned in the agreement. Nevertheless, it can be assumed that royal officials were responsible for implementing all these provisions. They participated in the process of settling accounts with the administrators and tenants, in which the Hospitallers were not involved.

The final clause of the agreement related to the transfer of two-thirds of all Templars' movable property acquired by the Hospitallers. The division was to be based on inventories drawn up at the time of the transfer, meaning it only concerned items remaining in the houses and farms once the process was complete. Where equipment had been sold prior to the estates being leased, there was probably nothing left to divide. However, 19th-century literature stated that the king had seized all the Templars' movable property, which was obviously untrue. This has already been discussed by Borrelli de Serres, who highlighted the precise wording of the provision.[246]

As part of the settlement regarding movable property, it was decided that the new owners would have the right to purchase any necessary equipment, animals or furniture at a price determined by people selected by both parties. The money to pay off the resulting liabilities was to come from one-third of the remaining movable property belonging to the Hospitallers. If this sum was insufficient, the remaining liabilities were to be paid from other assets belonging to the Order. However, this solution did not apply to vessels, vestments, or liturgical books that constituted the furnishings of individual houses and were necessary for celebrating Mass and services. The planned division also did not apply to items and animals acquired by the Hospitallers after they took over the properties.

All these provisions introduced an extremely important change in the settlements between the king and the Order, consisting of removing from the debtor the obligation to seek the financial resources necessary to repay his liabilities. Although this was not explicitly stated in the agreement, it appears that from that moment on, the king's officials were to be responsible for actions aimed at recovering individual components of the Templars' assets, and the amount of money that would ultimately go to the royal treasury depended on the effectiveness of their efforts. This solution was beneficial for the Hospitallers (from their perspective, it effectively closed the settlement with the French crown) and, at the same time, risky for the monarch. It did not guarantee that all the amounts indicated in the first part of the agreement would be recovered. One may question the accuracy of the estimates of the additional costs to be incurred by the Hospitallers, as indicated in the document, but all we know on this matter is that both parties agreed to them. In any case, the agreement was intended to conclude the transfer of the Templar properties, but it turned out to be much more difficult than expected. However, the consequences of the new decisions had to be faced by the successor of Louis X, who died in June 1316.

3.3.2 The agreement with Philip V (1318)

The provisions of the 1316 agreement began to be implemented only at the end of the year, by which time Philip V had already ascended the French throne. On 22 December, he appointed three officials, led by Guillaume Clignet, to recover all Templar property still in unauthorised hands, as well as any income or debts owed to the Order which had not yet been repaid. In addition, they were tasked with collecting copies of inventories from people involved in procedures relating to the seizure of Templar properties and the management of their assets. They could appoint two assistants in each seneschalship and bailiwick.[247] The second part of the order reveals that inventories of Templar houses, compiled at various times, had not previously been gathered centrally, which is surprising given that these documents could have formed the basis for all settlements relating to the management and transfer of properties.

The commissioners were also responsible for implementing the agreement between the Hospitallers and Charles de Valois. Apparently, the Order had certain obligations relating to the Templars' estates towards the count as well, as the signed agreement was similar to that concluded with the king. It is known that the Hospitallers had reached an agreement with Charles de Valois by mid-December 1315. They undertook transferring the meadows of Chelles and an annual rent of 1200 l. t. to him.[248] However, this agreement was probably not implemented, which is why a new agreement modelled on those reached between the Hospitallers and Louis X was decided upon. Under this new agreement, the count was to receive one-third of the property and money due to the Order. In May 1317, Charles de Valois instructed his treasurer, Jean Billouart, to take possession of the money and other assets of the Templars on his behalf, as specified in the agreement with the king.[249] This mission was probably too demanding for one person, however, because a few months later, in February 1318, Bernard Raymond Caldier received the same order, but only in relation to the south of France.[250] Later documents indicate that, in subsequent years, both envoys fulfilled the duties assigned to them.[251] However, they did not participate in any investigations relating to the Templar properties, only collecting the sums due to the count from the royal commissioners responsible for implementing the provisions of the 1316 agreement.[252]

In July 1317, Philip V issued further orders detailing the envoys' role in implementing the agreement's terms. These concerned the transfer of one-ninth of the goods and money collected to Charles de Valois, as well as the procedure for collecting rent from the former Templar estates.[253] The commissioners were to collect the two-thirds due to him from houses that had been leased continuously since the proceedings, directly from the tenants. Where the new owners had removed the tenants or sold part of the farms or land, the sums due were to be collected from the Hospitallers' other income.

In the spring of 1317, Guillaume Clignet began to carry out the king's orders. In April, he appointed five commissioners to act on his behalf and recover all debts owed to the Templars throughout the kingdom. In his instructions, he informed them that he would provide documentation to serve as the basis for their initial actions. It is unclear whether this referred to confirmations of existing obligations towards the dissolved Order that had been found and handed over to royal officials by the Hospitallers, or to some other documents that had previously been sought by the king's people. Either way, gathering the relevant materials from across the kingdom was certainly a very demanding and engaging undertaking. It is likely that Guillaume Clignet only had access to some of the documentation. The commissioners were also expected to conduct their own investigations and send all money collected to Paris on an ongoing basis.[254]

Later, Guillaume Clignet appointed other officials who, in accordance with royal instructions, were responsible for conducting proceedings in individual bailiwicks and seneschalships. Little is known about how they fulfilled their missions. Only a few documents from the first half of 1318 survive, describing the procedures followed by the envoys. In March of that year, for example, two sergeants who had been entrusted a few months earlier by Guillaume Clignet with the mission of seizing two-thirds of the income from the lease of Templar estates in the seneschalships of Périgord and Quercy[255] summoned the commanders of all the houses taken over by the Hospitallers to Cahors to determine their dues jointly. In the presence of the judge and other witnesses, the commanders informed Arnaud de Gironde, a money changer and expert chosen by the parties, of the sums they were to pay under the agreement with the king. The monarch's envoys accepted the calculations, and the relevant sums were paid promptly.[256] Transferring the debt from La Chapelle de Demigny in Burgundy was equally straightforward. A receipt issued by the king's envoy in January 1318 has survived.[257] However, the Hospitallers were unable to raise the necessary funds everywhere. In such cases, the commissioners participated in the sale of some of the movable property and the leasing of land, in accordance with their instructions. An example of this occurred in May 1318 in Pézeans, where the Hospitaller commander presented the value of the property and income of the house to the king's envoy. He then stated that the resources at his disposal did not allow for the repayment of the debt. Consequently, they sold and leased part of the property together with the commissioner. Only then could the latter collect the appropriate amount.[258] Such situations undoubtedly prolonged the settlement process. Given the Order's general problems with repaying its debts to the French monarchy, it can be assumed that such situations occurred quite often.

The royal commissioners were also responsible for collecting outstanding debts owed to the Templars. The enforcement proceedings they conducted were often complicated, frequently requiring the king's personal intervention. One example is the case of Gilles and Jean de Compiègne, who owed the Templars over 4000 l. t. On 16 March 1318, Philip V ordered Guillaume Clignet and the other commissioners appointed to collect Templar debts to enforce them as quickly as possible. The money collected was to be used to repay the monarch's debts to others. In November of that year, Guillaume Clignet instructed his envoys to carry out enforcement proceedings against the heirs of the two debtors. In March 1319, the king issued a similar order concerning the same case, specifying the amount to be collected. Further letters from Philip V relating to these proceedings were dated 25 June, 2 July, and 17 July, and concerned details of further settlements. The monarch's orders were finally carried out on 29 July.[259] It therefore appears that collecting this one debt alone required almost a year and a half of effort involving the king. Although no other documents from these proceedings survive, it is easy to imagine that many of them involved similar complications and required the involvement of the state apparatus at various levels.

There were also other kinds of problems. Some debtors tried to exploit the fluid situation surrounding the transfer of the dissolved Order's assets to avoid paying their debts. In December 1317, Philip V issued an order concerning the collection of outstanding debts for the lease of Templar houses. This order emphasised that nobody had been exempted from repaying their debts to the Order, despite some claiming that they had been granted special concessions in this matter.[260] The king's letter indicates that this was not an isolated incident, but rather a broader issue.

The pope also became involved in the settlement between Philip V and the Hospitallers. His correspondence reveals that both the Order and the French ruler kept him updated on the issues arising from the implementation of the agreement with Louis X. In a letter dated 18 May 1317, John XXII requested that Philip V instruct his officials to cease harassing the Hospitallers residing in former Templar estates due to the Order's outstanding debts to the monarch. Royal envoys were forcing the Order to repay its debts in Parisian currency, even though they should have allowed it to pay in the local currency. The pope also wrote that the king's people were seizing the property of the Hospitallers if they failed to make their payments. He demanded that this practice be abandoned, believing it to be detrimental to the cause of the Holy Land.[261] We do not know how Philip V responded to this request, but it is possible that he requested the reform of the Order at this time. He wanted to introduce changes to the French province of the Hospitallers, enabling them to repay their outstanding debts.[262] Consequently, in July 1317, John XXII met with the Order's dignitaries and reformed its structure, dividing the French province into three and determining their respective shares in repaying existing debts.[263] In a letter dated 3 August, in which he informed the monarch of the decisions taken, he also requested his assistance in finding a solution that would enable the Hospitallers to repay the agreed sums. He drew attention to properties seized by the king's men who had stopped paying the workers' wages. Consequently, the necessary work was not carried out, resulting in the houses falling into disrepair. Therefore, the pope requested solutions that would allow normal management and contribute to the Order's debts being repaid more quickly.[264] Clearly, John XXII was aware of the difficulties faced by the French Hospitallers, yet he also recognised the importance of their fulfilling their obligations to Philip V.

The pope did not stop at reorganising the French province of the Order. He also became involved in settling accounts between the Hospitallers and the monarch. He intervened in the dispute between the Order and royal officials regarding the payment of leases on Templar estates, among other things. In accordance with the provisions of the 1316 agreement, Philip V's commissioners demanded that the new owners pay for the entire year in which they took over the estates. This was in line with the previously adopted principle that tenants did not pay in full for the first year of use of the farms, a principle that was offset by payments for the final year. Consequently, the Hospitallers were required to pay their dues for months during which the estates were already in their possession, and in some cases, were no longer leased. The Order did not agree with this solution and, in the second half of 1317, lodged a complaint with Parliament in Paris, reporting this to the pope at the same time. At the end of September that year, John XXII once again defended the French Hospitallers, asking Philip V to abandon a practice that he believed to be contrary to the agreement concluded with Louis X.[265] A few weeks later, Parliament issued a ruling on the matter. It confirmed the king's right to collect his share of the previous year's revenues, except in cases where the land had not been cultivated or there had been no tenants on the estate.[266] While this solution imposed certain restrictions on fee collection, it was certainly not satisfactory for the Hospitallers. The pope also protested strongly against it in a letter dated 5 December. He considered the requirement to pay the full year's dues to be unlawful and called for this solution to be abandoned.[267] However, the king of France apparently did not heed this appeal because, on 12 January 1318, he issued an order instructing compliance with the Parliament's ruling, stipulating that all sums collected contrary to its wording should be returned to the Hospitallers.[268]

As well as solving general problems, John XXII was also engaged in resolving local conflicts. One example of this was his involvement in the dispute over *jus patronatus* concerning one of the churches in Normandy, which had been taken over by the Hospitallers from the Templars. When the new owners nominated their candidate for rector, a knight whose father had originally given the church to the Templars objected. He claimed that, following the dissolution of the Order, it should be returned to him. However, the royal officials to whom the complaint was referred ruled that the right of patronage in the duchy of Normandy belonged to the king and seized the church. Following this decision, the Hospitallers once again turned to the pope for help. John XXII sent a letter to the king, demanding the immediate return of the church to the Order.[269] In later letters, he also requested the intervention of the bishop of Bayeux.[270] It is not known how this dispute ended, nor whether the pope took any further action in this regard. Nevertheless, this demonstrates his determination to defend the interests of the French Hospitallers, even in minor matters.

It was perhaps John XXII's subsequent interventions that prompted Philip V to open negotiations with the Hospitallers regarding an amendment to the 1316 agreement. These negotiations culminated in the signing of a new agreement on 6 March 1318.[271] This document has also often been misread and misinterpreted as two earlier agreements.[272] Like them, it therefore requires reanalysis.

The source indicates that the Hospitallers initiated the agreement. It states that the 1316 agreement was made to repay the 260,000 l. t. owed by the Order to the king. However, disputes arose between Philip V's people and the brothers over the division of house equipment, making the implementation of its provisions problematic. For this reason, the Hospitallers proposed new terms to facilitate mutual settlements.

It was agreed that all that had been received by either party under previous agreements, up to the time of signing this agreement, would remain in their possession. This applied to settlements with former administrators of Templar estates, unpaid debts, and sold movable property, as well as sums collected in accordance with Parliament's 11 October 1317 decision, or contrary to it. It was also decided that the king's officials would collect rent for Templar houses from previous settlement periods until the beginning of April 1318. Any remaining liabilities were to continue to be collected as set out in the 1316 agreement. The only difference was that, from that point onwards, these sums would go entirely to the royal treasury. The only exception was the amounts that the Hospitallers had agreed to pay to Charles de Valois. Philip V agreed to fulfil the terms of the Hospitallers' agreement with the count, paying him one-ninth of all sums collected. The king also decided that these transfers would not place an additional burden on the Order. The Hospitallers, on the other hand, undertook to pay Philip V 50,000 l. t. in six instalments spread over three years. Once these payments had been made, the Order would finally be released from all financial obligations to the French crown relating to the acquisition of the Templar properties.

The adopted solutions certainly simplified the process of settling accounts between the Order, the king and Charles de Valois. In this respect, they benefited both parties. However, the formulas for paying part of the debt in cash was reinstated, despite not being provided for in the 1316 agreement. Following the papal reform, it was probably deemed easier for the Hospitallers to raise the necessary funds than to continue participating in the complicated process of recovering Templar property and subsequent settlements with the king and the count, which entailed the risk of new conflicts. The document also shows that the amount of debt remained unchanged. Only the method of repayment was adjusted. Therefore, the calculations of some researchers who assume that Philip V imposed an additional 50,000 l. t. on the Hospitallers and that the Order owed the French crown a total of 310,000 l. t. are incorrect.[273] Through this agreement, the monarch did not seek to enrich himself further at the expense of the Hospitallers, but merely agreed to the Order's proposal to simplify the settlement process. His favourable attitude towards the Hospitallers is confirmed by the donation he made to them around this time: his share of the income from the former Templar house of La Brosse near Paris.[274]

Following in the footsteps of his predecessors, Philip V referred to Philip the Fair's decision of 1314 and once again transferred the money that the Order had promised to repay to count of La Marche. Therefore, despite the promise made in 1315 by Louis X, it seems that the obligation to the king's brother had not yet been fulfilled. In October 1318, Philip V instructed his brother's treasurer to enforce payment from the Hospitallers' debtors so that they would be able to settle their own debts.[275] There is no information about the measures taken to implement this order. It is also unclear what these measures would have entailed. All we know is that the monarch issued similar orders to other officials at that time. In March 1319, in a letter addressed to the bailiff of Rouen, Philip V ordered that the Hospitallers be allowed to sell part of the forest belonging to the commandery of Sainte-Vaubourg, in order to repay their debt to the count of La Marche.[276] These orders all testify to the awareness of the Hospitallers' continuing inability to accumulate financial resources.

Implementing the provisions of the 1318 agreement began with a significant delay. More than a year after it was signed, the king informed his officials of the provisions of the new agreement with the Hospitallers. A letter containing an order to implement the agreement's provisions, addressed to the bailiffs in the duchy of Normandy, was dated 19 May 1319.[277] The reason for this delay is unclear. It cannot be ruled out that, due to a lack of source material, we do not have a complete picture of the situation, and that the king had, in fact, already issued orders on this matter earlier. However, the content of the May order suggests that this was not the case.

Preserved sources indicate that, after the agreement was signed, estimates were made of the expected revenues from its implementation in different parts of the kingdom. However, it is unclear what these estimates were based on. Documents relating to financial settlements between Philip V and the duke of Burgundy refer several times to the sum of 7000 l. t., which royal officials were to recover from the former estates of the Templars in the duchy. However, the documents suggest that officials were aware of the potential challenges in achieving the desired outcome of the investigations.[278] Indeed, this was not successful everywhere. For example, the actions of the commissioners in the seneschalship of Toulouse ended in failure; it had been expected that at least 3770 l. 16 s. 2 d. t. would be collected, a sum that Philip V had promised to transfer in full to the commander of the crossbowmen stationed in Flanders.[279] However, by May 1321, Guillaume Clignet had handed over only 1289 l. 10 s. t.,[280] so in 1323, Charles IV ordered the remaining sum to be collected in the seneschalships of Périgord and Quercy.[281] This illustrates the nature of the agreements of 1316 and 1318. By signing them, both Philip the Fair's sons took on the task of recovering the Templar property, which proved difficult to achieve. It required a great deal of time and the involvement of the state apparatus, yet ultimately it did not bring the expected profits. The situation was supposed to improve with the 1318 decision to settle part of the Hospitallers' debt in cash, but this did not solve all the problems. From the monarchs' and the state's point of view, the agreements with the Order seem to be quite disadvantageous in terms of their finances.

Meanwhile, thanks to the reforms of John XXII and possibly an agreement with Philip V, the Hospitallers enjoyed greater financial freedom than before. One example of a decision that may indicate a changing situation was the case of the lands belonging to the commandery of Montmorency near Paris. Jean de Montmorency, the Lord of Montmorency, seized lands that had been taken over by the Hospitallers from their previous owners in 1318. He claimed that neither the Hospitallers nor the previous owners had redeemed them from him. Simon Le Rat ultimately took ownership after paying 1600 l. t.[282] On the other hand, in 1320, the Order sold a house belonging to the former Templar estate in Châlons for 400 l. t.[283] These transactions demonstrate that they had already gained the ability to dispose of their own properties by this time. However, this did not solve the Order's financial problems or put an end to the settlement of accounts with the French crown, which continued for several more years.

3.3.3 Renaud de Saint-Ouen's mission (1322–1325) and the final decisions

Following the death of Philip V, his brother and successor, Charles IV, continued the process of recovering the Templars' assets. We are familiar with the events that took place in southwestern France (*in Lingua Occitana*). In October 1322, the king ordered an investigation into any unpaid debts owed to the Templars, as well as any thefts or abuses committed on their estates since the beginning of the proceedings by the administrators of the estates, their tenants, or the collectors. The king's envoys were also tasked with enforcing the collection of these debts, the proceeds of which were to go to the royal treasury and, in part, to Charles de Valois, as stipulated in the 1318 agreement. Renaud de Saint-Ouen was appointed commissioner to carry out this mission. Preserved sources indicate that, from at least September 1323, he was accompanied by Benoît Brocart. At the same time, the king entrusted them with another task: collecting money from Jewish estates in southwestern France.[284] Although Benoît Brocart was referred to in subsequent documents as the commissioner for Templar properties,[285] he is not mentioned in the financial report prepared by Renaud de Saint-Ouen. This suggests that he was primarily, if not exclusively, involved in matters relating to Jewish properties and did not participate in the investigation into Templar properties.

The report on the nearly three-year investigation, repeatedly referred to in the work, enables the commissioners' actions to be reconstructed precisely. This extensive document is currently stored in the Archives départementales de Tarn-et-Garonne under the reference number H 317. Previously, part of the municipal archives in Castelsarrasin, it was found there by Gaulejac in the 1920s.[286] It takes the form of a parchment *rotulus* consisting of 17 sheets of various sizes, stapled together and written on both sides. One side lists the income and expenses related to the investigation, while the other contains additional information and copies of documents issued in connection with the proceedings. These include procurations issued by the king and Charles de Valois, a record of sums due to the count, receipts issued by his representative and others to whom Renaud de Saint-Ouen transferred money, letters from the monarch, and detailed accounts of some of the income and expenses included in the main part of the report.

The condition of the document does not allow for its complete reading. The parchment is damaged and partly missing due to moisture and mold. This is most evident on the first surviving page, which is only partially legible. Based on its content, it can be assumed that other pages from the beginning of the document are missing, although it is unclear how many. There are also losses in other parts of the manuscript, but these only affect individual words. However, most of the numerous notes in the margins are illegible. It seems that these were only made to facilitate reading the report and do not add any new content.

Renaud de Saint-Ouen's report tells us that he was active in the seneschalships from Périgord in the northwest to Carcassonne and Beaucaire in the southeast. However, the attached documentation shows that they were also supposed to include the seneschalships of Saintonge and Poitou. For some reason, however, the local officials tried to prevent him from operating in their territories.[287] It is unclear whether this obstacle was overcome, as the report makes no mention of the outcome of the investigations in any of these seneschalships. Nevertheless, it cannot be ruled out that they were mentioned in a part of the document that has not survived to the present day. If so, proceedings in these areas would have taken place only during the first few months of Renaud de Saint-Ouen's mission.

The investigation lasted three years, from October 1322 to September 1325. The first royal procuration for Renaud de Saint-Ouen was issued on 18 October 1322.[288] Shortly thereafter, most likely, the newly appointed commissioner left Paris for southern France, where he remained until mid-May of the following year. He then returned to Paris, where he received new procuration from the monarch and appeared before Parliament in matters related to the ongoing investigation.

On 25 July 1323, he travelled south again, returning on 31 March 1324. This time, he spent four and a half months in Paris (until 17 August), presenting a report of his activities to date. The next royal authorisation is dated 10 September, meaning the commissioner took a short break from the investigation. Ten days after it was issued, he set off on another journey south, returning on 22 July1325. Shortly afterwards, he presented the final account of his mission, which was accepted on 17 September that year.[289] Renaud de Saint-Ouen later appeared in royal documents only as commissioner for Jewish properties.[290] He thus spent a little over two years in the south.

When the investigation began, the king's envoy had to overcome various formal obstacles. The lieutenant of the seneschal of Toulouse, who was involved in military operations in Gascony at that time, initially refused to consent to action in the territory under his jurisdiction because he had not received any instructions from his superior in this matter.[291] The seneschal of Rodez, in turn, demanded to see the original royal letters authorising Renaud de Saint-Ouen to conduct the investigation.[292] While such situations undoubtedly prolonged the proceedings and increased their cost – the report shows that the notary's journey to deliver the original procuration from the monarch to Rodez took six days and cost 30 s. t.[293] – they did not prevent the commissioner from carrying out his duties in the seneschalships where he had initially encountered obstacles. The exceptions were most likely the aforementioned seneschalships of Saintonge and Poitou.

Apart from Renaud de Saint-Ouen, many other people were involved in the investigation. These included sergeants and notaries who participated in all procedures relating to the search for debtors and the enforcement of claims,[294] heralds who publicly announced calls for the disclosure of debts owed to the Order,[295] servants who accompanied the commissioner,[296] and lawyers who advised him and participated in court proceedings.[297] The document shows that even a Templar chaplain and donat in Montpellier took part in tracking down the Order's debtors. He was paid for a 20-day journey, during which he carried out the tasks entrusted to him.[298] The document also mentions eight deputies (*substitutis*) of Renaud de Saint-Ouen who conducted activities in the designated seneschalships.[299] Due to gaps in the manuscript and the illegibility of some names, it is unfortunately impossible to determine the total number of participants in the investigation.

The first actions taken were probably based on documents handed over by previous commissioners and collectors of outstanding Templar debts. Renaud de Saint-Ouen continued some of the executions that had been started by the previous commissioners and collectors, and in other cases, he used their findings.[300] However, most of the information was obtained on an ongoing basis by reviewing the records of local notaries, who were paid for their assistance in identifying outstanding debts.[301] Inventories of Templar houses[302] and accounts drawn up by former Order's estate administrators[303] were also analysed. Renaud de Saint-Ouen also managed to recover documents drawn up by the envoys of the former administrators of the Order's estates. These documents contained information about debts that had been repaid but not settled by those administrators.[304] Heralds were also paid to publicly announce the proceedings and call for the disclosure of thefts and debts.[305]

Those who responded to the call and helped to recover the money could expect a reward of one-fifth of the recovered amounts. Records show that this remuneration was paid to five people: four notaries[306] and a Hospitaller brother, Pierre de Châlus, the commander of the house in Toulouse, who handed over documents concerning unpaid loans granted by the Templar Gérard Lavigne to several people to the commissioners.[307] However, it is unclear whether this solution applied to all those who shared information about unpaid debts, since the text also mentions others people who secretly handed important documents over to the commissioners without receiving any remuneration.[308] Perhaps, therefore, it was a matter of individual arrangements.

The report shows that, in most cases, debtors – and often their heirs – paid the sums owed without much protest. Some agreed to repay the debt in instalments, while others requested partial remission due to poverty.[309] However, there were also those who consistently denied any obligation to pay and refused to settle the debt, appealing to higher authorities. This significantly prolonged and complicated the work of the commissioners. The most difficult cases were referred to Parliament of Paris. One such case was that of the debt of count of Périgord, Archambaud IV, whose father borrowed 285 l. 4 s. 5 d. t. from Gérard Lavigne in 1297, but did not repay it until his death in 1311. The debtor's son refused to repay the debt, even after proceedings in the Toulouse court confirmed his obligation. The count therefore asked the king for permission to appeal to Parliament, which he received. Consequently, Renaud de Saint-Ouen spent several months in Paris at the turn of 1322 and 1323, appearing before Parliament regarding the count's debt and similar cases. According to his report, the count of Périgord was ultimately forced to reach an agreement with the king's people regarding the repayment of his debt.[310]

In a few cases, the commissioner was forced to seize or sell the property of debtors. One example is Bertrand de Goth, who refused to return money unjustly taken from several Templar houses, most likely by his father, Arnaud de Goth. Ultimately, some of his lands were seized to pay off his debts.[311] Similar consequences befell Philippe Claveau of La Villedieu-du-Temple, who refused to acknowledge his obligations. This resulted in legal proceedings that generated further costs. Renaud de Saint-Ouen ordered the sale of Philippe Claveau's house, land, vineyards, and even bedding.[312]

However, there were cases in which the commissioners were unable to recover the sums owed. For instance, the proceedings concerning the fraud committed by the first accuser of the Templars, Esquieu de Floyran, were unsuccessful. After the trial, Philip the Fair granted him the Templar estates in Montricoux, from which he was to derive an income of 500 l. t. In reality, however, the income amounted to 1100 l. t., a fact that Esquieu de Floyran concealed. Consequently, in 1322, the estates were taken away from him and transferred to the Hospitallers.[313] Together with Charles IV, they decided to place the estates under the temporary control of Alphonse of Spain until the disputes surrounding the property were resolved. The following year, during an investigation led by Renaud de Saint-Ouen, the commissioners attempted to recover the dishonestly taken money by Esquieu de Floyran. However, they were unsuccessful due to a change in ownership.[314] Esquieu de

Floyran was also accused of misappropriating some of the house's furnishings in Montricoux. A separate proceeding was conducted in this case.[315] Unfortunately, Renaud de Saint-Ouen's report does not contain any information about the outcome of either proceeding, so it is not known whether the defendant ultimately returned all the money he owed.

Only part of the money collected by the commissioner made it to the royal treasury. It was sent to Paris via the Scala Company (*societas de Scala*).[316] Between June 1323 and September 1325, the *Journaux du Trésor* recorded 11 payments totalling 773 l. 18 s. p. (967 l. 7 s. 6 d. t.).[317] Renaud de Saint-Ouen was also responsible for ongoing settlements with Charles de Valois' envoy and for transferring the remainder of the amount promised to the commander of the crossbowmen stationed in Flanders by Philip V, which Guillaume Clignet had previously failed to collect.[318] In the end, after deducting the very high costs, which will be discussed later, the commissioner collected 2646 l. 3 s 4 d. t. to be divided between the king and Charles de Valois. The report indicates that part of the debt was to be repaid later, but it is unclear whether or when this happened. In any case, the final amount was very small compared to the sums mentioned in earlier agreements between the French monarchs and the Hospitallers. Furthermore, at the settlement stage, it was reduced further by the salaries paid to the officials controlling the accounts. However, it should be noted that funds from the Templars' estates and receivables had been collected for several years, so it is likely that most of the money had already entered the royal treasury by this time.

During Renaud de Saint-Ouen's mission, attempts were also being made elsewhere in the country to recover funds owed to the French monarchy as part of settlements with the Hospitallers. Between 1324 and 1325, a similar investigation was conducted in the Paris region. As a result, 31 l. 15 s. 7 d. p. (c. 39 l. 14. s. 5 d. t.) were paid into the royal treasury between January and September 1325.[319] The *Journaux du Trésor* also recorded other individual payments, probably resulting from proceedings in other parts of the country. For instance, in December 1324, one of the administrators of two Templar houses near Paris submitted a final account of his activities,[320] and the heirs of the bishop of Bayeux repaid part of his debt incurred with the administrators of the Templars' estates.[321] Based on these references, Jules Viard calculated that, during the first four years of Charles IV's reign (i.e., from 1322 to 1325), debts owed to the Order totalling 6309 l. 10 s. 6 d. p. (c. 7886 l. 18 s. t.) were collected.[322] Taking into account the difference between the final financial result of the proceedings conducted by Renaud de Saint-Ouen, as indicated in his accounts, and the sum of his payments as recorded in the *Journaux du Trésor*, it can be assumed that the total revenue from Templar properties and receivables was higher than Viard calculated. However, from the perspective of the French monarchy, this was not significant.

Preserved documents show that, in 1325, Charles IV decided to finalise the settlement with the Hospitallers. Alongside accepting the financial report from Renaud de Saint-Ouen's mission, other summaries were prepared at that time. Former commissioners, including Guillaume Clignet, submitted final reports on their activities.[323] In September of that year, Guillaume Pisdoe and Rénier Bourdon, the former general administrators of the Templar estates in France, also prepared a summary of their activities.[324] Considering the amount of money that had been recovered from the Templars' assets and debts, there was probably a need to find a solution that would provide adequate financial compensation for the monarch and enable the closure of the case of the assets of the Order, which had been dissolved several years earlier. As Eugène Mannier established, in 1325, the Hospitallers agreed to grant Charles IV and his wife an annuity of 1200 l. t. from the income of several Templar houses, including Sennevières and Beauvais-en-Gâtinais. In return, the king released the Hospitallers from all obligations arising from previous agreements.[325] It is impossible to assess the extent to which this agreement reflected the calculations of royal officials at the time, or whether it was beneficial to either party. However, it was clearly in the interests of both the Hospitallers and the monarch to bring the protracted settlement process involving the royal administration to an end.

Luttrell believes that the Hospitallers ultimately failed to repay their debts to the king of France.[326] A similar assumption was made by Demurger.[327] However, both researchers appear to have overlooked the terms of the 1316 and 1318 agreements, which stipulated that the royal administration would enforce debts relating to Templar properties, included in the Hospitallers' liabilities. Therefore, the Order did not collect money itself and transfer them to the royal treasury, which could lead to erroneous conclusions about the outcome of the bilateral settlements.

Signing the agreement with the Hospitallers did not mean that the process of recovering the Templar property was completely over. Charles IV's officials continued to pursue legal action to enforce the obligations. Debtors continued to repay their debts for several more years.[328] In 1329, Guillaume Clignet handed over valuables that had been part of the furnishings of one of the Templar churches to the royal treasury.[329] This suggests that the Hospitallers themselves had to settle the last obligations. The latest mention of the Templar properties in the *Registres du Trésor des Chartes* dates from September 1332, when Philip VI (1328–1350), successor to Charles IV, confirmed the sale of property owned by Bertrand de Crandelain – referred to in the document as "tenant of the Templar estates in Laon and Ardon" – to pay his debt to the king, amounting to 160 l. 12 d. p. (200 l. 1 s. 3 d. t.).[330] It therefore seems that as many as five successive French rulers were involved in settling the financial consequences of the proceedings against the Order.

Apart from settling accounts with the king in the 1320s, the Hospitallers were also involved in various court proceedings concerning disputes that began during the Templars' time or during their trial. For instance, Guillaume Bacon, a descendant of the founder of the commandery of Baugy, asserted his claim to the property as early as 1322. Ultimately, however, he withdrew from the dispute.[331] On 1 February 1323, the Parliament of Paris ruled on a dispute concerning land belonging to the chapter of Saint-Pierre of Beauvais, which had been seized by the Templars of Ivry.[332] A few months later, a final judgement was handed down in a case brought by a man who claimed he had been granted a lease on a Templar farm that had been taken from him by the Hospitallers.[333] In 1324, the Hospitallers filed a complaint against a royal official who had not paid them rent for certain properties since they took over the Templars' estates.[334] Similar trials were held in subsequent years. In 1326, the proceedings concerning conflicts over property in the vicinity of Toulouse and the estates belonging to the commandery of Cours, mentioned in earlier chapters, came to an end.[335] However, it was not until 1329 that the dispute between the Templars and lord of Montlaur concerning their rights of justice in La Sauvetat was resolved. The verdict favoured the Hospitallers.[336] However, new problems arose concerning the obligations of the abolished Order. For instance, in 1328, Otto de Grandson's heirs claimed the annuity granted to him for life by Jacques de Molay, which they believed should continue to be paid.[337] However, these were all isolated cases, most of which dragged on for a long time for various reasons. After 1325, the sources provide no information about any systematic efforts to recover Templar property and settle related debts.

3.4 Costs of recovering Templar property

As discussed in previous chapters, the effective recovery of Templar assets stolen over several years of proceedings, and the collection of money owed to the Order, required significant involvement from the royal administration. This entailed growing costs. It can be assumed that, at least up to a certain point, these costs were mostly or even entirely borne by the beneficiaries of this process, i.e., the Hospitallers. It is reasonable to assume that the expenses relating to investigations, court proceedings, and executions constituted a large proportion of the 60,000 l. t. that the Hospitallers undertook to transfer to Louis X. Unfortunately, no accounts have survived that would enable us to estimate the total cost of the activities carried out over a period of more than ten years by three successive monarchs. The only document that indicates the scale of expenditure involved is Renaud de Saint-Ouen's report of his mission. As the items included in it were probably similar to those in other proceedings of this type, it is worth taking a closer look at them.

The total expenses incurred during the two-and-a-half-year period of the commissioners' work amounted to 1026 l. 3 s. 4 d. ob. t. These primarily consisted of salaries and travel expenses for those involved in conducting individual proceedings. The commissioner himself received 7 s. 6 d. t. per day during his stay in Paris and 12 s. 6 d. t. when he was outside the city. His remuneration remained the same throughout the proceedings, despite the fact that, as noted in the report, from September 1324 he was simultaneously dealing with the cases of the Templar properties and the Jews. In total, he was paid 572 l. 3 s. 6 d. t.[338] Additionally, he was paid 38 l. 10 s. t. for the loss of four horses he had travelled on. They had all been purchased during the mission and were so exhausted from work that they were sold for small sums.[339] The accounts also show that he received additional money for personally participating in the proceedings against the count of Périgord. He was paid 61 l. t. for the trips he made in connection with this, i.e., 1 l. t. per day.[340] The document also reveals the salaries of Renaud de Saint-Ouen's deputies. They received 10 s. t. per day of work.[341]

Most of the expenses were for the salaries of a large group of sergeants and notaries who were involved in all stages of the proceedings. Initially, the former set out on a journey to summon anyone with knowledge of Templar debts or property thefts to disclose this information. They received 1 to 2 s. t. per day for this work, and the rate was most likely dependent on the number of places they visited and the distances they travelled in a day.[342] If they travelled on horseback, they were paid 3 s. t. per day.[343] Heralds, who publicly announced the commissioners' summonses, received separate remuneration.[344] The sergeants then took part in delivering various types of summons and transporting documents. In this case, they received 2 or 3 s. t. per day of travel.[345] Additional costs also arose, for example when one of the sergeants and his servant had to wait four days in Toulouse for documents to be prepared so that they were to be taken to Paris. They were paid an extra 20 s. t. to cover these expenses.[346]

During the initial stage of the proceedings, notaries were primarily responsible for reviewing books and court records to identify unpaid debts. Those who searched their own documents were paid between 18 d. t. and several s. t., depending on the time spent and probably also on the volume of the books.[347] The remuneration for reviewing court records or other notaries' documentation started at 2 s. t.[348] Once this work was complete, notaries' main task was to prepare and copy various types of documents. They were paid between 2 and 20 s. t. for these activities.[349] They usually received 5 s. t. per day for participating in other activities, including various enforcement proceedings.[350]

Other people also took part in the proceedings. Among them were the servants who had accompanied Renaud de Saint-Ouen on his journey. Four of these servants were listed in the account, each having performed their duties for three months. Three received remunerations of 20 s. t. and one received 25 s. t.[351] Expenses also included payment for a guide who led the commissioner to the residence of one of the debtors. He was paid 15 s. t. for the five-day journey.[352] The payroll also included two lawyers. One advised the commissioner during the trial against the count of Périgord and received 50 s. t. for this,[353] while the other appeared in court in various cases concerning the Templar properties and the investigation. He was paid 20 s. t. for this work.[354]

In addition to salaries, the list of expenses included the purchase of paper, parchment, and wax. Several livres were paid for these items throughout the proceedings.[355] Additional costs included 10 s. 6 d. t. for renting a horse to transport a debtor to Cahors for trial,[356] and 162 l. 18 s. 8 d. t.[357] Furthermore, Renaud de Saint-Ouen's report did not include expenses related to the transfer of the money he collected and subsequent settlements. In March 1325, the Scali company received 80 l. p. (100 l. t.) for transferring payments from the commissioner in Toulouse to the Paris treasury.[358] It is unclear whether this was a one-off payment, or if the bankers received any other remuneration. The *Journaux du Trésor* also mentions the remuneration of officials who checked the commissioners' reports. One of these officials, the notary Denis de *Lorryaco*, who was referred to as the *corrector et ordinator* of the accounts concerning the recovery of Templar property, received 5 s. p. (6 s. 3 d. t.) per day for his work. Therefore, for the period from 16 July 1322, to 1 July 1329, he was paid 481 l. p. (601 l. 5 s. t.).[359] He also received three additional sums totalling 73 l. 46 s. 5 d. p. (94 l. 3 s. t.).[360] Three other controllers, each of whom performed their duties for one year, were paid a total of 83 l. p. (103 l. 15 s. t.).[361] Taking all these amounts into account – 637 l. 46 s. 5 d. p. (799 l. 3 s. t.) – the total comes to 1825 l. 6 s. 4 d. ob. t. Comparing this with the total proceeds from the proceedings – 3672 l. 6 s. 8 d. ob. t. – shows that the expenses accounted for almost half of it. It can be assumed that this proportion changed over time, as part of the debt was to be repaid later, which should not have incurred additional costs. However, we do not know whether the liabilities were settled or whether further action by royal officials was required.

It is not known who covered the costs of the investigations and executions. While it seems likely that the Hospitallers covered the costs in the first years after the proceedings ended, one might also wonder whether the monarchs were responsible for covering the costs under the agreements in which Louis X and later Philip V agreed to collect the debts of the Hospitallers from the Templars independently. Apart from the 1316 agreement, which mentioned 60,000 l. t. charged to the Order, there is no mention of this in any other documents. In any case, the cited accounts show that the costs of recovering the Templar property significantly reduced the value of their estate in the final stage of the process.

In addition to summarising the total expenses incurred throughout the investigation, Renaud de Saint-Ouen's report offers an alternative view on the issue of costs. The information in the document enables the identification of expenses associated with the conduct of individual cases, providing insight into the possible cost of proceedings lasting several years mentioned in earlier chapters. For instance, the recovery of the count of Périgord's debt, totalling 285 l. 4 s. 5 d. t., cost a total of 85 l. 8 s. 6 d. t.,[362] which included the commissioner's travel expenses (61 l. t.), the preparation of various case-related documents (6 l. 9 s. t.), and the remuneration of other persons involved in the case. The document shows that the count of Périgord reimbursed the commissioner 48 l. t. for part of the proceedings before Parliament in Paris.[363] However, it is not known who covered the rest of the expenses. The proceedings against Esquieu de Floyran, who was receiving excessive income from the Montricoux estate, cost 6 l. 3 s. t., of which 3 l. 19 s. t. was spent on preparing and copying court documents and 2 l. 4 s. t. on travel.[364] The report notes that the attempt at enforcement was unsuccessful because the property in Montricoux was no longer in Esquieu de Floyran's possession at that time, but it is not known how much was expected to be obtained from him. Therefore, no payment was recorded in the document. Based on the account, it is impossible to determine how many of the proceedings ended in a similar manner. However, it is certain that some debts could not be recovered despite attempts being made and various people being involved, which in turn generated further costs.

The list of expenses incurred in connection with the case of Pierre de Verderonne, the custodian of the grange of Bonnefare, who died without presenting an account of his activities, was slightly shorter. Preparing three documents and paying the notary for two days' work cost a total of 3 l. t., but his heirs handed over 54 l. t. to the commissioners.[365] This was therefore one of the less complicated proceedings, which certainly prevailed in Renaud de Saint-Ouen's report and, in general, throughout the process of recovering the Order's properties. However, the other two examples cited here, as well as the report of the entire mission, show that this was not always the case and that the final financial outcome of the entire undertaking was determined by more complex cases.

3.5 Gains and losses of the Hospitallers

Within several months of the announcement of the bull *Ad providam*, the Hospitallers took possession of the vast majority of former Templar houses in the kingdom of France. Despite various problems in the following years, they gradually regained other assets of their predecessors. After more than a decade, they finally settled their accounts with the French crown. Nevertheless, according to contemporary commentators, the Hospitallers lost more than they gained by taking over the Templar properties. Giovanni Villani wrote in his chronicle that they were poorer than before.[366] However, as Luttrell points out, this comment is general in nature and applies not only to the kingdom of France, but to other countries too.[367] Schein, in turn, considered it to be "pure exaggeration."[368] However, this opinion was also shared by an anonymous continuator of Guillaume de Nangis' chronicle. According to him, the situation of the Hospitallers worsened after the transfer of the Templar properties. However, he did not explain why.[369] Many historians have adopted this point of view, believing that the Hospitallers fell into serious financial difficulties as a result of the settlements related to the acquisition of the Templar properties. These difficulties lasted for many years.[370] In this context, Theresa M. Vann referred to the opinion of some researchers who claim that the numerous court proceedings conducted since the time of the Templars and settled after the transfer were one of the reasons for the new owners' difficult situation.[371] While such situations undoubtedly burdened the Hospitallers, there is no evidence in the available sources to suggest that they had such a significant impact on the Order's finances.

However, some literature also claims that, despite temporary difficulties, the Order became significantly wealthier, as evidenced primarily by the situation in France, where the Hospitallers received twice as many houses as they had previously.[372] This is demonstrated by the inventories of the Order's assets in the kingdom in 1333 and 1373.[373] These inventories show that the income of the French Hospitallers increased significantly, and that their assets remained largely unchanged for over half a century. This indicates stability rather than crisis.

How can we explain the radically different interpretations of researchers? How did the acquisition of the Templar properties actually affect the Hospitaller's situation? Luttrell has written the most extensively on this subject recently. He believes that the Order became enormously wealthy, although this was associated with high short-term costs.[374] However, the impoverishment that affected the functioning of the entire institution for several decades, as described by other researchers, seems to be more than just "short-term" problems. Therefore, let us take another look at the financial situation of the Hospitallers in the second decade of the 14th century.

The first funds from the French Templar estates were probably transferred to the Hospitallers by Clement V as early as 1309. The *passagium particulare*, which was being prepared at the time, the conquest of Rhodes and the subsequent fortification of the island required enormous financial outlays.[375] In 1312, there was no longer any question of taking over further sums from the Templars' treasury or income from their commanderies collected during the trial. In France, however, the Hospitallers were given almost all of the land and houses belonging to the dissolved Order, as well as some of its former furnishings. Initially, they also received financial support to restore the properties to a usable condition. At the same time, they undertook to repay the substantial sum resulting from the agreement with Philip the Fair in 1313. This was certainly a serious challenge for them at that time. However, they could easily have met this demand by selling some of the properties they had acquired from the Templars. Unfortunately, the pope forbade them to do so. According to Menache, Clement V wanted to protect the Order from potential pressure from secular rulers.[376] This may have been one of the motives behind the decision taken in 1312, but there are also other possible reasons for introducing such a ban. For example, the pope may have wanted to avoid being accused of squandering the assets of the dissolved Templar Order completely. It may also have formed part of the reforms announced at the Council of Vienne. The Hospitallers were thus forced to maintain their possessions, which facilitated control over the Order's finances and, in theory at least, guaranteed that the properties previously belonging to the Templars could be used for the crusades in future, as desired by Clement V and announced in his bulls. The situation of the Hospitallers was further complicated by the fact that, at the beginning of 1313, Philip the Fair and his vassals prohibited them from acquiring properties in their territories other than that which they were to receive from the Templars. This solution was approved by the Church.[377] As a result, the French Hospitallers became very wealthy, but in practice they were unable to utilise their wealth as was most needed at the time.

Despite these limitations, the leaders of the Order approached the issue of taking over the Templar properties with great enthusiasm. On 28 March 1313, after talks with the king of France regarding the financial settlement had concluded, Albrecht von Schwarzburg arrived at the pope's court. Clement V was already familiar with the terms of the 21 March agreement and discussed them with his guests. According to the Aragonese envoys, Albrecht von Schwarzburg told the pope that the decision to transfer the Templar properties to his Order was the greatest gift since the Donation of Constantine.[378] Clearly, therefore, Philip the Fair's demands were not an insurmountable obstacle in his opinion.

However, the following years proved difficult for the Hospitallers. The need to repay 200,000 l. t. to Philip the Fair, coupled with other significant expenses related to the acquisition of Templar properties in the kingdom of France and the functioning of the entire Order and its military activities, proved challenging.[379] Consequently, the Hospitallers debts grew very quickly. They asked the pope several times for permission to use some of the former French Templar houses as collateral to repay their debts to Italian bankers. In the spring of 1314, for example, Clement V agreed to cover the debts owed to the Peruzzi and Bardi families of Florence in this way.[380] For the same reason, in July 1315, the Hospitallers transferred to the Genoese merchant Antonio Pessagno the right to collect income from a dozen or so Templar houses in various parts of France for five years.[381] In 1314, Foulques de

Villaret also sold a vineyard belonging to the Templars in Marseille to pay off the dissolved Order's debts to local merchants.[382] However, it is unclear whether the Grand Master obtained the pope's consent for this transaction in advance, or if it was exempt from Clement V's ban as part of the property transfer settlements. The latter would certainly have provided significant relief for the Hospitallers.

However, despite the implementation of these measures, the financial situation of the Order remained unchanged. Furthermore, at that time, the French Hospitallers were faced with the high costs of recovering the assets of the Templars, as well as the ongoing inquisitorial proceedings. Although the 1316 and 1318 agreements with Philip the Fair's sons provided solutions that freed the Order from the need to collect the entire amount owed to the French monarchy alone, part of the debt continued to be collected from the income of individual commanderies and by seizing their equipment, which hampered their functioning. In response to this situation, John XXII introduced a reform of the French province of the Hospitallers. The bull of 21 July 1317 contained the papal decision on this matter and listed the Order's most serious obligations. As well as debts to Italian bankers, it mentioned the need to support former Templars still living in their houses, among other things.[383] Regarding the latter issue, John XXII attempted to assist the Order by ordering a reduction in the pensions paid to former brothers. The pope also made other decisions to streamline the process of settling accounts with creditors yet still did not lift the ban on selling properties owned by the Hospitallers.[384] In his bulls of 1318, he ordered the cancellation of the sale of certain properties, citing his predecessor's decision. Furthermore, he appointed *judices conservatores*, as well as special commissions, to oversee the implementation of this decision.[385] However, John XXII ultimately had to change his policy on this issue. By 1320, the Order's debt had risen to over 575,000 florins (approximately 383,000 l. t.), of which 360,000 (240,000 l. t.) was owed to Florentine bankers.[386] Consequently, the pope agreed to the pledging and sale of certain properties. That same year, he purchased a house in Cahors and its associated properties from the Order for 2500 florins (approximately 1667 l. t.), subsequently transferring them to the Carthusians.[387] The following year, he permitted the Hospitallers to mortgage some of their possessions to enable them to repay their debts to the Florentine bankers over the next four years.[388] In 1322, he allowed the sale or transfer of less useful properties into lifetime leases, which was to enable them to repay debts amounting to approximately 500,000 florins (more than 333,000 l. t.).[389] Thanks to this and the consistent actions of the Order's leaders over the following years, the Hospitallers managed to get rid of their outstanding liabilities.[390] However, as shown by the aforementioned property inventories conducted in the fourth and eighth decades of the 14th century, their holdings in the kingdom of France did not decrease significantly. While it is true that Italian bankers such as Antonio Pessagno continued to collect income from some of the houses for several years, this did not disrupt the functioning of the Order as much as earlier efforts to improve its financial situation.

Therefore, it seems that in 1313, the French Hospitallers received enormous wealth, which would certainly have enabled them to significantly reduce or even repay the debts they owed at that time, not only to Philip the Fair, but also – and perhaps most importantly – to Italian bankers. However, this proved impossible due to Clement V's and, later, John XXII's decision to prohibit the sale and pledge of the received assets. The prolonged financial crisis was only resolved when the pope relented and permitted the sale of certain properties. On the other hand, the papal policy of asset sales restriction resulted in the French Hospitallers retaining their possessions for several decades after the Templar properties were transferred. Therefore, the seemingly contradictory views expressed by historians since the 19th century regarding the impact of the acquisition of Templar properties on the Hospitallers' situation are, in fact, complementary. In fact, they are two sides of the same coin. However, their common denominator is not the provisions of the bull *Ad providam* or the related debt to the French monarchs, but the restrictions imposed on the Order by the popes.

Notes

1 *Papsttum*, vol. 2, nos. 125–148, pp. 230–306. On the activity of the Aragonese envoys at the Council and the content of the reports they produced, see also M. Satora, *Sprawa*, pp. 214–233.

2 *Papsttum*, vol. 2, no. 127, p. 248. See also M. Satora, *Sprawa*, pp. 163–265.

3 On Guillaume de Plaisians' participation in various missions to the papal curia, see, for example, M. Satora, 'Dyplomaci Filipa IV Pięknego (1285–1314) – mechanizmy wyboru', in: *Między misją a profesją. Ewolucja roli dyplomaty w stosunkach międzynarodowych na przestrzeni wieków*, ed. R. Simiński, A. Szczepańska-Dudziak (Szczecin 2016), pp. 27–28.

4 *Papsttum*, vol. 2, no. 128, p. 250. See also J. Lecler, *Histoire*, p. 64; J. M. Sans i Travé, *El procés*, pp. 250–251; M. Vilar Bonet, *Els Béns*, p. 62; M. Satora, *Sprawa*, p. 219.

5 *Papsttum*, vol. 2, no. 132, pp. 258–259; *The Chronicle of Walter of Guisborough Previously Edited as the Chronicle of Walter of Hemingford or Hemingburgh*, ed. H. Rothwell (London 1957), p. 396. See also M. Barber, *The Trial* (2006), pp. 264–265; M. Satora, *Sprawa*, pp. 87–88.

6 *Papsttum*, vol. 2, no. 127, p. 246.

7 *Papsttum*, vol. 2, no. 127, p. 247. Forey erroneously attributed this statement to Cardinal Bérenger Frédol – *The Fall*, p. 158.

8 *Papsttum*, vol. 2, no. 132, p. 260.

9 *Papsttum*, vol. 2, no. 126, p. 243. For more on this conversation and Cardinal Bérenger Frédol's remarks, see M. Satora, *Sprawa*, pp. 217–218.

10 *Livre*, pp. 289, 291. See also A. J. Forey, 'The Military Orders in the Crusading Proposals', p. 332.

11 E. Boutaric, 'Notices et extraits', no. 37, p. 202. See also J. Lecler, *Histoire*, p. 70.

12 'Les papiers de Guillaume de Nogaret et de Guillaume de Plaisians au Trésor des chartes', ed. C. V. Langlois, *Notices et extraits des manuscrits de la Bibliothèque Impériale*, 39 (1908), no. 303, p. 235.

13 *Papsttum*, vol. 2, no. 132, p. 260; *Papsttum*, vol. 2, no. 133, p. 265. See also G. Lizerand, *Clément V*, p. 261; E. Müller, *Das Konzil*, pp. 130, 143; J. Lecler, *Histoire*, p. 67; M. Barber, *The Trial* (2006), p. 263; M. Satora, *Sprawa*, pp. 222–223.

14 *Papsttum*, vol. 2, no. 138, pp. 277. See also G. Lizerand, *Clément V*, p. 264; M. Barber, *The Trial* (2006), p. 265.

15 J. Lecler, *Histoire*, p. 77; J. Favier, *Un conseiller*, p. 656; L. Wetzel, *Le Concile*, p. 89; A. Luttrell, 'Gli Ospitalieri e l'eredità dei Templari, 1305–1378', in: *I Templari. Mito e storia*, ed. G. Minucci, F. Sardi (Siena 1989), pp. 67–86.

16 *Papsttum*, vol. 2, no. 138, p. 278.
17 For more on the composition and objectives of the missions sent by the French court during Philip the Fair's reign, see M. Satora, *Dyplomaci*, pp. 29–30.
18 P. Dupuy, *Histoire de la condamnation*, no. 110, p. 417; *Auberti Miraei opera diplomatica et historica*, ed. J. F. Foppens, vol. 3 (Bruxelles 1734), p. 428; *Le dossier*, no. 11, pp. 196–199; H. Prutz, *Entwicklung*, pp. 221–222; G. Bordonove, *La Tragédie*, pp. 327–328 (French translation). The letter was also quoted extensively in: C. Mansuet Jeune, *Histoire*, vol. 2, p. 291; G. Lizerand, *Clément V*, p. 264; J. Lecler, *Histoire*, p. 78.
19 J. Lecler, *Histoire*, p. 78.
20 K. Schottmüller, *Der Untergang*, vol. 1, p. 521; J. Favier, *Un conseiller*, p. 145; J. Favier, *Philippe le Bel*, p. 89. Barber used the term "thinly disguised ultimatum" – *The Trial* (2006), p. 266.
21 This observation was first made by Georges Lizerand, *Clément V*, p. 264; *Le dossier*, p. XI (editor's commentary), but was later ignored by researchers. See, for example, M. Barber, *The Trial* (2006), p. 266.
22 On the interpretation of Philip's letter, see also M. Satora, *Sprawa*, pp. 168–169.
23 P. Dupuy, *Histoire de la condamnation*, no. 110, pp. 416–417; *Auberti Miraei opera*, vol. 3, pp. 428–429; B. Barbiche, *Les actes*, vol. 3, no. 2427, p. 79. The letter is quoted extensively in J. Lecler, *Histoire*, p. 78. See also M. Satora, *Sprawa*, p. 169.
24 *Papsttum*, vol. 2, no. 139, p. 285.
25 *Papsttum*, vol. 2, pp. 280–281, 284. See also J. Lecler, *Histoire*, p. 79; M. Satora, *Sprawa*, pp. 169–170.
26 G. Lizerand, *Clément V*, pp. 264–265. Jean Favier believes that Enguerrand de Marigny spoke to the pope most likely about Templars' goods, given that the dissolution of the Order had already been agreed upon during an earlier visit by royal envoys – *Un conseiller*, p. 657.
27 Louis X wrote about the talks concerning the obligations of the Hospitallers towards the king of France in one of his letters – AN, JJ 52, no. 131; *Registres*, vol. 2.1, no. 181, p. 40.
28 *Papsttum*, vol. 2, no. 140, p. 286.
29 *Papsttum*, vol. 2, no. 140, p. 287. See also G. Lizerand, *Clément V*, p. 266; M. Satora, *Sprawa*, pp. 89–90.
30 *Papsttum*, vol. 2, no. 144, pp. 292–293; *The Chronicle of Walter of Guisborough*, p. 396. See also G. Lizerand, *Clément V*, pp. 266–268; M. Barber, *The Trial* (2006), p. 267; M. Satora, *Sprawa*, pp. 89–90.
31 See the latest edition of the bull, together with a list of the most important earlier editions and an English translation, in: E. A. R. Brown, A. Forey, '*Vox in excelso* and the Suppresion of the Knights Templar: The Bull, Its History, and a New Edition', *Medieval Studies*, 80 (2018), pp. 1–58.
32 See, for example, E. A. R. Brown, A. Forey, '*Vox in excelso*'; A. Gilmour-Bryson, '*Vox in excelso* deconstructed: Exactly What Did Clement V Say?', in: *On the Margins of Crusading. The Military Orders, the Papacy and the Christian World*, ed. H. Nicholson (Farnham 2011), pp. 75–88.
33 *Papsttum*, vol. 2, no. 144, pp. 292–293. See also S. Menache, *Clement V*, p. 115; M. Satora, *Sprawa*, p. 172. Clement V only announced his decision to impose a tithe in a bull issued in December 1312. On this topic, see Reg. Clem. V, vol. 7, nos. 8781–8783, pp. 301–303; Reg. Clem. V, vol. 8 (Rome 1888), nos. 8986–8987, pp. 32–35; G. Lizerand, *Clément V*, Appendice, no. 33, pp. 476–478; B. Barbiche, *Les actes*, vol. 3, nos. 2457–2458, pp. 92–93; N. Housley, *The Avignon Papacy*, pp. 14–15; E. A. R. Brown, 'Royal Salvation', p. 19.
34 *Papsttum*, vol. 2, no. 144, pp. 293–294.
35 *Papsttum*, vol. 2, no. 145, p. 295. See also L. Wetzel, *Le Concile*, p. 92; M. Satora, *Sprawa*, pp. 172–173, 232.

36 *Papsttum*, vol. 2, no. 146, pp. 299–300.
37 On this topic, see J. Favier, *Un conseiller*, pp. 658, 660; J. Favier, *Les papes d'Avignon*, p. 91.
38 M. Barber, *The Trial* (2006), p. 270.
39 *Papsttum*, vol. 2, no. 146, p. 299. See also G. Lizerand, *Clément V*, p. 270; J. Lecler, *Histoire*, p. 90; L. Wetzel, *Le Concile*, pp. 92–93; S. Menache, 'The Hospitallers', p. 159, n. 42; M. Barber, *The Trial* (2006), p. 270; M. Satora, *Sprawa*, p. 173.
40 *Papsttum*, vol. 2, no. 146, p. 300. See also M. Vilar Bonet, *Els Béns*, p. 74; M. Satora, *Sprawa*, p. 232.
41 *Corpus documentorum inquisitionis haereticiae pravitatis Neerlandicae*, ed. P. Frédéricq, vol. 2 (Ghent 1889), no. 41, pp. 67–70. See the list of other editions in: E. A. R. Brown, A. Forey, '*Vox in excelso*', p. 4, n. 6. See also J. Lecler, *Histoire*, p. 91; T. M. Vann, 'The Assimilation of Templar Properties by the Order of the Hospital', in: *The Debate on the Trial of the Templars (1307–1314)*, ed. J. Burgtorf, P. F. Crawford, H. J. Nicholson (Farnham 2010), p. 340.
42 *The Chronicle of Walter of Guisborough*, p. 396.
43 See, for example, E. Bellomo, 'Colliding Perceptions', pp. 280–284.
44 P. Dupuy, *Histoire de la condamnation*, no. 112, pp. 426–428; *Codice diplomatico*, vol. 2, no. 23, pp. 26–30. See also J. M. A. Delaville Le Roulx, *Les hospitaliers*, p. 32.
45 Reg. Clem. V, vol. 7, no. 8784, pp. 303–305; *Conciliorum oecumenicorum decreta*, ed. G. Alberigo et al. (Basel 1962), pp. 323–325. On preserved copies of this bull, see E. A. R. Brown, A. Forey, '*Vox in excelso*', p. 5, n. 7.
46 Reg. Clem. V, vol. 8, no. 9835, p. 354. See also J. M. A. Delaville Le Roulx, *Les hospitaliers*, p. 21, n. 1.
47 Reg. Clem. V, vol. 8, no. 8974, pp. 29–30; E. Müller, *Das Konzil*, p. 229; A. Luttrell, 'Gli Ospitalieri', p. 76; A. Luttrell, 'The Hospitallers and the Papacy', p. 616; A. Demurger, *Les Hospitaliers*, pp. 449–450.
48 Reg. Clem. V, vol. 8, no. 9984, pp. 420–423; A. Theiner, *Annales Ecclesiastici*, vol. 23, *1286–1312* (Bar-le-Duc 1871), p. 511. See also E. Müller, *Das Konzil*, pp. 227–231; A. Luttrell, 'The Hospitallers and the Papacy', p. 617; A. Demurger, *Les Templiers*, p. 471.
49 See Section 2.2.3.
50 Reg. Clem. V, vol. 7, no. 7952, pp. 82–83; ADHG, H 116, no. 7; A. Theiner, *Annales*, pp. 510–511; A. de Loisine, 'Bulles de papes pour l'ordre du Temple conservées aux Archives nationales (1155–1312)', *Bulletin philologique et historique du comité des travaux historiques*, 31 (1917), no. 174, p. 234; *Conciliorum*, pp. 325–326; B. Barbiche, *Les actes*, vol. 3, no. 2443, p. 86; A. Goineaud-Bérard, *Templiers et Hospitaliers en Perigord* (Bordeaux 2002), Annexe, no. 8, p. 235. See also J. M. A. Delaville Le Roulx, *Les hospitaliers*, p. 32.
51 See the letter to Philip the Fair – G. Lizerand, *Clément V*, Appendice, no. 34, pp. 474–476 (incorrectly dated to 17 May); A. de Loisine, 'Bulles', no. 173, pp. 233–234; and letters addressed to other monarchs – P. Dupuy, *Histoire de la condamnation*, no. 115, pp. 449–450; *Foedera*, vol. 2.1, p. 6; *Corpus*, vol. 2, no. 42, pp. 70–71; A. de Loisine, 'Bulles', no. 175, p. 234; letters addressed to bishops – ADHG, H 116, no. 5; A. de Loisine, 'Bulles', nos. 171–172, p. 233; A. Goineaud-Bérard, *Templiers*, Annexe, no. 8, p. 235.
52 Reg. Clem. V, vol. 8, no. 8973, pp. 28–29; B. Barbiche, *Les actes*, vol. 3, no. 2461, p. 94.
53 J. Favier, *Un conseiller*, p. 659.
54 P. Dupuy, *Histoire de la condamnation*, no. 116, pp. 450–451; R. A. de Vertot, *Histoire*, vol. 1, *Preuves*, pp. 647–648; *Auberti Miraei opera*, vol. 3, p. 429; *Codice diplomatico*, vol. 2, no. 27, p. 34; *Le dossier*, no. 11, pp. 198–203; E. Müller, *Das Konzil*, pp. 703–704; G. Bordonove, *La Tragédie*, p. 335 (French translation). See also A. Luttrell, 'The Hospitallers and the Papacy', pp. 616–617.
55 P. Dupuy, *Histoire de la condamnation*, no. 117, pp. 451–458; R. A. de Vertot, *Histoire*, vol. 1, *Preuves*, pp. 656–662; *Codice diplomatico*, vol. 2, no. 29, pp. 36–40. See also J. M. A. Delaville Le Roulx, *Les hospitaliers*, p. 32.

56 *Recueil general des titres, concernant les fonctions, rangs, dignitez, seances et privileges des charges des presidens tresoriers de France, generaux des finances, et grands voyers des generalitez du royaume*, ed. S. Fournival (Paris 1655), pp. 35–36; P. Dupuy, *Histoire de la condamnation*, no. 123, pp. 468–469; M. Félibien, *Histoire de la ville de Paris*, vol. 3, *Preuves* (Paris 1725), p. 320; L. Delisle, *Mémoire*, no. 35, pp. 228–229; *Registres*, vol. 1, no. 1528, pp. 292–293; *The Templars*, no. 78, pp. 323–324 (English translation). See also E. Mannier, *Ordre de Malte*, pp. XVIII–XIX; H. de Curzon, *La maison*, p. 202.

57 *Acta Aragonensia*, vol. 1, no. 216, p. 325; J. M. A. Delaville Le Roulx, *Les hospitaliers*, p. 34, n. 4.

58 J. Delaville Le Roulx, 'La suppression', p. 26; *Procès-verbal de remise de maisons diverses des Templiers aux chevaliers hospitaliers de Saint-Jean De Jérusalem dans le Poitou (20 mai de l'année 1313)*, ed. C. Tranchant (Poitiers 1882), p. 4; A. Pétel, *Les Hospitaliers de Saint-Jean de Jérusalem, seigneurs de Sancey, aujourd'hui Saint-Julien (Aube)* (Troyes 1903), p. 6; A. Demurger, *Les Templiers*, p. 472; A. Demurger, 'Le concile de Vienne, la dévolution des biens du Temple et le sort des Templiers', in: *Templiers: De Jérusalem aux commanderies de Champagne*, ed. A. Baudin, G. Brunel, N. Dohrmann (Paris 2012), p. 156; A. Demurger, *Les Hospitaliers*, p. 456.

59 C. V. Langlois, 'Le procès', p. 418; R. Pernoud, *Les Templiers*, p. 89.

60 *Procès-verbal*, p. 4.

61 L. Delisle, *Mémoire*, p. 93; G. Bordonove, *La Tragédie*, p. 339.

62 A. Luttrell, 'The Hospitallers and the Papacy', p. 618.

63 A. Luttrell, 'Observations', p. 371.

64 C. V. Langlois, 'Le procès', p. 396; I. de La Torre, 'The Templars' Banking Activities', p. 186.

65 E. Mannier, *Ordre de Malte*, p. XIX; H. de Curzon, *La maison*, p. 202; L. L. L. Lavocat, *Procès*, p. 395; H. C. Lea, *A History*, vol. 3, pp. 252, 329; J. M. A. Delaville Le Roulx, *Les hospitaliers*, p. 34.

66 K. Schottmüller, *Der Untergang*, vol. 1, pp. 65, 538.

67 L. L. Borrelli de Serres, *Recherches*, vol. 3, pp. 37–38.

68 C. Mansuet Jeune, *Histoire*, vol. 2, p. 325; G. Lizerand, *Clément V*, p. 343 (the author did not specify the amount of the dowry).

69 E. A. R. Brown, *Customary Aids*, p. 19, n. 30.

70 *The Chronicle of Amadi*, transl. N. Coureas, P. Edbury (Nicosia 2015), p. 263. See also H. de Curzon, *La maison*, p. 257; L. L. L. Lavocat, *Procès*, pp. 117–118, 395.

71 H. de Curzon, *La maison*, pp. 257–258.

72 See, for example, K. Schottmüller, *Der Untergang*, vol. 1, p. 65; L. Delisle, *Mémoire*, p. 72; G. Lizerand, *Clément V*, p. 83; M. L. Bulst-Thiele, *Sacrae domus militiae Templi Hierosolymitani magistri: Untersuchungen zur Geschichte des Templerordens 1118/19–1314* (Göttingen 1974), p. 302; A. Demurger, *Les Templiers*, p. 427; A. Demurger, *Jacques de Molay: Le crépuscule des Templiers* (Paris 2007), pp. 225–227; P. Josserand, *Jacques de Molay*, pp. 205–206. For a different interpretation of this passage and its credibility, see B. Frale, *L'ultima battaglia dei Templari. Dal codice ombra d'obedienza militare alla construzione del processo per eresia* (Rome 2001), pp. 48–59; A. Luttreil, 'Observations', pp. 367–368. There are also references in literature that Philip actually owed the Templars 400,000 l. t. – K. Elm, 'Der Templerprozeß', p. 97.

73 See Section 3.3.1.

74 C. V. Langlois, 'Le procès', p. 418.

75 L. L. Borrelli de Serres, *Recherches*, vol. 3, p. 36. See also examples of accounts from the 1290s in L. Delisle, *Mémoire*, p. 89; J. Piquet, *Des banquiers*, p. 215. On the method of keeping the royal account in Parisian Temple, see also J. R. Strayer, *The Reign*, p. 144.

76 In one of his letters, Louis X mentioned that this issue had been raised during the discussions that accompanied the Council – AN, JJ 52, no. 131; *Registres*, vol. 2.1, no. 181, p. 40.

77 A. Luttrell, 'Observations', p. 371.
78 L. L. Borrelli de Serres, *Recherches*, vol. 3, p. 36.
79 E. Boutaric, 'Notices et extraits', no. 44, p. 231.
80 L. Delisle, *Mémoire*, pp. 90–91; L. L. Borrelli de Serres, *Recherches*, vol. 3, pp. 41, 45–46.
81 J. Raybaud, *Histoire*, vol 1, pp. 239–240.
82 G. Lizerand, *Clément V*, p. 342; M. Barber, *The Trial* (2006), p. 271.
83 H. Prutz, *Entwicklung*, no. 20, p. 292; G. Lizerand, *Clément V*, Appendice, no. 35, pp. 482–483; B. Barbiche, *Les actes*, vol. 3, no. 2465, p. 95. See also M. Barber, *The Trial* (2006), p. 271; A. Luttrell, 'The Hospitallers and the Papacy', pp. 614, 619.
84 ADHG, H 128, fol. 156.
85 *Recueil general*, pp. 36–38; P. Dupuy, *Histoire de la condamnation*, no. 120, pp. 462–463; M. Félibien, *Histoire*, vol. 3, pp. 319–320; R. A. de Vertot, *Histoire*, vol. 1, *Preuves*, pp. 648–650; *Codice diplomatico*, vol. 2, no. 28, pp. 34–35; *Les Olim*, vol. 2 (1847), pp. 580–582; *Actes*, no. 4089, p. 105.
86 ADHG, H 128, fol. 5v.
87 ADR, 48H25; BnF, NAL 58, fols. 324–325; *Cartulaire des Hospitaliers (Ordre de Saint-Jean de Jérusalem) du Velay*, ed. A. Chassaing (Paris 1888), no. 71, p. 123. See also L. Niepce, *Le Grand-prieuré d'Auvergne*, p. 85; J. Raybaud, *Histoire*, vol. 1, p. 244.
88 M. Miguet, *Templiers et Hospitaliers en Normandie*, Pièces annexes, no. 2, p. 229.
89 *Papsttum*, vol. 2, no. 116, p. 220.
90 AN, K 39, no. 1; *Monuments historiques*, no. 1081, p. 367 (Jules Tardif mistakenly attributed this order to Louis d'Evreux). See also J. M. Roger, 'La dévolution', p. 244.
91 A. Trudon des Ormes, *Étude*, p. 272.
92 *Cartulaire des Hospitaliers*, no. 70, pp. 122–123; L. Niepce, *Le Grand-prieuré d'Auvergne*, p. 85.
93 J. Raybaud, *Histoire*, vol. 1, pp. 240–241.
94 ADR, 48H1827–1828; ADHG, H Malte, La Cavalerie, liasse 15, no. 1; BnF, ms. lat. 9035, no. 32; BnF, NAL 25, fols. 243–248; A. Du Bourg, 'Prise de possession', pp. 177–184; *Procès-verbal*; B. de Gaulejac, *La liquidation*, Pièces justificatives, no. 2, pp. 92–98; M. Miguet, *Templiers et Hospitaliers en Normandie*, Pièces annexes, no. 2, pp. 228–229; J. M. Roger, 'La prise de possession', Pièces justificatives, nos. 1–2, pp. 239–242. These issues have been discussed in detail in works concerning the acquisition of Templar properties by the Hospitallers in various regions of France. See, for example, J. Raybaud, *Histoire*, vol. 1, pp. 241–243; B. de Gaulejac, *La liquidation*, pp. 34–35; J. M. Roger, 'La prise de possession', p. 238; J. M. Roger, 'La dévolution', p. 244; P. Josserand, 'Les Templiers en Bretagne', p. 16.
95 Nine inventories have been preserved: **Ansigny** (15 May 1313) – *Documents inédits*, no. 25, pp. 94–96; J. H. Geslin de Bourgogne, *Anciens évêchés de Bretagne*, vol. 6, *Bretagne féodale et militaire* (Saint-Brieuc 1879), pp. 218–221; **Toulouse** (8 May 1313; 21 December 1313) – A. Du Bourg, 'Prise de possession', pp. 177–184. Jochen Burgtorf lists four inventories from Toulouse copied by marquis of Albon ('The Trial Inventories', p. 108, n. 22), however, the *Cartulaire de l'Ordre du Temple* most likely contains two parts of the May 1313 inventory (BnF, NAL 32, fols. 526–537, 546–548), a December 1313 inventory (BnF, NAL 32, fols. 539–545) and an account from 1314 by the Hospitaller treasurer managing the Templar estates in Toulouse (BnF, NAL 32, fols. 549–558); **Bret** (15 May 1313) – J. M. Roger, 'L'inventaire', pp. 363–367; **Cenan** (17 maja 1313) – J. M. Roger, 'La prise de possession', Pièces justificatives, no. 1, pp. 239–240; **Joigny** (6 June 1313) – *Inventaire des ornements et vases sacrés de la chapelle de la commanderie de Joigny, au commencement du XIVe siècle*, ed. A. Tardif, *Annales archéologiques*, 7 (1847), pp. 85–86; **Larramet** (18 May 1313) – BnF, NAL 33, fols. 302–314; **La Lande-de-Parthenay** (20 May 1313) – *Documents*

inédits, pp. 92–94; **Larmont** (May 1313) – BnF, NAL 33, fols. 359–362; **Sours** (27 May 1313) – AN, S 4999 A, no. 79; BnF, NAL 46, fols. 77–84.

96 ADHG, H Malte, Douzens 3, no. 1; B. de Gaulejac, *La liquidation*, Pièces justificatives, no. 3, p. 99. See also J. Raybaud, *Histoire*, vol. 1, p. 244 (The order is incorrectly dated 18 July).

97 *Inventaire d'anciens comptes*, p. 265.

98 ADHG, H Malte, Douzens 3, no. 2; B. de Gaulejac, *La liquidation*, Pièces justificatives, no. 6, pp. 103–104.

99 A. Luttrell, 'The Hospitallers in Cyprus after 1291', in: A. Luttrell, *The Hospitallers in Cyprus, Rhodes, Greece and the West, 1291–1440. Collected Studies* (London 1978), pp. 167–168; P. W. Edbury, *The Kingdom of Cyprus and the Crusaders, 1191–1374* (Cambridge 1991); p. 136; T. M. Vann, 'The Assimilation', p. 342.

100 Reg. Clem. V, vol. 8, no. 9386, pp. 205–206; *Codice diplomatico*, vol. 2, no. 5, p. 399. See also G. Lizerand, *Clément V*, p. 342.

101 J. M. A. Delaville Le Roulx, *Les hospitaliers*, p. 40; K. Toomaspoeg, 'Le patrimoine des grands ordres militaires en Sicile, 1145–1492', *Mélanges de l'École française de Rome. Moyen-Age*, 113 (2001), no. 1, pp. 335–337; J. M. Roger, 'La réforme de l'Hôpital par Jean XXII: Le démembrement des prieurés de Saint-Gilles et de France (21 juillet 1317)', in: *On the Margins of Crusading: The Military Orders, the Papacy and the Christian World*, ed. H. Nicholson (Farnham 2011), pp. 122–123.

102 H. J. Nicholson, *The Knights*, p. 189; P. Slavin, 'The Fate', pp. 220–221; J. M. Jefferson, *The Templar Estates*, pp. 162–164.

103 *Foedera*, vol. 2.1, p. 10 (document from August 1313); *Foedera*, vol. 2.1, pp. 54–55 (document from November 1313). For more on this topic, see C. Perkins, 'The Wealth', pp. 252–263; J. M. A. Delaville Le Roulx, *Les hospitaliers*, pp. 36–39; A. M. Leys, *The Forfeiture*, pp. 161–163; J. S. Hamilton, 'King Edward II', pp. 223–224; H. J. Nicholson, *The Knights*, p. 189; S. Phillips, 'The Hospitallers' Acquisition of the Templar Lands in England', in: *The Debate on the Trial of the Templars (1307–1314)*, ed. J. Burgtorf, P. F. Crawford, H. J. Nicholson (Farnham 2010), pp. 237–246.

104 A. Demurger, *Les Hospitaliers*, p. 456.

105 H. C. Lea, *A History*, vol. 3, p. 330; J. M. A. Delaville Le Roulx, *Les hospitaliers*, pp. 39–40; M. Starnawska, 'The Commanderies ot the Templars in the Polish Lands and Their History after the End of the Order', in: *The Debate on the Trial of the Templars (1307–1314)*, ed. J. Burgtorf, P. F. Crawford, H. J. Nicholson (Farnham 2010), pp. 301–314; A. Demurger, *Les Hospitaliers*, p. 455.

106 For more on the negotiations regarding the distribution of goods across the Iberian Peninsula, as well as their final outcome, see J. M. A. Delaville Le Roulx, *Les hospitaliers*, pp. 42–47; C. B. Goñi, 'La Orden del Hospital y la recepción de los bienes templarios en la Península Ibérica', *Hispania Sacra*, 51 (1999), no. 104, pp. 531–556; A. Forey, *The Fall*, pp. 156–209; J. M. Sans i Travé, *La fi*, pp. 323–333; C. Porro, 'Reassessing', pp. 177–182; A. Demurger, *Les Hospitaliers*, pp. 460–462.

107 M. Barber, *The Trial* (2006), p. 272.

108 H. C. Lea, *A History*, vol. 3, p. 329.

109 K. Schottmüller, *Der Untergang*, vol. 1, p. 541; A. Demurger, 'Dal Tempio all'Ospedale', p. 96.

110 A. Demurger, *Les Hospitaliers*, p. 457.

111 J. N. Hillgarth, *Ramon Lull*, p. 78; S. Schein, *Fideles Crucis*, p. 242.

112 *Procès-verbal*, pp. 4–5.

113 A. Du Bourg, *Histoire*, p. 10; J. M. Roger, 'La prise de possession', p. 228; B. Suau, 'La maison du Temple à Toulouse: un site méconnu', *Mémoires de société archéologique du Midi de la France*, 70 (2010), p. 214.

114 BnF, NAL 32, fol. 536; A. Du Bourg, 'Prise de possession', pp. 178–183.

115 Appendix, fol. 1v.

116 ADHG, H 123, no. 5.
117 ADHG, H 89 II, p. 8.
118 ADHG, H 89 II, p. 8; ADHG, H 123, no. 10; B. de Gaulejac, *La liquidation*, Pièces justificatives, no. 31, p. 164. On the papal ban on selling Templar assets taken over by the Hospitallers, see Section 3.5.
119 ADHG, H 89 II, pp. 15–17; B. de Gaulejac, *La liquidation*, Pièces justificatives, nos. 32, 34–35, pp. 166–167, 169–170. The provisions of this agreement were implemented over the following months.
120 ADHG, H 89 II, pp. 11–12. On the royal measures taken in connection with the religious house in Toulouse between 1324 and 1326, see also B. de Gaulejac, *La liquidation*, pp. 81–82.
121 *Registres*, vol. 2.1, nos. 277–278, pp. 60–61. Antonio Pessagno also took control of other houses that are not mentioned in either document – J. M. Roger, 'La prise de possession', p. 228; J. M. Roger, 'Antonio Pessagno', in: *Prier et combattre: Dictionnaire européen des ordres militaires au Moyen Âge*, ed. N. Bériou, P. Josserand (Paris 2009), p. 98.
122 J. M. Roger, 'La prise de possession', p. 228.
123 A. Demurger, 'Dal Tempio all'Ospedale', p. 97.
124 E. Mannier, *Ordre de Malte*, p. 20; L. L. L. Lavocat, *Procès*, pp. 399–400.
125 C. Métais, *Les Templiers*, no. 192, p. 200. See also E. Mannier, *Ordre de Malte*, p. 125.
126 E. Mannier, *Ordre de Malte*, p. 371; C. Schmidt, 'Les commanderies et les hôspitaux dans l'Yonne', in: *Inventaire sommaire des archives départementales postérieures à 1790. Yonne, Archives hospitalières: série H, suppl.*, vol. 4, ed. F. Molard (Auxerre 1897), p. XVIII.
127 J. U. Devals, '*Montricoux*', *Mémoires de l'Académie impériale des sciences, inscriptions et belles-lettres de Toulouse,* 2 (1864), p. 151.
128 ADHG H. Malte Lacapelle 5, liasse 7, no. 4; E. Lalou, *Itinéraire*, vol. 2, p. 407.
129 *Papsttum*, vol. 2, no. 57, p. 84; *The Templars*, no. 70, p. 257. See also A. Demurger, *La persécution*, p. 25.
130 ADHG H. Malte Lacapelle 5, liasse 7, no. 4; E. Lalou, *Itinéraire*, vol. 2, p. 407.
131 J. U. Devals, '*Montricoux*', p. 151.
132 Appendix, fol. 9 r.
133 ADHG, H 89 II, p. 11; B. de Gaulejac, *La liquidation*, Pièces justificatives, no. 33, p. 168.
134 J. U. Devals, '*Montricoux*', p. 152.
135 L. Delisle, *Mémoire*, pp. 90–91; L. L. Borrelli de Serres, *Recherches*, vol. 3, pp. 41, 45–46.
136 L. L. Borrelli de Serres, *Recherches*, vol. 3, p. 41, n. 1.
137 The document was dated 15 August 1317 – AN, J 1036, no. 7; AN, J 1044, no. 22 (second copy). See also H. de Curzon, *La maison*, p. 244; J. M. A. Delaville Le Roulx, *Les hospitaliers*, p. 36; J. M. Roger, 'La prise de possession', p. 228; A. Demurger, *Les Hospitaliers*, p. 457; L. Mercuri, *L'Enclos du Temple: topografia e forme di un'assenza della Parigi medieval* (Rome 2025), p. 96.
138 *Codice diplomatico*, vol. 2, no. 56, pp. 73–74; Jean XXII, *Lettres communes analysées d'après les registres dits d'Avignon et du Vatican*, ed. G. Mollat, vol. 3 (Paris 1906), no. 10673, p. 37. See also J. M. A. Delaville Le Roulx, *Les hospitaliers*, p. 36; L. Mercuri, *L'Enclos*, p. 96.
139 J. M. A. Delaville Le Roulx, *Les hospitaliers*, p. 36, n. 5.
140 L. L. Borrelli de Serres, *Recherches*, vol. 3, p. 83.
141 H. de Curzon, *La maison*, p. 244; A. Demurger, *Les Hospitaliers*, p. 457; L. Mercuri, *L'Enclos*, p. 96.
142 ADR, 48H1827–1828; BnF, NAL 33, fol. 304 (**Larramet**); BnF, NAL 33, fol. 359 (**Larmont**); BnF, NAL 34, fol. 506 (**Lectoure**); BnF, NAL 34, fol. 509 (**Fleurance**); BnF, NAL 32, fols. 526–527; A. Du Bourg, 'Prise de possession', pp. 177–178 (**Toulouse**); B. de Gaulejac, *La liquidation*, Pièces justificatives, no. 2, p. 92 (**Lomiers**).

143 BnF, NAL 33, fols. 302–314 (**Larramet**); BnF, NAL 33, fols. 359–362 (**Larmont**).
144 BnF, NAL 32, fols. 526–537, 546–548; A. Du Bourg, 'Prise de possession', pp. 178–183.
145 BnF, NAL 34, fol. 506.
146 BnF, NAL 34, fols. 508–510.
147 All three inventories were compiled by Guillaume Hervé. Their dates correspond to the dates of transfer of the houses indicated in the protocol – *Documents inédits*, no. 25, pp. 92–93 (**Ansigny** and **La Lande-de-Parthenay**); *Procès-verbal*, pp. 6, 9.
148 J. H. Geslin de Bourgogne, *Anciens évêchés*, p. 219 (**Ansigny**); J. M. Roger, 'L'inventaire', pp. 366–367 (**Bret**); J. M. Roger, 'La prise de possession', Pièces justificatives, no. 1, p. 240 (**Cenan**). In La Lande-de-Parthenay, Jean Alexandre, the tenant, and his wife witnessed the writing of the minutes. However, the document does not indicate that either of them provided any information – *Documents inédits*, no. 25, p. 94.
149 AN, S 4999 A, no. 79; BnF, NAL 46, fol. 77.
150 *Inventaire des ornements*, p. 85.
151 *Procès-verbal*, p. 16.
152 J. M. Roger, 'La prise de possession', p. 238.
153 J. Burgtorf, 'The Trial Inventories', p. 112.
154 M. Miguet, *Templiers et Hospitaliers en Normandie*, Pièces annexes, no. 2, p. 229.
155 J. M. Roger, 'La prise de possession', Pièces justificatives, no. 2, pp. 242 and 237 (editor's commentary).
156 J. M. Roger, 'La prise de possession', Pièces justificatives, no. 2, pp. 243 and 237 (editor's commentary).
157 ADHG, H Malte, Douzens 3, no. 2; B. de Gaulejac, *La liquidation*, Pièces justificatives, no. 6, pp. 103–104.
158 Appendix, fol. 12r.
159 Appendix, fol. 2r.
160 Appendix, fol. 1v.
161 J. Raybaud, *Histoire*, vol. 1, p. 245.
162 Appendix, fol. 4v.
163 Reg. Clem. V, vol. 8, nos. 8961–8962; B. Barbiche, *Les actes*, vol. 3, nos. 2453–2454, p. 91.
164 ADHG, H 128, fol. 5v.
165 ADHG, fol. 4v.
166 See Section 2.1.3.
167 ADHG, H 128, fols. 96v, 115v.
168 ADHG, H 89 II, p. 7; ADHG, H 123, no. 3; ADHG, H 128, fol. 45. B. de Gaulejac, *La liquidation*, Pièces justificatives, no. 5, p. 102. See also J. Raybaud, *Histoire*, vol. 1, p. 245.
169 ADHG, H 128, fol. 65v; B. de Gaulejac, *La liquidation*, Pièces justificatives, no. 4, pp. 100–101.
170 ADHG, H 128, fols. 156r–157v.
171 ADHG, H 123, no. 4.
172 M. Miguet, *Templiers et Hospitaliers en Normandie*, Pièces annexes, no. 6, pp. 328–331.
173 Reg. Clem. V, vol. 7, no. 7806, p. 71; ADHG, H 129, fols. 69r-79r.
174 ADHG, H. 123, no. 4; B. de Gaulejac, *La liquidation*, Pièces justificatives, nos. 9–10, pp. 118–119.
175 The letter was dated 8 July 1314 – ADHG, H 123, no. 6; B. de Gaulejac, *La liquidation*, Pièces justificatives, no. 10, p. 119. See also J. Raybaud, *Histoire*, vol. 1, p. 250.
176 ADHG, H Malte, Douzens 3, no. 14; B. de Gaulejac, *La liquidation*, Pièces justificatives, no. 8, pp. 107–117. See also J. Raybaud, *Histoire*, vol. 1, pp. 238–239.
177 ADHG, H 129, fols. 84–88v.

178 A. Pétel, *La Commanderie, Pièces Justificatives*, nos. 8–9, pp. 137–138. See also A. Pétel, *La Commanderie*, pp. 75–77.
179 Reg. Clem. V, vol. 8, no. 8975, p. 30; B. Barbiche, *Les actes*, vol. 3, no. 2455, pp. 91–92.
180 *Registres*, vol. 2.1, no. 2764, p. 532.
181 ADHG, H. Malte, Douzens 3, no. 1; B. de Gaulejac, *La liquidation*, p. 40.
182 Appendix, fol. 10r.
183 E. Mannier, *Ordre de Malte*, p. 200.
184 *Registres*, vol. 2.1, no. 2762, pp. 530–531; *Registres*, vol. 2.1, no. 2925, p. 572; Appendix, fols. 1r, 6r, etc. The case of the deceased regional administrator, whose debts to the former managers were settled by his sons in 1317, was also mentioned by Demurger – 'Dal Tempio all'Ospedale', p. 95.
185 *Registres*, vol. 2.1, no. 2764, p. 532.
186 *Inventaire d'anciens comptes*, p. 265.
187 A. Du Bourg, 'Prise de possession', p. 174.
188 E. Mannier, *Ordre de Malte*, pp. XVII–XVIII; K. Schottmüller, *Der Untergang* vol. 1, p. 539; L. L. L. Lavocat, *Procès*, p. 395; G. Bordonove, *La Tragédie*, p. 339.
189 *Tres calices argenteos, quandam crucem anctam munitam lapidibus preciosis incastratam in auro et argento* – A. Higounet-Nadal, 'L'inventaire', p. 258. See also J. Delmas, 'L'inventaire des biens de la commanderie de Sainte-Eulalie du Larzac en 1308', in: *La Commanderie, institution des ordres militaires dans l'Occident médiéval*, ed. A. Luttrell and L. Pessouyre (Paris 2002), p. 322.
190 *Une croix d'argent et I vaisel d'argent (…) I mecel, I antefenier, I sautier, I breviaire et I ordenaire (…) I qualice d'argent doré* – A. Pétel, 'Templiers et Hospitaliers dans le diocèse de Troyes. Comptes', pp. 346–347, 350.
191 **Ansigny**: *un calice doré efors et deans, et une patenne dorée (…) une petite crois cuverte d'argent* – *Documents inédits*, no. 25, p. 94; J. H. Geslin de Bourgogne, *Anciens évêchés*, pp. 218–219; **Toulouse**: *unum calicem, cum sua patella de argento, deauratum itnus et pomelum deauratum cum opera cum cruce in pede (…) unum calicem de argento deauratum intus et foris cum platina sua (…) unum turribulum argenti (…) duo vasa eborea cum reliquiis (…) quamdam magnam crucem de cristallo (…) duo candelabra de cristallo (…) unam pectem de ebore* – A. Du Bourg, 'Prise de possession', p. 181; **Bret**: *un calice doré dedans* – J. M. Roger, 'L'inventaire', p. 366; **Cenan**: *un calice doré dedans é defors (…) crois couverte d'argent doree, ou il ha reliques (…) un ensanser d'argent* – A. Du Bourg, 'La prise de possession', Pièces justificatives, no. 1, p. 239; **Joigny**: *une croiz d'argent (…) ung vaisselet d'argent, deus bureites d'argent (…) ung parement à l'autel, d'or* – *Inventaire des ornements*, pp. 85–86; **Larramet**: *unum calicem cum sua patena, argenti, intus de auratum (…) quoddam pecten eburneum* – BnF, NAL 33, fol. 311; **La Lande-de-Parthenay**: *un calice doré dedans (…) doues crois ouvertes d'argent dorées, ou il ha reliques* – *Documents inédits*, no. 25, p. 93; **Larmont**: *unum calicem argenti, cum sua patena, intus deauratum* – BnF, NAL 33, fol. 359; **Sours**: *unus calix de argento cum platena* – AN, S 4999 A, no. 79; BnF, NAL 46, fol. 82.
192 See A. M. Legras, J. L. Lemaître, 'La pratique liturgique des Templiers et des Hospitaliers de Saint-Jean de Jérusalem', in: *L'écrit dans la société médiévale. Textes en hommage à Lucie Fossier*, ed. C. Bourlet, A. Dufour (Paris 1991), pp. 121–126. The article does not include the inventories form the following houses: **Sours**: *unum missale, unum graduale, unus antiphonarius, unus legendarius, unum psalterum, unum collectarium, unum commune sanctorum, quedeam hystoria de Sancto Ludovico* – AN, S 4999 A, no. 79; BnF, NAL 46, fol. 82; **Larramet**: *unum librum missalem (…) unum officierium (…) unum epistolerium et evangelisterium (…) unum breviarium (…) unum sanctorale (…) unum psalterium* – BnF, NAL 33, fols. 311–312; **Larmont**: *duos psalteros veteres (…) unum missal antiquum (…) unum alium missal cum camisia de lino (…) unum*

librum de cantu (…) unum epistolerium et evangelisterium mixtum (…) unum responsorium, cum media poste (…) unum leccionarium veterem – BnF, NAL 33, fols. 359–360.

193 *Inventaire des ornements*, p. 86.

194 BnF, NAL 32, fol. 527; A. Du Bourg, 'Prise de possession', p. 178.

195 BnF, NAL 32, fol. 533; A. Du Bourg, 'Prise de possession', p. 181.

196 *Le Procès*, vol. 2, p. 218; *Processus*, vol. 1, p. 910.

197 J. M. Roger, 'L'inventaire', p. 367.

198 *unum minhotum altaris, signatum, signo Templi consuam* – BnF, NAL 33, fol. 359.

199 BnF, NAL 32, fol. 529; A. Du Bourg, 'Prise de possession', p. 179.

200 *Les Olim*, vol. 2, p. 581.

201 ADHG, H 123, no. 7; BnF, NAL 32, fols. 549–558; B. de Gaulejac, *La liquidation*, Pièces justificatives no. 12, pp. 126–127.

202 ADHG, H 123, no. 7; BnF, NAL 32, fol. 554; B. de Gaulejac, *La liquidation*, Pièces justificatives, no. 12, p. 127.

203 This explanation was presented by Antoine Du Bourg, *Histoire*, p. 74. It was also adopted by Forey, 'Templars', p. 97.

204 ADHG, H 123, no. 7; BnF, NAL 32, fols. 555–556; B. de Gaulejac, *La liquidation*, Pièces justificatives, no. 12, p. 127.

205 ADHG, H 123, no. 7; BnF, NAL 32, fol. 553; B. de Gaulejac, *La liquidation*, Pièces justificatives, no. 12, p. 127.

206 It is difficult to determine the exact date of this council. It is not mentioned in any literature – H. Vidal, 'Les conciles méridionaux aux XIIIe et XIVe sièces', *Cahiers de Fanjeaux*, 29 (1994), pp. 147–180. On the conclusion of the proceedings against the Templars in the province of Narbonne, see B. Alart, 'Suppression de l'ordre du Temple en Roussillon', *Bulletin de la Société agricole, scientifique et littéraire des Pyrénées-Orientales*, 15 (1867), pp. 68–71; A. Forey, 'Templars', p. 91; A. Demurger, *La persécution*, pp. 273–274.

207 ADHG, H 123, no. 7; BnF, NAL 32, fol. 556; B. de Gaulejac, *La liquidation*, Pièces justificatives, no. 12, p. 127.

208 ADHG, H 123, no. 7; BnF, NAL 32, fol. 553; B. de Gaulejac, *La liquidation*, Pièces justificatives, no. 12, p. 126.

209 On the material conditions of the Templars after the end of the trial, see A. Demurger, *Les Templiers*, pp. 476–479; A. Forey, 'Templars'. Other relevant works are listed in note 1 of this article.

210 See, fo example, Jean XXII, *Lettres*, vol. 2, Paris 1905, no. 6974, p. 134; Jean XXII, *Lettres*, vol. 3, no. 13307, p. 277. See also A. Demurger, *Les Templiers*, p. 475.

211 Jean XXII, *Lettres*, vol. 1, Paris 1904, no. 2510, p. 233; Jean XXII, *Lettres*, vol. 1, nos. 3182–3192, p. 292; Jean XXII, *Lettres*, vol. 2, no. 7918, p. 230. See also G. Mollat, 'Dispersion définitive des Templiers après leur suppression', *Comptes rendus des séances de l'Académie des Inscriptions et Belles-Lettres*, 96 (1952), no. 3, p. 377.

212 *Lettres secrètes*, no. 1181, cols. 985–986.

213 *Le procès*, vol. 1, p. 202; *Processus*, vol. 1, p. 282.

214 Jean XXII, *Lettres*, vol. 2, no. 6974, p. 134; G. Mollat, 'Dispersion', p. 377.

215 A. Luttrell, 'Gli Ospitalieri', pp. 80–81; A. J. Forey, 'Ex-Templars in England', *Journal of Ecclesiastical History*, 53 (2002), no. 1, p. 28; A. Demurger, *Les Templiers*, pp. 476–477; R. Vinas, 'Le destin des templiers du Roussillon, 1276–1330', *Cahiers de Fanjeaux*, 41 (2006), pp. 198–203.

216 *Codice diplomatico*, vol. 2, no. 52, p. 69; Jean XXII, *Lettres*, vol. 2, nos. 8721–8723, pp. 310–311; *Bullarium Franciscanum romanorum pontificum constitutiones epistolas, ac diplomata continens*, ed. G. Gacinto Sbaraglia, C. Eubel, vol. 5 (Rome 1898), no. 347, pp. 160–162; *Lettres de Jean XXII (1316–1334)*, ed. A. Fayen, vol. 1 (Rome 1908), no. 666, p. 263. See also G. Mollat, 'Dispersion', p. 378; A. J. Forey, 'Ex-Templars', pp. 30–31; A. Forey, 'Templars', pp. 101–102.

217 V. Bessey, *Les commanderies,* no. 2, pp. 316, 319; A. Demurger, *La persécution*, pp. 274–275. For more on the pensions of former Templars, see A. Forey, 'Templars', p. 97.
218 On this topic, see A. Forey, 'Templars', pp. 102–104.
219 *Codice diplomatico*, vol. 2, no. 53, pp. 70–72; *Documents concernants les Templiers extraits des Archives de Malte*, ed. J. Delaville le Roulx (Paris 1882), no. 40, p. 51; H. Prutz, *Entwicklung*, no. 21, pp. 293–294. See also G. Mollat, 'Dispersion', p. 379; A. J. Forey, 'Ex-Templars', pp. 31–33.
220 In 1318, John XXII instructed the archbishop of Narbonne to provide for the maintenance of 22 brothers who had been imprisoned in his province shortly before – Jean XXII, *Lettres*, vol. 2, no. 6974, p. 134. See also A. Forey, 'Templars', p. 95.
221 See, for example, Jean XXII, *Lettres*, vol. 2, no. 7918, p. 230.
222 V. Bessey, *Les commanderies*, no. 2, pp. 316–317, 319; V. Bessey, *Les commanderies*, no. 4, p. 323.
223 E. Mannier, *Ordre de Malte*, p. XXI; H. C. Lea, *A History*, vol. 3, p. 329; J. M. A. Delaville Le Roulx, *Les hospitaliers*, p. 34; N. Housley, *The Avignon Papacy*, pp. 281–282; M. Miguet, *Templiers et Hospitaliers en Normandie*, p. 51.
224 This was referred to in the royal ordinance dated 28 November 1314 – E. A. R. Brown, 'Royal Salvation', pp. 22–23, 51. For more on the reasons behind Philip the Fair's decision, see E. A. R. Brown,'Philip the Fair's Sons, Their Statuses, and Their Landed Endowments', *Medieval Prosopography*, 32 (2017), pp. 210–217.
225 AN, JJ 52, no. 131; *Registres*, vol. 2.1, no. 181, p. 40.
226 ADHG, H 123, no. 8; B. de Gaulejac, *La liquidation*, Pièces justificatives, no. 14, pp. 130–132.
227 ADHG, H Malte, Douzens 3, no. 5; B. de Gaulejac, *La liquidation*, Pièces justificatives, no. 13, p. 129.
228 J. Raybaud, *Histoire*, vol. 1, p. 250.
229 BnF, ms. lat. 9035, no. 33 (dated 27 August); BnF, NAL 69, fols. 86–89.
230 ADHG, H Malte, Douzens 3, no. 5 (dated 28 August); ADHG, H Malte, Douzens 3, no. 17 (dated 26 August); BnF, NAL 69, fols. 86–89; B. de Gaulejac, *La liquidation*, Pièces justificatives, no. 16, pp. 134–136. See also J. Raybaud, *Histoire*, vol. 1, p. 250.
231 Order dated 29 August 1315 – ADHG, H Malte, Douzens 3, no. 17; BnF, NAL 69, fols. 90–92; B. de Gaulejac, *La liquidation*, Pièces justificatives, no. 17, pp. 137–138.
232 BnF, ms. lat. 9035, no. 33; BnF, NAL 69, fols. 88–89.
233 *Registres*, vol. 2.1, no. 2764, p. 532.
234 J. Raybaud, *Histoire*, vol. 1, p. 249.
235 *Archives historiques*, no. 75, pp. 174–180.
236 *Registres*, vol. 2.1, no. 648, p. 145.
237 M. Miguet, *Templiers et Hospitaliers en Normandie*, Pièces annexes, no. 2, p. 430.
238 M. Miguet, *Templiers et Hospitaliers en Normandie*, Pièces annexes, no. 2, pp. 408–409.
239 M. Miguet, *Templiers et Hospitaliers en Normandie*, Pièces annexes, no. 2, pp. 50–52, 408.
240 M. Miguet, *Templiers et Hospitaliers en Normandie*, Pièces annexes, no. 2, p. 50.
241 *Les Olim*, vol. 3.2, pp. 989–990; *Actes*, no. 4420, p. 136. For more on the conflict and its causes, see A. Trudon des Ormes, *Étude*, pp. 205–209.
242 A. Trudon des Ormes, *Étude*, pp. 209–210, n. 1.
243 P. Dupuy, *Histoire de la condamnation*, no. 124, pp. 471–474; M. Félibien, *Histoire*, vol. 3, pp. 320–322; *Monuments historiques*, no. 1102, p. 369; L. Delisle, *Mémoire*, no. 36, pp. 229–233; *The Templars*, no. 79, pp. 324–328 (English translation). See also E. Mannier, *Ordre de Malte*, pp. XIX–XX; H. de Curzon, *La maison*, pp. 202–203; L. L. L. Lavocat, *Procès*, p. 397; J. M. A. Delaville Le Roulx, *Les hospitaliers*, p. 35; J. Raybaud, *Histoire*, vol. 1, pp. 251–252. On the agreement between Louis X and the Hospitallers and the process of transferring properties during this monarch's reign, see also B. de Gaulejac, *La liquidation*, pp. 50–59.

244 A. Luttrell, 'Observations', p. 371.
245 H. de Curzon, *La maison*, p. 202; L. L. L. Lavocat, *Procès*, p. 397; B. Causse, *Eglise*, vol. 1, p. 249; S. Menache, 'The Hospitallers', p. 161.
246 L. L. Borrelli de Serres, *Recherches*, vol. 3, p. 42, n. 3.
247 ADHG, H 124, no. 4.
248 The agreement was dated 17 December 1315 – AN, J 164, no. 35. See also J. Petit, *Charles de Valois (1270–1325)* (Paris 1900), p. 133; G. Lizerand, *Clément V*, p. 345, n. 2; B. de Gaulejac, *La liquidation*, p. 58.
249 *Monuments historiques*, no. 1117, p. 370.
250 Appendix, fol. 9v; ADHG, H 123, no. 9; B. de Gaulejac, *La liquidation*, Pièces justificatives, no. 25, p. 152.
251 J. Petit, *Charles de Valois*, Pièces justificatives, no. 18, pp. 392–393; Appendix, fols. 13r, 1v, 3v, 9v.
252 On 26 February 1318, Guillaume Clignet ordered his subordinates in southern France to pay Charles de Valois the sums owed to him – ADHG, H 123, no. 9; B. de Gaulejac, *La liquidation*, Pièces justificatives, no. 26, pp. 153–154. On 3 March, Philip V instructed judicial officers to assist Bernard Raymond Caldier in collecting debts relating to the furnishings of the Templars' houses – ADHG, H 123, no. 9; B. de Gaulejac, *La liquidation*, Pièces justificatives, no. 27, p. 155. See also B. de Gaulejac, *La liquidation*, pp. 58–59.
253 ADHG, H Malte, Pézeans 2, pièce 82; B. de Gaulejac, *La liquidation*, Pièces justificatives, no. 19, pp. 141–142; B. de Gaulejac, *La liquidation*, Pièces justificatives, no. 23, pp. 148–149.
254 ADHG, H 124, no. 6; B. de Gaulejac, *La liquidation*, Pièces justificatives, no. 18, pp. 139–140.
255 ADHG, H 124; B. de Gaulejac, *La liquidation*, Pièces justificatives, no. 21, pp. 144–145.
256 ADHG, H 124. See also B. de Gaulejac, *La liquidation*, p. 63.
257 BnF, NAL 57, fols. 40–41.
258 ADHG, H Malte, Pézeans 2, pièce 82; B. de Gaulejac, *La liquidation*, Pièces justificatives, no. 29, pp. 158–162.
259 *Registres*, vol. 2.1, no. 2826, pp. 547–548.
260 ADHG, H 124, no. 5; B. de Gaulejac, *La liquidation*, Pièces justificatives, no. 22, pp. 146–147.
261 *Lettres secrètes*, vol. 1, no. 236, cols. 186–187; B. Barbiche, *Les actes*, vol. 3, no. 2501, p. 110. See also B. de Gaulejac, *La liquidation*, p. 60; N. Housley, *The Avignon Papacy*, p. 281.
262 We learn about the king's request through the pope's response, dated 3 August 1317: *Codice diplomatico*, vol. 2, no. 41, pp. 60–61.
263 For more on the circumstances surrounding the introduction of the reform and the content of the provisions of 21 July 1317, see J. M. A. Delaville Le Roulx, *Les hospitaliers*, pp. 21–22; J. M. Roger, 'La réforme de l'Hôpital', pp. 101–138.
264 *Codice diplomatico*, vol. 2, no. 41, pp. 60–61; *Lettres secrètes*, vol. 1, no. 333, cols. 253–254. See also N. Housley, *The Avignon Papacy*, p. 281.
265 The papal letter of 29 September 1317 concerned the actions of the king's officials in the seneschalship of Beaucaire – *Lettres secrètes*, vol. 1, no. 398, col. 316. See also B. de Gaulejac, *La liquidation*, p. 61; J. M. A. Delaville Le Roulx, *Les hospitaliers*, p. 35, n. 5; N. Housley, *The Avignon Papacy*, p. 282.
266 *Les Olim*, vol. 2, pp. 643–645; *Actes*, no. 4483, pp. 143–144. See also L. L. Borrelli de Serres, *Recherches*, vol. 3, p. 43. Barber mistakenly believed that this document confirmed an earlier agreement between the king and the Hospitallers, as approved by the Parliament of Paris – *The Trial* (2006), p. 272.
267 *Lettres secrètes*, vol. 1, nos. 453–454, cols. 361–367. See also B. de Gaulejac, *La liquidation*, p. 61; J. M. A. Delaville Le Roulx, *Les hospitaliers*, p. 36, n. 2.

268 ADHG, H 124, no. 7; B. de Gaulejac, *La liquidation*, Pièces justificatives, no. 4, pp. 150–151.

269 The exact timing of the dispute and the point at which the pope intervened is not known. The editor of the letter suggested that it was created between 1316 and 1318 – *Lettres secrètes*, vol. 1, nos. 917–918, cols. 794–796.

270 *Lettres secrètes*, vol. 1, no. 918, cols. 796–798, *Lettres secrètes*, vol. 1, no. 986, cols. 852–853.

271 P. Dupuy, *Histoire de la condamnation*, no. 124, pp. 474–478; M. Félibien, *Histoire*, vol. 3, pp. 322–325; R. A. de Vertot, *Histoire*, vol. 1, *Preuves*, p. 650; L. Delisle, *Mémoire*, no. 37, pp. 234–238. See also H. de Curzon, *La maison*, p. 203; J. M. A. Delaville Le Roulx, *Les hospitaliers*, p. 36; B. de Gaulejac, *La liquidation*, pp. 61–62.

272 See, for example, examples of misinterpretations from 19th-century literature, provided by L. L. Borrelli de Serres, *Recherches*, vol. 3, p. 43, n. 3.

273 J. M. A. Delaville Le Roulx, *Les hospitaliers*, p. 34; A. Forey, *The Military Orders. From the Twelfth*, p. 230; M. Miguet, *Templiers et Hospitaliers en Normandie*, p. 51; A. Demurger, 'Le concile', p. 156; A. Luttrell, 'Observations', p. 369.

274 C. V. Langlois, *Registres*, no. 1021, pp. 372–373; *Registres*, vol. 2.1, no. 1806, p. 340.

275 ADHG, H Malte, Pézeans 1, pièce 25; B. de Gaulejac, *La liquidation*, Pièces justificatives, no. 30, p. 160.

276 M. Miguet, *Templiers et Hospitaliers en Normandie*, pp. 50–52, 408.

277 *Registres*, vol. 2.1, no. 2762, p. 531.

278 *Les journaux du trésor de Charles IV*, no. 2508, col. 436; *Les journaux du trésor de Charles IV*, no. 6449, col. 1075; *Les journaux du trésor de Charles IV*, no. 9515, col. 1526.

279 The exact amount varies from one document to another. The *Journaux du Trésor* mention 3787 l. 16 s. 2 d. t. (*Les journaux du trésor de Charles IV*, no. 3575, col. 616), while a royal letter from 1322, included in Renaud de Saint-Ouen's report, gives the amount as 3780 l. 16 s. 2 d. t. (Appendix, fol. 7v). Another letter from the same monarch, written at the end of 1323, gives the amount as 3770 l. 16 s. 2 d. t. (Appendix, fol. 5v). The latter sum is also given in a fragment of the settlement for 1323 – Appendix, fol. 13r. See also B. de Gaulejac, *La liquidation*, p. 78, n. 5.

280 *Les journaux du trésor de Charles IV*, no. 3575, col. 616; Appendix, fol. 13r.

281 Appendix, fol. 5v.

282 E. Mannier, *Ordre de Malte*, p. 20; L. L. L. Lavocat, *Procès*, pp. 399–400.

283 *Registres*, vol. 2.1, no. 3449, p. 716.

284 On the collection of money from Jewish properties by both commissioners, and more broadly on actions against French Jews during the reign of Charles IV, see Y. Dossant, 'Les Juifs à Toulouse: un demi-siècle d'histoire communautaire', *Cahiers de Fenjeaux*, 12 (1977), pp. 117–139; E. A. R. Brown, 'Philip V, Charles IV, and the Jews of France: The Alleged Expulsion of 1322', *Speculum*, 66 (1991), no. 2, pp. 294–329.

285 *Registres*, vol. 3.1; *Règne de Philippe de Valois*, no. 426, p. 54; *Les journaux du trésor de Charles IV*, no. 5909, col. 987.

286 B. de Gaulejac, *La liquidation*, p. 70.

287 Appendix, fol. 18v.

288 Appendix, fol. 13r.

289 Appendix, fols. 13r, 18r, 19r; *Registres*, vol. 3.1, no. 426, p. 54. See also B. de Gaulejac, *La liquidation*, p. 71.

290 C. Devic, J. Vaissète, *Histoire*, vol. 10, *Preuves de l'Histoire du Languedoc*, no. 231, col. 631; *Les journaux du trésor de Charles IV*, no. 9460, col. 1514; *Les journaux du trésor de Charles IV*, no. 9647, col. 1548.

291 Appendix, fol. 18v. On the formal problems encountered by the commissioner, see also B. de Gaulejac, *La liquidation*, p. 71.

292 Appendix, fol. 18v.

293 Appendix, fol. 18v.
294 E.g. Appendix, fols. 9r,18v, etc.
295 Appendix, fols. 8r, 9r.
296 Appendix, fol. 18v.
297 Appendix, fol. 9r.
298 Appendix, fol. 12v.
299 Appendix, fols. 3r, 4r, 5r, 12r, 17r, 4v, 18v.
300 Appendix, fol. 2r.
301 Some notaries reviewed their registers themselves, while others only made them available to the commissioner's envoys – Appendix, fol. 9r.
302 The document shows that Renaud de Saint-Ouen ordered copies of the inventories of several Templar houses to be made – Appendix, fols. 11r, 12r., 18r. Unfortunately, these copies were not included in the documentation. It is unclear whether these were inventories drawn up at the beginning of the proceedings, at a later stage or when the properties were transferred to the Hospitallers. The text only mentions that the copied inventory was drawn up by the king's envoys at the time of the Templars' arrest in one case – Appendix, fol. 18r.
303 E.g. Appendix, fol. 12r.
304 Appendix, fol. 18r.
305 Appendix, fols. 8r, 9r.
306 Appendix, fols. 5r, 12 r. 18r.
307 Appendix, fol. 2r.
308 Appendix, fol. 18r.
309 Some debtors resolved the issue with the commissioners (Appendix, fols. 2r, 3r, 4r, etc.), while others appealed to the king – Appendix, fols. 4r, 10r.
310 Appendix, fols. 6r, 3v.
311 Appendix, fol. 10r.
312 Appendix, fols. 1r, 8r, 9r.
313 J. U. Devals, '*Montricoux*', p. 151.
314 Appendix, fol. 9r.
315 Appendix, fol. 11r.
316 *Les journaux du trésor de Charles IV*, no. 7275, col. 1195.
317 *Les journaux du trésor de Charles IV*, no. 3232, col. 559; *Les journaux du trésor de Charles IV*, nos. 4888–4889, col. 815; *Les journaux du trésor de Charles IV*, nos. 5730–5731, col. 959; *Les journaux du trésor de Charles IV*, no. 5818, col. 973; *Les journaux du trésor de Charles IV*, nos. 6982–6983, col. 147; *Les journaux du trésor de Charles IV*, no. 7961, col. 302; *Les journaux du trésor de Charles IV*, no. 1813, col. 308; *Les journaux du trésor de Charles IV*, no. 8454, col. 1376; *Les journaux du trésor de Charles IV*, no. 8456, col. 1376; *Les journaux du trésor de Charles IV*, no. 8459, col. 1377; *Les journaux du trésor de Charles IV*, no. 8509, col. 1387.
318 Appendix, fols. 5v, 7v.
319 *Les journaux du trésor de Charles IV*, no. 6725, col. 1107; *Les journaux du trésor de Charles IV*, no. 7113, col. 1169; *Les journaux du trésor de Charles IV*, no. 8413, col. 1370; *Les journaux du trésor de Charles IV*, no. 8458, col. 1377.
320 *Les journaux du trésor de Charles IV*, no. 6426, col. 1071.
321 *Les journaux du trésor de Charles IV*, no. 6415, col. 1069.
322 *Les journaux du trésor de Charles IV*, p. XXIV.
323 *Les journaux du trésor de Charles IV*, no. 8242, col. 1343 (Report by Guillaume Clignet and Jean de Lignières); *Les journaux du trésor de Charles IV*, no. 8687, col. 1409 (Report presented by the heirs of Raymond Dupuy).
324 *Inventaire d'anciens comptes*, p. 265.
325 E. Mannier, *Ordre de Malte*, pp. XX–XXI; H. de Curzon, *La maison*, p. 203; L. L. L. Lavocat, *Procès*, p. 399.

326 A. Luttrell, 'The Hospitallers and the Papacy', p. 618; A. Luttrell, 'Observations', p. 370.
327 A. Demurger, 'Le concile', p. 156.
328 *Les journaux du trésor de Charles IV*, no. 9971, col. 1598; *Les journaux du trésor de Charles IV*, no. 10172, col. 1633; *Les journaux du trésor de Charles IV*, no. 1278, col. 1658; *Les journaux du trésor de Philippe VI de Valois suivis de l'ordinarium thesauri de 1338–1339*, ed. J. Viard (Paris 1899), no. 75, p. 15.
329 *Inventaire d'anciens comptes*, p. 369.
330 *Registres*, vol. 3.3, no. 1628, p. 207.
331 J. M. A. Delaville Le Roulx, *Les hospitaliers*, p. 158.
332 *Actes*, no. 7053, p. 496.
333 The decision was dated 21 May – *Actes*, no. 7219, p. 523.
334 *Actes*, no. 7405, p. 552.
335 On the dispute over the estates near Toulouse, see Section 3.2.2. On the conflict over the property belonging to the commandery of Cours, see Section 2.3.
336 *Cartulaire des Hospitaliers*, no. 79, p. 149. See also T. M. Vann, 'The Assimilation', p. 342.
337 J. B. de Vaivre, *La Commanderie*, pp. 38–39; A. Demurger, 'Othon de Grandson', pp. 45–46.
338 Appendix, fols. 13r, 18r.
339 Appendix, fols. 13r, 18r.
340 Appendix, fol. 3v.
341 Appendix, fols. 8r, 12v.
342 Appendix, fol. 8r.
343 Appendix, fols. 7r, 8r.
344 Appendix, fol. 8r, 9r.
345 Appendix, fols. 8r, 10r, 12r, 12v, etc.
346 Appendix, fol. 7r.
347 Appendix, fol. 9r.
348 Appendix, fol. 9r.
349 Appendix, fols. 8r, 9r, etc.
350 Appendix, fol. 18v.
351 Appendix, fol.18v.
352 Appendix, fol.18v.
353 Appendix, fol. 3v.
354 Appendix, fol. 18v.
355 Appendix, fols. 10r, 18v. It is not possible to indicate the total amount spent on these materials, since only the total cost of preparing some documents and the paper or parchment used has been indicated in these documents – Appendix, fols. 10r, 13r, 18r, 12v.
356 Appendix, fol. 9r.
357 Appendix, fols. 1v-2v.
358 *Les journaux du trésor de Charles IV*, no. 7275, col. 1195.
359 *Les journaux du trésor de Charles IV*, no. 5825, cols. 974–975; *Les journaux du trésor de Charles IV*, no. 7112, cols. 1168–1169; *Les journaux du trésor de Charles IV*, no. 8457, col. 1376; *Les journaux du trésor de Charles IV*, no. 10208, col. 1642; *Les journaux du trésor de Philippe VI*, no. 15, p. 4; *Les journaux du trésor de Philippe VI*, no. 41, p. 8; *Les journaux du trésor de Philippe VI*, no. 126, p. 26.
360 *Les journaux du trésor de Charles IV*, no. 6791, col. 1117; *Les journaux du trésor de Charles IV*, no. 10275, col. 1657; *Les journaux du trésor de Philippe VI*, no. 105, p. 23.
361 *Les journaux du trésor de Charles IV*, no. 3304, col. 573; *Les journaux du trésor de Charles IV*, no. 5469, col. 911; *Les journaux du trésor de Charles IV*, no. 8506, col. 1387. The first of these was Michel Poulin, who received remuneration for the period

1322–1323. According to L. L. Borrelli de Serres (*Recherches*, vol. 3, p. 39) he oversaw work during the years 1320–1323. However, this is not evident in the document cited by the researcher.

362 Appendix, fols. 10r, 3v.

363 Appendix, fol. 6r.

364 Appendix, fol. 9r.

365 Appendix, fols. 2r, 10r.

366 Giovanni Villani, *Nuova cronica*, ed. G. Porta, vol. 2 (Parma 1990), p. 184; M. Barber, *The Trial* (2006), p. 272.

367 A. Luttrell, 'The Hospitallers and the Papacy', p. 619, n. 127.

368 S. Schein, *Fideles Crucis*, p. 245.

369 *Chronique latine de Guillaume de Nangis, de 1113 à 1300 avec les continuations de cette chronique de 1300 à 1368*, ed. H. Géraud, vol. 2 (Paris 1843), p. 392.

370 R. A. de Vertot, *Histoire*, vol. 1, p. 543; A. Theiner, *Annales*, p. 511; H. de Curzon, *La maison*, p. 200; C. V. Langlois, 'Le procès', pp. 418–419; H. C. Lea, *A History*, vol. 3, p. 330; J. M. A. Delaville Le Roulx, *Les hospitaliers*, p. 51; J. Glénisson, 'L'enquête pontificale de 1373 sur les possessions des Hospitaliers de Saint-Jean de Jérusalem', *Bibliothèque de l'École des chartes*, 129 (1971), p. 90; M. Miguet, *Templiers et Hospitaliers en Normandie*, p. 51.

371 The author did not indicate in which works such opinions appeared – T. M. Vann, 'The assimilation', p. 343.

372 K. Schottmüller, *Der Untergang*, vol. 1, p. 541; L. L. Borrelli de Serres, *Recherches*, vol. 3, p. 44; A. Luttrell, 'Gli Ospitalieri', p. 75; A. Demurger, *Les Hospitaliers*, p. 463.

373 For more on the Templar houses owned by the Hospitallers in the kingdom of France at various periods during the 14th century, see A. de Charmasse, *État des possessions*; *L'Enquête pontificale*, pp. 93–96; J. M. Roger, 'Les maisons', pp. 49–54; J. M. Roger, 'Les biens', pp. 243–298; J. M. Roger, 'La prisée des biens', pp. 349–432; R. Favreau, 'L'enquête pontificale', pp. 447–538.

374 A. Luttrell, 'The Hospitallers and the Papacy', p. 620.

375 According to Anthony Luttrell, the three-year conquest of Rhodes costed 154,000 florins – 'Papauté et Hôpital: l'enquéte e 1373', in: *L'Enquête pontificale de 1373 sur l'Ordre des Hospitaliers*, ed. A. M. Legras, vol. 1, *L'enquête dans le prieuré de France* (Paris 1987), p. 11, n. 1. This was, of course, only part of the expenses related to the military activities of the Order during that period.

376 S. Menache, 'The Hospitallers', p. 161.

377 *Papsttum*, vol. 2, no. 115, p. 219.

378 *Papsttum*, vol. 2, no. 116, pp. 220. See also A. Luttrell, 'The Hospitallers of Rhodes: Perspectives, Problems, Possibilities', in: *Die geistlichen Ritterorden Europas*, ed. J. Fleckenstein, M. Hellmann (Sigmaringen 1980), pp. 251–252.

379 A. Luttrell, 'The Hospitallers and the Papacy', pp. 618–619; A. Luttrell, 'Observations', p. 370; A. Demurger, *Les Hospitaliers*, pp. 457–458.

380 Reg. Clem. V, vol. 9 (Rome 1892), nos. 10327–10330, pp. 106–107. See also A. Luttrell, 'The Hospitallers and the Papacy', p. 618, n. 126.

381 *Registres*, vol. 2.1, nos. 277–278, pp. 60–61. He also took control of other houses not mentioned in either document, some of which remained in his possession until the end of the 1340s. – J. M. Roger, 'La prise de possession', p. 228; J. M. Roger, 'Antonio Pessagno', p. 98.

382 T. M. Vann, 'The assimilation', p. 343.

383 Jean XXII, *Lettres*, vol. 1, no. 4463, p. 409. See also J. B. de Vaivre, *La Commanderie*, pp. 36–37. On the reform of the French province of the Hospital see Section 3.3.2.

384 For more on the pope's efforts to improve the financial situation of the Hospitallers, see J. M. A. Delaville Le Roulx, *Les hospitaliers*, pp. 22–24; N. Housley, *The Avignon Papacy*, pp. 283–284.

385 ADHG, H 34, no. 9; Jean XXII, *Lettres*, vol. 2, no. 7316, p. 169; Jean XXII, *Lettres*, vol. 2, nos. 7322–7323, pp. 169–170; no. 7406, pp. 198–199; Jean XXII, *Lettres*, vol. 3, nos. 10461–10463, pp. 17–18. See also J. M. A. Delaville Le Roulx, *Les hospitaliers*, p. 21, n. 2 and 3.

386 *Lettres secrètes*, vol. 1, no. 1227, col. 1019; J. M. A. Delaville Le Roulx, *Les hospitaliers*, pp. 23, 53; A. Luttrell, 'The Hospitallers and the Papacy', p. 612; A. Luttrell, 'The Hospitallers and Their Florentine Bankers, 1306–1346', in: *Karissime Gotifride: Historical Essays Presented to Professor Godfrey Wettinger*, ed. P. Xuereb (Malta 1999), pp. 17–24; A. Luttrell, 'Observations', p. 370.

387 J. Raybaud, *Histoire*, vol. 1, p. 268.

388 Jean XXII, *Lettres*, vol. 3, nos. 13407–13410, p. 287; J. M. A. Delaville Le Roulx, *Les hospitaliers*, p. 54; N. Housley, *The Avignon papacy*, p. 284.

389 Jean XXII, *Lettres*, vol. 4, Paris 1910, no. 16588, p. 206. J. M. A. Delaville Le Roulx, *Les hospitaliers*, p. 54; N. Housley, *The Avignon Papacy*, p. 284.

390 J. M. A. Delaville Le Roulx, *Les hospitaliers*, pp. 55–56.

Conclusion

Taking a closer look at the material aspects of the French Templar trial reveals that, even after hundreds of years of research, new insights can be gained, and new answers can be found to familiar questions. French archives still contain documents whose analysis improves our understanding of the reasons behind and consequences of the dramatic end of one of the largest Military Orders. The conclusions drawn from these documents certainly do not exhaust the subject matter – the political aspect of the Templar affair has been deliberately omitted – and, in many cases, remains speculative. However, they may stimulate further discussion and research. So, what became of the Templar properties following the sudden arrest of its owners in October 1307? This book provides the following answer to this question:

Two persons initiated proceedings against the Templars: Philip the Fair, King of France, who ordered the arrest of Templar brothers in France, and Pope Clement V, who ordered an investigation into all members of the Order. They were most likely both involved in these actions for the same reason: money. From the outset, they both declared their willingness to transfer the Templars' assets to the Holy Land for the future crusade. However, over time, it became clear that, despite their seemingly common goals, their ideas on how to achieve them, and the decisions they made in this regard, were completely different.

In 1305, the king of France became involved in planning a new crusade. Attacking the Templars, whose existence as an independent Order was being questioned at the time, and who were facing serious charges of heresy, seemed an easy way to obtain the funds necessary for the new expedition to the East. While it cannot be ruled out that the monarch hoped to seize some of their properties or money for his own purposes – after all, the pope had saved his finances more than once with Church funds – this was certainly not his only or main goal. Regardless of Philip the Fair's intentions regarding the properties seized in October 1307, it quickly became clear that there were significant obstacles to their realisation. Right at the beginning of the proceedings, at least some of his vassals demanded their share, probably expecting to gain temporary profits from the controlled estates or fearing restrictions on their traditional rights as territorial rulers. Soon afterwards, the pope also demanded that the French Templar estates be transferred to him, contrary to the customary practice in such cases. Ultimately, Philip the Fair's plans were thwarted

DOI: 10.4324/9781003742241-5

by the Masters of Theology at the University of Paris, who were asked to resolve the procedural issues that had arisen. Their opinion marked the beginning of a new stage in the proceedings, during which the administration of Templar houses would be handled jointly by representatives of the king, the pope, and the French bishops, at least temporarily. The involvement of such a large number of people in properties administration, combined with the change in management system that was also implemented at that time, made it practically impossible to maintain real control over what was happening in individual commanderies, with widespread negligence and theft. Contrary to initial assumptions, the monarch swiftly lost actual control over what happened to the Templar properties within his kingdom. The same was true of the money collected from the Order's estates on an ongoing basis. Sources suggest that, unlike other rulers, Philip the Fair handed over control to the pope. The funds collected went straight to Clement V's treasury, as agreed at Poitiers in the summer of 1308. Any hopes the French king had of taking over at least part of the properties – or of ensuring that it would fall into the hands of one of his sons as the future king of Jerusalem – were finally buried at the Council of Vienne, during which the pope decided to transfer all remaining Templar properties to the Hospitallers. Philip agreed to this but demanded the return of the money owed to him from the settlement of funds held in the Templar treasury in Paris. It is unclear whether these expectations corresponded to the actual state of affairs or if this was to be his share of the spoils, or perhaps a form of compensation for the state apparatus's involvement in various activities related to the Templar's case over several years, including the management of their properties and the accompanying difficulties and disputes. In any case, once the king's demands had been accepted, he ensured that the transfer of properties was efficient and swift, and that officials helped the Hospitallers enforce their rights and recover the assets and debts owed to the Templars. They did not renounce the payments specified in the 1313 agreement but tried to make it as easy as possible for the Hospitallers to repay them by increasingly involving the state apparatus in the complicated process of recovering the assets of the dissolved Order. This only ended in 1325, but the outcome is unknown.

From the perspective of the French monarchy, dealing with the Templar properties proved to be a challenging task that did not yield significant benefits. Even if the 200,000 l. t. that Philip the Fair demanded from the Hospitallers were to be his profit from the trial, their recovery was so spread out over time and involved such complications that, in the end, the amounts flowing into the royal treasury were almost negligible. All financial hopes that the French ruler had pinned on the proceedings against the Templars, initiated in 1307, both in terms of raising funds for the crusade and perhaps his own personal gain, proved to be in vain.

The issue of the Order's properties appeared very different to the pope. Clement V sacrificed the Templars to fulfil his dream of organising a new crusade. When, in October 1307, Philip the Fair presented him with a plan to quickly obtain the funds to carry out the crusade, he did not hesitate for long. The decision to initiate proceedings against the Order, leading to its dissolution and the confiscation of its properties, was made easier for the pope by the Templars' opposition to his plans to reform the Military Orders by taking away some of their resources. Admittedly, this solution was much more costly than possible changes to the structure of the religious communities, but it offered the chance to take full control of all their assets – a very tempting prospect indeed.

Clement V was well aware of the risks involved in allowing a secular ruler with serious financial problems to participate in proceedings against the Templars, which is why he tried to take full control of the seized properties from the outset. According to the Templars' accuser, Esquieu de Floyran, Clement V even wanted to confiscate part of the properties belonging to the heretical Order. However, the verdict of the Parisian university masters forced him to abandon these plans. Nevertheless, it ensured his influence over what happened to the seized properties. At the meeting in Poitiers, the pope had the final say on matters relating to the Templar properties. He decided how it was to be managed and what would happen to the income derived from it. All the money was to go to his treasury, and only he could decide how to use it further. This enabled him to fund the Hospitallers' military expedition and, in subsequent years, amass substantial funds, which he intended to use to organise the *passagium generale*. An obstacle to the realisation of his plans was undoubtedly the involvement of French bishops in the administration of the Templars' estates. However, the decision to involve them was probably forced by organisational considerations, as the pope was unable to establish an efficient system for administering estates scattered throughout the kingdom without their assistance. Alternatively, it may have been the result of a compromise with the French king, whereby a third party was brought in to oversee the actions of the other two. Clement V was obviously aware that such a solution would result in losses, and that the group of people who could derive private benefits from the managed assets would grow significantly, but he clearly had no alternative.

The decisions made in Vienne can be seen because of the pope's disappointment with preparations for the new crusade. Realising that this would take time and that secular rulers were ready to seize Templar assets intended for the Holy Land, Clement V ensured they were given to an Order capable of defending itself against monarchical pressure and abuse. Almost immediately after the council ended, the pope decided to distribute the money he had collected over several years to finance the crusade. As was his custom, he gave most of it to his relatives and close friends, leaving only a portion to his nephew for use when the crusade was organised. Clement V's greatest dream thus remained unfulfilled. In this context, the years of proceedings against the Templars and the efforts to take control over their properties were ultimately pointless.

The Hospitallers certainly benefited from the trial of the Templars. Perhaps as early as 1309, they began receiving money from the estates of the imprisoned Templars. Later, they also received the Templar properties, but this decision came with significant restrictions on their independence. In France, the Hospitallers swiftly took possession of the Templars' houses; however, they were also burdened with substantial debts. Repaying these, alongside the difficult financial situation of the entire Order and the papal ban on selling new properties, proved to be a significant challenge. It took them several years to repay the French monarchy, but they ultimately emerged from these difficulties much richer than before. However, they failed to use the goods they had received for the intended purpose, i.e., to organise a new crusade to the East. The intentions of Philip the Fair and Clement V were therefore not realised, and the proceedings against the Templars, which lasted several years, merely provided an opportunity to squander a large portion of their vast fortunes.

Appendix
Account of Renaud de Saint-Ouen's mission (ADTG, H 317)

The recto pages of the manuscript contain a summary of the amounts collected and expenses incurred at various stages of the investigation:

- List of debs collected by Renaud de Saint-Ouen in 1322 (fols. 1r–2r);
- List of debts collected by Renaud de Saint-Ouen between 14 May 1323 and 31 March 1324, when he arrived in Paris to present an account of his activities: in the seneschalship of Toulouse (fol. 2r), disclosed by Hospitaller brother Pierre de Châlus to former commissioners, Jean de Crépy and Bernard Raymond Caldier (fols. 2r–3r), in the seneschalships of Quercy and Périgord, including those collected by Renaud de Saint-Ouen's deputy, Gérard Morel (fol. 3r), in Limousin, including those collected by Gérard Morel (fol. 4r), in the seneschalships of Lomagne and Agenais, including those collected by Renaud de Saint-Ouen's deputies, Raymond de *Borda* and Guillaume de Vigneaux (fol. 4r), in the seneschalships of Carcassonne and Béziers, including those collected by Renaud de Saint-Ouen's deputy, Bernard Leroi (fol. 4r), in seneschalship of Beaucaire, including those collected by Renaud de Saint-Ouen's deputies, Raymond de Lagardiolle and François Martin (fol. 4r), collected by Renaud de Saint-Ouen's deputy, Jean Martin in Comminges, Cousernas and the Foix region (fol. 5r), found in the court records of Montricoux (fol. 5r), disclosed and collected by notaries Arnaud Leroi and Bernard de *Barta Martino* (fol. 5r), related to the actions carried out against various persons (fol. 6r);
- Total amount of sums collected between 14 May 1323 and 31 March 1324 (fol. 7r);
- List of expenses incurred in connection with Renaud de Saint-Ouen's activities in 1322–1324: for the salaries of other sergeants and notaries delivering summonses to debtors (fol. 7r), for the salaries of persons delivering summonses to notaries to review their records in order to find debts owed to the Templars (fol. 7r–8r), in connection with the case of Pierre d'Escobet, who owed 100 florins to the Templar brother, Bernard de Roche (fol. 8r), in connection with the collection of the debt of the tenant of the Templar house of Gimbrède, Fort Sans de la Porte d'Astaffort (fol. 8r), for the preparation of various documents (fol. 8r), in connection with the case of Pierre des Bordes (fol. 8r),

in connection with the case of Philippe Claveau (fol. 8r), in connection with the case of P. de *Spahone* (fol. 8r), for the preparation of various documents, and the salaries of notaries and heralds publicly announcing the commissioner's summonses (fol. 9r), in connection with the case of Esquieu de Floyran (fol. 9r), for salaries for reviewing notaries' records in search of debts owed to the Templars (fol. 9r), for other reasons (fol. 9r), in connection with the case of the count of Périgord (fol. 10r), for other reasons (fol. 10r);

- Total amount of the aforementioned expenses (fol. 10r);
- List of expenses incurred by Renaud de Saint-Ouen in the seneschalship of Toulouse in 1323 including salaries, preparation of documents, materials, etc. (fols. 10r–11r);
- List of expenses incurred by Renaud de Saint-Ouen in the seneschalships of Quercy and Périgord in 1323 for salaries, preparation and copying of various documents (fol. 11r);
- List of expenses incurred by Renaud de Saint-Ouen in Limousin in March 1323 for salaries and preparation of various documents (fol. 12r);
- List of expenses incurred by Renaud de Saint-Ouen in Provence in 1323 for salaries, preparation and copying of various documents (fol. 12r);
- List of expenses incurred by Renaud de Saint-Ouen for salaries of deputy commissioners (fol. 12r);
- Total amount of all the aforementioned payments and costs incurred in 1323 (fol. 12r);
- Summary of amounts dues to Renaud de Saint-Ouen as salary for the investigation conducted in the south of France and related stays in Paris, as well as for the purchase of horses used for transportation and the preparation of three copies of his accounts (fol. 13r);
- Summary of all collected sums and expenses (fol. 13r);
- List of payments made to the royal treasury in connection with Renaud de Saint-Ouen's mission in 1323 and 1324 (fol. 13r);
- List of sums transferred by Renaud de Saint-Ouen to the commander of the crossbowmen in Flanders, Pierre de Galard, and his envoys on the king's orders in 1323 and 1324 (fol. 13r);
- Total amount of payments and sums due to Renaud de Saint-Ouen (fols. 14r–15r);
- List of debts collected by Renaud de Saint-Ouen between 23 August 1323 and 22 July 1325 (fols. 15r–17r);
- List of expenses incurred in connection with Renaud de Saint-Ouen's activities between 23 August 1323 and 22 July 1325 for preparation of documents, materials and salaries for persons who participated in the collection of unpaid debts (fol. 18r);
- Summary of amounts dues to Renaud de Saint-Ouen as salary for the investigation conducted in the south of France concerning debts owed to the Templars and Jews between 20 September 1324 and 22 July 1325, his 57-day stay in Paris to settle accounts for the mission, as well as for the purchase of horses used for transportation and preparation of documents (fol. 18r);

- List of payments made to the royal treasury in connection with Renaud de Saint-Ouen's mission in 1325 (fol. 19r);
- Final summary of sums due to Renaud de Saint-Ouen for the entire mission (fol. 19r).

The reverse pages of the manuscript contain documents supplementing the financial report from the mission of Renaud de Saint-Ouen:

- Summary of amounts due and paid to Bernard Raymond Caldier, envoy of count of Valois, as part of his 1/9 share of the debts collected by Renaud de Saint-Ouen, and a list of costs reducing them (fols. 1v–2v);
- List of sums included in the list of debts collected by Renaud de Saint-Ouen between 14 May 1323 and 31 March 1324, of which Bernard Raymond Caldier did not receive 1/9 (fol. 2v);
- Receipt from Bernard Raymond Caldier for certain sums received from Renaud de Saint-Ouen in 1323 (fol. 3v);
- List of expenses incurred in connection with the case of the count of Périgord, mentioned in the list of sums collected related to the actions carried out against various persons (fol. 3v);
- List of payments and expenses incurred by the tenant of the Templar house of Magnac, Pierre de Mons, reducing his debt mentioned in the list of sums collected in Limousin between 14 May 1323 and 31 March 1324 (fol. 4v);
- List of payments and expenses incurred by the tenant of the Templar house of Puybonnieux, Pierre de Fougeré?, reducing his debt mentioned in the list of sums collected in Limousin between 14 May 1323 and 31 March 1324 (fol. 4v);
- List of payments and expenses incurred by the tenant of the Templar houses of Bellechassagne, Foulventour and La Bussière-Rapy, Pierre la Rivière de *Brinis*, reducing his debt mentioned in the list of sums collected in Limousin between 14 May 1323 and 31 March 1324 (fol. 4v);
- List of payments and expenses incurred by the tenants of the Templar houses of Mons, Bonnefare and Chaumont, Jean *Ribier* and Raynaud la Maynardie, reducing their debt mentioned in the list of sums collected in Limousin between 14 May 1323 and 31 March 1324 (fol. 4v);
- List of payments and expenses incurred by the tenants of the Templar house of Le Palais, Étienne *Belleti*; Pierre *Fabri*, reducing their debt mentioned in the list of sums collected in Limousin between 14 May 1323 and 31 March 1324 (fol. 4v);
- List of debts collected by Renaud de Saint-Ouen's deputies in the seneschalships of Agenais and Bordeaux, Raymond de *Borda* and Guillaume de Vigneaux, the total amount of which is included in the list of debts collected in the seneschalships of Lomagne and Agenais between 14 May 1323 and 31 March 1324 (fol. 4v);
- List of sums collected by Renaud de Saint-Ouen's deputy in the seneschalship of Beaucaire, François Martin, the total amount of which is included in the list of debs collected in the seneschalship of Beaucaire between 14 May 1323 and 31 March 1324 (fol. 4v);

- List of sums collected and spent by François Martin, the total amount of which is included in the list of debs collected in the seneschalship of Beaucaire between 14 May 1323 and 31 March 1324 (fols. 4v–5v);
- Order of King Charles IV and the seneschal of Toulouse from 1323 concerning the transfer of money collected by Renaud de Saint-Ouen in the seneschalships of Toulouse, Périgord and Cahors to the commander of the crossbowmen in Flanders, Pierre de Galard (fol. 5v);
- Receipt of Pierre de Galard for money received from Renaud de Saint-Ouen in 1323 (fols. 5v–7v);
- Letter of Pierre de Galard, from 1323, in which he informs about the appointment of two procurators, who were to collect on his behalf the money granted to him by the king, originating from the Templar estates (fol. 7v);
- Order of Charles IV and the seneschal of Toulouse from 1322 concerning the transfer of money collected by Renaud de Saint-Ouen to Pierre de Galard (fols. 7v–8v);
- Receipt from the royal treasury for one of the sums paid by Renaud de Saint-Ouen (fol. 8v);
- Confirmation of the payment from the royal treasury to Pierre de Galard of money previously paid by Renaud de Saint-Ouen (fol. 8v);
- List of expenses for the salaries of sergeants delivering summonses to debtors and the preparation of various documents, the total amount of which (XIII l. XI s. IIII d. t.) was included in the list of expenses incurred in 1322–1324 (fol. 8v);
- List of expenses for the salaries of other sergeants and notaries delivering summonses to debtors, the total amount of which (VIII l. V s.) was included in the list of expenses incurred in 1322–1324 (fol. 8v);
- Eight receipts from Bernard Raymond Caldier for sums received from Renaud de Saint-Ouen or directly from debtors as part of 1/9 of the amount owed to the count of Valois in 1322 and 1323, and the total amount of money paid to him (fol. 9v);
- Charles se Valois's order to Bernard Raymond Caldier to collect on his behalf the sums owed to him from the money derived from the Templars' estates collected in several seneschalships in southern France (1318) (fol. 9v);
- List of expenses and amount of salary for François Martin, the total sum of which has been included in the list of expenses incurred by Renaud de Saint-Ouen for salaries of deputy commissioners in 1322–1324 (fol. 12v);
- List of six documents whose total cost (VI s.) is included in the list of expenses incurred in connection with Renaud de Saint-Ouen's activities between 23 August 1323 and 17 September 1325 for preparation of documents, materials and salaries for persons who helped to collect unpaid debts (fol. 18v);
- Information about the content of two others documents whose total cost (VI s.) is included in the list of expenses incurred in connection with Renaud de Saint-Ouen's activities between 23 August 1323 and 17 September 1325 for preparation of documents, materials and salaries for persons who helped to collect unpaid debts (fol. 18v);

- List of sums paid to persons who participated in the collection of debts owed, the total amount of which (XXII l. XIIII s. VIII d. t.) is included in the list of expenses incurred in connection with Renaud de Saint-Ouen's activities between 23 August 1323 and 17 September 1325 for preparation of documents, materials and salaries (fol. 18v).

All editor's notes are written in italics. Notes in the margins of the manuscript and in the text are written in square brackets.

The division into paragraphs was introduced by the editor.

Passages crossed out in the manuscript are crossed out in the edition.

Passages underlined in the manuscript are underlined with a straight line in the edition.

Passages added in the manuscript above or below the text and on the scratched-out text are underlined with a wavy line in the edition.

The spelling of currency names has been standardized using the following abbreviations:

d. – denarius
l. – libra
o. – obolus
s. – solidus
t. – turonenis

Other abbreviations used in the manuscript have been resolved.

Fol. 1

The card is only partially preserved and severely damaged. On most of the page the text is illegible or only partially legible.

~~Summa totalis IIIe XVIII l. XVII s. VIII d. ob., de qua cadunt pro nona parte domini comitis Valesii XLVI l. X s. IX d. ob. pict. et restant pro Rege IIIe LXXII l. VI s. X d. ob. t.~~

Ab heredibus Davini de Roaxio[1] burgensis Tholose, quondam curatoris bonorum dicti Templi solventibus pro Fortio Sancii de Porta de [*In the left margin:* Sequela firme domus de Gimbreda] Hasta Forti, olim firmario domus Templi de Gimbreda[2] in Leomania,[3] pro resta dicte firme de annis M° CCC° XI° et XII°, de qua [*In the left margin*: II^{us} in ordine litterarum et rotulorum camera restituorum] prefatus Fortius et dicti heredes compotum reddiderunt dicto commissario et magistro Bernardo Raymundi Calderie, ut per dictum compotum [*In the left margin:* A tergo] apparet et de hiis fit mentio superius et in dorso presentis rotuli, ubi totius fuerat veritas declarata per revelationem magistri Raymundi de Borda ~~deducta nona parte domini comitis Valesii, quam dictus magister Bernardus habuerat per manus heredum predictorum:~~ II^{c} LXIX l. XIII s. VI d. t.

Item de summa LXXVII l. XIIII s. X d. t. de tempore Burgensis, in quibus Raymonus Gonterii, Germanus Redditoris et Pontius Martini arrendatores grangie de Caventhis olim Templi fuerant honorati per dictum Davinum in suis compotis redditis magistro Guillelmo de Gisortio[4] ratione dicte firme, recepit dictus comissarius ab heredibus dicti Davini solventibus pro dictis firmariis ~~pro parte regia de~~ LVI l. ~~dicte monete, que restabant ad solvendum XLIX l. XV s. VI d. ob. pict.~~ dicte monete Burgensis valentes ad bonam monetam C ~~l. XVI s. V d. ob. t.~~ XLIIII l. XVI s. t. De residuo vero prefati heredes reddiderunt rationem in quibusdam compotis per eos redditis Renerio Burdonis ~~excepta nona parte dicti comitis dictarum LVI l. ad dictum dominum comitem pertinens.~~

Item de summa IIII^{xx} l. t. de tempore Burgensis, in quibus Stephanis de Ruppibus mercator Tholose fuerat honoratus per dictum Davinum in suis compotis supradictis pro peccunia eisdem Stephano tradita de bonis dicti Templi ad portandum Parisius, de qua summa Davinus postmodum habuit ab eodem L l. dicte monete, de quibus prefati heredes reddiderunt rationem in suis compotis memoratis dicto Renerio, recepit dominus comissarius a dictis heredibus ~~pro parte Regis de~~ XXX l. dicte monete, que restabant ad solvendum, ~~deducta nona parte domini comitis Valesii XXVI l. XIII s. IIII d. dicte monete Burgensis~~ valentes ad bonam monetam XXIIII l. t.

A domino Petro de Bordis milite, fratre domini Bertrandi de Bordis quondam cardinalis habuit et recepit dictus commissarius pro parte Regis tantum VIII^{xx} l. t. ratione cuiusdam compositionis facte inter procuratorem suum et dictum commissarium super eo, quod idem miles receperat per annum et medium decimas ecclesie de Roillaco[5] in Leomania pertinentes ad domum Templi de Gimbreda post mortem dicti cardinalis, cui collate fuerant ad vitam per fratrem Bernardum de Rupe[6] preceptorem dicti loci, et hec revelavit magister Raymonus de Borda notarius, clericus tunc dicti militis, sub conditione, quod de hiis debuit habere quintam partem ratione sue revelationis et laboris: [*In the left margin*: Infra est] ~~et super expensis per dictum comissarium factis et pro salariis notariuorum et servientium habuit X l. t.~~ [*words scratched out*] IX^{xx} l. t.

Item de superlectilibus repertis in domo Philippi Clavelli de Villa Dei[7] et de quibusdam terris, quas ipse vendidit Symoni [*name illegible*] necnon domine de Fronton[8] et Guillelmo Bernardi de Gimellis[9] ratione plurimum expensis factarum per eundem in persecutione negocii dicti Philippi, de quo superius fit mentio: XVIII l. t.

Fol. 2

Ab heredibus magistri Petri de Verdelone[10] quondam custode bonorum mobilium grangie Templi de Bona Fara[11] diocesis Petragoricensis[12] ~~de~~ LIIII l. XV s. VIII d. t., in quibus tenebantur per finem sui compoti redditi dicto commissario ratione dictorum mobilium: ~~pro parte domini Regis tantum XLVIII l. XIII s. XI d.~~

~~Ab heredibus domini Davini de Roaxio per manus Karoli de Troga~~[13] ~~pro expensis factis contra eos XLVIII s. t.~~

~~A Fortio Sancii de Porta pro expensis contra eum factis: C s. t.~~

~~A domino Othone de Monte Alto procuratore domine Ermessandis filie et heredis Arnaldi Bariani quondam curatoris bonorum Templi pro expensis factis in auditione compoti per eum redditi, de quo superius fit mencio in recepta, in quinta particula: L s. t.~~

~~A domino Guiraudo capellano Castri Novi~~[14] ~~procuratore domini Gauberti Vaquerii rectoris dicti loci pro expensis factis contra eum ratione mille florenorum auri, quas debet per sua [*sic for* suas] litteras, quas habet dominus G[uillelmus] Cligneti, duas cartones avene valentes L s. t., pro istis quatuor partibus:~~ XII l. VIII s. t. [*In the right margin*: Inferius in recepta sequente]

[*In the left margin*: LIIII s. II d.] Summa ab alia: ~~V^{e}~~ [*words scratched out and crossed-out*] ~~s. IIII d. ob~~ V^{c} IIII^{xx} XI l. V s. II d. t.

Totalis summa recepte per dictum commissarium facte domini nostri Regis in anno vicessimo secondo [*words scratched out and crossed-out*] [*In the left margin:* (*characters illegible due to paper damage*) XXI d.] non deducta nona parte domini comitis Valesii, de qua dictus commissarius est honoratus: mille decem l. II s. IX d. t.

Sequitur alia recepta per dictum commissarium facta in senescallia Tholosana a dicta die XIIII^{am} Madii anno domini M^{o} CCC^{o} vicessimo tertio usque ad diem ultimam Martii eodem anno, qua venerit Parisius, compotum redditur pro parte domini Regis tantum:

[*In the left margin*: Hoc per IX^{am} literram] Guillelma Oleria uxor Petri de Marcelhano[15] debebat VI l. XVII s. VIII d. t. pro baralia et obliis grangie de Taysoneriis[16] quondam Templi de anno XII°, ~~de~~ quod dictus commissarius habuit. ~~pro VIII^{te} partibus Regis VI l. II s. IIII d. ob. t. Residuum habuit dominus comes Valesii pro nona parte sua.~~

Bernardus d'Antoela, Raymudnus Robleni et Petrus Navarro de Villa Dei emerunt domum Philippi Clavelli a predicto commissario pretio L l. t., quas [*In the left margin*: Hoc per litteram X^{am}] solverunt in deductione debiti superius in recepta predicta declarati.

Item Arnaudus de Duro Forti[17] emit unam petiam terre pretio IX l. t., quas solvit ex causa predicta.

Item Guillelmus Bridoera emit unum ortum pretio CX s. t., quos solvit prout supra et ex dicta causa ~~et de hoc habuit dictus comissarius pro Rege LVII l. VI s. VIII d. t. de residuo prout supra.~~

Magister Andus de Ruppe Forti[18] receperat per quinques annos [*In the left margin*: Hoc per litteram XI^{am}], ut dicebatur, redditus bastide de Planha[19] pertinentes ad domum Templi de Monte Salnerio[20] valent in dictis quinque annis XX l. t., quas solverat fratri Johanni de Affariis hospitalario post compositionem inter dominum Regem et Hospitalem factam, ~~et de hiis~~ quas dictus frater solvit dicto comissario ~~pro~~ parte Regis ~~XVII l. XV s. VI d. ob. t. de residuo prout supra.~~

Raymonus Athonis de Ruallibus[21] fuit honoratus in compotis Davini de Roaxio quondam curatoris bonorum Templi in senescallia Tholosana CXII l. t. monete currentis tempore Burgensis valent ad t. bonos IIII^{xx} IX l. XII s. Et de hoc composuit cum [*In the left margin*: Hoc per literram XII^{am}] dicto commissario Tholosa eius uxor et solvere promisit ad tres terminos sibi datos et pro primo termino solvit XXX l. t., ~~de quibus habuit dictus~~ [*In the left margin*: debitum] ~~commisasrius pro Rege: XXVI l. XIII s. IIII d. t. de residuo prout supra~~ residuum debent.

Heredes Davini de Roaxio fuerunt condempnati per dictem commissarum ad solvendum XI l. t. monete Burgensis restans de L l. t., quas dictus Davinus receperat ab Arnaldo Auriberii pro Brugueria de Arameto[22] et de hoc non posuerat in suis compoto nisi XXXIX l. t. dicte monete Burgensis, que quedam XI l. t. valent ad bonam monetam VIII l. XVI s. t., quas ~~de quibus magister B[ernardus]~~ ~~R[aymundi] Calderie habuit pro nona parte domini comitis Valesii per manus dictorum heredum XIX s. VI d. ob. t. et~~ dictus commissarius habuit ~~nomine Regio residuum, quod astendit VII l. XVI s. V d. ob. t.~~

[*Letters illegible due to paper damage*] debebat ratione firme domus Templi Lane Arquerii[23] de anno M° CCC° IX° per compotos dicti Davini VIII l. VI s. VIII d. t., ~~de quibus~~ quas dictus commissarius habuit ~~pro parte Regis VII l. IX s. II d. t. de residuo prout supra.~~

Garsias Amerii debebat totidem ex causa predicta et de hoc solvit dicto comissario XXVI s. t., residuum debet.

Raymonus de Campis Aquis[24] quondam firmarius Ville Dei fuit honoratus in compotis dicti Davini de VII^{xx} l. t. monete Burgensis pro resta dicte firme, de quibus dictus comissarius habuit tam per manus Guillelmi de Roaxio, magistri Bernardi de Salvio[25] et ~~de~~ Pictavine de Sancto Licerio[26] quam de quibusdam bonis mobilibus heredum dicti Raymoni venditis per dictum commissarium ~~pro Rege~~ XXIIII l. XI s. VII d. t., et de vino et blado vendito apud Villam Dei per Hugonem d'Arboy ex causa predicta VII l. XII s. VI d. t. [*words scratched out and crossed-out*] ~~dicti Raymoni de Campis Aquis per manus Barali Ville Dei et Hugonis d'Arboiz servientis de vino et blado venditis per eos de bonis dictorum heredum ex causa predicta: VII l. XII s. VI d. t.~~ Residuum debetur ~~ad huc excepta IX^{am} parte domini comitis Valesii.~~

Summa istius recepte senescallie Tholosane: ~~pro parte Regis tantum VIII^{xx} XII l. XIII s. VII d. ob~~. VIII^{xx} XII l. V d. t.

Sequitur recepta senescallie Caturcensis et Petragoricensis facta in anno proxime dicto et primo de quibusdam debitis revelatis per fratrem Petrum de Carlutio[27] cum litteris et instrumentis traditis per eundem magistris Johanni de Cryspeyo[28] et Bernardo R[aymundi] Calderie tunc commissariis super hoc deputatis, qui dicto fratri promiserunt reddere quintam partem dictorum debitorum pro sua revelatione et expensis factis in dictis litteris et instrumentis perquirendis:

[*In the left margin*: Per litteram VIII^{am} hoc habuit de XVIII l.] Item dominus Helias Talarandi[29] quondam comes Petragoricensis debuit fratri Geraldo la Vina[30] Templario III^{c} XL l. t. debiles per litteras factas Idus Ianuarii anno M^{o} [*In the left margin*: Item de VIII^{xx} l. III s. VII d. ob. per XII^{am}] CC^{o} XC^{o} VII° valent de augmento monete V^{c} XV l. XIII s. IIII d. t. debiles,

Fol. 3

que ascendunt ad bonam monetam II^{c} IIII^{xx} V l. IIII s. V d. ob. t., ~~et de hiis habuit dictus magister Bernardus ex causa predicta pro domino comite Valesii XIX l. XIII s. IX d. t. et~~ quas dictus commissarius habuit. ~~Pro toto residuo: IIe LXV l. X s. IX d. t.~~

Stephanus de Ruppe, Peturs Suriz et quidem alii consortes sui debebant dicto fratri per litteras factas anno M^{o} CCC^{o} VI° IIII° [*letter scratched out*] Nonas [*letters scratched out*] Februarii V^{c} XL l. t. debilis, de quibus solverant dicto fratri ante captionem Templariorum II^{c} XL l. t., sicut monstraverunt per legitima documenta. Et super residuo fuit facta compositio cum dicto commissario per eosdem ad C l. t. parvorum, ~~de quibus solverunt dicto magistro Bernardo pro nona parte domini comitis Valesii XI l. II s. II d. ob. t. residuum~~ quas habuit dictus commissarius tam pro dicto fratre Petro quam pro dicto domino nostro Rege scilicet ~~LXVIII l. XVII s. X d. b. t.~~

Stephanus de Felenor[31] debebat dicto fratri cum instrumento facto sub anno M^{o} CCC^{o} VI° C l. t. debilis, pro quibus fuit diu litigatum coram Petro de Sancto Plancato[32] et magistro Geraldo Morelli substitutis per dictum commissarium et deinde fuit cum eis facta compositio ad XXIX l. t., quas dictus commissarius habuit ~~XXX l. t., de quibus quinta pars partem dicto fratri ascendit CXVI s. Et IX^{a} pars residua domini comi1tis est II s. VI d. ob.~~

Eblo de Sancto Rupperio[33] debebat dicto fratri cum litteris factis die Martis ante festum Epiphanie anno M^{o} CC^{o} XC^{o} IIII° C s. petragoricenses, de quibus finavit cum dicto substituto ad IIII l. t.

Summa istarum IIII^{or} partium: IIII^{c} XVIII l. IIII s. V d. ob. ~~Summa totalis ab alia grossa: Ve IIII^{xx}X l. IIII s. X d. ob. t.~~

[*In the left margin*: ~~Summa totalis ab alia: Ve IIII^{xx} X l. IIII s. X d. ob. t.,~~ (*word illegible*) ~~aliter summa: M VIe l. V s. VII d. ob., de qua cadunt pro IX^{a} parte domini~~

~~comitis Valesii. IXª pars est CLXXVII l. XVI s. VI II d. ob., restant pro Rege M IIIIᵉ XXII l. XI s. V d.] Totalis summa summarum predictarum mille sexente l. septem s. septem d. et ob. t., de qua cadunt pro nona parte domini comitis Valesii CLXXVII l. XVI s. II d. ob. t., et restant pro domino nostro Rege mille quadrigente viginti due l. undecim s. quinque d. t.~~

Item Jacobus Magistri debebat preceptori domus Templi de Monte Rocoso[34] pro censu bladi LX s. catalanenses, pro quibus Guillelmus Margerranii de Caloata, qui tenet bona dicti debitoris, finavit et solvit XL s. t.

Item Arnaldus de Campanhaco[35] de Sancto Anthonino[36] debebat dicto preceptori ex mutuo XIIII l. t., pro quibus Girardus Sarreti de Nigrapellitia[37] detentor bonorum ipsius Arnaldi finavit et solvit VI l. t.

Item Helias de Solo fuit dealtus coram dicto substituto super eo, quod habuerat, ut dicebatur, quedam mobilia de bonis domus Templi quondam de Bella Fara prope Petragoris et de hoc finavit et composuit cum eo ad XII l. t., quas habuit dictus commissarius per manus dicti substituti.

Item Raymonus de Arnaldo debebat ex causa cuiusdam financie facte cum Aymerico de Ponte de Petragoris olim receptore debitorum Templi super quibusdam bonis mobilibus per ipsum habitis de domo Sancti Pauli[38] quondam Templi LVI s. t., quas solvit.

Item dominus Petrus de Castilione[39] miles fuit delatus coram dicto substituto super eo, quod habuerat, ut dicebatur, unum roncinum de bonis Templi quondam, pro quo fuit condempnatus per dictum magistrum Reginaldium in VIII s. t., ~~et in VI l. t. pro expensis,~~ quas solvit: ~~XIIII l. t.~~

~~Item Helias de Aguete de Petragoris futi delatus per dictum substitutum coram ipso commissario dicentem ipsum H[eliam] habuisse plura de bonis dicti Templi, super quibus fuit inquesta facta, set nichil fuit probatum~~ [*In the left margin*: Inferius sunt iste expense (*word illegible*) dictus comes nihil habuit in eis] ~~contra ipsum, ymo suas deffensiones probatas. Et ab hoc fuit per dictum commissarium~~ [*lettres scratched out*] ~~finaliter absolutus, set pro expensis pro ab hoc factis per ipsum commissarium in suis deffensionibus audiendis solvit dicto commissario X l. t. per manum Johannis Fabri et pro confirmatione dicte summe Parisius impetranda solvit per manus G[uiardi] de Suessone VI: VII l. X s. t.~~

Summa ab alia: ~~LIIII l. VI s. t., de quibus sunt XXIII l. X s. pro expensis et de residuo, quod est~~ XXX l. XVI s., ~~debet dictus comes habere IXᵐ partem, que ascendit LXVIII s. V d. pict. t.~~

~~Summa recepte senescallie Catturcenis et Petragoricensis: IIIIᵉXXI l. XIIII s. VII d. ob. t., IIIIᵉ XLIX l. V d. ob. t.~~

Fol. 4

Recepta facta in Lemovicino,[40] de qua nihil habuit dominus comes Valesii ex causis in dorso superius expressatis:

[*In the left margin*: A tergo] Petrus de Montibus firmarius domus Templi de Mannaco[41] anno M° CCC°XII° debebat pro resta dicte firme, que ascendebat in universe CIIII l. [*In the left margin*: A tergo] per compotum Guidonis Pignete, quam solvit IIII l. X s. t., de residuo redditur ratione per partes a tergo declaratas.

Dominus Petrus de Faugeraco[42] presbiter quondam firmarius domus Templi de Podio Bonionis[43] fuit honoratus in compoto Aymerici de Ponte et G[uidonis] Pignete de quibusdam summis in dorso rotuli declaratis, restantibus de precio dicte firme, quas conpsumpserat in operibus dicte domus, prout executores ipsius asseruerunt et monstraverunt non tamen ad plenum coram dicto substitute, qui cum consilio Andree Russi canonici Petragoris, clerici domini Regis admisit eos ad compositionem C l. t., quas dictus commissarius habuit et receipt de bonis mobilibus et immobilibus executionis predicte venditis pluribus personis tam per dictum substitutum quam per Guiardum de Suessone, Guillelmum [*In the left margin*: A tergo] Fulcardi servientes et alias a dicto commissario super hoc deputato, de aliis redditur ratione per partes in dorso rotuli declaratas: C l. t.

Guillelmus Bonelli debebat per litteram, quam dictus Guido restituit, pro venditione cuiusdam gagerie seu e~~n~~iecti per dictum Guidonem sibi venditi de bonis dicti Templi LV l. t., de quibus dictus commissarius habuit tam per manus dicti substituti quam dicti Guiardi et aliorum, residuum habuit dictus Guido: XL l. t. XVII s. t.

Petrus de Rupperia de Brinis firmarius domorum Templi de Pulcra Cassanea,[44] Fonte Laventour[45] et de Buxeria Raspit[46] debebat de resta dicte firme per compotum Aymerici de Ponte de Petragoris, quam habuit idem commissarius tam per manus dicti Petri quam dicti substitute XXXV l. t., de hiis vero et aliis veritas in dorso rotuli declaratur.

Johanes Ribier et Raymondus la Maynardie firmarii domorum Templi de Montibus[47] et de Bellafar debebant per dictum compotum predicti A[ymerici] pro resta dicte firme, quam habuit dictus commissarius per manus dicti sui substituti et dicti Raymondi, de qua firma fit mencio in dorso rotuli: XIIII l. t.

Dulcetus de Valle debebat per litteram, quam restituit dictus Guido, XXXII s. t. debilium currentium anno millessimo CCC° IIII°, de quibus finavit ad XV s. t., quos solvit: XV s. t.

Guillelmus de Matasanges debebat per litteram, quam restituit dictus Guido, XX l. t., de quibus probavit solutionem Templariis esse factam, exeptis X s. t., quos solvit: X s. t.

Helias de Valencia[48] debebat per litteras, quas restituit dictus Guido, LXXIIII l. t. debilis, quas habuerat anno M° CCC° V° et pro hoc se obligaverat in summa IIII^{c} LXII sestarios siliginis, item in II^{c} IIII^{xx} sextarios avene et in LXX l. t., pro quibus heredes eius finaverunt cum dicto substitute, qui cum consilio domini Andree Russi canonici Petragoris, clerici domini Regis inspecta summa peccunie, quam habuerat necnon modica mensura prime et eorum papuertate, et preterea quod se offerebant probare solutionem ipsos admisit in dubio ad compositionem IIII^{xx} l. t., quas solverunt pro suo labore redimendo.

Petrus Fabri et Stephanus Belleti firmarii de Palacio[49] debuerunt pro firma dicti loci de anno M° CCC° IX° VIII^{xx} l. t., item pro dicta firma anno M° CCC° X° VIII^{xx} l. et de anno M° CCC° XI° VII^{xx} l., et pro anno M° CCC° XII° LXIII l. VI s. VIII d., exepta capellania dicti loci, que fuit collata capellano per Summum Pontificem, de quibus dictus commissarius habuit per manus Guiardi de Suessone solventis pro Petre Belleti filio dicti Stephani: XX l. t., et Petrus Fabri debet ad huc alia viginti l. De residuo sunt liberati, prout in dorso rotuli contietur.

Summa recepte Lemovicensis[50]: II^{c}IIII^{xx}XV l. XII s. t.

Recepta senescallie Leomanie et Agenensis:[51]

[*In the left margin:* hoc per litteram XII^{am}] Bertrandus de Causenthis domicellus tenuit per unum annum, scilicet anno M° CCC°VIII°, domum Templi de Gimbreda nomine episcopi Lectorensis et fructus eius recolegit, de quibus dictus episcopus habuerat unam partem et pro residuo dictus Bertrandus debebat C l. t., prout magister Raymonus de Borda revelavit, qui pro sua revelatione debet habere quintam partem, et hoc dictus Bertrandus confessus fuit, ~~de quibus~~ quas solvit dicto commissario ~~IIII^{xx} VIII l. XVII s. IX d. ob. t. et residuum solvit magistro Bernardo Raymundi Calderie pro nona parte domini comitis Valesii scilicet XI l. II s. II d. ob.~~

Item dictus commissarius receipt a magistris Raymundo de Borda et Guillelmo de Vinealibus[52] notariis substitutis per eundem in dictis senescalliis L l. t., [*In the left margin*: a tergo] quas receperant a personis et in diversis partibus in dorso presentis rotuli registratis.

Item dictus Raymundus de Borda modo et forma, quibus supra revelavit dicto commissario et monstravit per instrumentum, quod Davinus de Roaxio receperat a Petro de Bordis domicello pro nemore de Gimbreda XL l. t. de tempore monete Burgensis et a Fortio Sancii de Porta firmario dicti loci pro resta dicte firme, de qua superius fit mencio in recepta anni M° CCC° vicesimo secundi in albo et in dorso XXXIX l. XVIII s. eiusdem monete, de quibus non computaverat dictus Davinus, et idcirco heredes ipsius fuerunt compulsi ad solvendum per dictum commissarium dictas summas, que ascendebant ad bonam monetam LXIII l. XVIII s. IIII d. ob. ~~de quibus magister Bernardus R~~[aymundi] ~~Calderie habuit pro nona parte domini comistis Valesii per manus dictorum heredum VII l. II s. ob. t. residuum habuit dictus commissaries, quod astendit: LVI l. XVI s. IIII d. t.~~

Summa recepte senescallie Leomanie et Ageni non deducta nona parte domini comitis Valesii, de qua dictus comissius est honoratus: II^c XIII l. XVIII s. IIII d. ob. t.

Recepta senescallie Carcassone[53] et Bitteris:[54]

Heredes Petri Catelli de Sancto Uberio[55] quondam curatoris bonorum Templi diocesis Agatensis[56] debabant per finem sui compoti redditi magistro [*In the left margin:* habuit de hoc XII l. XIII s. III d. ob.] G[uillelmo] de Gisorctio quondam XL l. t., quas ~~de quibus magister Bernardus Raymundi habuerat pro nona parte domini comitis Valesii IIII l. VIII s. X d. ob. et~~ dictus commissarius habuit. ~~Residuum, quod est XXXV l. XI s. I d. ob. t.~~

Petrus Bundei de Spondellano[57] firmarius domus Templi de Abeliano[58] debebat pro dicta firma de anno M° CCC° XII° XL l. t. pro compositionem factam inter ipsum et magistrum Bernardum Regis substitutum dicti commissarii, de quibus idem commissarius habuit tam per manus dicti substituti quam de quibusdam bonis mobilibus venditis apud Bitteris ad inquantum per Guiardum de Suessone, captis in domo dicti Petri de mandato dicti commissarii: XI l. IIII s. XI d., [*In the left margin*: debitum] de quibus prefatus dominus comes nichil habuit, quia residuum debetur ad huc et quia levari non potuit propter quasdam litteras regis directas [*In the left margin*: redditur inferius] senescallo et thesaurario Carcassone, quod darent dicto Petro tres terminus ad solvendum usque ad tres annos.

Item a Bernardo de Monte Olivo[59] tenente locum Aymerici Boffati quondam de Bitteris curatoris olim dicti Templi in dyocesis Carcassonenis [et] Bitterensis pro resta, quam debebat per finem sui compoti redditi magistro Bernardo Regis memorato, quem noluit acceptare: IIII l. IX s. VI d. t.

Summa istius recepte LV l. XIIII s. V d. t. non deducta IX^a parte supradicta senescallie Carcassone et Bitteris.

Recepta senescallie Bellicadri:[60]

Jacoba iusta uxor Johanis de Abbatio de Generaco[61] legaverat in suo testamento domui Templi dicti loci C s. t. anno M° CCC° VI°, quo decessit, de quibus Guillelmus Britone executor dicti testamenti composuit cum magistro Raymondo de Gardiola[62] dicti commissarii substituto ad XXX s. t., quas solvit.

Petrus Garnerii de Generaco dederat dicto Templo prius finem ipsius Petri LX s. t., de quibus solvit per compositionem factam cum dicto substitute XX s. t.

Durandus Pellicerii de Sancto Boneto[63] et Bernardus Plaucati de Sariaco[64] debebant pro pastuis dicti loci IIII l. X s. t. debilis, pro quibus dictus commissarius habuit per manus dicti substituti XXX s. t.

Raymondus de Tralio de Margaritiss[65] debebat pro erbagiis dicti Templi XXVI l. XIII s. IIII d. malgarenses, de quibus fuit absolutus per dictum commissarium, quia solverat Templariis ante captionem eorumdem, exeptis quas idem commissarius habuit XX s. t.

Item recepit idem commissarius a magistro Francisco Martini commissario per eum in dicta senescallia substituto XL l. t., quas idem Franciscus receperat a personis et ex causis in dorso rotuli presentis expressatis. Et ultra hoc receipt idem Franciscus a quibusdam aliis personis in dorso nominatis XXVII l. XVII s. VIII d., quas expendit et consumpsit pro partes in suo compoto declaratas, pro perquirendo dictis debitis et aliis per ipsum repertis, que nondum sunt levata [*sic for* levatis], de quibus omnibus reddidit compotum dicto commissario, prout in ipsius compoto continetur per finem, cuius debentur pro suis vadiis: XXXIX l. XVII s. V d. t., que quidam debita per € dictum sustitutum reperta non levata continenta in quodam rotulo, de quo fit mentio inferius in expensa.

Summa recepte senescallie Bellicadri computate: XXVII l. XVII s. VIII d. t.
Summa dictis LXXII l. XVII s. VIII d. t. ~~computatorum expensis dicti Francisci~~

Fol. 5

Recepta facta per magistrum Johannem Martini, commissarium substitutum per dictum magistrum R[eginaldum] in partibus convensis,[66] fuxensis,[67] coseransis:[68]

Petrus de Martenaco[69] debebat pro condempnatione curie Templi quondam Montis Salnerii XII s. t., quos solvit.

Raymundus Arnaldi debebat ex causa simili: VIII s. t.
Napros del Vinhau: XV s. t.
Guillelmus de Yspania:[70] III s. t.
Bartholomeus de Lauraco[71] pro clamore: XVIII d. t.
Vitalis de Faiola:[72] XVIII d. t.
Brimosa de la Rua: XVIII d. t.
Guillelmus de Casa pro pluribus clamoribus: VII s. t.
Sancius Benedicti: VI s. t.
Guillemus Cortes: XVI s. t.
Johanes Bernardi: XVIII d. t.
Petrus de Podio: VI s. t.
Petrus Lana: XV s. t.
Laurentius de Limite: III s.
Petrus et Ardus de Lassera:[73] XVIII d. t.
Raymonus Deleres: III s. t.
Petrus de Puiolio:[74] III s. t.
Guillelmus de Capite Subrano: XVI d. t.

Talhafer de Casa pro preventionibus finavit et solvit: VI s. t.

Dominicus Vaca ex causa simili: XX s. t.

Petrus Gosserii: V s. t.

Guillelmus Redelli: XVI d. t.

Bonus Homo Gaytonis pro clamore: XVI d. t.

Raymundus Gayta ex causa simili: XVI s. t.

Item idem ex alia parte: VIII s. t.

Bertrandus de Mala Cabana pro clamore, preventione et condempnatione finavit et solvit XXXVI s. t.

Petrus del Casser: XII s. t.

Talhafer de Casa et eius socii: LIIII s. t.

Homines de Aqua Tincta[75] fuerunt delati coram dicto magistro Johanne, quia cessaverant solvere quandam pensionem blade, quam facere tenebantur anno quoquam domum Templi [*part of the word scratched out*] de Aqua Tincta, per unum annum post captionem Templariorum et super hoc finaverunt eodem ad summam, quam solverunt: IX l. t.

Summa istius recepte: XXII l. V s. VI d.

Sequintur alia recepta facta de quibusdam debitis abstractis de libris curie Montis Ricosi quondam Templi:

Gausbertus de Cahusaco[76] de Monte Ricoso debebat pro uno clamore <u>X s.</u> caturcenses, pro quibus solvit <u>V s. caturcenses</u> valent <u>III s. IIII d. t.</u>

Guillelmus Cautel debebat ex causa acapitis <u>VI s. caturcenses,</u> pro quibus solvit per manum G[uillelmi] de Suossone III s. IIII d. t.

Johannes Mechi debebat ex causa predicta <u>XXIII s. caturcenses</u>, pro quibus solvit VII s. t.

Galferius de Laverina[77] debebat ex causa predicta <u>X s. I d. caturcenses</u>, pro quibus solvit III s. IIII d. t.

Durandus Bruni debebat ex causa predicta <u>XII s. X d. caturcenses</u>, pro quibus solvit III s. VI d. t.

Geraldus Juliani Junior debebat ex causa predicta <u>XI s. caturcenses</u>, pro quibus solvit per manus G[uiardi] de Suessone III s. t.

Durandus Cernel fuerat condempnatus per curiam dicti loci in quibusdam munitis summis, de quibus offerebat se probare solutionem, set in dubio solvit per compositionem, ad quam fuit admissus propter sua paupertatem, X s. t.

Guiotus Murat debebat pro clamore <u>V s. caturcenses</u>, pro quibus solvit II s. t.

Garsias d'Estiron[78] debebat <u>V s. caturcenses</u> per condempnationem curie dicti loci, pro quibus solvit per manus G[uiardi] de Suessone III s. t.

Petrus Carmanh debebat ex causa simili <u>V s. caturcenses</u>, pro quibus solvit per manus dicti G[uiardi] II s. t.

Petrus de Manus debebat pro clamore V s. caturcenses, pro quibus solvit per manus G[uiardi] III s. t.

Ademarius de la Gulha debebat per condempnatione XX s. caturcenses, pro quibus solvit VI s. t.

Raymundus Boerii Sartor debebat ex causa simili XXX s. caturcenses, pro quibus solvit X s. t.

Johannes de l'Estang debebat ex causa simili LX s. caturcenses, pro quibus solvit per manum dicti G[uiardi] XX s. t.

Petrus Lont et Bernarda uxor Johannis Lont debebant ex causa simili XXV s. caturcenses, pro quibus solvunt per manus magistri Jerardi Maurelli X s. t.

Guillelmus Cernel debebat ex causa simili LX s. caturcenses, pro quibus solvit per manus dicti magistri G[uiraudi] XXVI s. VIII d. t.

Guillelma de Roana[79] debebat ex causa simili X s. caturcenses, pro quibus solvit per manus dicti magistri G[uiraudi] IIII s. t.

Summa istius recepte: VI l. II d.

Recepta de quibusdam debitis revelatis et levatis per magistros Arnaldum Regis et Bernardum de Barta Martino notarios, qui de hoc habuerunt pro sua revelatione et pro suo salario quintam partem:

Bernardus de Aurida de Fuxio debebat pro condempnatione curie dicti loci quondam Templi IIII l. t.

Raymondus Vignerii de Huos[80] pro clamore: V s. t.

Dominicus Cleri pro una contumatia: II s. t.

Arnaldus et Vitalis de Ganties[81] pro clamore: V s. t.

Arnaldus Martini de Fica pro clamore: II s. t.

Guillamotus de Puiolio de Barta[82] pro clamore: V s. t.

Arnaldus de Bocio pro obliis casalis de Arguto: II s. VIII d. t.

Amelius Sancii pro obliis dicti casalis: X s. t. ~~Summa: CXI s. VIII d. de quibis dictus comissarius habuit deducere quinta parte IIII l. IX s. IIII d. t~~. Nichl deducitur hic.

Summa per se: CXI s. VIII d. t.

Fol. 6

Item recepit pro suis expensis partes a personis que inferius continentur:

Primo ab heredibus Davini de Roaxio per manus Karoli de Trecis: XLVIII s. t.

A Fortio Sancii de Porta de Lectora per manus Guillelmi de Vinealibus notarii: C s. t.

Ab heredibus Arnaldi Berrani per manus domini Othonis de Monte Alto: L s. t.

A domino Gauberto Vaquerii rectore ecclesie Castri Novi de Strictis Fontibus per manus Hugonis d'Arboy et capellani dicti rectoris, qui debet M florenos, per litteras, quas habuit dominus G[uillelmus] Cligneti, duos cartones avene valent L s. t.

A domino Petro de Bordis milite: X l. t.

A domino Petro de Castilione milite ~~VI l. t.~~ per manus magistri Geraldi Morelli: VI l. t.

Ab Helia de Aguete de Petragoris per manus Guiardi de Suessone pro quibusdam expensis factis contra dominum Heliam super eo quod imponebatur ei ipsum habuisse de bonis Templi et tunc non potuit probare contra eum set suam innocentiam monstravit et fuit absolutus per sententiam et solvit ex una parte X l. t. et pro impetrando confirmationem dicte sententie in Parlamento solvit VI l. p. valent VII l. X s. t.

Item a gentibus comitis Petragoricensis tam per manus domini Guiardi quam procuratoris dicti comitis pro expensis contra ipsum factis Parisius anno XXII° deffendendo causam appelationis per dictas genets interiecte in Parlamento a quadam summa per dictum commissarium lata pro debito supradicto, quod solvit idem comes: XLVIII l. t.

Ab heredibus Raymundi Bernardi de Manso[83] quondam curatoris bonorum Templi per manum Egidii de Vernino[84] pro expensis ~~contra eos~~ factis Tholose expectando eos per duas dies ad finem quod compotum redderunt de gestis per dominum parentem suum et per eos et alias nomine suo circa dictam curam quod tunc facere non curarunt: XL s. t.

Summa ab alia: IIII^{xx} XV l. XVIII s. t.

Fol. 7

Totalis summa ab alia grossa: ~~totalis pro Rege de qua IX^{a} pars fuit deducta~~ VII^{c} IIII^{xx} XVIII l. XIII s. IX d. ob. t. non deducta IX^{a} parte de ista summa VII^{c} IIII^{xx} XVIII l. XIII s. IX d. ob. t.

Universalis summa totius recepte, de qua prefatus magister R[eginaldus] est honoratus ~~due mille due mille ducente viginti una l. quinque s. duo d. et ob. t.~~ trecente quadriginti decem nonem l. quinquam d.

Sequintur expense per dominum comissarium facte pro negociis et expeditione comissionis supradicte:

Pro salario plurimum servientum missorum ad faciendum citationes contra debitores obligatos, de quibus fit mentio in recepta: XIII l. XI s. IIII d. t., [*In the left margin:* A tergo] quorum servientium nomina et partes summe salarii in dorso presentis rotuli continentur.

Item pro tribus instrumentis sententiarium latarum contra heredes Davini de Roaxio missis Parisius in camera computorum per Guillelmum de Campelli, uno super resta Raymundi Gonterii et suorum sociorum, alio super resta Stephani de Ruppibus nominati in recepta, et tertio super summa CXII l. t. posita in compotis dicti ~~domini~~ Davini super Raymundo Athonis de Rualibus de Tholosa: XV s. t.

Pro instrumento summe late contra Raymundum Garcie de Sancto Gironcio[85] et pro inquesta facta contra ipsum missis Parisius prout supra: XV s. t., super XXVII l. t. t. [*sic!*] redditis in recepta.

Pro copia inqueste facte contra Philippum Clavelli missa Parisius prout supra, super eo quod appellaverat a summa contra ipsum lata: XX s. t., de qua fit mentio superius in recepta.

Pro processu et summa facta contra Petrum de Scobeto[86] super centum florenis, quos debet ad huc, missis Parisius ut supra: X s.

Pro processu et summa Guiraudi de Tapiis,[87] Petri de Festis et eorum sociorum lata contra ipsos super petitionem XXIIII l. t. redditis ~~in recepta XI s. t.~~ in recepta, missa Parisius prout supra: XI s. t.

Pro expensis dicti Guillelmi et Petri, et eius famuli, qui remanserunt Tholose per IIII^or dies expectando dictas inquestas ~~XX s. t.~~ et instrumenta: XX s. t.

[*In the left margin:* XVIII l. II s. ~~t.~~ IIII d.] Summa istarum VII partium: XVIII l. II s. ~~t.~~ IIII d. t.

Item pro salario quorumdam aliorum servientum et notariorum missorum in diversis locis ad citandum et compellendum plures homines, de quibus [*In the left margin:* A tergo] fit mentio superius in recepta, et alios obligatos dicto Templo, quorum nomina et partes sunt a tergo: VIII l. V s. t.

Summa per se.

Sequitur alie expense facte pro citando notarios diversorum locorum ad finem, quod perquirerent libros suos, ut debita de eis astraherent, si que essent que debita continentur in quodam rotulo inferius inter partes expensis factarum pro scripturis expressato et superius in recepta:

Primo die sabati in festo Sancti Augustini per Sancio Guillelmi misso apud Boldracum,[88] Lanam Arquerii et Suessium,[89] ubi fuit per tres dies ad citandum notarios dictorum locorum, II s. per diem: VI s. t.

Veneris post festum Sancti Michaelis pro Guillelmo de Maurenchis[90] misso apud Bononiam[91] et apud Samatan,[92] ubi fuit per duos dies ad faciendum preconisationem consuetam, III s. per diem, quia eques erat: VI s. t.

Fol. 8

Veneris ante Sanctam Crucem pro Guillelmo Calhanelli misso apud Lautricum[93] ad citandum notarios et consules et faciendum fieri preconisationem consuetam, ubi fuit per tres dies: IIII s. VI d. t.

Martis post festum Natalis beate Marie pro Amelio Falbatii misso apud Tayssonnerias ex causa predicta, ubi fuit per tres dies: III s. t.

Martis in festo Sancto Mathei pro Franscisco Grandis misso apud Insulam Jordani[94] ex causa predicta pro duobus diebus: III s. t.

Mercurii post dictum festum pro Andrea Pechevin misso apud Boldracum ad compellendum [*letters scratched out*] consulis dicti loci, ubi fuit per tres dies: III s. t.

Eadem die pro dicto Andrea, qui ivit de dicto loco apud Borderias[95] in Bigoria[96] ex causa predicta: II s. t.

Lune ante Sanctum Simonem et Judam pro Guillelmo Sancii misso apud Montem Ricosem, ubi fuit per tres dies ex causa preditca: VI s. t.

Mercurii ante Omnium Sanctorum pro Guillelmo Callanelli misso apud Marestagnum[97] ex causa predicta, ubi fuit per duos dies: III s. t.

Lune ante dictum festum pro expensis Karoli de Troia missi apud Samatan, ubi fuit per tres dies ex causa predicta: IX s. t., quia eques erat.

Jovis post dictum festum pro Guillelmo Pecherennie misso apud Bononiam ad citandum magistrum Guillelmum de Sernihaco[98] notarium ex causa predicta, ubi fuit per tres dies: VI s. t.

Veneris sequenti pro Johane de Sancto Marcello[99] misso apud Sayssanum[100] in Astarac,[101] ubi fuit per IIII^or dies ex causa predicta: VIII s. t.

Mercurii ante Sanctum Martinum hyemalis pro Hugone d'Orban[102] misso apud Levinhacum,[103] Pibracum,[104] Sanctum Licium,[105] Plasenciam[106] et Sanctam Fidem,[107] ubi stetit per V dies ex causa predicta: X s. t.

Veneris sequenti pro Stephano Xpinni misso apud Castrum Novum de Manhoaco[108] et Sanctum Plancatum, ubi fuit per IIII^or dies ex hac causa: VIII s. t.

Martis post dictum festum pro Jacobo Alamanni misso apud Bonum Locum,[109] ubi fuit per unam diem ex causa simili: II s. t.

Jovis post Conversionem Sancti Pauli pro Guilloto de Lectora misso apud Astafortem[110] in Agenesio, ubi fuit una die ex causa predicta: II s. t.

Eadem die pro Pontio Estolti misso apud Miratorium[111] ex causa predicta pro una die: II s. t.

Item pro item pro [*sic!*] Jacobo Arquerii misso apud Sanctum Antonium,[112] Dunas,[113] Flamereux,[114] Donzacum[115] et Altum Villarem[116] in Leomania, ubi fuit per tres dies ex hac causa: VI s. t.

Mercurii post Sanctum Valentinum pro Johane Candelorii misso apud Castrum Mairanum,[117] Montem Astrucum,[118] Rapistagnum,[119] Insulam Albigensis,[120] Galhacum[121] et Corduam,[122] ubi fuit per sex dies ex hac causa: XII s. t.

Die X^a Februari pro Andrea Pechevin misso apud Sayas,[123] Podium Togesii[124] et Bellum Fortem,[125] ubi fuit per IIII^or dies ex causa predicta: VIII s. t.

Summa istarum partium: CX s. VI d. t.

Expense facte contra Petrum de Scobeto de Miratorio in Leomania pro C florenis, quos debet pro fratre Bernardo de Ruppe olim Templario:

Die Veneris post festum Natalis beate Marie pro salario Fabri Michaelis servientis missi apud Miratorium in Leomania contra dictum Petrum ex causa predicta, ubi fuit per V dies: XV s. t.

Die Lune ante festum Sancti Martini pro Johanne Garaudi misso de Insula Jordani apud Tholosam pro negotio dicti Petri pro duobus diebus: IIII s. t.

Die III[a] Februarii pro Guiardo de Suessone et Hugone d'Arboy servientibus missis contra dictum Petrum, ubi fuerunt per quinque dies ex hac causa V s. t. per diem pro ambobus: XXV s. t.

Summa ab alia: XLIIII s. t.

Expense facte contra Fortium Sancii de Porta de Astaforti in Agenio [*sic for* Agenesio] firmarium de Gimbreda ratione reste, que soluta fuerit per ipsum et heredes Davini de Roaxia, de qua fit mentio superius in recepta:

Die Jovis post festum beati Michaelis pro Bemondo Sancii misso apud Astafortem in Agenesio contra dominum Fortium, ubi fuit per VI dies: XII s. t.

Die ultima Decembris pro dicto Raymondo misso iterato contra dictum Fortium ex causa predicta pro alios sex dies: XII s. t.

Die III[a] Februarii pro dicto Raymondo misso apud Lectoram et Astafortem contra dictum Fortium ex causa predicta: XII s. t.

Pro uno instrumento compoti dicti Fortii et pro salario et expensis magistri Guillelmi de Vinealibus notarii, qui fuit apud Lectoram per quinque dies eundo de Tholosa ad recipiendum dictum instrumentum X s. t. per diem et X s. pro instrumento: LX s. t.

Summa ab alia: IIII l. XVI s. t.

Sequintur alie expense facte contra diversos homines, de quibus conscit per instrumenta et alias scripturas:

Pro copia informationis facte contra homines de Martino et pro uno magno instrumento facto super XLVII l. t., quas solverunt, prout continetur in recepta: XX s. t.

Summa per se.

Pro uno instrumento citationis facte contra uxorem et executorem Raymondi Athonis quondam comissarii super facto Templi, quod venirent Parisius redditum compotum de administratione per eum: II s. t.

Pro uno instrumento citationis Arnaldi Bernardi de Manso filii et heredis Raymundi Bernardi quondam curatoris bonorum Templi, quod veniret Parisius redditurі rationem de administratione per eundem: II s. t.

Pro uno magno instrumento sententie Raymundi Gonterii et Germani Raditoris late super summa LVI l. t., que redduntur superius in recepta: VI s. t.

Pro instrumento sententie late contra Raymundum Garcie super XXVII l. t., quas solvit, prout continentum superius in recepta: IIII s. t.

Pro quodam magno instrumento appellationis facte per heredes Davini de Roaxio a sentenciis supradictis: X s. t.

Summa ab alia: XXIIII s. t.

Expense facte contra dictum Petrum de Bordis super summa VIIIxx l. t., que redduntur superius in recepta et X l. pro expensis:

Die Martis ante festum Natalis beate Marie pro Thoma d'Auchi serviente misso contra dictum Petrum de Bordis, ubi fuit per II dies: VI s. t.

Die ultima Novembris pro Hugone d'Arboy misso contra dictum dominum P[etrum] pro duobus diebus: IIII s. t.

Die Mercurii post festum Sancti Vincentii pro Audeto Revelli misso apud Astafortem ad citandum testes contra dictum dominum P[etrum], ubi fuit per tres dies: VI s. t.

Die crastina Conversionis Sancti Pauli pro Laurentio Laboratoris misso apud Rolhacum ex causa predicta per duos dies: IIII s. t.

Pro salario et expensis magistrorum Guillelmi de Vinealibus et Arnaldi de Sancta Mera[126] notariorum, qui fecerunt inquestam contra dictum dominum P[etrum], ubi fuerunt per X dies apud Gimbredam, Astafortem et Rolhacum in Leomania, scilicet pro dicto Guillelmo X s. t. per diem et pro dicto Arnaldo V s. t. per diem: VII l. X s. t.

Pro IIIIor instrumentis factis per magistrum Johanem de Alta Fagia contra dictum dominum P[etrum] ad probandum intentionem Regis et pro salario dicti notarii, qui fuit per duos dies ad ea facienda: XXX s. t.

Pro copia dicte inqueste: XV s. t.

Summa istarum expensarum: X l. XV s. t.

Expense facte contra Philippum Clavelli pro summa, in qua fuit condempnatus, de qua fit mentio superius in recepta, ubi redduntur expense:

Pro uno instrumento facto per Petrum Chalonis de venditione vinee dicti Philippi: XII d. t.

Pro citatione facienda contra detentores bonorum dicti Philippi pro summas redditis in recepta: II s. t.

Pro salario magistri Guillelmi de Vinealibus notarii, qui fuit per sex dies ad faciendum inquestam contra dictum Philippum, X s. t. per diem: LX s. t.

Pro instrumento sententie late contra dictum Philippum: XX s. catalanenses valent XIII s. IIII d. t.

Summa ab alia: LXXVI s. IIII d. t.

Pro salario Petri Magistri missi apud Taissonnarias ad citandum P. de Spahone et ejus consortes ratione territorii de Alito, quod fuit de bonis Templi quondam, quod detinet sine causa, ut apparet per inquestam inde factam per magistrum Petrum de Cayra[127] commissarium super hoc auctoritate Regis deputatum: VIII s. t.

Pro copia dicte inqueste facta super hoc per dictum magistrum P[etrum]: III floreni auri ad argentum valent LVI s. III d. t.

Pro copia cuiusdam alterius inqueste facte super eodem per magistrum Dominicum de Ecclesia commissarium ad hoc deputatum per Davinum de Roaxio quondam: V s. t.

Pro aliis scripturis factis coram magistro ~~Sfa~~ Stephano Abbati judice Tholose et magistro Petro Rubei commissariis super hoc deputatis per senescallus Tholose: V s. t.

Summa: LXXIIII s. III d. t.

Fol. 9

Pro tribus instrumentis preconisationum [*sic for* preconisationis] factis apud Grimontem per Petrum Salas notarium et pro salario ~~istius~~ ipsius notarii et Geraldi de Acromonte[128] preconis dicti loci per tres dies ex parte Regis contra illos, qui haberent aliqua de bonis dicti Templi: XV s. t.

Pro quodam alio instrumento facto apud Samatan super eodem et pro salario notarii et preconis dicti loci de una die: sex s. t.

Pro quodam alio instrumento preconisationis facte [*sic for* facto] apud Petragoris et pro salario preconis et notarii, qui fuerunt per unam diem ad hoc faciendum super eodem facto: XV s. t.

Pro quodam alio instrumento facto contra archiepiscopum Burdegalensem[129] super quibusdam bonis Templi, que administravit, de quibus nullum compotum reddidit et pro salario notarii, qui dictum instrumentum fecit: X s. t.

Pro duobus instrumentis factis per Raymundum Adelli notarium Insule Jordani de XXII cartonibus frumenti, quos debet Bernardus Berthena, cuius bona Guillelmus Feriacteri de Gimonte[130] tenet: VI s. t.

Pro sex instrumentis factis par Raymundum de Cererio notario Montis Rocosii de debitorum dicti loci, qui ascendunt XI^{xx} XII l. t. et pro salario dicti notarii: XVIII s. t.

Pro uno magno instrumento ad sigillum curie Petragoricensis officialis, in quo Helias Budelli est [*In the left margin*: (*characters illegible due to paper damage*) ligatura (*characters illegible*) est pars nona] obligatus fratri Geraldo de Verina[131] in IX^{c} s. petragoricenses:V s. t.

Pro quadam littera ad dictum sigillum, in qua Reginaldus de Ponte est obligatus dicto fratri in XX sextariis frumenti: XII d. t.

Pro tribus instrumentis debitorum traditis ad levandum Bernardo de Lorda[132] clerico, notario Tholose, quorum unum continens V^{c} LX l., aliud C florenos et aliud XI l. t. in partibus agenensis: XVI s. t., de quibus idem Bernardus nichil potuit explectare propter gerram domini Jordani de Insula et sociorum eius.

Summa: IIII l. XII s. ~~X d.~~

Pro una littera senescallie Tholose data contra dominum Petrum de Bordis: III s. t.

Pro alia littera eiusdem senescalli data contra archiepiscopum Auxitanum:[133] III s. t.

Pro transcripto compositionis Hospitaliorum sub sigillo maiori senescallie Tholose: II s. t.

Pro transcripto littere domini P[etri] de Galardo sub sigillo vicarii Tholose: III s. t.

Summa: XI s. t.

Pro copia processus facti contra Esquinum de Florano per Guillelmum de Vinealibus notarium et Petrum Chalonis super facto de Monte Ricoso quondam Templi, super qua habet, ut dicit, V^{c} l. annuatim et valent M C l. t., et pro salariis dictorum notariorum X dierum: L s. t.

Pro copia processus et summe late contra ipsum Esquinum pro Hospitalariis, pro iudice maiori senescallie Caturcensis et pro corrigendo dictam copiam cum originalis per magistrum Olivierum de Sancto Johanne[134] notarium Tholose et Guillelmum de Vinealibus notarium Regis, qui vacaverunt ad hoc pro duos dies: XXV s. t.

Pro IIII^{or} instrumentis factis super executione inchoata contra ipsum per Guirardum de Suessone: IIII s. t.

Pro expensis notariorum qui dicta instrumenta receperunt: XX s. t.

Pro expensis dicti Guiardi, qui fuit per octo dies ad dictam executionem faciendum: XXIIII s. t., de quibus est sciendum, quod nichil ~~poru~~ potuit recuperare propter quandam litteram, quam dominus Esquinus impetravit in requestis per magistrum Jacobum de Jarssenis[135] et quia postmodum domus illa fuit data domino Alphonoso de Yspanna per dominum nostrum Regem et per Hospitalarios.

Summa: VI l. III s. t.

Item pro salario Petri Chalonis notarii Ville Dei, qui perquisivit libros Philippi Clavelli notarii dicti loci: V s. t.

Pro salario Petri Guillelmi de Fabrica, qui perquisivit libros notarii de Samatan: II s. t.

Pro expensis Vitalis de Silhaco,[136] qui perquisivit libros curie de Marestagno per duos dies: IIII s. t.

Pro salario Petri Dossene, qui perquisivit libros notariorum de Carbona:[137] II s. VI d. t.

Pro salario Petri Magoti notarii Tholose, qui ~~pers~~ perquisivit libros suos: III s.

Pro salario magistri Arnaldi Garcie notarii Tholose, qui perquisivit libros Raymundi de Casilhaco[138] et Petri de Monte Sorio:[139] IIII s. t.

Pro salario Guillelmi de Fonte notarii Tholose, qui perquisivit libros suos: XVIII d. t.

Pro Bernardo Grandis notario, qui perquisivit libros curie Lane Arquerii: II s. t.

Et ~~pro~~ pro perquirendis libris magistri Guillelmi de Sernihaco notarii Bononie: XVIII d.

Bernardo de Arpaiano notario Bononie pro perquirendis libris suis: III s.

Pontio de Sotulo notario Castri Sarraceni[140] pro perquirendis libris notariorum dicti loci: IIII s. Bernardo Jordani notario Tholose pro perquirendis libris curie Montis Salnerii pro duos dies: VI s.

Eidem pro perquirendis libris curie de Cadelhano[141] et de Plauterio: IIII s.

Eidem pro perquirendis libris magistri Bertrandi de Carcanos:[142] V s.

Petro de Podio pro perquirendis libris notarii Calciata:[143] IIII s.

Bartholomeo de Croso[144] notario de Fonte Novo[145] pro perquirendis libris suis: III s. VI d.

Guillelmo Costa notario pro perquirendis libris curie de Capella[146] in Caturcinio[147] et debita abstrahendis per duos dies: VI s. t.

Bernardo Vasconis notario Montis Ricosi pro perquirendis libris suis et debitis abstrahendis per sex dies: XVIII s. t.

Arnaldo Bernardi notario de Lectora pro perquirendis libris curie de Gimbreda in Leomania per quinque dies: XV s. t.

Bernardo Baconis notario de Saissano pro perquirendis libris suis: XX d. t.

Summa: IIII l. XV s. VIII d. t.

Salaria servientium, notariorum et aliorum, de quibus extant littere solutionum: [*words scratched out*]

Die XVII Octobris Guillelmo Martini preconi Ville Dei pro vendendo superlectilibus Philippi Clavelli, de quibus fit mentio superius in recepta: III s. IIII d.

Petro Chalonis notario pro scribendo dicta bona: II s. VI d.

Die XVIII Octobris Karolo de Troia servienti pro executione facta contra dictum Philippum per V dies: X s. t., et pro suis expensis: XV s. t.

Die Martis in crastinum Sancti Lucherii Petro Banguesie servienti ex causa predicta X s. t., et pro expensis ipsius: XV s. t.

Die Jovis post festum Omnium Sanctorum Guillelmo de Alberic notario ~~Insule~~ Insule Jordani pro perquirendis libris dicti loci: XVI s. VIII d. t.

Veneris sequent~~e~~i Guillelmo Pecherennie servienti misso contra homines de Taissonerias: V s. t.

Eadem die Stephano Xpinni servienti misso contra homines Lane Arquerii: V s.

Johanni de Claris Vallibus[148] servienti pro ducendo Philippum Clavelli de Caturco[149] apud Villam Dei: XXIIII s.

Sabati ante festum Beati Andree Petro Burgundi servienti pro suo salario deservito in Caturcinio: XXII s. t.

Petro de Sancto Plancato commissario misso in Caturcinio ad perquirednum debita Templi: X [*number scratched out*] X l. t.

Die XIIIIª Decembirs Johanni de Fabrica pro locagio unius equi ad ducendum dictum Philippum Clavelli apud Caturcum: X s. VI d. t.

Die Mercurii post festum Epiphanie Domini magistro Bernardino de Cleissano[150] advocato Tholose pro patrocinio prestito in causis dicti Templi: L s. t.

Die Martis post septuagesima Bernardo de Borda clerico pro suis expensis factis eundo apud Lectoram pro negotio ~~Sancii~~ Fortii Sancii de Porta: XX s. t.

Die Jovis in festo beati Mathie Guioto de Suessone servienti misso contra comitem Petragoricensem: X s. t.

Guillelmo de Vinealibus notario et Hugoni d'Arboy servienti misso in Brathona pro debitis dicti Templi: XL s. t.

Die ultima Februarii Guillelmo Peles servienti misso in Agenesio ad senescallum Agenensium: X s. t.

Die IIIIª Martii Guillelmo de Vinealibus notario misso in Carcassesio[151] pro negocio dicti Templi: XXX s. t.

Lune in crastinum Pasche Bernardo de Barta Martino notario pro perquiredis libris suis: XII s. t.

Mercurii sequentis Johanni de Sancto Marcello et Guillelmo Calhanelli servientibus pro executione per eos facta super bonis Bernardi Busca: XVII s. VI d.

Die Vª Aprilis anno XXIIIº Petro Burgesie servienti pro pluribus executionibus per eum factis contra diversos homines ~~de Martino~~ obligatos Templo: CI s. t.

Die VIII^{a} Aprilis Guillelmo de Vinealibus pro suis expensis contra homines de Martino:[152] XXIII s.

Eidem pro suis expensis factis contra Fortium Sancii de Porta: XVI s. III d.

Die XII^{a} Aprilis Johanni de Alta Fagia[153] notario pro suo salario deservito contra dominum Petrum de Bordis militum: L s. t.

Martis post octavam Pasche Johanni de Pruvinis[154] servienti Tholose pro suo salario executionis facte contra comitem Petragoricensem per decem dies: L s.

Die XVI^{a} Aprilis Geraldo Morelli notario pro salario ipsius et Petri de Aureliano[155] servientis, qui fuerunt per X dies tam contra comitem Petragoricensem quam contra archiepiscopum Burdegalensem: VI l. t.

Die XXIII^{a} Aprilis Guiardo de Suessone per suo salario deservitio in executione dicti comitis: L s. t.

Martis post festum beati Marchi evangeliste Helie de Erguant servienti misso ad citandum testes contra dominum Petrum de Castellione super una equa, quam habuerat a fratre Gerardo de Verina V s. t., de quo redduntur VIII l. superius in recepta.

Summa: LVI l. IIII s. IX d. t.

Fol. 10

Expense scripturarum factarum contra comitem Petragoricensem:

Pro tribus intreumentis citationum factarum contra comitem Petragoricensem per Guillelmum de Vinealibus notarium et pro expensis et salario dicti notarii, qui fuit per decem dies ad hoc: L s. t.

Pro salario Johannis de Alta Fagia notarii, qui fecit processus contra dictum comitem per II dies: X s.

Pro quodam magno instrumento facto per dictum notarium super responsione appellationis dicti comitis et pro salario dicti notarii unius diei: XV s.

Pro uno alio instrumento facto per Petrum de Puni notario Petragoris super eo, quod mater dicti comitis et eius procurator promiserunt solvere debitum ab eo petitum: X s. t.

Pro salario dicti notarii, qui vacavit ad hoc per unum diem: V s. t.

Pro IIII^{or} instrumentis factis per Guillelmum de Brolio[156] notario de Calciata super executione facta contra dictum comitem per Guiardum de Suessone et pro salario dicti notarii duorum dierum: XX s. t.

Pro quodam alio instrumento facto per Petrum de Campis notarium regium super copia littere regie dicto comiti concessa de appellatione sui procuratoris et pro salario dicti notarii: IIII s. t.

Pro quodam alio magno instrumento facto per Johannem Fabri notarium Petragoris super presentatione dicte littere et super responsione dicti commissarii super hoc facta. Et pro salrio dicti notarii qui vacavit ad hoc per unum diem: XV s. t.

Summa: VI l. IX s. t.

Pro quodam magno instrumento facto per Johannem Fabri notarium Petragoris super compoto heredum magistri Petri de Verdelone reddito per eosdem. Et pro salario dicti notarii unius diei: XX s. t.

Pro aliis duobus instrumentis per dictum notarium factis super eodem negotio et pro salario dicti notarii alterius diei: viginti s. t.

Summa: XL s. t.

Pro quodam alio instrumento magno facto per Guillelmum Janmar notarium regium super litteris archiepiscopi Burdegalensis, quas dicebat se habere de compoto per eum reddito Hospitalariis ratione bonorum Templi sue diocesis per eum administratorum et pro salario dicti notarii duorum dierum: XX s. t.

Item pro pluribus aliis scripturis contra eum factis et recuperatis super eodem facto: X s. t.

Item pro uno magno rotulo, in quo debita, que dictus commissarius reperiit [*sic for* reperit], sunt scripta et pro pergameno ad hoc faciendum: XL s. t.

Summa: IIII l. X s.

Summa totalis[*part of the word scratched out*] expensarum predictarum: VII^{xx} IIII l. XII s. X d. t.

[*About 1/6 of the page is blank*]

Sequntur expense per dictum commissarium facte anno M° CCC° XXIII° in senescallia Tholosana:

Die ultima Julii pro media duodena pergameni: II s. t.

Pro una manu papiri: XV d.

Pro cera rubea ad sigillandum: VII d. t.

Die prima Augusti pro expensis Bobini de Ponte missi apud Villam Dei ad recuperandum quedam instrumenta a notariis isti loci pro duobus diebus: IIII s.

Pro VII instrumentis a dictis notariis recuperatis de minutis debitis testamentorum: V s. VIII d.

Die Mercruii post festum Sancti Petri ad Vincula pro salario Guillelmi Cadeplon missi apud Vasegiam[157] ad citandum Guillelmum de Roaxio super hec, que debebat, pro una die: II s.

Pro sigillo baiuli dicti loci et pro serviente, qui fecit citationem: VIII d. t.

Pro uno instrumento continente LXXII l., quas debet Bernardus de Sancto Ruffo,[158] facto per Petrum de Caturco: III s. t.

Die X^a Augusti pro expensis Jacobi Armanni missi apud Cymorram[159] ad citadnum Guillelmam Aleriam pro hec, que debebat et solvit in recepta, pro tribus diebus: IIII s. VI d.

Die XII^a Augusti pro salario Guiardi de Suessone missi apud Villam Dei ad citandum emptores Philippi Clavelli per hec, que debebant et solverunt, pro tribus diebus, quibus steterat et pro salario servientis dicti loci: XIX s. t.

Die XVIII^a Augusti pro salario dicti Guiardi missi apud Calciatam contra magistrum Guillelmum de Tisseris procuratorem comitis Petragoricensis pro hec, que debebat, ubi fuit per IIII^{or} dies: XX s. t.

Eadem di~~em~~ pro expensis Petri Fabri missi apud Bastidam Templi[160] contra dominum Arnaldum Belli pro hec, que debebat, pro tribus diebus, quibus fuit illuc: VI s. t.

Die XXIIII^a Augusti pro salario Guiardi de Suessone missi apud Sanctum Tyberium contra heredes Petri Catelli pro hec, que debebant et solverunt in recepta Carcassone, ubi fuit pro [*sic for* pro] octo dies: XL s. t.

Eadem die pro salario Colini Lescapele missi contra fratrem Johannem de Affariis, ubi fuit per duos dies ratione summe, quam debebat et solvit: VI s. t.

Die prima Septembris pro salario Andree Peschemin missi apud Cambonum[161] ad citandum dominum Gaillardum de Causenthis pro hec, que debebat, pro duobus diebus: IIII s. t.

Eadem die pro salario Guillellmi Callanelli missi apud Bonum Locum et Vasegiam ad citandum heredes Davini de Roaxio pro hec, que debebant et solverunt, pro duobus diebus: VI s.

Pro transcriptis duorum instrumentorum et unius magni rotuli de facto Templi Lane Arquerii et pertinentis eiusdem: VIII s. t.

Die VIII^a Septembris pro salario Guiardi de Suessone missi contra heredes Dominici de Vallatis pro hec, que solverunt, ubi fuit per duos dies: X s. t.

Die Sabbati post festum beati Mathei Apostoli pro expensis Thome Britonis missi apud Carbonam contra notarium dicti loci: II s. t.

Die Jovis post festum beati Francisci pro salario dicti Thome missi in Leomania ad citandum quosdam homines, qui tenentur ratione dicti Templi, pro V diebus: X s. t.

Die Mercurii ante festum beati Luche pro expensis magistri Bernardi Regis, qui citavit dominum Petrum de Bordis ratione unius equi quem habuit de bonis dicti Templi: V s. t.

Pro copia littere vicecomitis Leomanie, per quam inhibuit suis subditis ne parerent comissioni: VIII d. t.

Die ultima Octobris pro salario Guiardi de Suessone missi apud Calciatam et Nigram Pellitiam contra Guillelmum Marmgerrani et Guirrardum Sarreti pro hoc, que solvent [*sic for* solverunt], ubi fuit per IIII^{or} dies: XX s. t.

Eadem die pro una manu papiri et duabus pellibus pergameni et cera ad sigillandum: III s. t.

Die ultima Novembris pro expensis magistri Guillelmi de Vinealibus notarii et Petri de Borda servientis missorum in Leomania ad capiendum terram vicecomitis pro redditibus domorum Templi de Burdegalis et de Arcinis,[162] quos recepit per plures annos et de hoc nihil solvit, ubi fuerunt per sex dies: LX s. t.

Die Martis post festum Nativitatis Domini pro expensis Johannis le Bidan missi apud Ventilhacum[163] contra magistrum Michaelem de Rotondo: VI s. t.

Die Mercurii sequenti pro expensis Hugonis Bergonda missi apud Gymontem contra Raymundum des Campis Aquis: VI s.

Item eidem Hugoni ex causa predicta pro decem diebus, quibus stetit illuc executionem faciendo: XXX s. t.

Pro salario Bernardi de Murello[164] notarii de Gimonte, qui fecit instrumenta preconisationis bonorum dicti Raymondi: III s. t.

Fol. 11

Pro Robino Cordelerii serviente Tholose et eius familia, qui fuerunt in dicta executione per VI dies: XL s.

Pro instrumetno debiti, quod debebat Guillema Aleria, restituto: [*In the left margin:* VI[a] ligature IIII instrumenta reddita camere in VI (*characters illegible due tu paper damage*) instrumentarum] II s.

Pro instrumento debiti, quod debebat Dominicus de Vallatis: II s. t.

Pro instrumento debitorum Guillelmi de Roaxio et Bartholomei eius fratris: II s. t.

Pro instrumento bastide de Maseriis: V s. t.

Pro aliis tribus instrumentis debitorum: II s. t.

Pro salario magistri Almerii de Sancto Johanne, qui fecit instrumentum computi Guilellmi de Roaxio, et pro copia dicti instrumenti: III s. t.

Pro salario magistri Garnerii de Moriaco[165] notarii de Ruthena[166] deserviti in perquirendo libros suos et pro rotulo sue relationis: XV s. t.

Pro una littera emanata a commissariis senescallie Tholosane contra heredes et executores archiepiscopi Auxitensis: XII d. t.

Pro copia revocationis et suspensionis comissionum: XII d. t.

Pro quadam informatione et aliis scripturis factis contra Philippum Clavelli: V s. t.

Pro [*In the left margin: text illegible due to paper damage*] duobus instrumentis debitorum Bernardi et Johannis Sarraceni quondam de Monte Salvio[167] et alii ab hoc factis: II s. t.

Pro [*word scratched out*] XII instrumentis continentibus debita Templi quondam a notariis Ville Dei recuperatis: XXX s. t.

Pro [*words scratched out*] XII instrumentis ab Arnadlo Garcie recuperates, continentibus plures summas de bonis et debitis domino Regi pertinentis ratione dicti Templi: XXX s. t.

Pro pluribus infromationibus inquestis et aliis scripturis factis contra dominum Petrum de Bordis super hiis, que detinet indebite de bonis dicti Templi: XL s. t.

Pro duobus intrumentis a Guillelmo de Salerna recuperatis: [*number illegible*] s. t.

Pro tribus instrumentis a Petro Berrani notario Alte Rippe[168] recuperatis: III s. t.
Pro sex instrumentis a diversis notariis recuperatis: X s. t.

Summa expensarum senescallie Tholosane: XXIIII l. V s. IIII d. t.

[*About 1/5 of the page is blank*]

Sequntur expense per dictum comissarium facte in senescallias Caturcensi, Petragoricensi.

Et primo anno Domini M° CCC° XXIII°:

Die XXI° julii pro expensis Guiardi de Suessone misso apud Petragorum ad habendum copias inventariorum domorum Templi de Andrivals,[169] de Podio Martini[170] et de Soleto,[171] ubi fuit per XII dies: LX s. t.

Et pro dictis copiis dictorum inventariorum: VI s. t.

Die XXV^a Julii pro expensis Thome Britonis missi apud Villam Dei ad habendum duo instrumenta debitorum dicti [*In the left margin:* in secunda ligatura] Templi contra magistrum Arnaldum Fabri, ubi fuit per IIII^or [dies]: XII s.

Et pro dictis duobis instrumentis: IIII s. t.

Die VI^a Octobris pro expensis Guiardi de Suessone et dicti Thome missorum apud Bastidam Francesiam[172] contra Guillelmum Fabri filium et heredem dicti magistri Arnaldi, ubi fuerunt per IIII^or dies: XXXII s. t.

Et pro uno magno instrumento contra ipsum facto: X s. t.

Die XIIII^a Novembris pro expensis Colini Lescapele servientis missi apud Villam Francesiam contra dictum Guillelmum, ubi fuit per tres dies: IX s. t.

Die XV^a Decembris pro expensis dicti Colini missi apud Caturcum ad habendum copiam recepte [*name illegible*] de Gerondia receptoris olim debitorum Templi senescallie Caturcensis pro ~~X~~ V diebus: XV s. t.

Et pro dicta copia: V s. t.

Die XVIII^a Decembris pro expensis Bernardi de Podio missi apud Caturcum ad citandum dominum Geraldum de Sabanaco[173] olim curatorem Templi ad reddendum compotum, quod Raymundus de Podio receptor suis quondam et alii receptores per ipsum deputati nolebant obedire, et pro salario Guillelmi de Gonte Alto[174] servientis de Caturco, qui fecit dictam citationem: X s. t.

Die XX^a Decembris pro expensis Hugonis Burgondi missi apud Calciatam et Montem Ricosum ad habendum inquestam factam contra Sycardum de Masuris ratione Templi: VIII s. t.

Pro uno instrumento de decimis domus Templi de Curtibus[175] diocesis [*In the left margin:* (*word illegible*) de Octobirs: VI^a ligatura] Agenensis: XII d. t.

Pro salario magistri Oliverii de Sancto Johanne notarii, qui fecit transcriptum inqueste facte contra dominum Petrum de Bordis super uno equo et aliis rebus, quas habuit de domo Templi de Gimbreda: VI s. t.

Pro tribus instrumentis sigillatis sigillo regis Petragoris continentibus debita dicti Templi factis per Johannem Fabri notarium regis dicti loci: XV s. t.

Pro quondam magno instrumento de restis traditis [*In the left margin:* III instrumenta: VIII^a^ ligature] Guidoni Pigneta per Aymericum de Ponte receptorem olim debitorum dicti Templi in dicosesis Petragoricensis: X s. t.

Pro copia compoti Aymerici de Ponte redditi Bernardo de Clavelli quondam comissario de quibusdam receptis per dictum Aymericum factis post compotum redditum per eundem magistro Guillelmo de Gysorcio: III s. t.

Pro quodam instrumento facto super executione inchoacta contra Sycardum de Masuris de Monte Ricoso ratione quorumdam debitorum ab eo petitorum ratione dicti Templi, quam executionem dominus Rex revocavit ex eo, quod dictus locus fuit datus domino Alphonso de Yspania: II s. t.

Pro copia processus facti contra dominum Petrum de Castilione militum pretextu XIIII l. t., in quibus fuit finaliter condemnatus: VIII s. t.

Pro copia processus facti contra Heliam de Chavantone et contra heredes magistri Gaufridi de Ripperia[176] ratione bonorum mobilium domus Templi de Soleto dyocesis Petragoricensis, que habuerunt: VIII s. t.

Die Martis in carniprivio pro salario Guillelmi Pictavini servientis, qui fecit executionem contra Johannem Fabri notarium pro tribus instrumentis per eum superius restitutis: III s. t.

Pro expensis Guillelmi de Vinealibus notarii missi apud Turrem Albam[177] contra heredes magistri Gaufridi de Rupperia ratione bonorum mobilium domus Templi de Soleto, ubi fuit per duos dies: X s. t.

Pro instrumento appellationis dictorum heredum et responsionis partis Regis: X s. t.

Pro copia inventarii bonorum mobilium domus Templi de Bona Fara facta per magistrum Petrum de Verdalone: IIII s. t.

Pro copia compoti Bernardi de Chamellis[178] redditi Arnaldo de Proboleno thesaurario Caturci de hoc, que dictus Bernardus receperat de bonis dicti Templi: V s. t.

Pro informationibus et processibus factis contra Esquinum de Florano ratione bonorum domus Templi de Monte Ricoso, que habuit indebite: X s. t.

Pro IIII^or^ instrumentis factis contra priorem de Murello[179] Stephanum de Molinis, Guidonem et Petrum de Alvernia necnon contra Fulconem de Barra: VIII s. t., qui quidem omnis sunt obligati ratione dicti Templi, prout in rotulo debitorum continetur.

Summa expensarum senescallie Caturcensis et Petragoricensis: XIII l. XIIII s. t.

Fol. 12

Sequntur expense per dictum commissarum facte in Lemovicinio anno Millessimo CCC° XXIII°, mense Martii:

Die prima Martii pro una littera sub sigillo regio curie Lemovicensis de X l. t., quas habuit et receipt indebite frater Johannes de Monte Boscherii[180] hospitalarius a Petro de Montibus firmario de Manhaco quondam Templi: III s. t.

Pro copia compoti Guidonis Bozonis olim receptoris debitorum Templi quondam dyocesis Lemovicensis: II s. t.

Pro copia quarundam litterarum sub sigillo regio baillivie Lemovicensis factarum super solutionibus factis per Stephanum de Molinis firmarium domorum Templi de Carreris[181] [et] de Mortua Sama:[182] IIII s. t.

Pro alia copia, cum publico instrumento, facta de litteris solutionum factarum per Johannem de Manso firmario domorum quondam Templi de Manso Dei[183] et de Lobers:[184] II s. t.

Pro salario Guillelmi Pictavini servientis missi ad citandum homines in recepta Lemovicensis superius nominatos, in diversis locis, ubi fuit per spatium decem dierum continuorum: XX s. t.

Pro [*words scratched out and crossed-out*] dicto Guillelmo misso de Lemovico apud Inucheriam[185] contra Petrum et Guidonem de Alvernia fratres de Inucheria, qui debent ~~pro resta~~ VI^{xx} VI l. II s. XI d. ratione firme domus Templi de Paulhaco:[186] V s. t.

[*Letters scratched out*] Pro [*words sratched out*] salario Aymerici Gramani notarii de Lemovico, qui perquisivit libros suos per unum diem: [*words scratched out and crossed-out*] IIII s. t.

Pro copia processus facti contra Guichardum de Combornio[187] super XLV l., quas debet cum litteris per G[uidonem] Pignete restitutis: XII d. t.

Pro copia processus facti contra Stephanum Boleti et Petrum Fabri firmarios domus Templi de Palacio pro resta dicte firme, quam debet: VI s. t.

Pro copia processus facti contra Stephanum de Molinis firmarium domorum Templi de Carreris et de Mortua Sama ratione restarum, de quibus est per compotum Aymerici de Ponte de Petragoris honoratus: IIII s. t.

Pro copia processus facti contra Petrum et Guidonem de Alvernia fratres ratione firme superius expressate: VI s. t.

Pro rationibus factis contra Stephanum de Molinis contra [*sic for* coram] senescallo Lemovicensi super appellatione per ipsum interposita de executione contra ipsum ichoacta ratione restarum predictarum: III s. t.

Pro quadam informatione facta contra Foulcandum de Drolio[188] super sexagina l. ab eo petitis cum litteris per Guidonem Pignete restitutis: IIII s. t.

Pro quodam rotulo [*words scratched out*] pergameni, in quo debita Templi, quod que [*sic!*] debenture, per dominum G[eraldum] Morelli reperta tam in diocesis Petragoricensis quam Lemovicensis et Burdegalensis registrantur: II s. t.

Item pro rotulo inventarii facti de instructis et litteris dicto comissario et eius substitutis per notarium et alias restitutis: X s. t.

Summa expensarum factarum in Lemovicino: LXXV s. t.

Expense facte in Provincia anno XXIII°:

Die septima Septembris pro salario Bernardi Picardi missi apud Limosum[189] ad habendum copiam inqueste facte contra firmarium dicti loci per IIII^{or} dies: VIII s.

Item pro dicta copia et salario dicti notarii: XV s.

Item die XVIª Septembris pro salario dicti Bernardi missi apud Nemausum [*letters scratched out*] ad magistrum Bernardum Gardiola notarium pro inquirendo super bonis Templi, pro X diebus: XX s.

Item die Xª Octobris pro salario dicti Bernardi missi apud Bitteris ad citandum heredes Aymerici Boffati, pro VI diebus: XII s.

Item die XIIª Octobirs pro salario Guillelmi de Silvanes[190] missi apud Narbonam ad citandum heredes Bernardi Raditis, pro VI diebus: XVIII s.

Item die Jovis ante festum Omnium Sanctorum pro expensis Guillelmi Calhanelli apud Bitteris ad citandum plures homines traditis in restis per dominum B[ernardum] Raditoris, pro quinque diebus: X s.

Item pro salario Megrini Magulfi servientis regii de Neumausus deservito in pluribus citationibus faciendo XXIXª die Octobris: XII s.

Item pro salario Bernardi Picardi missi apud Avinionensem [civitatem?] contra magistrum Bertrandum de Sancto Genesio[191] super facto Lane Arquerii, pro XII diebus: XVIII s. t.

Item pro salario Martini Bofface missi contra P[etrum] Bundei per duos dies et pro uno instrument, in quo dictus P[etrus] est obligatus in XXXIII l. t.: XI s. t.

Item die IXª Novembris pro salario Roggerii Normanni missi apud Carcassonam ad senescallum dicti loci pro facto Petri Bundei et apud Nemausum pro negotiis dicti Templi, pro XV diebus, quibus stetit: XXX s.

Item die Mercurii post octavas Omnium Sanctorum pro salario Guiardi de Suessone servientis, pro XXXIIII diebus, quibus vacavit ad negotia dicti Templi: VI l. t.

Item pro transcripto littere compoti Petri Catelli sub sigillo Regis de Bitteris: III s. t.

Item pro copia processus facti contra dominum Guillelmum de Nemausus [*letters scratched out*] et inventariorum domorum Templi senescallie Nemausensis facta per Bernardum Petri clericum de Nemausus: XX s. t.

Item pro copia antiquorum compotorum Bernardi Raserii de Narbona curatoris bonorum Templi dyociesis Narbonensis, Bitterensis et Carcassone: X s. t.

Pro copia sui ultimi compoti: III s. t.

Item pro uno magno instrumento ~~magno~~ facto per Oliverium de Sancto Johanne Tholose notarium super hoc, quod dominus Bernardus post suam curam finitam receperat, de quibus [*sic for* quo] sui heredes tenentur reddere rationem: XVI s. t.

Item pro copia compoti Bernardi de Monte Olivo burgensis Narbone tenens locum Aymerici Boffati de Bitteris quondam curatoris bonorum dyocesis Bitterensis: V s. t.

Item pro copia litterarum solutionis fa Item pro vadiis LXXII dierum cte Aymerico Boffati predicto per firmarium de Limoso III s. t.

Item pro copia litterarum solutionum factarum per Bernardum Raditoris predicto magistro Guillelmo de Gysorcio et aliis curatores et receptores dicti Templi: XIIII s. t.

Item pro copia instrumentorum per Heliam Biretii notarium et aliis notarios de arrendaveritis et firmis Templi quondam dyocesis [*In the left margin:* XIIIª ligatura: instrumentum est cum aliis in inventario] Carcassone: VIII s. t.

Item pro quodam instrumento continento VIIIc L sestarios bladi: V s. t.

Item pro quodam rotulo, in quo debita senescallie Bellicadri reperta per magistrum Franciscum Martini sunt registrata: XV s. t.

Item pro alio rotulo, in quo debita senescallie Carcassone et Bitteris reperta per magistrum Bernardum Regis sunt inserta: VIII s. t.

Summa: XIX l. IIII s.

[*In the left margin:* A tergo] Item pro expensis et salario magistri Francisci Martini commisarii per dominum R[eginaldum] substituti in senescallia Bellicadri de factum circa habendam commissionem per partes a tergo declaratas et de quibus fit mentio superius in recepta dicte senescallie, in qua dominus R[eginaldus] honorat se de tota recepta dicti Franscisci [*sic for* Francisci]: XXVII l. XVII s. VIII d.

Item solvit Raymundo de Borda clerico, notario substituto per dictum commissarium in ducatu Aquitanie pro quinta parte sibi promissa ratione sue revelationis facte per eundem contra dominum Petrum de Bordis, qui solvit VIII^{xx} l. t. et contra Fortium Sancii de Porta, qui solvit XXII l. XII s. t., que summe continentur superius in recepta XLV l. XII s. VI d., ut apparet per litteras dicti Raymundi factas die Mercurii post festum Assumptionis Beate Marie anno M° CCC° XXIII°: XLV l. XII s. VI d. t.

Item Guillelmo de Vinealibus clerico, notario regio ratione sui salarii et laboris deserviti et impensi in spatio VI^{xx} dierum, quibus vacavit circa negotia dicti Templi tam cum dicto commissario quam sine ipso, non computatis suis expensis, quas eidem dictus commissarius ministravit V s. t. per diem pro toto: XXX l. t., ut apparet per litteras dicti Guillelmi datas XV^{a} die Ianuaris anno que supra.

[*Characters illegible due to paper damage*] [Item pro] magistro Johanne Martini notario in diversis partibus per dictum commissarium destinato pro suis vadiis XL dierum circa dicta negotia deserviti: XX l. t., [*characters illegible due to paper damage*] [ut apparat per] litteras datas XIX^{a} die Februarii anno proxime supradicto.

Summa istarum trium partium solutarum: IIII^{xx} XV l. XII s. VI d. t.
Summa expensarum in anno M° CCC° XXIII° factarum: VII^{xx} XVI l. X s. X d.
Summa totalis expensarum et solutionum predictarum: III^{c} XXIX l. XVI d. t.

Fol. 13

Pro vadiis dicti comissarii de II^{c} VIII diebus, quibus vacavit ad negotium dicte comissionis, scilicet [a] die XVIII^{a} Octobris anno M° CCC° XXII° usque ad diem XIIII^{am} Madii anno M° CCC° XXIII°, qua die venit Parisius pro sua comissione removanda et pro deffendendo iure regio contra comitem Petragoricensem et quosdam alios qui per eum fuerant condempnati et appellaverant in Parlamento, pro die qualibet XII s. VI d. t., valent pro toto VI^{xx} X l. t.

Item pro vadiis LXXII dierum, quibus remansit Parisius ex causa predicta, scilicet de die XIIII^{a} Madii predicta usque ad diem XXV^{am} Julii anno predicto, VII s. VI d. t. per diem, valent pro toto XXVII l. t.

Item pro suis vadiis II^{c} XL VIII dierum, quibus vacavit ad negotium dicte comissionis post eius revocationem, scilicet de dicta die XXV^{a} Julii usque ad diem ultimam Martii eodem anno, qua venit Parisius pro compotis presentibus reddendis, ~~per~~ XII s. VI d. t. per diem, valent pro toto VII^{xx} XV l. t.

Item pro vadiis VII^{xx} VIII dierum, quibus remansit Parisius pro dictis compotis faciendis et reddendis, scilicet a dicta die ultima Martii usque ad diem Lune post festum beati Bartholomei apostoli, que fuit XXVII^{a} die Augusti anno M° CCC° XXIIII°, VII s. VI d. t. per diem, valent pro toto LV l. X s. t.

Item pro ~~scriptura et~~ pergameno et scriptura compotorum presentium ter scriptorum: LV s. t.

Item pro detrimento unius equi baiardi, qui deconstabat XXXV l. t. et emptus fuerat apud Ruas a Petro Alamanni dicti loci, qui quidem equus fuit sic deterioratus propter laborem, quod non poterit vendi nisi XX l. t.: XV l. t.

Item pro detrimento cuiusdem equi morelli, quem emit ab Arnaldo de Sancto Polito scutifero in foro Tholose pretio XV l. t., et non fuit venditus in foro Parisius nisi C s. t. propter deteriorationem laboris: X l. t.

Totalis summa expensarum, vadiorum, pergameni, scripture computorum et detrimenti equorum, deductis quatuor l. t., quas lucratus est in quodam alio equo liardo vendito Parisius: VII^{c} XVIII l. XI s. IIII d. t.

Quibus deductis de summa totius recepte, que est II^{m} III^{c} IIII^{xx} XIX l. V d. restant penes eundem commissarium tam pro domino Rege quam pro domino comite Valesii M VI^{c} IIII^{xx} l. IX s. I d. t., de quibus cadunt pro nona parte dominum comitum Valesii, quam dictus commissarius dicit se solvisse magistro Bernardo Raymundi Calderie collectori dicte none partis de mandato Regis per litteras suas, quarum tenor est superius a tergo, de qua solutione dicte none partis debet facere fidem: IX^{xx}VI l. XIIII s. IIII d. t.

Et sic debet pro domino nostro Rege: XIIII^{c} IIII^{xx} XIII l. XIIII s. IX d. t.

Sequntur pecunia soluta in thesauro Parisius:

Primo pro unam cedulam ipsius thesauri scriptam Sabbato IIII^{a} die julii anno M° CCC° XXIII°: L l. t.

Item pro aliam cedulam ipsius thesauri scriptam Mercurii XXVII^{a} die Julii eodem anno: VI^{c} l. t.

Item pro aliam cedulam ipsius thesauri scriptam Jovis V^{a} die Aprilis anno M° CCC° XXIII° ante Pascha floridum: CXII l. parisiensis VIII d. parisiensis valent VII^{xx} l. X d. t.

Item pro aliam cedulam thesauri scriptam Martis [*words scratched out and crossed-out*] XXVIII die Augusti CCC^{o} XXIIII°: IIII^{xx} l. parisiensis valent C l. t.

~~Item thesaurus Tholose per litteram suam scriptam XXXIa die Januarii Mo CCCo XXIIIo C l. t.~~

[*In the left margin:* Summa dictarum solutionum in thesauro, quarum cedule hic (*word illegible*) IX^{c} IIII^{xx} X l. t. X d. de residuum XIIII^{c} IIII^{xx} et cetera, quas debet ut supra bene ostendit solutiones, que nondum sunt acceptarum qua usquam habeantur littere originales de mandato Regis [*words illegibles*] remanserunt penes senescallum Tholose, cui propter hoc scribitur ex parte gentium compotorum ut mittat dictas originales litteras] Item pro aliam cedulam thesauri scriptam ~~Summa per se~~ Martis XVIII^{a} die Septembris anno XXIIII°: C l. t.

Pro cambio II^{c} X florenorum auri ad mutonem quorum quilibet decostabat XV s. VI d. parisienses et eas reddidit in thesauro Parisius anno M^{o} CCC^{o} XXIII° ante festum beati Johannis Babtiste tam per manus domini Petri de Galardo quam Robillardi de Bononia[192] quemlibet pro XV s. parisiensibus: VII l. XI s. III d. t.

Item pro cambio VI^{xx} X turonensis argenti quorum quilibet decostabat XVI d. t. et eos tradidit ibidem, et illo tunc per dictas manus: X s. X d. t.

Item pro cambio VII^{xx} IIII florenorum aurorum ad mutonem quorum quilibet decostabat XVI s. parisienisum et eos tradidit in dicto thesauro anno M^{o} CCC^{o} XXIII° circa festum Pasche Domini quemlibet pro XV s. VI d. parisiensibus dumtaxat: IIII l. X s. t.

Summa: XII l. XII s. I d. t.

[*In the left margin:* Remisit dictus senescallus litteras predictas quas (*word illegible*) reddidit magister Reginaldus de Sancto ~~vacat quibus inferius est~~ Audoeno, prout patet in serie] Summa pecunie soluti thesauri et cambii monete: M II l. XII s. XI d. t.

~~Item pro resta, que dicto commissario debetur per finem sui compoti ultimi redditi domino Guillelmo Cligneti prima die Martii anno Mo CCCo XXIo de gestis per eum in senescallia Tholosana super facto Templi per commissionem dicti domini G[uillelmi] sibi factam CI l. XI s. VIII d. ob. pict. t.~~

Item solvit dictus commissarius domino Petro de Gallardo[193] militi balistarum magistro et aliis eius nomine de mandato senescalli Tholose per eius litteras scriptas die ultima Decembris anno M^{o} CCC^{o} XXIII° sibi facti. In deductione M VIII^{c} IIII^{xx} I l. VI s. VI d. t. restantum ad solvendum de III^{m} VII^{c} LXX l. XVI s. VI d. sibi debitis pro stipendiis per eum et gentes suas in fronteriis Flandrie deservitis, de quibus habuerat per dominum Guillelmum Cligneti M II^{c} IIII^{xx} IX l. X s. t. Et tamen idem magister pro dicto domino G[uillelmo] totam summam reddi fecerat in thesauro ac si eam integre recepisset per compotum thesauri de termino Nativitatis Domini anno XVIII° sicut patet per litteras regias, quas ~~dictus senescallus retinuit~~ retinuimus et sunt cum aliis litteris istius compoti scriptas XXVI^{a} die Julii anno M° CCC° XXIII°. Et per litteras recognitionis dicti domini P[etri] factis die Jovis post Nativitatis Domini anno proxime dicto quas retinuimus et sunt cum litteris istius compoti: VI^{c} XIIII l. t.

Item Arnaudo de Roquapina[194] procuratore dicti domini P[etri] per suas litteras factas Mercurii post Epiphanie anno proxime dicto, quas retinuimus et sunt ut supra cum procuratione, quod habebat dictus Arnaldus a dicto domino P[etro] pro dicta summa recipienda: LX s. t.

Item Johanni de Stratis scutifero dicti domini P[etri] per suas litteras factas Sabbato post Sanctum Hilarium anno proxime dicto, quas retinuimus ut supra cum litteris clausis dicti domini P[etri] de mandato: XII l. t.

Summa: VI^{c} XXIX l. t. ab alia.
Item pro resta dicto commissario debita pro finem sui compoti ultimi redditi domino G[uillelmo] Cligneti anno XXI°: CI l. XI s. VIII d. ob. pict. t.

Fol. 14

[*In the left margin*: Audita XXIII^{a} Augusti anno XXIIII] Summa totalis solutionum factarum in thesauro et domino P[etro] de Gallardo nec non cambii monete et reste dicto commissario superius debite: mille septuagente triginta tres l. quatuor s. septem d. ob. pict. t.

Line of text under the stitching.

Fol. 15

[*In the left margin*: Expense] Totalis summa est: II^{m} IIII^{c} LI l. XVI s. ~~R. ei debuit LII l. XV s. VII d.,~~ debentur eidem R[eginaldo]: II^{c} XXXIX l. IX s. VI d.

~~Sequitur recepta facta~~ Compotus factus per magistrum Reginaldum de Sancto Audoeno de debitis Templi ~~ultra hec de quibus in suo primo compoto reddidit rationem~~ Lingue Occitane per ipsum receptis virtute commissionis regie sibi facte ab anno XXIIII° X^{a} die Septembris ~~tam super facto Templi Lingue Occitane quam Judeorum, que commisio~~ usque ad diem XXII^{am} Julii anno XXV°, cuius tenor a tergo, continentur ~~in dorso sui compoti redditi de bonis Judeorum receptis per eum et levatis.~~

[*In the left margin:* Alibi est] ~~Primo debet prefatus commissarius pro resta sui compoti redditi de bonis Judeorum senescallie Tholosane per ipsum receptis a die~~

~~X^a Septembris anno XXIIII° usque ad diem XXII^am Julii anno XXV°: XXVIII l. XVIII s. XI d. t.~~

Recepit prefatus commissarius ~~ab ann~~ die XXIII^a Augusti anno XXIII°, quando reddidit compotum suum primum, usque ad diem, quando presens compotus fuit auditus:

~~Item pro~~ Petro Bundei de Insula Jordani firmario ~~de Lar~~ grangie de Larmonte[195] quondam Templi per manus Vitalis Baterii debitoris

Fol. 16

[*Text under the stitching*] usque ad diem XV^am Augisti XXV II [*text under the stitching*] dicti Petri in deductione IX^xx II l. t., quas debuit per compotum Davinum de Roaxio curatoris Templi, ~~ratione dicte firme, de qua fit mentio in~~ de quibus redduntur LXXI s. IIII d. in principio compoti precedenti dicti Reginaldi, in quatuor partibus: X sol. III d. t.

Ab heredibus Remundi Delga de Insula Albigesii pro legato per ipusm facto domui Templi de Vaour:[196] XLVIII s. VII d. ob. t.

Ab heredibus magistri Raymundi Arnaldi de Columbino pro legato facto preceptori Ville Dei: IX l. t.

A Guillelmo filio et herede de Amici de Cantamerla de Ventillaco pro compositione quorumdam linthaminum et vestium lineorum, que dicebatur habuisse de domo Templi Ville Dei: X l. t.

A magistro Michaele de Rotundo pro resta VI^xx l. t., quas debuerat ratione emptionis cuiusdam terre, que fuerat heredum Gaillardi de Nogareto,[197] de quibus solverat magistro Johanni de Crispeyo commisario domini G[uillelmi] Cligneti XXXIIII l. VIII s. t. et in compoto precedenti redduntur LXI l. I s. X d. t., hic pro residuis XXIIII l. X s. II d.

Ab heredibus Davini de Roaxio et Raymundi de Campis Aquis in deductione septies viginti l. t. debilis monete currentis tempore Burgensis valent CXII l. t. fortis, de quibus idem Raymundus servat honoratus in compotis dicti Davini, sicut in compoto precedenti declarator, in quo redduntur triginta duo l. quatuor s. VII d. t. inter partes recepte anni Millessimi CCC^i XXIII^i facte in senescallia Tholosana per manus diversorum hominum et in diversis partibus XL l. t., residuum debetur videlicet domino comiti Valesii pro sua nona parte totius dicte summe XII l. VIII s. X d. ob. t. et domino nostro Regi pro toto, residuo XXVII l. VII s. ob. t.

Item a Petro Dantoere firmario domus Sancti Medardi[198] in Lemovicino de anno XI° pro resta sue firme de decem l., quas debebat VI l. X s. t., residuum fuit sibi remissum propter sua paupertatam [*sic for* suam paupertatem].

Item ab uxore et executore defuncti Raymundi Athonis de Ruallibus in deductione centum duodecim l. t. Burgensis valent ad bonas turonenses IIII^xx IX l. XII s. t., [*In the left margin:* debitum] de quibus idem R[aymundus] fuit in dicti D[avini] compoto Honoratus, sicut in prefati Reginaldi compoto precedenti et in capitulo proxime dicto continentur, in quo redduntur de hec XXX l. t. tam pro domino Rege quam pro domino comite Valesii. Et hic pro domino Rege solo LII l. VII d. t., residuum restat pro domino comite supradicto.

Item ab Ymberto Lobeti de Dampno Petro[199] in Lemovicino in deductione C l. t. debilis, quas Yterius Prepositi socius suus debuerat fratri Petro Maliani[200] Templario ex causa mutui cum quibusdam aliis codebitoris suis, qui debent residuum per litteras camere restitutionis, quas Guidonis Pignete reddiderat: IIII l. t.

[*In the left margin:* (*word illegible*) contra heredes Raymundi de Podio de Caturco] Item a Bernardo Mercerii et eius sociis de Calciata in deductione IIII^{xx} XV l. catalanensium, quas debuerunt preceptori Montis Ricosi C s. catalaneneses valent XLVI s. VIII d. t., residuum habuit R[aymundus] de Podio quondam de Caturco, receptor pro domino Geraldo de Sabanaco curatore Templi quondam.

Item a Guiraudo Sarreti de Nigra Pellitia pro dicto preceptore L s. t., unum cifum argenti pretio XLI s. t. et IX s. t. in moneta curribili L s. t.

Item de Aymerico de Mueg custode domus de Ausone[201] propre Pictavis in deductione XIIII l., quas debebat per finem sui compoti redditi Ade de Berrone commissario domini G[uillelmi] [*In the left margin:* (*word illegible*) contra dominum Amelium de Sella] Cligneti, unum roncinum venditum apud Lemovicum ad mercatum: LX s. t.

Item a domino Amelio de Sella firmario de Foresta[202] et de Roca[203] in deductione plurimum restarum, quas debet per compotum curatoris, unum coopertorium vetus venditum apud Lemovicum ad mercatum: XXVIII s. t.

Item a Petro Bundei de Spondeillano, firmario domus Templi de Abeliano de XL l. t., quas debebat pro resta dicte firme, de qua fit mentio in compoto precedenti, in capitulo de recepta senescallie Carcassone et Bitteris, ubi redduntur ~~residuum~~ soli XI l. IIII s. XI d. pro toto, residuum XXVIII l. XV s. I d. t.

Item a Stephano de Molinis de Sancto Leonardo[204] firmario domorum quondam Templi de Mortua Sama et de Carreriis pro resta dicte firme: XL l. t. de annis M° CCC° IX° et X°. De residuo reddunt rationem Aymericus de Ponte de Petragoris et G[uillelmus] Almanni de Pictavis, exceptis quibusdam superantibus factis per dictum firmarium in reperatione et sustentatione domorum predictorum.

Item de Aymerico de Ponte de Petragoris olim receptore dicti Templi pro viginti una l. tribus s. et quatuor d. monete Burgensis, quos habuerat a magistro Petro Daniele firmario domus Templi de Pogia[205] et eos omiserat in suis compotis per oblivionem ut dicebatur allocare: XVI l. XVIII s. VIII d. t.

Item a Guillelmo Alamanni de Pictavis et ab heredibus Johannis de Genis[206] dicti loci receptoris olim Templi pro XXX^{ta} l. et X s. monete Burgensis, [*In the left margin: words illegible*] quos habuerant a Guillelmo Baysadona de Subterranea[207] firmario de Fonte Laventour et de Buxeria Raspit et eos in suis compotis pro oblivionem ut dicebatur omiserant allocare in deductione

Fol. 17

II^{xx} l. t., quas dictus Guillelmus debebat pro resta dicte firme: XXIIII l. VIII s. t.

Item ab heredibus et bonorum detentoribus dicti Guillelmi per manus magistri Geraldi Morelli substitute a dicto commissario in senescallia Lemovicensi ex causa proximo dicta: LX l. t., de superfluo nichil potuit levare propter sui paupertatem.

Item a domino Gaillardo de Causenthis et Bertrando eius fratre, custode quondam domus Templi de Gimbreda in Leomania pro bonis mobilibus dicte domus, que dicebatur habuisse: C l. t.

Item a Guillelmo Bonelli et Petro Cabernerii custodibus et firmariis domorum Templi quondam de Rellaco et de Manso Dei pro resta dicte firme et custodia bonorum ipsarum domorum de annis M° CCC° VII° et VIII° per compotorum curatorum senescallie Petragoricensis et Lemovicensis, qui reddunt de residuo rationem per manus Geraldi Morelli clerici substituti a dicto R[eginaldo] in dictis senescallias: XVIII l. t.

Item ab Hugone Guilebaudi firmario de Pogia quondam Templi pro resta dicte firme de annus M° CCC° [*In the left margin*: (*characters illegible due to paper damage*) VI s. ~~XI d.~~ ob.] VIII° et IX° per manus dicti Geraldi: XVIII l. t.

Item a Fulcone de Chasteluz[208] ex eadem causa per manus isti Geraldi: VI^{xx} l. t.

Summa ~~tam recepta reste quam~~ recepte: V^{c}IIII^{xx}V l. VI s. ob.

Fol. 18

Sequntur expense per dictum commissarium facte ratione sue commissionis memorate:

Primo pro redimendis decem octo litteris continentibus plures summas pecunie, quas nonnulli commissarii per curatores Templi quodam deputatis receperunt in Lingua Occitana de debitis dicti Templi, de quibus nullam rationem dicuntur reddidisse: XVIII s. t.

Pro copiis inventariorum factorum per gentes regias de bonis mobilibus repertis in domibus quodam Templi de Monte Salnerio, de Boldraco, de Lana Arquerii, de Serinolio, de Avello, de Cambono: XVII s. t.

Pro inventario et copia factorum per magistrum Michaelem de Rotondo et Petrum Chalonis notarios Ville Dei contra Raymundum de Campis Aquis super summa VII^{xx} l. t. ~~de quibus~~ quas debebat, de quibus ratio redditur in recepta superius et pro salario dictorum notariorum de tribus diebus, quibus vacaverunt circa: ~~litteram~~ XLVI s. t.

Pro redimendis sex instrumentis continentibus quedam debita dicti Templi, que debenture, inter que est unum instrumentum continens IIII^{xx} XVI l. t., quas Petrus de Cabanesio[209] debet, restitutum per Guidonem Pigneta de Lemovico, que quidam instrumenta fuerunt dicto commissario restituta per quosdam homines religiosos ~~in secr~~ et aliis in secreto: XXIIII s. t.

Pro duabus litteris obligatoriis continentibus XLV l. t., quas magister Aubertus de Tyfaugiis[210] debuit dicto Templo et pro una lettra continente X l., quas Aloudetus Suriz subvicarius Tholose recepit a Petro Marssolli de Bononia, qui eas debebat domino nostro Regi ratione dicti Templi: IIII s. t.

Pro copia quarumdam litterarum ~~litterarum~~ in iuditio Carcassone dicto commissario productarum per dominum Petrum de Bordis militem, dominum de Lonaco[211] prope Tholosam ad sui deffensionem super hoc, que dictus commissarius petebat a dicto milite fructus ~~pro de~~ et redditus plurimarum domorum Templi senescallie Agenensis, quos dictus ~~d~~ miles habuit et collegit per quinque annos in preiuditium Regis pretextu cuiusdam donationis, sicut dictus miles assuerit dudum facte domino Bertrando de Bordis quondam cardinali fratri suo per fratrem Bernardum de Ruppe tunc preceptorem Provincie existentem in carcere episcopi Vasatensis[212] post generalem captionem Templariorum, qui redditus valent communiter annuatim IIII^{c} l. t., de quibus dictus commissarius reddit in suo compoto precedenti VIII^{xx} l. t., quas habuit a dicto milite per compotum inter eas factam super fructibus unius de domibus antedictis vocate de Rollaco, quam ~~tenuerat~~ dictus miles tenuerat per annum et medium sive pluri et alias adhuc tenet indebite, quia dicte littere fuerunt scripte fraudulenter sub data temporis ~~predicte~~ prestiti ante captionem predictam et tunc fuerunt sigillate in carcere memorato et preterea dictus ~~dictus~~ Templarius non habebat conferendi potestatem et nichilhominus hoc fecit per violentiam compulsus, ut apparet per informationem inde factam per dominum commissarium et in suo compoto precedenti restitutam: XX s. t.

Pro copia cuiusdam processus facti coram senescallo Tholose contra Philippum Clavelli et Johanem Trepati, qui debent XII sestarios frumenti et pro decem instrumentis recuperatis per dictum commissarium in secreto a diversis personis, quibus fuerant in deposito tradita per dictum Philippum de debitis ipsius, que sibi debebantur et debenture: XXVII s. t.

Pro tribus instrumentis preconisationum factarum apud Vaurum[213] de bonis Raymundi Fabri notarii, qui est obligatus Regi ratione Templi una cum Petro Bundei in summa IX^{xx} l. t., de quibus fit mentio superius in recepta: VI s., et pro salario Petri Bingesii servientis, qui diversas preconisationes fecit per tres dies: XV s. t.

Pro quinque magnis instrumentis factis per Geraldum Morellum notarium regium super pluribus executionibus inchoactis contra Guidonem de Alvernia de Inucheria in Lemovicino filium et heredem Petri de Alvernia quondam firmarium domus Templi de Pullaco pretextu VIII^{c} XLII l. t., de quibus fuit honoratus in compotis Guillelmi Almanni de ~~Provins~~ Pictavis, Aymerici de Ponte de Petragoris et Guidonis Bozonis, et Guidonis Pigneta de Lemovico curatorum dicti Templi ratione dicte firme, a quibus executionibus appllavit et ob hoc est adiournatus per dictum commissarium ad primam diem Octobri anno XXV° in camera compotorum: XXVIII s. t., et pro salario dicti Geraldi notarii, qui vaccavit per spatium quinque dierum: XXV s. t.

Pro sex aliis instrumentis et litteris in droso rotuli declaratis: VI s. t.

Pro quadam informatione facta per magistrum Raymundum de Borda et Guillelmum de Vinealibus notarios Tholose regios per dictum commissarium deputatos contra dominum Bernardum de Durfora[214] militem, dominum de Flamerenthis in Leomania super depopulatione et abstrusione nemoris domus Templi de Gimbreda, de quo dictus miles habuit usquam ad valorem II^{c} l. t. ~~et~~ V s. t., et pro expensis dictorum notariuorum, qui vacaverunt ad hoc per quinque dies tam eundo quam ibi stando et Tholosam revertendo: L s. t.

Pro copia plurimum litterarum facta sub sigillo regio Lemovicensi de pluribus summis, quas Guido Bozonis de Lemovico receptor olim Templi habuit et recepit de debitis dicti Templi et expendit, de quibus non reddidit rationem, ymmo dictas litteras retinet in preiuditium domini nostri Regis et ob hoc est adiournatus prout Guido de Alvernia supradictus: XX s. t.

Pro copia duarum litterarum in tergo presentis rotuli declaratarum: VI s. t.

Pro copia cuisdam processus facti contra Durandum Payrola de Insula Albegesii curatorem olim Templi super pluribus restis per eum traditis ad levandum, que sibi solute fuerunt, sicut asserunt et probare se offerunt homines per eum honorati: XV s. t., et pro salario ~~per~~ Perroti Bosseleti missi apud Agenium ad citandum Durandum, qui erat ibi receptor regius, ad domino Johanne de Blayvilla, qui non permisit ipsum Durandum Tholose coram dicto commissario super hoc comparere per quatuor diebus: XII s. t.

Pro copia plurimum arrendamentorum de domibus Templi quondam factorum per Arnaldum Berrani tunc curatorem dicti Templi in Provincia et alibi: XVIII s. t.

Pro copia cuiusdam processus facti per magistrum Johannem Martini et Remundum de Meranis[215] notarios contra comitem Armaniaci,[216] qui habuit de bonis mobilibus et redditibus domus Templi de Aqua Tincta prope Auxium per sui potentiam post captionem Templariorum usque ad valorem IIII^c l. t. et amplius, et pro salario dictorum notariorum, qui vacaverunt ad hoc per sex dies: LIIII s. t.

Pro copia cujusdam informationis facte per dictos Johannem et Reymundum contra archiepiscopum Auxitanum quondam super eo, quod habuit et recepit per quatuor annos redditus domus Templi Aque Tincte supradicte ~~qui~~ post captionem Templariorum, qui valent annuatim quinquaguinta cartones frumenti, et quilibet carto valent IIII^or sestaria parisiensis, de quibus redduntur Regi ~~tam~~ IIII^c XXX l. t., ~~tam~~ per Guillelmum de Ruella commissarium domini G[uillelmi] Cligneti C l. t. et per dominum Reginaldum III^c XXX l., in quibusdam compotum dicto domino G[uillelmo] redditum per eosdam, et pro salario dictorum notariorum, qui vacaverunt ad hoc per sex dies: LXXIIII s. t.

Pro quadam inquesta facta s per magistrum Petrum et Guillelmum de Brolio notarios contra Guillelmum Fabri de Villa Francesia in Caturcino super pluribus debitis, que ascendunt ducentas l. t. petitas pro preceptore domus Templi Ville Dei et pro salario dictorum notariorum, qui vaccaverunt per quinque dies: LXVI s. t.

Pro copia inventarii facti per gentes regias de bonis domus Templi de Monte Frino[217] in Provincia tempore captionis Templariorum: X s. t.

Pro copia inventariorum, ut permittitur facti, de bonis domus Templi de Argentia[218] in Provincia: VIII s. t.

Pro copia inventarii facti de bonis domus Templi de Campo Publico[219] in Provincia et pro copia compoti custodis dicte domus: XXIIII s. t.

Pro copia compoti redditi gentibus regiis per custodes domus Templi de Monte Frino in anno M^o CCC^o VIII°: XXX s. t.

Pro salario et expensis magistri Johannis Martini notarii factis in ~~lex~~ exhigendo et levando XXII l. V s. VI d. t. de debitis Templi iudicature Rinaris per ipsum revelatis, que redduntur in compoto precedenti in particulam, qui incipit: Recepta facta per magistrum Johannem Martini, et pro quinta parte sibi promissa per dictum commissarium per litteras dicti magistri Johannis: LXIIII s. V d. ob. t.

Pro quinta parte CXI s. VIII d. t., que redduntur in dicto compoto, in particulam subsequenti, quas magister Arnaldus Regis et Bernardus de Barta Martino revelarunt et levarunt, que quinta pars fuit eis promissa per dictum commissarium per litteras ipsorum: XXII s. V d. t.

Pro salario, vadiis et expensis magistri Geraldi Morelli notarii et Guillelmi Pictavini servientis deservitis in spatio quadraginta dierum, quibus fuerunt per diversa temporum intervalla in exhigendo et levando VI^{xx} l. t. a Fulcone de Chatelluz et LX l. ab hominibus de Subterranea, et XVIII l. t. ab Hugone Guilebaudi, que redduntur superius in recepta: XX l. t. pro litteras dicti notarii.

Pro tribus libris papiri ad scribendum processus et debita dicti Templi et pro pluribus aliis scripturis camere compotorum restitutorum: XX s. t.

[*In the left margin:* LVI l. XIIII s. X d. ob. t.] Summa: LVI l. XIIII s. X d. ob. t.

Item pro salariis et expensis plurimum servientum et aliorum in dorso rotuli nominatorum, qui per dictum commissarium missi fuerunt ad faciendum citationes et ad alia negotia commissionis expedienda contra diversos homines et per diversas partes ex causis, qui et que a tergo continentur: XXII l. XIIII s. VIII d. t.

Somma [*sic for* summa] totalis expensarum predictarum: LXXIX l. IX s. VI d. ob.

Item pro vadiis dicti commissarii deservitis tam circa dicta debita Templi quam circa debita Judeorum, de quibus reddidit compotum, perquirenda et levanda, circa que fuit a XX^{a} die Septembri anno XXIIII°, qua recessit de Parisius ad tres equos, usque ad diem XXII^{am} Julii anno XXV°, qua venit Parisius ultima vice pro reddenda ratione de predictis, in cuius temporis spatio sunt III^{c} VI dies, decem s. p. per diem, pro toto: VII^{xx} XIII l. p. valent IX^{xx} XI l. V s. t.

Item pro vadiis suis de quinquaginta ~~sex~~ septem diebus, quibus fuit Parisius ad unum equum solum ratione predicta, sex s. p. per diem, pro toto: XXI l. VIII s. VI d. t.

Item pro pergameno et scriptura compotorum redditorum per prefatum commissarium de bonis Judeorum et debitis supradictis: XL s. t.

Item pro detrimento unius modici palefredi minelli empti apud Yssodunum[220] a Guillelmo Hostelerii pretio XIII l. t., vendito Tholose in foro dicti loci VII l. X s. t., pro hec: VII l. X s. t.

Pro detrimento cuiusdam alterius palefredi bayardi empti in nundinis Moysiaci[221] a Johanne de Petragoris pretio XX l. t., venditi Tholose pretio XIIII l. t., pro hec: VI l. t.

Summa: II^{c} XXVIII l. II s. VI d.

Totalis summa expensarum, vadiorum et equorum detrimento: III^{c} VII l. XII s. ob. t.

Restat de receptis supra eum: II^{c} LXXVII l. XIIII s. t.

Fol. 19

Sequitur pecunia soluta in thesauro regio Parisius per cedulas redditas in camera, que sequntur:

Primo pro denariis solutis in thesauro per manus heredum Roberti de Cultura cum eiusdem thesauri cedula scripta Martis XI^{a} die Junii CCC XXV°: XXXV l. t.

Item in dicto thesauro cum cedula scripta Veneris XIIII^{a} die Junii anno domini M^{o} CCC XXV°: LX l. t.

[*In the left margin:* Redditur in thesauro] Item per Matheum Scoti clericum: XXV l. t.

[*In the left margin:* Redditur in thesauro] Item per heredes prefati Roberti de Cultura: C l. t.

Item in dicto thesauro cum cedula thesauri scripta Martis X^{a} die Septembris anno XXV°: XXXII l. p. valent XL l. t.

Item in dicto thesauro cum cedula thesauri scripta Martis X^{a} die Septembris anno XXV°: L l. p. valent LXII l. X s. t.

Item pro decasu XI^{c} XX^{ti} obolorum argenti traditorum dictis heredibus quandolibet pro sex d. p.: XLVI s. VIII d. t., et quibus decostabat VIII d. t.

Item pro decasu LXVIII florenorum de Florentia, ~~traditorum in thesauro~~ quorum quilibet decostitit XVIII s. t., traditorum in thesauro pro XVII s. VI d. t.: XXXIV s. t.

Item pro decasu XXIIII florenorum ad mutonem traditorum dicto Matheo, quemlibet pro XVI s. VIII d. p., et quilibet decostiterat XXI s. t.: IIII s. t.

Item pro decasu XXXVIII florenorum ad mutonem traditorum dicto thesauro sub dicto pretio: VI s. IIII d. t.

Item pro decasu LX florenorum ad mutonem traditorum dicto thesauro prout supra: X s. t.

Summa: II^{c} II l. XI s. t.
Item debentur ei per thesaurum VI^{xx} VI l. t.
Summa solutionum ~~et~~ cum decasu monete: III^{c} XXVII l. XI s. t.
Item summa expensarum, vadiorum cum detrimento equorum fuit, ut superius apparet: III^{c} VII l. XII s. ob. t.
Summa totalis solutinum, expensorum, vadiorum cum decasu monete et equorum detrimento: VI^{c} XXXV l. III s. ob. t.

Et sic facta deductione de summa recepte, que fuit V^{c} IIII^{xx} V l. VI s. ob., ad dictas solutionis et expensis, restant que debentur ei per presentem compotum XLIX l. ~~XVII s.~~ XVII s. t.

Et per compotum precedentem: II^{c} XXXIX l. IX s. VI d. t.

Et per compotum primo redditum per eum domino G[uillelmo] Cligneti: LII l. X s. II d. t.

Et per alium compotum redditum per eum dicto domino G[uillelmo]: CI l. XI s. VIII d. ob. pict. t.

[*In the left margin*: Redditus XVII^{a} die Septembris anno XXV° ad cameram compotorum]

Summa totius debiti, quod debetur eidem R[eginaldo]: IIII^{c} LXII l. VIII s. IIII d. ob. pict. t.

Et ipse debet per compotos redditos per eum de facto Judeorum LXXII l. VII s. II d. ob. ex una parte et XXVIII l. XVIII s. XI d. t. ex alia parte, quibus deductis de debito supradicto, restant que debentur eidem R[eginaldo] III^{c} LVIII l. VI s. V d. ob. pict. t.

Fol. 1v

The card is only partially preserved and severely damaged. On most of the page the text is illegible or only partially legible.

Item pro denariis solutis Bernardo de Feneris ex causa predicta declarata per sua litteras datas die IIII^{a} Decembris anno XXII°: XXX l. t. [*characters illegible due to paper damage*]

Item pro denariis solutis, ut dicitur, Bernardo de Estena et Bartholomeo Egidia ex causa predita: L l. t., de quibus L. l. heredes memorati facere debent fidem vel eis reddere.

Item Johanni Bozonis [*characters illegible due to paper damage*] domus Templi de Gimbreda pro suis vadiis et incheriis per eum factis in redditibus dicte domus: XVII l. X s. t., cum litteris curie [*word illegible due to paper damage*] Tholose die XVI^{a} Septembris anno M^{o} CCC^{o} XIII°.

Item pro denariis solutis Bertrando de Calveto sibi debitis pro incheriis dicte domus per litteras dicte curie datas die ultima Novembris: XXII l. X s. anno M^{o} CCC^{o} [*characters illegible due to paper damage*].

Item pro denariis solutis magistro Bernardo Amerii notario Fossereti[222] sibi debitis ratione suorum vadiorum deservitorum in faciendo quandam informationem super [*characters illegible due to paper damage*] de Gimbreda, cum instrumento facto XII^{a} die Novembris anno M^{o} CCC^{o} XXII°: C s. t.

Item pro denariis solutis Aloudeto Soriz subvicaris Tholose debitis pro suis vadiis deservitis in custodia dicti nemoris, cum instrumento facto XXVI die Aprilis anno Domini M^{o} CCC^{o} XXIII°: C l. t.

Item pro denariis solutis Guillelmo de Salerna et Petro Maioris collectoribus debitorum quondam pro Guillelmum de Berrellis ratione firme Ville Dei anno IX°, cum libris eorumdem datis die XIII Novembris anno M^{o} CCC^{o} X^{o}: XIX l. t.

Item pro denariis restitutis per dictum D[avinum] fratribus Guillelmo Robaldi preceptore Ville Dei, Bernardo de Sancto Mauricio[223] preceptore Castri Sarraceni et Petro de Carlutio preceptore Tholose Hospitalariis de bonis Templi, quando fuerunt adepti possessionem dicti Templi, cum litteris ipsorum datis XXIIII^{a} die Januarii anno M° CCC° XIII°: C l. t.

Item pro expensis per dictos Davinum et eius heredes factis in executione cuiusdam summe IIII^{c} XV l. t., per heredes Arnaldi Bernardi de Manso debitorum ratione cuiusdam compromissi facti inter ipsos et [*word illegible*] per magistrum G[uillelmum] de Gisortio quondam pro quibusdam pecunie summis, de quibus dictus Arnaldus Bernardi et eius [*paper damage*] fuerant in ipsius D[avini] compoti honorati, que summa IIII^{c} XV l. reddita tam in manus domini G[uillelmi] Cligneti quam domini P[etri] de Gallardo [*word illegible*] in compoto magistri Reginaldi ultimo reddito eidem domino G[uillelmo] [*words scratched out*]: IIII^{xx} VII l. XVIII s. III d. t., [*paper damage*] de quibus exponendo fit mentio in ultimis compotis heredum dicti Davini redditis R[enerio] Burdonis [curatori] de bonis Templi senescallie [*paper damage*]. Et sic ascendunt dicte partes ipsis heredibus defalcate: IX^{c} XIIII l. X s. VIII d. t. monete predicte Burgensis, et resta dictarum [*paper damage*] fuit et est: IIII^{c} XXXV l. IX s. IIII d. t. currentes tempore Burgensis valent ad bonas turonenses III^{c} XL VIII l. VII s. V d. ob. t. [*paper damage*] Magister B[ernardus] R[aymundi] Calderie habuit per manus dictorum heredum IX^{am} partem, que ascendit XXXVIII l. XIIII s. II d. bonorum. Et sic [*paper damage*] pro domino nostro Rege: III^{c} IX l. XIII s. [*characters illegible*] d. ob. t., de quibus redduntur in albo: II^{c} XXXIX l. XIII s. IIII d. t. et [*paper damage*] quod ascendebat LXX l. t. fuit dictis heredibus in suis compotis allocatum pro mutuo facto Arnaldo de Proboleno ol[im] [*paper damage*] nomine Regio pro guerra Flandrie sicut in ipsius A[rnaldi] compotis continentur.

Unde super hoc est notandum quod magister Raymundus de Borda debebat habere quintam partem dictarum III^{c} XLVIII l. VII s. V d. t., quia sibi fuit promiss[um] per dominum commissarium pro eo, quia dictum debitum revelavit et instruxit, docuit et monstravit, qualiter debebatur et potatur recuperari, quia heredes dicti D[avini] premissa denegabant et se dicebant ignorare propter mortem patris sui. Quare quidam quinta pars ascendit LXIX l. XIII s. V d. et de residuo, quod ascendit II^{c} LXXVIII l. XIIII s., prefatus magister R[aymundus] debebat habere nomine dicti domini comitis nonam partem, que est dumtaxat XXX l. XIX s. V d., et sic apparet quod ipse habuit plus debito VII l. XIIII s. X d. t.

Item de XXII l. X s. t. superius in albo redditur per dictum Fortium, quas dictus R[aymundus] de Borda revelavit, debet habere dictus R[aymundus] quintam partem ex causa predicta, que ascendit IIII l. X s., et dictus magister B[ernardus] de residuo nonam partem debuit habere, que est XL s., et habuit L s., et sic plus habuit X s. t., quam debebat.

Item de XL l. t. monete Burg~~degal~~ensis redditur inferius in albo per heredes D[avini] de Roaxio pro nemore de Gimbreda et de XXXIX l. XVIII s. eiusdem monete pro resta dicte firme, que ascendunt ad bonos t. LXIII l. XVIII s. IIII d. ob.

t. debebat habere dictus R[aymundus] de Borda, qui premissa revelavit et monstravit pro sua quinta parte XII l. XV s. VIII d. t., et de

[*In the left margin:* Usque hic (*word illegible*) primi rotuli]

Fol. 2v

residuo dictus magister B[ernardus] debebat habere IX^am partem, que est CXIII s. VII d. ob. t. sine pluri et ipse habuit VII l. II s. ob. t., et sic habuit plus quam debuit XXVIII s. V d. t.

Item de IX^xx l. t. solutis per dominum Petrum de Bordis, de quibus idem R[aymundus] de Borda debet habere quintam pertem ex causa predicta, que est XXXVI l., et dictus magister B[ernardus nonam] partem residui, que est XVI l. sine pluri, et habuit XX l., et sic plus habuit, quam debit IIII l. t.

Item de C l. t. per Bertrandum de Causenthis inferius in albo solutis, de quibus idem R[aymundus] de Borda debet habere XX l. pro sua quinta parte ex causa predicta et de IIII^XX l. restans dictus magister B[ernardus] debebat habere: VIII l. XVII s. IX d. pict. t., et ipse habuit XI l. II s. II d. ob. t., et sic habuit plus debito XLIIII s. V d. pict. t.

Item de debito comitis Petragoricensis inferius in albo reddito per fratrem Petrum de Carlutio revelato habuit dictus magister B[ernardus] plus debito XXII s. XI d. t. sicut apper[et] per suas litteras inferius registratas.

Item de C l. t. solutis ibidem per Stephanum de Ruppe, quas revelavit dictus frater, de quibus [debebat] habere XX l. t. pro sua quinta parte et dictus magister B[ernardus] pro sua IX^a parte [*paper damage*], XVII s. IX d. pict. t. sine pluri habuit idem magister B[ernardus] XI l. II s. II d. ob. t., et sic plus debito XXII s. XI d. t.

Summa de pluri receptis per dictum magistrum B[ernardum] quam debito: XVIII l. III s. VI d.

Que summa debet defalcare de partibus infrascriptis et in albo positis, de quibus nichil habuit, que ascendunt IIII^c XXXV l. XI s. t., de quibus etiam [*words illegible*]: XLVIII l. VII s. X d. ob., et sic restant XXX l. IIII s. IIII d. ob. de dicta IX^a parte, que dicto domino comiti deberentur, si ad nonam partem expensis per dictum commissarium factarum et in albo positarum non tenentur. Que quidam expensis ascendunt pro anno M^o CCC^o XXII° VII^xx IIII l. XII s.VIII d. et pro anno M^o CCC^o XXIII°: LXVIII l. XVI s. IIII d. t., et pro vadiis comissariorum: VIII^xx XV l. t. Et sic est totalis summa expensis et vadiorum: III^c LXXVIII l. IX s. t., de quibus IX^a pars est XLII l. I s., et in casu predicto deberet dictus dominus comes XI l. XVI s. VII d. ob.

Partes IIII^{c} XXXV l. XI s., de quibus nona pars domino comiti [*word illigible*] et nichil habuit de hiisdam [*sic for* hiis] ex causis superius expressatis, que partes recepte fuerunt in hunc modum:

Primo in senescallia Caturcensi et Petragoricensi:

A Stephano de Felenor: XXIII l. IIII s.
Ab Eblone de Sancto Ruperio deducta quinta parte fratris Petri: LXIIII s.
A Jacobo Magistri: XL s.
Ab Arnaldo de Campenaco: VI l.
Ab Helia de Solo: XII l.
A Bernardo de Arnaldo: LVI s.
A domino Petro de Castilione: VIII l.

Summa: LVIII l. IIII s.

Item in Lemovicino fuerunt recepte per partes in albo positas, ut apparet per easdem: II^{c} IIII^{xx} XV l. XII s.

Item in senescallia Leomanie et Agenensis a commissaris ibi deputatis: L l. t., de aliis vero ibi solitis et receptis habuit dictus dominus comes partem suam.

Item a magistro Johanne Martini: XXII l. V s. VI d.

Item de debitis Montis Ricosii: VI l. II d., et a magistro Arnaldo Regis: IIII l. IX s. IIII d.

Item de LI l. V s. VI d. receptis in senescallie Carcassone et Bitteris nichil debet habere, quia iam habuit partem suam vel adhuc debetur per illos qui solverunt.

Item de XVI l. receptis in senescallia Bellicadri nichil habuit nec habere debet, quia commissarius plus expendit ibi quam ascendit pro aliis debitis, que reperit perquirendis, que debeatur, de quibus patitur adhuc habere partem suam, et si forte debetur habere IX^{a} partem de eiusdem, apparet per summa predicta ipsum plus habuisse quam ascendit.

Fol. 3v

Littera magistri B[ernardus] R[aymundi] Calderie de XVII l., de quas fit mentio in albo:

Universis presentes litteras inspecturas Bernardus Raymundi Calderie collector none partis bonorum Templi quondam atque debitorum pro domino comite Valesii, salutem et presentibus dare fidem. Notum facimus quod magister Reginaldus de Sancto Audoeno clericus et commissarius domini nostri Regis super facto dicti Templi pro nona parte [*paper damage*] t., quas habuit a Tholosa uxor Raymundi Athonis de Ruallibus quondam, item pro nona parte centum l. t. per ipsum habitis receptis a domino Galhardo [*paper damage*] et Bertrando eius fratre, pro nona parte CLX l. III s. VII d. ob. t., quas habuit a gentibus comitis Petragoricensis XXXII l. IIII s. VI d. t. parvorum nobis solut[orum], de quibus tenemus nos nomine que supra, quod contentis et de hoc dictum dominum nostrum Regem et dictum commissarium absoluimus et quittamus. In [*paper damage*] testimonium sigillum nostrum presentibus litteris duximus apponendum. Datum Tholose die Jovis ante festum Nativitatis Domini anno eiusdem M° CCC° XXIII°.

Partes LXXVI l. XIII s. t., de quibus fit mentio in albo pro expensis factis contra comitem Petragoricensis:

Primo pro scripturis in albo superius declaratis: VI l. IX s.

Pro vadiis dicti commissarii VIII dierum, quibus fuit in primo viagio quam etiam ad loca dicti comitis: VIII l.

Pro suis vadiis IIII^or^ dierum de secondo viagio apud ~~Rabatanis~~ Calciatam: IIII l.

Pro suis vadiis XII dierum, quibus vacavit Tholose ad processum dicte cause: XII l.

Pro salario magistri Bernardini de Clayssano iurisperiti consiliarii dicti commissarii: L s. t.

Pro vadiis ipsius commissarii de quinque diebus, quibus fuit ad faciendum compotum apud Montem Albanum:[224] C s. t.

Pro vadiis suis II dierum, quibus expectavit procuratorem apud Petragoris ad solvendum: XL s. t.

Pro suis vadiis VII dierum, quibus fuit eundo de Petragoris apud Parisius ad deffendendum causam appellationis: VII l.

Pro suis vadiis XV dierum, quibus fuit Parisius ad dictam appelationem prosequendum: XV l.

Pro vadiis suis IIII^or^ dierum, quibus fuit in alio viagio de Tholosa apud Calciatam ad computandum cum procuratoris dicti comitis de hoc, que recepit ab eodem: IIII l.

Pro actis factis ad mittendum Parisius pro appelationem prosequendum: XL s.

Pro salario Guillelmi Pechevernie, Arnaldi Aneti et Johannis Condelerii, qui fuerunt per V dies in executionem predictam: XL s. t.

Pro salario magistrorum Petri de Podio et Guillelmi de Brolio notariorum, qui fuerunt in dicta executione per duos dies: XL s.

Pro sigillo et scriptura littere regie in transcripto: XIIII s.

Pro vadiis dicti commissarii IIII dierum, quibus fuit in ultimo viagio ad habendum ultimam solutionem apud Calciatam et ad faciendum aliam compositionem cum illis, qui tenebant bona dicti comitis obligata: IIII l. t.

Fol. 4v

Partes CIIII l. solutis per Petrum de Montibus firmarium de Mannaco Templi quondam:

Primo soluit Guidoni Pignete de Lemovico: LXIII l.
Item eidem ex alia parte [*characters illegible*]
Item Hospitaliariis: X l.
Item posuit in reparatione dicti domus et ecclesie dicti loci IIII l. X s., et alias IIII l. X s. redduntur in albo.

Partes firme domus Templi de Podio Bonionis, quam tenuit dictus P[etrus] de Faugeraco anno M° CCC° IX°, pretio III^{c} l., de quibus solvit Aymerico de Ponte de Petragoris II^{c} XLI l. X s.:

Item posuit in expensis dicti domus et in expensis donatoris LVIII l. X s., prout dictus A[ymericus] testificatur.

Item anno Domini M° CCC° X° tenuit dictam firmam pro III^{c} l., de quibus solvit dicto Aymerico C IIII^{xx} IIII l. et Johanni Berengarii[225] servienti armorum, tunc baillivo de Lemovico C l. et posuit in expensis donatoris XVI l., prout dominus Aymericus testificatur.

Item anno Domini M° CCC° ~~XX~~ XII° tenuit dictam domum pro III^{c} l., de quibus solvit Guidoni Pignete II^{c} XIII l. X s. et debuit de resta IIII^{xx} VI l. X s.

Item pro stagno dicti loci, quem tenuit illo anno et emolumentum habuit: IIII l. t.

Pro que resta et aliis, quod in compoto Aymerici dicitur, quod opera videantur ex executoris non poterant ad hoc vacare et habebant iustam causam incontinuationis propter lapsum temporis ad C l., que redduntur in albo de anno VIII° debuit respondere G[uillelmo] Alamanni de Pictavis[226] et de anno XI° reddidit rationem Ay[merico] de Ponte, G[uidioni] Pignete, [*words scratched out et crossed-out*] et sic fuit quinque anni.

Ratio firme de Pulcra Cassanea, de Fonte Laventour et de Busseria Raspit, quam tenuit Peturs la Ribera de Brinis anno M° CCC° IX°, pretio IIII^{c} XXX l., de quibus habuit A[ymericus] de Ponte III^{c} LV l. XVIII s. XI d. et deduxit ei pro Eblone de Cressalon[227] donato dicte domus X l., pro Robino Anglia L s., pro Petro Faure L s., et pro operibus dicte domus XXXIX l. XVI s., et pro incheriis XX l.

Item anno Domini Millesimo CCC° XI° tenuit dictam firmam de Fonte Laventour et de Buxeria Raspit pro III^{c} l., de quibus solvit dicto Guidoni VIII^{xx} IV l. II s. et pro capellanis et VII donatis finivit summe deducte per dictum G[uidonum]: IIII^{xx} XI l. XVIII s., et pro operibus XLIIII l.

Item anno XII° sequenti tenuit dictam firmam pro II^{c} XXXIII l. VI s. VIII d., de quibus habuit dictus Guido VIII^{xx} V l. VI s. VIII d.

Item XXX l. t. et Hospitalii habuerunt XXXIII l. t., et sic debuit XXXIX l. monete Burgensis, quas posuerat, ut dicebat, in operibus et expensis donatoris, et hoc ~~propter~~ probare se offerebat, sed ad percedendum sibi in laboribus et expensis finivit in dubio ad XXXV l. t., que redduntur in albo pro omnibus supradictis.

Ratio firme domorum Templi de Montibus, de Bellafar et de Chalmonte,[228] quam tenuit anno ~~pro~~ Mº XIº Johannes Ribier et Raymundus la Maynarda pro III^{c} IIII^{xx} X l., de quibus habuit dictus Guido II^{c} XXVII l.

Item eidem G[uidoni]: XII l.

Item fuerunt sibi deducte pro operibus LVIII l. t. ex una parte.

Item pro expensis donatoris: XXVI l. X s.

Item pro aliis operibus et incheriis fuerunt sibi deducte per dictum Geraldum de Sabanaco LVII l. t. X s., et sic debuerunt de resta IX l. t. monete Burgensis.

Item anno XIIº sequenti dictus Johannes tenuit firmam de Chalmonte pro XXXIII l. VI s. VIII d. t., de quibus habuit dictus Guido XXV l. VI s. VIII d. et debuit VIII l. t. monete Burgensis, pro quibus finavit ad XIIII l., que redduntur in albo.

Pro Petri Fabri et Stephano Beleti firmariis de Palacio modus, per quem fuerunt liberati:

Primo de VIII^{xx} ~~VIII~~ l. t. debitis pro anno IXº habuit ~~de Petra~~ A[ymericus] de Ponte de Petragoris tunc receptor XXIIII l. XIII s. et pro operibus dicte domus C l.

Item de VIII^{xx} l. pro anno Xº habuit predictus A[ymericus] LXXV l. XVIII d. et G[uidonis] Pigneta XL l.

Item de VII^{xx} l. pro anno XIº habuerunt dicti ~~dicti~~ Gudio et G. ~~Pignete~~ Paupereti de Lemovico IIII^{xx} IX l. IIII s. VI d.

Item de LXIII l. VI s. VIII d. pro anno XIIº habuit dictus Guido XL~~VI~~V l. VI s. VIII d.

Summa totius debiti: V^{c} XXIII l. VI s. VIII d.
Summa solutionum et operum: III^{c} LXXIIII l. V s. VIII d.

Resta fuit VII^{xx} IX l. XII d., de qua fuerunt eis deducte pro dampno grandinis et tempestatis, que cecidit in anno Xº: III^{xx} l., et in anno XIIº: XIX l. XII d., et debuerunt L l. t. de tempore Burgensis valent XL l. t. bonorum, de quibus fit mentio in recepta.

Et sciendum est quod Guillelmus Alamanni de Pictavis habuit reddere rationem de anno VIIIº pro tota senescallia Caturcensi, Petragoricensi et Lemovicensi.

Partes L l. t. receptarum per magistros Raymundum de Borda et Guillelmum de Vinealibus commissarios in senescallia Agenensi et Burdegalensi a personis qui sequntur:

A Richardo de Vano Flore de Agenio pro una olla metallic, quam habuerat de bonis domus Templi de Argenteno:[229] XLVIII s. t.

Ab heredibus Petri de Mellerone de Sairaco, firmario domus Templi de Argenteno pro resta dicte firme: IIII l. X s.

A Thalasono de Lorda commissario per dominum Geraldum de Buciaco[230] quondam curatorem Templi in diocesis Agenensis deputato pro resta sui compoti: LXXII s. t.

A domino Bernardo de Monte Calvo[231] firmario domus Templi ~~q~~ de Bono Fonte[232] pro resta dicte firme: XVI l. t.

A Bernardo Lati de Nayraco[233] pro quadam compositione facta cum dictis commissariis super quodam debito petito ab eodem tempore Templariorum: IIII l. t.

A Raymundo de Campis pro quadam condampnatione facta contra eum per curatorem Templi quondam de Gimbreda: L s. t.

Ab heredibus Arnaldi de Clambus pro eadem causa: XX s. t.

A domino Guillelmo Amerii condomino de Cuco:[234] XL s. t.

Ab Arnaldo de Bordis de Clusello[235] ex causa simili: XX s. t.

Ab heredibus Arnaldi de Claraco[236] ex causa predicta: XL s. t.

Ab Arnaldo de Tutella[237] de Ralhaco[238] ex eadem causa: XX s. t.

A Bernardo de Stagno de Castro Rubeo[239] ex causa simili: IIII l. t.

A Johanne de Papone de Layraco[240] pro nemore de Gimbreda: IIII l. t.

A Stephano de Maneul de Lectora ex causa predicta: XL s. t.

[*In the left margin*: Partes] Partes XL l. in albo positarum per magistrum Franciscum Martini commissarium senescallie Bellicadri receptarum a personis et ex causis, que sequuntur:

A Bernardo Lamberti pro X s. et una libra cere per ipsum legatis prius eius finem subsidio Terre Sancte: XVI s. malgarenses.

A Johanne Condereris ex dicta causa: XXV s.

Ab Alemanda uxore Guillelmi Macfredi ex causa predicta: XX s.

A Guillelmo de Galantis ex dicta causa: XLVIII s.

Ab heredibus Bernardi Furnerii: XXX s.

Ab heredibus Johannis de Pomeriis:[241] XV s.

Ab heredibus Petri Claperada: X s.

A detentoribus bonorum magistri Petri Fabri: C s.

Ab herede Petri Berengarii: XIII s.

A detentoribus bonorum Petri Gaudi: XXX s.

Ab heredibus Furmini Tegularii: X s.

A detentoris bonorum Johannis, Petri, Raymundi et Garssendis uxore quondam Bernardi de Rino: XX s.

A detentoribus Pontii Maurelli: XXXV s.

Ab herede Guillelmi Poneti et Dulcis eius uxore: X s.

Ab heredibus Andree de Narbone: XIX s.

Ab herede Jacobi Malmorceri: L s.

Ad heredibus Petri Maurelli de Fabricis:[242] XX s.

Ab hereditibus Raymundi Alemanni de Guihano: VII s.

A detentoribus bonorum Guillelmi de Amiliano:[243] V s.

A detentoris bonorum Bernardi de Cornelhano:[244] XII s.

A heredibus domini Bernardi Sequiti quondam: X s.

A detentoris bonorum Durandi Redilhan: XX s.

Ab herede Bernardi Arbosserii: XX s.

A detentoris bonorum Guillelmi Pomelli: L s.

Ab heredibus Andree Boerii, Pontii Boerii et Arnaudi Boerii: XX s.

Ab herede Bartrandi Fabri: X s.

Ab herede Raymundi Hugonis: X s.

Ab herede Stephani Bosc: XX s.

Ab herede Guillelmi Caiol: X s.

Ab heredibus Pontii Boneti: XX s.

Ab herede Johannis Figuri: XX s.

Ab herede Bernardi de Comba:[245] X s.

Ab heredibus Guillelmi Guasii: XX s.

Ab heredibus Bernardi de Narbone de Monte Ferrario:[246] XX s.

Ab heredibus Guillelmi Ayssare: XX s.

Ab heredibus Guillelmi Egidii: XX s.

Ab heredibus Stephani Sartori: V s. malgarenses

Partes XXVII l. XVII s. VIII d. t. per dictum substitutum receptarum et expensarum, in albo positarum, a personis infrascriptis:

A Durando Pageti ex causa legati per ipsum prius finem suum facti subsidio Terre Sancte: XXV s.

Ab herede Stephani Bamardi: XVIII s.

Ab herede Petri Tegularii: XX s.

Ab herede Bernardi Figerii: X s.

Ab heredibus Johannis de Fructibus: XX s.

Ab herede Mathei Granoardi: XXVI s.

A Raymundo Alemanni de Guihaco: VII s.

Ab herede Andree Sabaterii: XX s.

A detentoris bonorum Audeberti Domicelli: XXX s.

Ab herede Raymundi Magistri: XV s.

A Guillelmo Thome et Tyberio Thome de Aquis Mortuis[247] pro herbagiis domus Templi Sancti Egidii:[248] XIII l. t.

Ab heredibus Petri Martini ex causa legati prius finem suum facti subsidio Terre Sancte, prius quam Hospitalarii habuerunt bona Templi: VI s.

A Raymundo Franchi originario Montis Pessulani:[249] X s.

A Petro Bausili: X s.

A Raymundo Gervasii: XXV s.

A Petro Figareda: XII s.

Ab herede Petri Textorii: XIIII s. VI d.

Ab heredibus Bernardi Nicholaii: XXXV s.

Ab heredibus Bernardi Pagesii: XVI s.

Ab heredibus Petri Boissera: XXV s.

Ab herede Jacobe uxore quondam Guillelmi Maroni: IIII l. X s.

Fol. 5v

A Bernardo Caureti: L s.

A Bernardo Berengarii: X s.

A Johanne Chabondi: XXVIII s.

Ab Emengarde uxore Johannis Amelerii: XXV s.

A Johanne Michaeli: XXIII s. VI d.

[*About 1/2 of the page is blank*]

Forma mandati Regii et senescalii Tholosani, de quo fit mentio in albo rotuli presentis:

Johannes de Tria dominus de Mauciaco Castro[250] miles et senescallus Tholosanus et Albiensis[251] domini nostri Francie et Navarre Regis universis et singulis commissariis et receptoribus bonorum et debitorum Templi quondam tam auctoritate Regis quam nostra deputatis, salutem. Litteras Regis nos recepisse noveritis sub hiis verbis: Karolus dei gratia Francie et Navarre Rex senescallo Tholose vel eius locum tenenti ac deputato super levatione et receptione bonorum et debitorum quondam Templi, salutem. Cum dudum per litteras inclite memorie Carissimi Domini et germani nostri Philippi dilecto Guillelmo Cligneti militi nostro tunc super hoc deputato mandatum fuisset, ut ipse de denariis ex inde pervenientibus dilecto et fideli Petro de Gallardo militi nostro balistiorumque [*sic for* balistarumque] nostrorum magistro tria milia septingetas septuaginta l. sexdecim s. et sex d. t. pro stipendiis per eum et gentes suas in fronteris Flandrensis deservitis absque expectatione mandati alterius liberaret, quam summam dictus magister ac si eam integre recepisset pro dicto G[uillelmo] et in eius exhonorationem per compotum thesauri de termino Natalis Domini anno XVIII° reddi fecit, dicens, quod

Petrus mille ducentas octoginta nonem l. et decem s. t. in una parte per dictum G[uillelmum] et sexcentas l. t. in alia parte per magistrum Reginaldum de Sancto Audoeno iam redditas per compotum thesauri de termino presenti anni III° receperit, sicut de premissis tam per scripta thesauri quam per cedulam dicti G[uillelmi] testimonia[*letter scratched out*]lem quam in ipso thesauro retinere fecimus apparuit evidenter, mandamus vobis atque committimus, quatenus prefato balistiorum [*sic for* balistarum] magistro vel eius mandato octingenatas octaginta unam l. sex s. et sex d. t. resta de priori summa de bonis et debitis ipsis in dicta senescallia vel in senescallia Petragoricensi et Caturcensi iam levatis vel quam primum levandis absque difficultate aliqua persolvatis presentes et sua de solito litteras retenturas, per quarum exhibitionem iƀd, quod ei solveritis in vestris compotis precipimus allocari. Datum Parisius die XXVI Julii, anno Domini M° CCC° XXIII°, virtute quarum litterarum vobis et cuilibet vestrum mandamus quatenus contenta in dictis litteris secundam formam earum compleatis et exequamini taliter quod non possitis de negligentia reprehendi. In quorum testimonium sigillum Regis nostre senescallie predicte presenti littere apponi fecimus et appendi. Datum Tholose die ultima Decembris, anno Domini M° CCC° XXIII°.

Sequuntur littere solutionum, de quibus fit mentio in albo:

A tous ceus qui ces lettres veront Pierres de Gailart chevalier et mestre des arbalestes notre seigneur le Roy de France et de Navarre, salut. Savoir faisons a tous que nous avons eu et receve de mestre Regnaut de Saint Oyen cleric et commisseur du dit nostre seigneur le Roy sur le fait du Temple sis cens quatorze livres tournois en rabatant de greigneur somme, en quoi le dit nostre seigneur le Roy estoit tenuz a nous de la quele il nous a assigne sur le fait du Temple, si comme il apperet per ses lettres des queles li diz commissaires a copie par devans lui, c'est a savoir par les parties, qui ci apres sensinent: Premierment le samedi apres la Saint Michiel darrenerement passee II^{c} libres tournois, que nous avons eues devant par diverses parties et par diverses mains, par compte fait entre nous et lui. Item le mercredi

Line of text under the stitching

Fol. 6v

Page blank

Fol. 7v

Roquepine notre escuier come par la main du dit commissaire par compte fait entre nous et li le dit jour a Hireul. Item le mardi veille Saint Thomas par la main du dit Ernaut: <u>LX l. t.</u> Item par la main du dit commissaire le jeudi apres Noel a

Tholouse: XXX l. III s. VI d. t., des queles VI^{c} XIIII l. nous nous tenons pour bien paiez et enquitons le dit notre seigneur le Roy et le dit comissaire. En tesmoing de ce nous avons mis notre scel en ces presentes lettres le jeudi dessu dit l'an mil CCC XXIII.

Nous Pierre de Gaillart chevalier du Roy de France notre seigneur, mestre de ses arbelestes faisons assavoir a tous que comme le Roy nos seigneur me feust tenuz en une certaine somme d'argent, la quele somme il nous assigne a prendre suiz les biens jadiz du Temple, que je establiz et a establiz mes procures et messaiges pour recevoir la dit somme d'argent ou partie de celle Pierre Morant seigneur de Ponpignam[252] et Ernaut de Requepine mon escuier ou li un de euls et est assavoir que tout ce que il ou li uns d'euls deuz recevra j'eu quite le dit notre seigneur le Roy et le dit commissaire. En tesmoing de ce nous avons mis en ces presentes lettres mon scel. Donne a Huereaul le mercredi apres la Sainte Luce Virge l'an de grace mil CCC vint et trois.

Tenor litterarum regiarum et senescalli Tholose, de quibus fit mentio in albo:

Johannes de Tria dominus de Mouciaco Castro miles Domini nostri Francie et Navarre Regis, senescallus Tholosanus et Albiensis nobilo viro vicario Tholose aut eius locum tenenti et magistro Reginaldo de Sancto Audoeno comissario deputato super executione ~~bonorum~~ debitorum quondam ~~quon~~ Templi, salute et dilectionis [affectum]. Litteras Regis nos recepisse noveritis sub hiis verbis: Karolus Dei gratia Francie et Navarre Rex senescallo Tholosano vel eius locum tenenti, salutem. Cum de summa trium milium septigentarum octoginta l. sexdecim s. et duorum d. t., quam dudum inclite memorie Dominus et germanus noster carissimus Philippus dictorum regnorum Rex dilecto et fideli Petro de Galardo militi nostro balistiorumque [*sic for* balistarumque] nostrorum magistro per suas [*word scratched out*] litteras et ex certis causis in eisdem contentis per dilectum Guillelmum Cligneti militem nostrum tunc circa levationem et receptionem bonorum et debitorum Templariorum quondam Regni Francie super intendens de bonis et debitis ipsis in dicta senescallia levatis et levandis voluit et mandavit exsolvi, duo milia quadrigenta decem octo l. sex s. et duo d. t. remaneant exsolvendi, prout per cedulam testimonialem dicti G[uillelmi] datum die Sabbati post festum beatorum apostolorum Philippi et Jacobi, anno CCC° vicesimo primo dicitur apperere. Cupientes ipsi magistro balistiorum [*sic for* balistarum] de dicto residuo solutionem fieri condecentem, mandamus vobis atque committimus presertim cum dictus G[uillelmus] circa levationem dictorum bonorum et debitorum predictorum ad presens [*letters illegible*] non habeat, quatinus de bonis et debitis predictis in vostra senescallia usquam ad predictam summam residuam vel plurem si possit fieri explectetis celeriter et levatis tamquam ad thesaurum nostrum Parisius transmittatis inhibi per dilectos et fideles thesaurarios nostros prefato balistarum magistro vel eius mandato et non aliter liberandi, quibus [*word illegible*] presenti in mandatis, ut ipsam summam residuam in usus alios non [*letters scratched out*] convertant. Datum Parisius die IIII^{a} Augusti anno Domini M^{o} XXII°. Suarum auctoritate vobis mandamus, quatinus de bonis et debitis predictis in dicta senescallia existentibus usque ad predictam summam residuam vel pluris,

Fol. 8v

si fieri possit explectatis taliter et levatis eam, quam nobis celeriter transmittatis, ut eam ad thesauro Regni Parisius transmitter possumus iuxta ipsarum litterarum regiarum continentiam et tenorem. Datum Tholose, die IIII^{a} Novembris, anno Domini M^{o} CCC^{o} vicesimo secundo.

Cedule thesauri, de quibus fit mentio in albo:

Thesaurarii Domini Regis Parisius reddiderunt executionem Regis Philippi Pulcri de bonis Templariorum Regni Francie pro magistro Reginaldo de Sancto Audoeno commissario super facto dictorum bonorum: XL l. parisiensis per Robillandum de Brionia[253] clericum compotorum scriptum Sabato, IIII^{a} die Junii, anno Domini M^{o} CCC^{o} XXIII°.

Thesaurarii Domini Regis Parisius reddiderunt executionem Regis Philippi Pulcri de bonis seu debitis Templariorum quondam Regni Francie in senescallia Tholosana pro magistro Reginaldo de Sancto Audoeno clerico: VI^{c} l. t. per dominum P[etrum] de Galardo magistrum balistiorum [*sic for* balistarum] scriptum Mercurii XXVII^{a} Julii, anno Domini M^{o} CCC^{o} vicesimo tertio.

Partes XIII [*character scratched out*] l. XI s. IIII d. t. positis in albo in nomina servientum, qui eas habuerunt:

Die II^{a} Augusti, anno vicesimo secundo pro salario Petri de Meuleto, qui fecit executionem contra heredes Guillelmi Catalani ratione XXXV s., quas solverunt: III s. t.

Die IIII^{a} Augusti Hugoni Bourgondi misso apud Caventhas contra Johannem Tinhes per tres dies: IIII s. VI d.

Die no[na Augusti] eidem H[ugoni] misso apud Marcam Fabam[254] contra heredes Arnaldi de Trilha,[255] pro VI diebus: IX s. t.

XVIII Augusti eidem H[ugoni] misso ap[ud] [*paper damage*] ad citandum comitem Petragoricensem: XVIII s. pro XII diebus.

Eadem die Jacobo Arquerii misso apud Ventilhacum contra magistrum Michaelum [de Rotondo] [*paper damage*]

Die vicesima seconda Augusti eidem Jacobo misso apud Moissiacum contra heredes Guillelmi de Spahone: IIII s.

Die ultima Augusti eid[em misso] apud Ventilhacum contra Guillelmum de Cantamerla:[256] IIII s. t.

Die IIII[a] Septembris Guillelmo Capde Perdonie misso apud Montem Salnerium contra Guillelmum de Artigalonga:[257] IIII s. VI d.

Eadem die Johanni de Sancto Marcello misso apud Capadellum contra dententores bonorum Bartholomei Costa: VIII s. t.

Eadem die Andree Pechevin misso apud Mirapiscem[258] contra Stephanum de Arneto:[259] IX s. t.

Die quinta Septembris Guillelmo Pecherennie miss[o apud] Sanctum Gaudentium[260] in Convenis contra Arnaldum de Sancto Paulo:[261] VIII s. t.

Eadem die Jacobo Arquerii misso apud Villam Franc[eisam contra] Petrum de Festis et eius socios: V s. IV d.

Die sexta Septembris eidem Jacobo misso apud Salas contra heredes Bernardi de Con[*paper damage*]: III s.

Eadem die Johanni de Grolayo[262] misso apud Villam Dei contra Bertrandi de Carreris: II s.

Die X[a] Septembris Hugoni d[e] [*paper damage*] apud Rapistagnum contra Pontium Alerii: XII s. t.

Eadem die Stephano Espinni misso apud Levinhacum contra debitoris Petri Bundei [*paper damage*].

Die XV[a] Septembris Jacobo Arquerii misso apud Bononiam contra Arnaldum de Lauguet[263] et Arnaldum de Valle Cava:[264] IIII s.

Eadem die Hug[oni] Burgundi misso apud Sanctum Gerontium et Montem Esquinum[265] contra Bertrandum Garcie: XVIII s. t.

Die vicesima Septembris Andree Peschevin et Johanni de Sancto Marcello, qui fuerunt per sex dies contra Raymundum Gonterii, Germanum Radditorum et Pontium Martini et contra Stephanum de Rupibus: XXXVI s. t.

Eadem die Johanni de Pruvinis et Petro Burgondi missis contra dominum Petrum de Bordis per quatuor dies: XXIIII s.

Die XXV Septembris Andree Pechevin misso apud Borderias contra Sancium Averis: XII s.

Eadem die Hugoni d'Arboy misso apud Carb[ina] contra Petrum Salbaterii: XII s. t.

Die prima Octobris Guillelmo Pecherennie misso apud Montem Salnerium contra consules dicti loci: VI s. t.

Die quarta Octobris Andree Pechevin misso apud Stellam contra Arnaldo de Sancto Quentino:[266] IIII s.

Die VIII[a] Octobris Johanni de Sancto [Mar]cello misso apud Cadelhanum contra plures homines dicti loci: IIII s. VI d.

Eadem die Henrico de Grolayo misso apud Plauterum contra plures homines dicti loci: IIII s. VI d.

Die XIX^{a} Octobris Jacobo Arguerii misso apud Corduam contra heredes domini Geraldi de Casali Bono:[267] X s. t.

Die XXIV^{a} Septembris [*sic for* Octobris] Hugoni d'Arboy misso apud Sanctum Gerontium contra Raymundum de Podio: VIII s. t.

Die ultima Octobirs eidem H[ugoni] misso apud Salvam Terram[268] contra Rogerium de Fontano: XII s. t.

Partes VIII l. V s. positarum in albo et nomina notariorum et servinetum, qui eas habuerunt:

Die Sabbati ante festum Sancte Marie Septembris Thome d'Auchi[269] serviente misso apud Bonum Locum contra heredes Davini de Roaxio [*paper damage*].

Die Lune post dictum festum Petro Sartoris misso apud Insulam Jordani contra Petrum Benedicti et Guillelmum Fabri: IIII s. VI d. t.

[*Paper damage*] ~~sanctam~~ Sanctam Crucem Guillelmo Calhanelli misso apud Vaour et alia loca Templi, que tenet dominus Bertrandus de Ruppe Negata:[270] VIII s.

Sabbati sequentis Guillelmo de Basso Loco[271] misso apud Mansum contra heredes Raymundi Bernardi quondam curatoris bonorum dicti Templi: IX s.

Martis in festo Sancti Mathei Thome d'Auchi et Guillelmo Pecherennie misso contra Rogerium Caverni, qui debet IIII^{c} XXVI l. ~~t.~~: XII s.

Mercuri post dictum festum Andree Pechevin misso apud Carbina contra Othonem de Benaco et Petrum Salbaterii: XII s. t.

Iovis post Sanctem Michelem Guillelmo de Vinealibus notario misso ad faciendum executionem super bonis Bernardi Busca: X s. t.

Lune ante Omnes Sanctos Pauci misso contra Arnaldum de Astarum arrendatione redituum comitis Petragoricensis: VII s. VI d.

Mercuri sequentis Pontio Fabri misso Insulam Jordani contra Michaelem de Condonna, qui debet XV cartones frumenti: VI s. t.

Iovis sequentis Guillelmo Calhanelli misso apud Auxium contra Arnaldum Divos, qui debet LX s. t. et VIII s. t.

Mercuri ante Sanctum Martinum Dominico de Cartone misso apud Insulam contra Geraldum de Alta Valle[272] pro XXXVI cartones frumenti, quos de[bet]: VI s. t.

Sabbati post Conversione Sancti Pauli Hugoni d'Arboy misso apud Astafortem in Leomania contra Petrum de Aula, qui debet XXX l. t. per librum curie de Gimbreda, pro sex diebus, III s. t. per diem: XVIII s. t.

Eadem die pro expensis magistri Guillelmi de Vinealibus notarii, qui fuit in Leomania per octo dies ratione debitorum, que debentur per homines dicte terre, contra quos vicecomes procedure non permisit: XL s. t.

Die Iovis ante ~~festum~~ Sanctum Valentinum Perroto de Lectoria misso apud Altum Villarem ad citandum ~~dictum~~ dominum Johanem Alatris curatorem bonorum [Templi de] Leomanie ad reddendum compotum de administratione per eundem circa dictam curiam, pro quinque diebus: X s. t.

Dies Veneris post Cineres Bernardo Rogi misso apud Gimbredam ad citandum Raymundum Guillelmi de Duro Forti super quibusdam bonis Templi, que habuit de duro [*sic for* domo] dicti loci et de Villa Dei, pro quatuor diebus: VIII s. t.

About 1/4 of the page is blank

Fol. 9v

Partes et littere solutionum factorum magistro B[ernardo] Raymundi Calderie pro IX^{a} parte domini comitis Valesii, de quibus fit mentio in albo superius, in summa totali recepte, facte in anno Domini M^{o} CCC^{o} XXII° ante expensis dicti domini:

Noverint universi, quod nos Bernardus Raymundi Calderie collector none partis de bonis Templi quondam pro domino comite Valesii habuimus et recepimus a magistro Reginaldo de Sancto Audoeno clerico commisario domini nostri Regis super dictis bonis IIII l. XIIII s. VI d. ob. t. pro nona parte dictum dominum comitem contingente de debitis per dictum magistrum Reginaldum levatis et receptis, de quibus nomine prefati domini comitis de Valesio prefatum magistrum Reginaldum absoluimus et quitamus. In quorum testimonium nos prefatus Bernardus Raymundi Calderie sigillum nostrum duximus apponendum Tholose XVIII^{a} die mensis Novembris, anno Domini M^{o} CCC^{o} XXII°: IIII l. XIIII s. VI d. ob.

Noverint universi, quod nos Bernardus etc. habuimus et recepimus a consulibus Montis Salnerii per manus magistri Reginaldi de Sancto Audoeno etc. XXII s. III d. t. pro IX^{a} parte X l. t., quas recipit a consulibus antedictis etc., de quibus etc. Datum Tholose die Sabbati ante festum beati Clementis papae Anno Domini M^{o} CCC^{o} XXII°: XXII s. III d.

Noverint universi, quod nos Bernardus Raymundi Calderie etc. habuimus et recepimus a discreto viro magistro Reginaldo de Sancto Audoeno etc. XIII s. IIII d. t. pro IX^{a} p[arte] sex l. t., quas Bertrandus de Bosco solvere debebat etc., in quorum testimonium etc. Datum Tholose die Lune ante festum Beati Andree apostoli, anno Domini M^{o} CCC^{o} vicesimo secondo: XIII s. IIII d.

Noverint universi, quod nos Bernardus etc. recepimus a magistro Reginaldo etc. XL s. t. pro IX^{a} parte XVIII l. t., quas habuit ab heredibus Bertrandi de Podio de Caturco, de quibus etc. Datum Tholose die Sabbati ante festum Natalis Domini, anno eiusdem M^{o} CCC^{o} XXII°: XL s.

Noverint etc., quod nos Bernardus etc. habuimus etc. a magistro Reginaldo etc. XII l. II s. VI d. t. pro IXª parte dictum dominum comitem contingente de debitis, que idem commissarius receperat, de quibus tenemus nos nomine quo supra, pro contentis etc. In quorum testimonium etc. Datum Tholose die ~~Sabbati in festo beati Gregorii~~ Martis post festum Epiphanie Domini, anno eiusdem Mº CCCº XXIIº: XII l. ~~X~~ II s. VI d.

Universis etc. Bernardus Calderie etc. notum facimus, quod magister Reginaldus de Sancto Audoeno etc. pro IXª parte debitorum, que receipt CXII s. IIII d. ob. t. nobis solvit de quaquidam IXª parte tenemus nos nomine quo supra, contentos etc. In quorum testimonium etc. Datum Tholose die Sabbati in festo beati Gregorii, anno Domini Mº CCCº XXIIº: CXII s. IIII d. ob.

Universis etc. Bernardus Calderie etc. notum facimus, quod magister Reginaldus de Sancto Audoeno etc. de hiis, que recepit etc. XII l. VIII s. VI d. t. nobis solvit, de quibus tenemus nos pro contentis etc. In cuius rei etc. Datum Tholose die quinta introitus mensis Aprilis, anno Domini Mº CCCº XXIIIº: XII l. VIII s. VI d. t.

Universis etc. Bernardus etc. notum facimus, quod magister Reginaldus etc. pro IXª parte X l. t., quas habuerat a Bertrando de Castro Novo[273] etc. et pro IXª parte XVII l. t., quas habuerat a domino comite Petragoricensis etc. LX s. t. nobis solvit, de quibus etc. Datum Tholose die VIIª introitus mensis Aprilis, anno Domini Mº CCCº XXIIIº: XL s. t.

Item pro nona parte XX s., quos receperat a Petro de Casa etc.: II s. III d. t.

Suma istarum partium: XLI l. XV s. IX d. t.

Tenor commissionis facte dicto magistro B[ernardo] R[aymundi] per prefatum dominum comitem Valesii, sequitur in huic modum:

Charles filz de Roy de France, contes de Valoys, d'Alencon,[274] de Chartres et d'Anjo[275] a notre ame et feal mestre Bernart Raymon Calderie, salut et amour. Nous vous mandons et commetons, que vous alliez ou envoiez es liens, es quiex les biens, que les Templiers avoient en la seneschautie de Petregort et de Caoursin en la seneschautie de Biaucaire, en la seneschautie de Tholose et d'Aubigois, en la seneschautie de Carcassone et de Bediers, en la seneschautie de Poito et de Sanctonge et en la seneschautie de Roergue,[276] quant il furent pris, pourront estre trouvez, es quieux biens nostre sire le Roy de France a les II pars et les Hospitaliers la tierce part per terram acoit sau [*word illegible*] euls, et de la part auz diz Hospitals le tiers est nostre pour cause du don, que nostre ame frere Lyenart de Tybertis lieu tenant du grant mestre de l'Ospital nous eu fist, si comme notre cher compere frere Symon le Rat grant prieur de France et plusieurs autres le scevent bien. Et recevez cuiellez levez et esploitiez par vous ou par autres souffisans pour nous et en notre nom et faites venir devers nous notre tiers devant dit. Et de toutes ces choses et tout ce qui y appertient faire et destablir et deputer a les faire en lieu de vous une autre persone souffisant ou plusieurs nous vous donnons peoir et prions par ces lettres meismes, si de citer comme nous pouons ceus, a qui messieur le Roy et les Hospitalers dessus diz ont commises leur parties diceus biens a lever, qu'il vous avisent, conseillent et adrecent en ceste besoigne a leur pooir et qu'il en facent autant pour vous, comme il feroient pour nous, et a touz autres qu'il en tendent a vous diligemment. Donne a Mortaigne,[277] l'an mil CCC XVII, XXIIII de fevrier.

About 1/3 of the page is blank

Fol. 10v–11v

Pages blank

Fol. 12v

About 1/3 of the page is blank

Partes XXVII l. XVII s. VIII d. t. positis in albo pro expensis magistri Francisci Martini, de quibus fit mentio in compoto dicti Francisci prefato magistro R[eginaldo] de Sancto Audoeno reddito et per eum curie restituto:

Primo pro expensis Johannis de Croxia[278] notarii regii, qui vacavit per sexdecem dies ad transcribendum debita reperta in libris notarii Montis Pessulani et domus Templi dicti loci per diem V s., pro toto: XL s.

Pro expensis domini Petri Bedeii cappellani et donati dicte domus, qui vacavit per XX dies ad indagandum homines qui ad dicta debita fierant obligatis pro villam Montis Pessulani et pro alia loca circum vicina: C s. t.

Pro salario Petri Gaillerdi servientis, qui cum eo ibat ad citandum homines predictis: XX s. t.

Pro salario Petri Clari servientis missi apud Aviorum ad citandum illos, quos Durandus Payrola tradidit in resta, pro V^que^ diebus: XV s. t.

Pro salario Gauberti Ruffi clerici de Monte Pessulano, qui vacavit per decem dies ad perquirendum illas, qui tenebant bona debitorum Montis Pessulani in dictis libris repertarum: XX s. t.

Pro scribendo compoto dicti Francisci et pergameno ad hoc: X s. t.

Summa: X l. V s. t.

Et ~~d~~ pro salario dicti magistri Francisci de ~~centum~~ VI^{xx} diebus, quibus vacavit a predicta X s. t. per diem LX l. t., de quibus habuit per manus domini Albertini Brachii Fortis ~~firma~~ tenentis bona firmariorum Montis Pessulani pro expensis L s. t. Et de hiis, que receperat retinuit in deductione dicti salarii: XVII l. XII s. VIII d. t.

Summa: XXVII l. XVII s. VIII d. t.

Fol. 13v–14v

Pages blank

Fol. 15v

At the top of the page on the right: le secont compte du Temple rondu en la chambre l'an XXV

In the centre of the page: Templum

Fol. 16v–17v

Pages blank

Fol. 18v

About 1/3 of the page is blank

Partes sex instrumentorum et litterarum, de quibus fit mentio in albo et pro quibus sex s. computantur:

In primo instrumento continetur ~~m~~, quod dictus Johannes Marchi tenens locum senescalli Tholosani fecit inhibere et inhibuit dicto commissario ne infra commissione procederet sine licentia senescalli, qui erat in guerra Vasconie.[279]

Per secundam litteram apparet, de quadam commissione facta Johanni Andoyni de Pictavis, per quam volebat impedire commissionem dicti R[eginaldi] in senescallia Pictaviensi et Xa[ntonensi].

Tertia littera ~~est~~ continet copiam cuiusdam littere regie, directe dicto R[eginaldo] de compellendo uxorem et executores Raymundi Athonis de Ruallibus pro CXII l., quas debebant et que redduntur tam in precedenti compoto quam presenti.

Quarta littera continet copiam cujusdam littere regie dicto R[eginaldo] directe contra comitem Petragoricensem pro II^{c} IIII^{xx}V l. t., quas debebat et que redduntur in compotum [*paper damage*].

Quintum instrumentum de banno apposito in bonis Stephanis de Molinis apud Santcum Leonardum pro XL l. t., quas debebat et qui in albo reddun[tur].

Sextum instrumentum est banno per dictum commissarium posito in bonis Petri de Sancto Leodegario[280] de Arnaco[281] pro XIIII l. t., quas debet domino [*paper damage*] ratione dicti Templi, sicut in dicto instrumento continentur.

Sequntur due alie littere, de quibus ~~a tergo~~ in albo fit mentio et pro quibus ibidem sex s. computantur:

Una est copia cuiusdam donationis facte per fratrem Bernardum de Ruppe Templarium existentem in carcere episcopi Vasatensis post generalem captionem Templ[ariorum] [*paper damage*] scilicet domino Galtero de Mota militi, de quibusdam redditibus Templi ~~quod~~ dyocesis Agenensis valentibus annuatim C l. t., quas dictus miles habuit et recepit a dicta captione citra usque nunc.

Alia littera est copia cuisdam littere, per quam apparet, quod dominus Bertrandus tunc episcopus Albiensis et camerarius pape ~~ha~~ necnon dominus Gui[llelmus] Arnaudus de Mota[282] tunc episcopus Vasatensis habuerunt totam vaxellam argenti et totam pecuniam repertis penes fratrem Bernardum de Rup[pe] Templarium tunc preceptorem Provincie, qui valebant circa mille l. t.

Partes et nomina servientum et aliorum, de quibus fit mentio in albo, qui dictam firmam habuerunt ex causis que sequntur:

Primo pro Thoma de Hospitali misso in Armaniaco ad citandum executores archiepiscopi Auxitani, ubi fuit per quinques dies: XV s.

Pro copia commissionis, quam habuit: II s. t.

Item pro magistro Bernardo Regis notario misso in Ruthena ad senescallum Ruthenensem, ut commissionem videret, sine cuius originali nolebat permittere ea uti in sua senescallia, pro sex diebus: XXX s.

Item pro salario Petri Boneti de Lemovicis, qui duxit dictem commissarum apud Roserium,[283] ad domum domini Amelii de Sella, qui debet domino Rege plures summas per finem compoti curatorum senescallie Lemo[vicensis], pro quinque diebus: XV s. t.

Pro salario magistri Raymundi de Puissaguello[284] advocati Tholose, qui fuit procurator causarum domorum Templi per plures dies: XX s. t.

Pro perga[meno], papiro et cera: III s. II d.

Pro expensis Thome de Hospitali missi de Tholosa apud Lemovicas ad magistrum Geraldum Morelli substitutum ibi pro commissario regio super negotio dicti

Templi, pro litteris, quas Guidonis Pigneta de Lemovicis olim receptor habebat de debitis Templi recuperandis, que littere fuerunt per dominum R[eginaldum] in [*paper damage*] restitute, pro IX diebus: XXVII s.

Pro expensis Compaigneti de Sancto Sulpitio[285] missi de Tholosa apud Sanctum Gerontium ad magistrum Johannem Martini deputatum [*paper damage*] R. pro faciendo preconisari, quod qui haberet aliquid de bonis Templi, ea dicto commissario revelaret, pro quatuor diebus: VIII s.

Pro salario [*words illegible, paper damage*] servientis misso apud Montem Albanum ad citandum Bernardum Rubei, qui dicebatur habuisse de bonis Templi Ville Dei: VI s.

Pro salario [*words illegible, paper damage*] Lemovicis, qui vendidit equum Aymerici de Mueg et coopertorium domini Amelii de Cella, de quibus fit mentio superius in recepta et pro [*paper damage*] equi de quinque diebus: X s. VI d. t.

Pro Jaquenieto de Turre serviente Gimontis misso apud Auxium ad citandum heredes comitis Armaniaci [*paper damge*] in albo expressata, pro quinque diebus: XV s. t.

Pro Geraldo Morelli notario, qui fuit per octo dies contra Guillelmum Bonelli et Petrum Cabernerii pro quibusdam [*letters illegible, paper damage*] que petebantur ab eis pro compoto Guidonis Pigneta receptoris olim Templi, de quibus redduntur in albo in recepta XVIII l. t.: XL s. t.

Pro salario [*paper damage*] Blanchi missi apud Insulam Jordani ad citandum Petrum Bundei pro IX^{xx} l., de quibus fit mentio in recepta: VI s. t.

Pro Thoma de Hospitali misso [apud] Bastidam de Gordano ad citandum Guillelmum de Redola pro XL l., quas debet, ubi fecit per sex dies: XVIII s. t.

Pro Alberrico Burgundi serviente [*words illegible*] qui fuit per tres dies apud Dauratum[286] contra heredes Thome Taillati pro XIIII l., quas debent: XV s. t.

Pro Thoma de Hospitali misso de [*word illegible*] apud Bitteris contra Petrum Bundei, qui debebat XL l., que redduntur in precedenti compoto et presenti, pro IX diebus: XXVII s. t.

Pro Petri de [*word illegible*] serviente, qui fuit per sex dies apud Petragoris contra Stephanum la Rocha pro C l., que redduntur in compoto precedenti: XVIII s. t.

Pro Geraldo Morelli, qui fuit [per] decem dies apud Brinas pro XIIII l. l. [*sic!*] t., quas Raymundus la Maynarda debebat et que in dicto compoto redduntur: L s. t.

Pro Johanne [*name illegible*] misso apud Montem Albanum ad citandum magistrum Bernardum Ruffi ~~pro q~~ notarium, qui dicebatur habere plures litteras dictis Templi: VI s.

Pro salario Johannis Mercerii famuli peditis, qui fuit cum dicto commissario per tres menses: XX s. t.

Pro salario Yvoneti Britonis famuli peditis, qui fuit cum eo per alios tres menses: XX s. t.

Pro salario Johannis de Trecis, qui fuit cum eodem per alios tres menses: XX s. t.

Pro salario Johannis Chapellet, qui fuit cum eo [per] alios tres menses: XXV s. t.

Pro expensis Perroti Pictavini missi de Parisius apud Inucheriam ad citandum Guidonem de Alvernia et apud Lemovicum ad citandum Guidonem Bozonis ex causis in albo rotuli declaratis, ubi fuit per sexdecim dies: XXXII s. t.

[Pro] sigillo prepositi de Inucheria [*paper damage*] littera rescriptionis eiusdem de citatione facta contra dominum Guidonem de Alvernia: XII d. t.

Pro quodam instrumento facto per Martialem Alemandi notarium regium de Lem[ovicis] super citatione facta contra dominum Guidonem Bozonis: V s. t.

Fol. 19v

Page blank.

Notes

1 Roaix (Vaucluse, arr. Carpentras).
2 Gimbrède (Gers, arr. Condom).
3 Lomagne – former vicounty in Gascony.
4 Gisors (Eure, arr. Les Andelys).
5 Rouillac – former village in today's Gimbrède.
6 Bernard de Roche, master of Provence (1300–1306), probably commander of Vaour and Montricoux – A. Demurger, *Le peuple*, pp. 375–376.
7 La Villedieu[-du-Temple] (Tarn-et-Garonne, arr. Montauban).
8 Fronton (Haute-Garonne, arr. Toulouse).
9 Gimeaux? (Puy-de-Dôme, arr. Riom).
10 Verderonne? (Oise, arr. Clermont).
11 Bonnefare (Dordogne, arr. Bergerac, comm. Saint-Michel-de-Montaigne).
12 Périgueux (Dordogne, arr. Périgueux).
13 Troyes (Aube, arr. Troyes).
14 Castelnau-d'Estrétefonds (Haute-Garonne, arr. Toulouse).
15 Marseillan (Hérault, arr. Montpellier).
16 Tachoires (Gers, arr. Mirande).
17 Durfort (Tarn, arr. Castres).
18 Rochefort – several localities in France bear this name.
19 Plagne (Haute-Garonne, arr. Muret).
20 Montsaunès (Haite-Garonne, arr. Saint-Gaudens).
21 Rieux[-Volvestre]? (Haute-Garonne, arr. Muret).
22 Larramet (Haute-Garonne, arr. Toulouse, comm. Tournefeuille).
23 Lalanne-Arqué (Gers, arr. Mirande).
24 Champeaux – several localities in France bear this name.
25 Sauviac (Gers, arr. Mirande or Gironde, arr. Langon).
26 Saint-Lizier (Ariège, arr. Saint-Girons).
27 Châlus (Haute-Vienne, arr. Limoges).
28 Crépy? – several localities in France bear this name.
29 Hélie IX Talleyrand, Count of Périgord (1294–1311).
30 Gérard Lavigne, admitted to the Order in 1270, died after 1295 – A. Demurger, *Le peuple*, p. 263.
31 Château de Fénelon in Sainte-Mondane (Dordogne, arr. Sarlat-la-Canéda).
32 Saint-Blancard (Gers, arr. Mirande).
33 Saint-Robert (Lot-et-Garonne, arr. Agen).
34 Montricoux (Tarn-et-Garonne, arr. Montauban).
35 Campagnac (Tarn, arr. Albi).
36 Saint-Antonin[-Noble-Val] (Tarn-et-Garonne, arr. Montauban).
37 Nègrepelisse (Tarn-et-Garonne, arr. Montauban).
38 Saint-Paul[-la-Roche] (Dordgone, arr. Nontron).
39 Castillon – several localities in southwestern France bear this name.

40 Limousin – region in southwestern central France.
41 Magnac (Haute-Vienne, arr. Limoges, comm. Magnac-Bourg).
42 Fougeré? (Maine-et-Loire, arr. Saumur).
43 Puybonnieux (Haute-Vienne, arr. Limoges, comm. Pageas).
44 Bellechassagne (Corrèze, arr. Ussel).
45 Foulventour (Haute-Vienne, arr. Bellac, comm. Saint-Hilaire-la-Treille).
46 La Bussière-Rapy (Haute-Vienne, arr. Bellac, comm. Saint-Amand-Magnezeix).
47 Le Mons (Corrèze, arr. Brive-la-Gaillarde, comm. Estivaux).
48 Valence – several localities in southern France bear this name.
49 Le Palais[-sur-Vienne] (Haute-Vienne, arr. Limoges).
50 Limoges (Haute-Vienne, arr. Limoges).
51 Agenais – ancient region in Guyenne.
52 Les Vigneaux? (Hautes-Alpes, arr. Briançon).
53 Carcassonne (Aude, arr. Carcassonne).
54 Béziers (Hérault, arr. Béziers).
55 Saint-Thibéry (Hérault, arr. Béziers).
56 Agde (Hérault, arr. Béziers).
57 Espondeilhan (Hérault, arr. Béziers).
58 Abeilhan (Hérault, arr. Béziers).
59 Montoulieu (Hérault, arr. Lodève).
60 Beaucaire (Gard, arr. Nîmes).
61 Générac (Gard, arr. Nîmes).
62 Lagardiolle (Tarn, arr. Castres).
63 Saint-Bonnet – several localities in southwestern France bear this name.
64 Sariac[-Magnoac] (Hautes-Pyrénées, arr. Tarbes).
65 Marguerittes (Gard, arr. Nîmes).
66 Comminges – historical region of southern France, part of Gascony, situated in today's deprtment of Haute-Garonne.
67 Foix – capital of ancient county, situated in today's department of Ariège.
68 Couserans – historical province in the western part of today's department of Ariège.
69 Marignac – several localities in southwestern France bear this name.
70 Spain – medieval Iberian Peninsula.
71 Laurac (Aude, arr. Carcassonne).
72 La Fajolle? (Aude, arr. Limoux).
73 Lasséran (Gers, arr. Mirande).
74 Pujols? (or Les Pujols?) – several localities in southwestern France bear this name in various forms.
75 Ayguetinte (Gers, arr. Auch).
76 Cahuzac – several localities in southwestern France bear this name.
77 Lavergne (Lot-et-Garonne, arr. Marmande or Lot, arr. Gourdon).
78 Ancient village, incorporated into today's Denguin (Pyrénées-Atlantiques, arr. Pau).
79 Roannes[-Saint-Mary]? (Loire, arr. Roannes-Saint-Mary).
80 Huos (Haute-Garonne, arr. Saint-Gaudens).
81 Ganties (Haute-Garonne, arr. Saint-Gaudens).
82 Labarthe – several localities in southwestern France bear this name.
83 Mas (or Le Mas) – several localities in southwestern France bear this name.
84 Vernines? (Puy-de-Dôme, arr. Issoire).
85 Saint-Girons (Ariège, arr. Saint-Girons).
86 Escobet, territory in today's Séailles (Gers, arr. Condom).
87 Tapia, hamlet near Dun (Ariège, arr. Pamiers).
88 Boudrac (Haute-Garonne, arr. Saint-Gaudens).
89 Seysses? (Haute-Garonne, arr. Muret).
90 Maurens (Haute-Garonne, arr. Toulouse).

91 Boulogne[-sur-Gesse] (Haute-Garonne, arr. Saint-Gaudens).
92 Samatan (Gers, arr. Auch).
93 Lautrec (Tarn, arr. Castres).
94 L'Isle-Jourdain (Gers, arr. Auch).
95 Bordères[-sur-l'Échez] (Hautes-Pyrénées, arr. Tarbes).
96 Bigorre – historical county, part of today's department of Hautes-Pyrénées.
97 Marestaing (Gers, arr. Auch).
98 Sernhac? (Garn, arr. Nîemes).
99 Saint-Marcel – several localities in southwestern France bear this name.
100 Seissan (Gers, arr. Mirande).
101 Astarac – historical county, located in Gascony.
102 Orban (Tarn, arr. Albi).
103 Lévignac (Haute-Garonne, arr. Touloue).
104 Pibrac (Haute-Garonne, arr. Touloue).
105 Saint-Lys (Haute-Garonne, arr. Muret).
106 Plaisance-du-Touch (Haute-Garonne, arr. Touloue).
107 Sainte-Foy[-de-Peyrolières] (Haute-Garonne, arr. Muret).
108 Castelnau-Magnoac (Hautes-Pyrénées, arr. Tarbes)
109 Bouloc (Haute-Garonne, arr. Touloue).
110 Astaffort (Lot-et-Garonne, arr. Agen).
111 Miradoux (Gers, arr. Condom).
112 Saint-Antoine (Gers, arr. Condom).
113 Dunes (Tarn-et-Garonne, arr. Castelsarrasin).
114 Flamarens (Gers, arr. Condom).
115 Donzac (Tarn-et-Garonne, arr. Castelsarrasin).
116 Auvillar (Tarn-et-Garonne, arr. Castelsarrasin).
117 Castelmaurou (Haute-Garonne, arr. Toulouse).
118 Montastruc-la-Conseillère (Haute-Garonne, arr. Toulouse).
119 Rabastens (Tarn, arr. Albi).
120 L'Isle-d'Albi, today: Lisle-sur-Tarn (Tarn, arr. Albi).
121 Gaillac (Tarn, arr. Albi).
122 Cordes[-sur-Ciel] (Tarn, arr. Albi).
123 Sajas (Haute-Garonne, arr. Muret).
124 Pouy-de-Touges (Haute-Garonne, arr. Muret).
125 Beaufort (Haute-Garonne, arr. Muret).
126 Sainte-Mère (Gers, arr. Condom).
127 Cayrac (Tarn-et-Garonne, arr. Montauban).
128 Gramont (Tarn-et-Garonne, arr. Castelsarrasin).
129 Arnaud IV de Canteloup, archbishop of Bordeaux (1306–1332).
130 Gimont (Gers, arr. Auch).
131 Gérard de Lavergne was a sergeant probably from the diocese of Périgueux. In 1307, and probably earlier, he was commander of the house in Périgueux – A. Demurger, *Le peuple*, p. 245.
132 Lourdes (Hautes-Pyrénées, arr. Argèles-Gazost).
133 Armanieu II d'Armaniac, archbishop of Auch (1261–1318).
134 Saint-Jean (Haute-Garonne, arr. Toulouse).
135 Jacques de Jasseines was a royal notary between 1301 and 1327 – L. Perrichet, *La Grande chancellerie de France des origines à 1328* (Paris 1912), p. 543.
136 Silhac? (Ardèche, arr. Privas).
137 Carbonne (Haute-Garonne, arr. Muret).
138 Cazilhac (Aude, arr. Carcassonne or Hérault, arr. Lodève).
139 Montsoreau? (Maine-et-Loire, arr. Saumur).
140 Castelsarrasin (Tarn-et-Garonne, arr. Castelsarrasin).

141 Cadeilhan (Gers, arr. Condom).
142 Carcans? (Gironde, arr. Lespare-Médoc).
143 Caussade (Tarn-et-Garonne, arr. Montauban).
144 Cros? – several localities in southern France bear this name in various forms.
145 Fonneuve – locality in Montauban (Tarn-et-Garonne, arr. Montauban).
146 Lacapelle[-Livron] (Tarn-et-Garonne, arr. Montauban).
147 Quercy – historical province located in southwestern France.
148 Clairvaux[-d'Aveyron]? (Aveyron, arr. Rodez).
149 Cahors (Lot, arr. Cahors).
150 Cleisan – former locality in today's Marseillan (Hérault, arr. Montpellier).
151 Carcassès – region of Carcassonne.
152 Martin? – several localities in southern France bear the name Saint-Martin.
153 Hautefage (Corrèze, arr. Tulle).
154 Provins (Seine-et-Marne, arr. Provins).
155 Orléans (Loiret, arr. Orléans).
156 Breuil – several plces in France bear this name.
157 Baziège (Haute-Garonne, arr. Toulouse).
158 Saint-Ruf – environs of Saint-Ruf Abbey in Avignon (Vaucluse, arr. Avignon).
159 Simorre (Gers, arr. Auch).
160 Lebastide-du-Temple (Tarn-et-Garonne, arr. Castelsarrasin).
161 Cambon – former village where the Templars' house of Cambon-du-Temple was localed (Tarn, arr. Abli, comm. La Fraysse).
162 Arcins (Gironde, arr. Lesparre-Médoc).
163 Ventilhac – former village in today's Barry-d'Islemade (Tarn-et-Garonne, arr. Castelsarrassin).
164 Muret (Haute-Garonne, arr. Muret).
165 Mauriac (Aveyron, arr. Millau, comm. Saint-Laurent-de-Lévézou?).
166 Rodez (Aveyron, arr. Rodez).
167 Montsalvy (Cantal, arr. Aurillac).
168 Auterive – several localities in southwestern France bear this name.
169 Commandery of Andrivaux in Chancelade (Dordogne, arr. Périgueux).
170 Commandery of Puymartin in La Chapelle-Faucher (Dordogne, arr. Nontron).
171 Commandery of Soulet in Gout-Rossignol (Dordogne, arr. Périgueux).
172 Lafrançaise (Tarn-et-Garonne, arr. Montauban).
173 Géraud de Sabanac – probable deputy to the seneschal of Périgord from 1298 to 1303 and royal collector de Bigorre in 1324 – P. de Bosredon, 'Liste chronologique des sénéchaux du Périgord', *Bulletin de la Société historique et archéologique du Périgord*, 18 (1891), p. 339; L. Delisle, 'Chronologie des baillis et des sénéchaux royaux depuis des origines jusqu'à l'evènement de Philippe de Valois', in: *Recueil des historiens des Gaules et de la France*, 24 (Paris 1905), pp. 215, 223.
174 Gontaud[-de-Nogaret] (Lot-et-Garonne, arr. Marmande).
175 Cours (Lot-et-Garonne, arr. Agen).
176 La Rivière (Gironde, arr. Libourne)?
177 La Tour-Blanche (Dordogne, arr. Périgueux).
178 Chomelix? (Haute-Loire, arr. Le Puy-en-Velay).
179 Priory of Saint-Germier of Muret.
180 Montboucher (Creuse, arr. Guéret).
181 Charrières (Creuse, arr. Guéret, comm. Saint-Moreil)
182 Mortessagne (Haute-Vienne, arr. Limoges, comm. Saint-Léonard-de-Noblat).
183 Le Grand-Madieu (Charente, arr. Confelons).
184 Loubert[-Madieu] – former village (Charente, arr. Confolens).
185 La Jonchère[-Saint-Maurcie] (Haute-Vienne, arr. Limoges).
186 Paulhac (Haute-Garonne, arr. Toulouse).

187 Guichard II de Combron (1260–1319), Lord of Treignac and Chamberet.
188 Droux (Haute-Vienne, arr. Bellac).
189 Limoux (Aude, arr. Limoux).
190 Sylvanès (Aveyron, arr. Millau)?
191 Saint-Geniès – several localities in southwestern France bear this name.
192 Boulogne – several localities in France bear this name.
193 Galard – family originating from Condom in Gascony.
194 Roquepine (Gers, arr. Condon).
195 Larmont – former village (Haute-Garonne, arr. Toulouse, comm. Le Castéra).
196 Vaour (Tarn, arr. Albi).
197 Nogaret (Haute-Garonne, arr. Toulouse).
198 Saint-Merd (Corrèze, arr. Ussel, comm. Saint-Merd-les-Oussines).
199 Dompierre[-les-Églises] (Haute-Vienne, arr. Bellac).
200 Commander of La Bussiè-Rapy, arrested in 1307 – A. Demurger, *Le peuple*, p. 275.
201 Auzon or Ozon (Vienne, arr. Châtellerault, comm. Châtellerault).
202 La-Fôret[-du-Temple] (Creuse, arr. Guéret).
203 La Roche (Indre, arr. Châteauroux, comm. Arthon).
204 Saint-Léonard[-de-Noblat]?
205 La Pouge (Creuse, arr. Guéret).
206 Génis? (Dordogne, arr. Nontron).
207 La Souterraine (Creuse, arr. Guéret).
208 Châtelus – several localities in France bear this name.
209 Chabanais (Charente, arr. Confolens).
210 Tiffauges (Vandée, arr. La-Roche-sur-Yon).
211 Launac (Haute-Garonne, arr. Toulouse).
212 Bazas (Gironde, arr. Langon).
213 Lavaur (Tarn, arr. Castres).
214 Durfort[-Lacapelette] (Tarn-et-Garonne, arr. Caltelsarrasin).
215 Méras (Ariège, arr. Saint-Girons).
216 Bernard VI, count of Armagnac (1280–1319).
217 Montfrin (Gard, arr. Nîmes).
218 Argence (Gard, arr. Nîmes, comm. Bellegarde).
219 Saint-Pierre-du-Campublic (Gard, arr. Nîmes).
220 Issoudun (Indre, arr. Issoudun).
221 Moissac (Tarn-et-Garonne, arr. Castelsarrasin).
222 Le Fousseret (Haute-Garonne, arr. Muret).
223 Saint-Maurice – several localities in France bear this name.
224 Montauban (Tarn-et-Garonne, arr. Montauban).
225 Jean Bérenger – bailiff of Limousin from 1307 to 1313 – L. Delisle, 'Chronologie', p. 203.
226 Poitiers (Vienne, arr. Poitiers).
227 Craisseron, stream in today's department of Drôme.
228 Chaumont (Corrèze, arr. Brive-la-Gaillare, comm. Troche).
229 Argentens (Lot-et-Garonne, arr. Nérac, comm. Nérac).
230 Bussy – several localities in France bear this name.
231 Moncaut (Haute-Garonne, arr. Muret).
232 Bonnefont (Hautes-Pyrénées, arr. Tarbes).
233 Nérac (Lot-et-Garonne, arr. Nérac).
234 Cuq-Toulza (Tarn, arr. Castres).
235 Cluzel, hamlet in today's Bon-Encontre (Lot-et-Garonne, arr. Agen).
236 Clarac – several localities in southwestern France bear this name.
237 Tulle (Corrèze, arr. Tulle).
238 Reilhac (Lot, arr. Figeac).
239 Castet-Arrouy? (Gers, arr. Condom).

240 Layrac (Lot-et-Garonne, arr. Agen).
241 Pommiers (Gard, arr. Le Vigan).
242 Fabrègues (Hérault, arr. Montpellier).
243 Millau (Aveyron, arr. Millau).
244 Corneilhan (Hérault, arr. Béziers)
245 Combe – several localities in France bear this name in different forms.
246 Montferrat – several localities in southern France bear this name.
247 Aigues-Mortes (Gard, arr. Nîmes).
248 Saint-Gilles (Gard, arr. Nîmes).
249 Montpellier (Hérault, arr. Montpellier).
250 Mouchy-le-Châtel. Jean de Trie was seneschal of Toulouse, probably between 1321 and 1325 – L. Delisle, 'Chronologie', pp. 265–266; G. Dupont-Ferrier, *Gallia regia ou État des officiers royaux des bailliages et des sénéchaussées de 1328 à 1515*, vol. 5 (Paris 1958), p. 476.
251 Albi (Tarn, arr. Albi).
252 Pompignan (Gard, arr. Le Vigan or Tarn-et-Garonne, arr. Montauban).
253 La Brionne? (Creuse, arr. Guéret).
254 Marquefave (Haute-Garonne, arr. Muret).
255 La Trille – several localities in southwestern France bear this name.
256 Cantemerle, castel in Macau (Girone, arr. Bordeaux)?
257 Artiguelongue, hamlet in today's Loundeville (Hautes-Pyrénées, arr. Bagnères-de-Bigorre).
258 Mirepoix – several localities in southwestern France bear this name.
259 Arnay? – several localities in Burgundy bear this name.
260 Saint-Gaudens (Haute-Garonne, arr. Saint-Gaudens).
261 Saint-Paul – several localities in southwestern France bear this name.
262 Groslay? (Val-d'Oise, arr. Sarcelles).
263 Launaguet (Haute-Garonne, arr. Toulouse).
264 Betcave[-Aguin] (Gers, arr. Auch).
265 Montesquiou (Gers, arr. Mirande).
266 Saint-Quentin – several localities in southwestern France bear this name.
267 Cazaubon (Gers, arr. Condon).
268 Sauveterre[-en-Rouergue] (Aveyron, arr. Villefranche-de-Rouergue).
269 Auch (Gers, arr. Auch).
270 Roquenégade (Aude, arr. Carcassonne, comm. Val-de-Dagne).
271 Bas – many localities in France bear this name.
272 Altavaux – priory of (Haute-Vienne, arr. Rochechouart, comm. Dournazac).
273 Castelnau? – many localities in southern France bear this name in different forms.
274 Alençon (Orne, arr. Alençon).
275 Anjou – former county with Angers (Maine-et-Loire, arr. Angers) as its capital.
276 Rouergue – former province of France, corresponding with the today's department of Aveyron.
277 Mortagne – several localities in France bear this name.
278 Creysse (Lot, arr. Gourdon or Dordogne, arr. Bergerac).
279 Gascony – duchy, part of the duchy of Aquitaine.
280 Saint-Léger (Lot-et-Garonne, arr. Nérac).
281 Arnac – several localities in southwestern France bear this name.
282 Guillaume V Arnaud de La Mothe, bishop of Bazas (1302–1313).
283 Rosières (Tarn, arr. Albi)?
284 Puisseguin (Gironde, arr. Libourne).
285 Saint-Sulpice – several localities in southwestern France bear this name.
286 Le Dorat (Haute-Vienne, arr. Bellac).

Bibliography

Archival sources

Archives départementales de la Haute-Garonne (ADHG)
  BH wms 731
  H Malte 34, 89 II, 116, 123, 125–129
    Douzens
    La Cavalerie
    Lacapelle
    Pézeans
Archvies départementales du département du Rhône et de la métropole de Lyon (ADR)
  48 H (Ordre de Malte)
Archives départementales de la Vienne (ADV)
  3 H 1
Archives départementales de Tarn-et-Garonne (ADTG)
  H 317
Archives nationales (AN)
  Serie J (Trésor des Chartes, Layettes) 164, 413, 1036, 1044
  Serie JJ (Trésor des Chartes, Registres) 52
  Seire K (« Monuments historiques ») 37, 37 C, 38, 39
  Serie M (Ordres militaires et hospitaliers) 1
  Serie S (Biens des établissements religieux supprimés) 4952, 4999 A
Bibliothèque nationale de France, Département des manuscrits (BnF)
  Clairambault 8, 34, 1313
  Ms. fr. 4628, 8551, 10430, 20334, 25993, 26627
  Ms. lat. 9035, 9800, 17062
  Nouvelles Acquisitions Latines (NAL, Cartulaire de l'Ordre du Temple) 25, 32–34, 46, 57–58, 69

Printed sources

Acta Aragonensia: Quellen zur deutschen, italienischen, französischen, spanischen Kirchen- und Kulturgeschichte aus der diplomatischen Korrespondenz Jaymes II., 1291–1327, ed. H. Finke, vol. 1–3 (Berlin: W. Rotschild, 1908).

Acta Clementis PP. V, ed. F. M. Delorme, A. L. Tautu (Vatican: Typis Polyglottis Vaticanis, 1955).

Actes du Parlament de Paris, ed. E. Boutaric, vol. 2, *1299–1328* (Paris: Plon, 1867).

Adae Murimuth Continuatio Chronicarum. Robertus de Avesbury de Gestis Mirabilibus Regis Edwardi Tertii, ed. E. Maunde Thomson (London: H. M. Stationery Office, 1889, repr. Cambridge: Cambridge University Press, 2012).

Archives historiques de la Saintonge et de l'Aunis, vol. 12, *Documents Relatifs à l'histoire de la Saintonge et de l'Aunis extraits des registres du Trésor des chartes*, ed. P. Guérin (Saintes: Z. Montreuil, 1884).

Auberti Miraei opera diplomatica et historica, ed. J. F. Foppens, vol. 1–4 (Bruxelles: Foppens, 1723–1748).

Barbiche, Bernard, *Les actes pontificaux originaux des Archives nationales de Paris*, vol. 1–3 (Città del Vaticano: Biblioteca apostolica vaticana, 1975–1982).

Boniface VIII en procès. Articles d'accusation et dépositions des témoins (1303–1311), ed. J. Coste (Rome: L'Erma di Bretchneider: 1995).

Boutaric, Edgard, 'Notices et extraits de documents inédits relatifs à l'histoire de France sous Philippe le Bel', *Notices et extraits des manuscrits de la Bibliothèque Impériale*, 20 (1865), pt. 2, pp. 83–237.

Bullarium Cyprium, vol. 1–3, ed. C. Schabel, C. Perrat, J. Richard (Nikosia: Cyprus Research Centre, 2010–2012).

Bullarium Franciscanum romanorum pontificum constitutiones epistolas, ac diplomata continens, ed. G. Giacinto Sbaraglia, C. Eubel, vol. 1–7 (Rome: Typis Sacrae Congregationis De Propaganda Fide, 1759–1904).

Cartulaire des Hospitaliers (Ordre de Saint-Jean de Jérusalem) du Velay, ed. A. Chassaing (Paris: A. Picard, 1888).

Cartulaire et archives des communes de l'ancien diocèse et de l'arrondissement administratif de Carcassonne, ed. A. Mahul, vol 1–8 (Paris: V. Didron, 1857–1882).

Cartulaire général de l'Ordre des Hospitaliers de S. Jean de Jérusalem 1100–1310, ed. J. Delaville le Roulx, vol. 1–4 (Paris: Ernest Leroux, 1894–1906).

Chronicon Galfridi le Baker de Swynebroke, ed. E. Maunde Thomson (Oxford: Clarendon Press 1889).

Chronique latine de Guillaume de Nangis, de 1113 à 1300 avec les continuations de cette chronique de 1300 à 1368, ed. H. Géraud, vol. 1–2 (Paris: J. Renouard, 1843).

Codice diplomatico del sacro militare ordine Gerosolimitano, ed. S. Paoli, vol. 1–2 (Lucca: Salvatore e Giandomenico Marescandoli, 1733–1737).

Conciliorum oecumenicorum decreta, ed. G. Alberigo et al. (Basel: Herder, 1962).

Corpus documentorum inquisitionis haereticiae pravitatis Neerlandicae, ed. P. Frédéricq, vol. 1–5 (Ghent: J. Vuylsteke, 1889–1906).

'Der Nachlass Clemens V und der in Betreff desselben von Johann XXII (1318–1321) geführte Process' ed. F. Ehrle, *Archiv fur Literatur und Kirchengeschichte des Mittelalters*, 5 (1889), pp. 1–166.

Documents concernants les Templiers extraits des Archives de Malte, ed. J. Delaville le Roulx (Paris: E. Plon, 1882).

Documents inédits pour servir à l'histoire du Poitou poubliés par la Société des antiquaires de l'Ouest (Poitiers 1876).

'Excerpta e memoriali historiarum auctore Johanne Parisiensi, Sancti Vistoris Parisiensis canonico regulari' ed. L. Delisle, in: *Recueil des historiens des Gaules et de la France*, ed. M. Bouquet et al., vol. 21 (Paris 1855), pp. 630–676.

Foedera, conventiones, literae et cuiuscunque generis acta publica inter reges Angliae et alios quosvis imperatores, reges ... ab anno 1101 ad nostra usque tempora (3rd ed.), ed. T. Rymer, vol. 1–10 (Hague: Neaulme, 1739–1745).

Formulaires de lettres du XIIe, du XIIIe et du XIVe siècle, ed. C. V. Langlois (Paris: Imprimerie nationale, 1890).

Gascon Register A (1318–1319). Edited from British Museum Cottonian M. S. Julius E.i., ed. G. P. Cuttino, vol. 1–3 (London: Oxford University Press, 1975–1976).

Inventaire d'anciens comptes royaux, ed. R. Mignon, C. V. Langlois (Paris: Imprimerie nationale, 1899).

Inventaire des ornements et vases sacrés de la chapelle de la commanderie de Joigny, au commencement du XIVe siècle, ed. A. Tardif, *Annales archéologiques*, 7 (1847), pp. 85–86.

Jean XXII, *Lettres communes analysées d'après les registres dits d'Avignon et du Vatican*, ed. G. Mollat, vol. 1–16 (Paris: De Boccard, 1904–1946).

Lalou, Élisabeth, *Itinéraire de Philippe IV le Bel*, vol. 1–2 (Paris: De Boccard, 2007).

Langlois, Charles-Victor, 'Registres perdus des archives de la Chambre des comptes de Paris', *Notices et extraits des manuscrits de la Bibliothèque nationale*, 40 (1917), pp. 33–380.

L'Enquête pontificale de 1373 sur l'Ordre des Hospitaliers de Saint-Jean de Jérusalem, ed. A. M. *Legras*, vol. 1, *L'enquête dans le prieuré de France* (Paris: Éditions du Centre national de la recherche scientifique, 1987).

Le dossier de l'affaire des Templiers, ed. and trans. G. Lizerand (Paris: Champion, 1923, repr. 1964, 1989).

Le Procès des Templiers, ed. J. Michelet, vol. 1–2 (Paris: Imprimerie nationale, 1841–1851).

Les journaux du trésor de Charles IV le Bel, ed. J. Viard (Paris: Imprimerie nationale, 1917).

Les journaux du trésor de Philippe IV le Bel, ed. J. Viard (Paris: Imprimerie nationale, 1940).

Les journaux du trésor de Philippe VI de Valois suivis de l'ordinarium thesauri de 1338–1339, ed. J. Viard (Paris: Imprimerie nationale, 1899).

Les Olim, ou Registres des arrêts rendus par la Cour du Roi: sous les règnes de Saint Louis, de Philippe Le Hardi, de Philippe Le Bel, de Louis Le Hutin et de Philippe Le Long, ed. A. A. Beugnot, vol. 1–3 (Paris: Imprimerie royale, 1839–1848).

'Les papiers de Guillaume de Nogaret et de Guillaume de Plaisians au Trésor des chartes' ed. C. V. Langlois, *Notices et extraits des manuscrits de la Bibliothèque Impériale*, 39 (1908), pp. 211–254.

Lettres de Jean XXII (1316–1334), ed. A. Fayen, vol. 1–2 (Rome: M. Bretschneider, 1908–1912).

Lettres de rois, reines et autres personnages des cours de France et d'Angleterre depuis Louis VII jusqu'à Henri IV tirées des archives de Londres, ed. J. J. Champillon-Figeac, vol. 1–2 (Paris 1839–1847).

Lettres secrètes et curiales du Pape Jean XXII (1316–1334), relatives à la France, ed. A. Coulon, S. Clémencet, vol. 1–5 (Paris: De Boccard, 1906–1967).

Livre de Guillaume le Maire, ed. C. Port, Mélanges historiques, choix de documents, vol. 2 (Paris: Imprimerie nationale, 1874).

Loisine, Auguste de, 'Bulles de papes pour l'ordre du Temple conservées aux Archives nationales (1155–1312)', *Bulletin philologique et historique du comité des travaux historiques*, 31 (1917), pp. 171–236.

Lucca, Tholomeus von, *Historia ecclesiastica nova nebst Fortsetzungen bis 1329*, ed. O. Clavout, L. Schmugge, Monumenta Germaniae Historica, Scriptores, vol. 39 (Hannover: Hahn, 2009).

Memorias de D. Fernando IV de Castilla, ed. A. Benavides, vol. 1–2 (Madrid: J. Rodriguez, 1860).

Monumenta Germaniae Historica. Constitutiones et Acta Publica Imperatorum et Regum, vol. 4.1, ed. J. Schwalm (Hannover: Hahnsche, 1906).

Monumenta Henricina, ed. A. J. Dias Dinis, vol. 1–15 (Coimbra: Atlântida, 1960–1974).

Monuments historiques: cartons des rois, ed. J. Tardif (Paris: J. Claye, 1866, repr. 1977).

Papsttum und Untergang des Templerordens, ed. H. Finke, vol. 1–2 (Müntzer: Aschendorff, 1907).

Procès-verbal de remise de maisons diverses des Templiers aux chevaliers hospitaliers de Saint-Jean De Jérusalem dans le Poitou (20 mai de l'année 1313), ed. C. Tranchant (Poitiers: Tolmer, 1882).

Processus contra Templarios in Francia. Procès-verbaux de la procédure menée par la commission pontificale à Paris (1309–1311), vol. 1–2, ed. M. Satora (Leiden: BRILL, 2020).

Recueil general des titres, concernant les fonctions, rangs, dignitez, seances et privileges des charges des presidens tresoriers de France, generaux des finances, et grands voyers des generalitez du royaume, ed. S. Fournival (Paris: A. Chouqueux, 1655).

Regestum Clementis papae V ex Vaticanis archetypis [...] edito, cura et studio monachorum ordinis sancti Benedicti, vol. 1–9 (Rome: Ex Typographia Vaticana, 1885–1892).

Registres du Trésor des chartes, ed. R. Fawtier, vol. 1–3 (Paris: SEVPEN, 1958–1984).

Registrum Simonis de Gandavo: diocesis Saresbiriensis, AD 1297–1315, ed. C. T. Flower, M. C. Burdett Dawes, vol. 1–2 (Oxford: Oxford University Press, 1914–1934).

The Chronicle of Amadi, transl. N. Coureas, P. Edbury (Nicosia: Cyprus Research Centre, 2015).

The Chronicle of Walter of Guisborough Previously Edited as the Chronicle of Walter of Hemingford or Hemingburgh, ed. H. Rothwell (London: Offices of the Society, 1957).

The Templars: Selected Sources, trans. and annotated by M. Barber, K. Bate (Manchester: Manchester Univeristy Press, 2002).

Thomae Walsingham, quondam monachi S. Albani, Historia Anglicana, ed. H. T. Riley, vol. 1–2 (London: Longmans, Green, Longman, Roberts, and Green, 1863–1864).

Villani, Giovanni, *Nuova cronica*, ed. G. Porta, vol. 1–3 (Parma: Guanda, 1990).

Vitae Paparum Avenionensium, ed. E. Baluze, reed. G. Mollat, vol. 1–4 (Paris: Letouzey et Ané, 1914–1927).

Secondary literature

Alart, Bernard, 'Suppression de l'ordre du Temple en Roussillon', *Bulletin de la Société agricole, scientifique et littéraire des Pyrénées-Orientales*, 15 (1867), pp. 25–115.

Baethgen, Friedrich, 'Neue Beiträge zur Geschichte des päpstlichen Finanzwesens um die Wende des 13. Jahrhunderts', *Quellen und Forschungen aus Italienischen Biblioteken und Archiven*, 24 (1932–1933), pp. 124–149.

Baix, François, 'Notes sur les clercs de la Chambre apostolique (XIIIe–XIVe siècles)', *Bulletin de l'Institut historique belge de Rome*, 27 (1952), pp. 17–25.

Barber, Malcolm, 'Supplying the Crusader States: The Role of the Templars', in: *The Horns of Hattin: proceedings of the second conference of the Society for the Study of the Crusades and the Latin East: Jerusalem and Haïfa, 2-6 July 1987,* ed. Benjamin Z. Kedar (Jerusalem: Israel exploration socjety, 1992), pp. 314–326, repr. in: *Medieval Warfare 1100–1300,* ed. J. France (Aldershot: Ashgate, 2006), pp. 585–597.

Barber, Malcolm, 'The Trial of the Templars Revisited', in: *The Military Orders*, vol. 2, *Welfare and Warfare*, ed. H. Nicholson (Aldershot: Ashgate, 1998), pp. 329–342.

Barber, Malcolm, *The Trial of the Templars* (2nd ed). (Cambridge: Cambridge University Press, 2006).

Beaucage, Benoît, 'La saisie des biens provençaux de l'ordre du Temple', in: *Normes et pouvoir à la fin du moyen âge: actes du Colloque « La recherche en études médiévales au Québec et en Ontario », 16-17 mai 1989, Montréal*, ed. M. C. Déprez-Masson (Montréal: CERES, 1989), pp. 85–103.

Bellomo, Elena, *The Templar Order in North-west Italy (1142-c. 1330)* (Leiden: BRILL, 2008).

Bellomo, Elena, 'Colliding Perceptions: Italian Views of the Templar Trial from Contemporary Authors to Angelo Fumagalli's Delle antichità longobardico-milanesi (1792)', in: *The Templars. The Rise, Fall, and Legacy of a Military Religious Order*, ed. J. Burgtorf, S. Lotan, E. Mallorquí-Ruscalleda (London–New York: Routledge, 2021), pp. 274–298.

Berchon, Ernest, 'Histoire du pape Clément V', *Actes de l'Académie nationale des Sciences, Belles Lettres et Arts de Bordeaux*, 3th series, 55 (1893), pp. 493–535; 56 (1894), pp. 5–171.

Bessey, Valérie, *Les commanderies de l'Hôpital en Picardie au temps des chevaliers de Rhodes, 1309–1522* (Millau: Conservatoire Larzac Templier et Hospitalier, 2005).

Blancard, Louis, 'Documents relatifs au procès des Templiers en Angleterre', *Revue des sociétés savantes*, 4th. ser. 6 (1867), pp. 414–423.

Bompaire, Marc, 'Trésor des Templiers et trésor des Juifs au XIVe siècle', *Bulletin de la Société française de numismatique*, 53 (1998), no. 7, pp. 185–188.

Bordonove, Georges, *La Tragédie des Templiers* (3rd ed.) (Paris: Tallandier, 2011).

Bordonove, Georges, *Philippe le Bel: Roi de fer* (2nd ed.) (Paris: Pygmalion, 2013).

Borrelli de Serres, Léon-Louis, *Recherches sur divers services publics du XII au XVIIe siècle*, vol. 1–3 (Paris: A. Picard et fils, 1895–1909).

Borrelli de Serres, Léon-Louis, 'Les variations monétaires sous Philippe le Bel et les sources de leur histoire', *Gazette numismatique française*, 6 (1902), pp. 9–67.

Bosredon, Philippe de, 'Liste chronologique des sénéchaux du Périgord', *Bulletin de la Société historique et archéologique du Périgord*, 18 (1891), pp. 330–342.

Bourgain, Louis, 'Contribution du clergé à l'impôt sous la monarchie française', *Revue des questions historiques*, 48 (1890), pp. 62–132.

Boutaric, Edgard, 'Clément V, Philippe le Bel et les Templiers', *Revue des questions historiques*, 10 (1871), pp. 301–342 and 11 (1872), pp. 5–41.

Brown, Elisabeth A. R., 'The Political Repercussions of Family Ties in the Early Fourteenth Century: The Marriage of Edward II of England and Isabelle of France', *Speculum*, 63 (1988), no. 3, pp. 573–595.

Brown, Elisabeth A. R., 'Philip V, Charles IV, and the Jews of France: The Alleged Expulsion of 1322', *Speculum*, 66 (1991), no. 2, pp. 294–329.

Brown, Elisabeth A. R., 'Royal Salvation and Needs of State in Early-Fourteenth-Century France', in: E. A. R. Brown, *The Monarchy of Capetian France and Royal Ceremonial* (Aldershot: Ashgate, 1991), IV, pp. 1–56, first published in: *Order and Innovation in the Middle Ages. Essays in Honor of Joseph R. Strayer*, ed. W. C. Jordan, B. McNab, T. F. Ruiz (Princeton: Princeton University Press, 1976), pp. 365–383.

Brown, Elisabeth A. R., *Customary Aids and Royal Finance in Capetian France: The Marriage Aid of Philip the Fair* (Cambridge: The Medieval academy of America, 1992).

Brown, Elisabeth A. R., 'Philip the Fair's Sons, Their Statuses, and Their Landed Endowments', *Medieval Prosopography*, 32 (2017), pp. 186–227.

Brown, Elisabeth A. R., Forey, Alan, '*Vox in excelso* and the Suppresion of the Knights Templar: The Bull, Its History, and a New Edition', *Medieval Studies*, 80 (2018), pp. 1–58.

Bryson, David, 'Three "Traitors" of the Temple: Was Their Truth the Whole Truth?', in: *The Debate on the Trial of the Templars (1307–1314)*, ed. J. Burgtorf, P. F. Crawford, H. J. Nicholson (Farnham: Ashgate, 2010), pp. 97–103.

Bryson, David Morrow, 'Clement V and the Road to Avignon, 1304–1309', in: *On the Margins of Crusading: The Military Orders, the Papacy and the Christian World*, ed. H. Nicholson (Farnham: Ashgate, 2011), pp. 61–73.

Bulst-Thiele, Marie Luise, *Sacrae domus militiae Templi Hierosolymitani magistri: Untersuchungen zur Geschichte des Templerordens 1118/19–1314* (Göttingen: Vandenhoeck und Ruprecht, 1974).

Burgtorf, Jochen, 'The Trial Inventories of the Templars' Houses in France: Select Aspects', in: *The Debate on the Trial of the Templars (1307–1314)*, ed. J. Burgtorf, P. F. Crawford, H. J. Nicholson (Farnham: Ashgate, 2010), pp. 105–115.

Carraz, Damien, 'Chartiers privés et autres documents familiaux conservés dans les archives templières. Le cas de quelques commanderies du Midi français', in: *Commilitones Christi. Miscellanea di studi per il Centro Italiano di Documentazione sull'Ordine del Tempio, MMXI–MMXVI*, ed. S. Sammarco (Rome: Lisanti editore, 2016), pp. 167–192.

Carraz, Damien, Chevalier, Marie-Anna, 'Le marquis d'Albon (1866–1912) et son Cartulaire général de l'ordre du Temple', *Hereditas Monasteriorum*, 1 (2012), pp. 107–128.

Carter, James Robert Jr., 'Gascon Archival Materials in a British Museum Manuscript', *Manuscripta*, 16 (1972), no. 3, pp. 145–155.

Caselli, Fausto Piola, 'L'espansione delle fonti finanziare della Chiesa nel XIV secolo', *Archivio della Società romana di storia patria*, 110 (1987), pp. 63–97.

Caselli, Fausto Piola, 'L'evoluzione della contabilità camerale nel periodo Avignonese', in: *Aux origines de l'État moderne. Le fonctionnement administratif de la papauté d'Avignon. Actes de la table ronde d'Avignon (23–24 janvier 1988)* (Rome: École française de Rome, 1990), pp. 411–437.

Causse, Bernard, *Eglise, finance, et royauté: la floraison des décimes dans la France au Moyen Age*, vol. 1–2 (Lille-Paris: ANRT, 1988).

Cazelles, Raymond, 'Les variations du prélèvement et de la répartition selon les équipes au pouvoir', in: *Genèse de l'État moderne: prélèvement* et *redistribution. Actes du colloque* de *Fontevraud, 1984*, ed. J. P. Genèt, M. Le Mené (Paris: Centre national de la recherche scientifique, 1987), pp. 203–207.

Chaplais, Pierre, 'Règlement des conflits internationaux franco – anglais au XIVe siècle (1293–1337)', *Le Moyen Âge*, 57 (1951), pp. 269–302.

Chaplais, Pierre, 'La souveraineté du roi de France et le pouvoir législatif en Guyenne au début du XIVe siècle', *Le Moyen Âge*, 69 (1963), pp. 449–469, repr. Chaplais, Pierre, *Essays in Medieval Diplomacy and Administration* (London: Hambledon Press, 1981), no. V.

Charmasse, Anatole de, *État des possessions des Templiers et des Hospitaliers en Maconnais, Charollais, Lyonnais, Forez et partie de la Bourgogne d'après une enquête de 1333* (Paris: H. Champion, 1878).

Clémens, Jacques, 'La rumeur agenaise de l'enfermement templier au début du XIVe siècle', *Revue de l'Agenais*, 123 (1996), pp. 219–233 and 124 (1997), pp. 23–40.

Clémens, Jacques, Demurger Alain, 'Esquieu de Floyran', in: *Prier et combattre: Dictionnaire européen des ordres militaires au Moyen Âge*, ed. N. Bériou, P. Josserand (Paris: Fayard, 2009), pp. 339–340.

Courtieu, Jean, Courtieu, Anne-Marie, *Sources parisiennes relatives à l'histoire de la Franche-Comté, incluant le catalogue des manuscrits relatifs à la Franche-Comté qui sont conservés dans les bibliothèques publiques de Paris, par Ulysse Robert, 1878* (Besançon: Presses universitaires franc-comtoises, 2001).

Crawford, Paul F., 'The University of Paris and the Trial of the Templars', in: *The Military Orders*, vol. 3, *History and Heritage*, ed. V. Mallia-Milanes (Aldershot: Ashgate, 2008), pp. 115–122.

Curzon, Henri de, *La maison de Temple de Paris. Histoire et description* (Paris: Hachette, 1888).

Dailliez, Laurent, *La France des Templiers* (Paris: Marabout, 1974).

Delaville Le Roulx, Joseph, *La France en Orient au XIVe siècle*, vol. 1–2 (Paris: E. Thorin, 1886).

Delaville Le Roulx, Joseph, 'La suppression des Templiers', *Revue des Questions historiques*, 68 (1890), pp. 29–61.

Delaville Le Roulx, Joseph Marie Antoine, *Les hospitaliers à Rhodes jusqu'à la mort de Philibert de Naillac (1310–1421)* (Paris: E. Leroux, 1913).

Delisle, Léopold, *Mémoire sur les opérations financières des Templiers* (Paris: Imprimerie nationale, 1889).

Delisle, Léopold, *Études sur la condition de la classe agricole et l'état de l'agriculture en Normandie au moyen-âge* (Paris: H. Champion, 1903).

Delisle, Léopold, 'Chronologie des baillis et des sénéchaux royaux depuis des origines jusqu'à l'evènement de Philippe de Valois', in: *Recueil des historiens des Gaules et de la France*, ed. M. Bouquet et al., vol. 24 (Paris 1905), pp. 15–270.

Delmas, Jean, 'L'inventaire des biens de la commanderie de Sainte-Eulalie du Larzac en 1308', in: *La Commanderie, institution des ordres militaires dans l'Occident médiéval*, ed. A. Luttrell, L. Pessouyre (Paris: Comité des travaux historiques et scientifiques, 2002), pp. 319–328.

Demurger, Alain, 'Dal Tempio all'Ospedale. Il destino delle commende templari nella contea di Auxerre (secoli XIV)', in: *Acri 1291. La fine della presenza degli ordini militari in Terra Santa e i nuovi orientamenti nel XIV secolo*, ed. F. Tommasi (Perugia: Quattroemme, 1996), pp. 93–98.

Demurger, Alain, 'Trésor des Templiers, trésor du roi. Mise au point sur les opérations financières des templiers', *Pouvoir et Gestion*, 5 (1997), pp. 73–85.

Demurger, Alain, 'Les ordres militaires et la croisade au début du XIVe siècle: Quelques remarques sur les traités de croisade de Jacques de Molay et de Foulques de Villaret', in: *Dei gesta per Francos. Etudes sur les croisades dédiées à Jean Richard – Crusade Studies in Honour of Jean Richard*, ed. M. Balard, B. Z. Kedar, J. Riley-Smith (Aldershot: Ashgate, 2001), pp. 117–128.

Demurger, Alain, *Chevaliers du Christ: Les ordres religieux-militaires au Moyen Âge (Xie-XVIe siècle)* (Paris: Seuil, 2002), repr. *Moynes et Guerriers. Les ordres religieux-militaires au Moyen Âge* (Paris: Seuil, 2014).

Demurger, Alain, *Les Templiers. Une chevalerie chrétienne au Moyen Âge* (Paris: Seuil, 2005).

Demurger, Alain, *Jacques de Molay: Le crépuscule des Templiers* (Paris: Payot & Rivages, 2007).

Demurger, Alain, 'Le concile de Vienne, la dévolution des biens du Temple et le sort des Templiers', in: *Templiers: De Jérusalem aux commanderies de Champagne*, ed. A. Baudin, G. Brunel, N. Dohrmann (Paris: Somogy, 2012), pp. 154–159.

Demurger, Alain, *Les Hospitaliers: De Jérusalem à Rhodes, 1050–1317* (Paris: Tallandier, 2013).

Demurger, Alain, *La persécution des templiers. Journal (1305–1314)* (Paris: Payot, 2015).

Demurger, Alain, 'Les ordres religieux-militaires et l'argent: sources et pratiques', in: *The Templars and Their Sources*, ed. K. Borchardt, K. Döring, P. Josserand, H. J. Nicholson (Farnham: Ashgate, 2017), pp. 166–183.

Demurger, Alain, 'Othon de Grandson et les templiers d'Épailly', in: *Communicating the Middle Ages: Essays in Honour of Sophia Menache*, ed. I. Shagrir, B. Z. Kedar, M. Balard (London–New York: Routledge, 2018), pp. 39–49.

Demurger, Alain, 'La "prisée" de la maison templière d'Épailly en 1308', *Bulletin archéologique et historique du Chatillonais*, 1 (2019), pp. 32–48.

Demurger, Alain, *Le peuple templier, 1307–1312. Catalogue prosopographique des templiers présents ou (et) cités dans les procès–verbaux des interrogatoires faits dans le royaume de France entre 1307 et 1312* (Paris: CNRS, 2019).

Devals, Jean Ursule, 'Montricoux', *Mémoires de l'Académie impériale des sciences, inscriptions et belles-lettres de Toulouse*, 2 (1864), pp. 122–162.

Devic, Claude, Vaissète, Joseph, *Histoire générale de Languedoc*, ed. E. Barry et al., vol. 1–16 (Toulouse: E. Privat, 1870–1905).

Dietz, Karlheinz, 'Die Templer und das Turiner Grabtuch', in: *The Templars and Their Sources*, ed. K. Borchardt, K. Döring, P. Josserand, H. J. Nicholson (Farnham: Ashgate, 2017), pp. 223–259.

Dieudonné, Adolphe, 'Les variations monétaires sous Philippe le Bel', *Le Moyne Âge*, 9 (1905), pp. 217–257.

Digard, Georges, *Philippe le Bel et le Saint-Siège de 1285 à 1304*, vol. 1–2 (Paris: Sirey, 1936).

Dossant Yves, 'Les Juifs à Toulouse: un demi-siècle d'histoire communautaire', *Cahiers de Fenjeaux*, 12 (1977), pp. 117–139.

Du Bourg, Antoine, 'Prise de Possession par les Hospitaliers de la Maison du Temple de Toulouse', *Mémoires de la Société archéologique du Midi de la France*, 11 (1874/1879), pp. 172–185.

Du Bourg, Antoine, *Histoire du Grand-Prieuré de Toulouse* (Toulouse: L. Sistac et J. Boubée, 1883).

Dubourg, Jacques, 'La commanderie de Romestaing', *Revue de l'Agenais*, 130 (2003), no. 2, pp. 127–144.

Dupont-Ferrier, Gustave, *Gallia regia ou État des officiers royaux des bailliages et des sénéchaussées de 1328 à 1515*, vol. 1–7 (Paris: Imprimerie nationale, 1942–1966).

Dupuy, Pierre, *Histoire du differend d'entre le pape Boniface VIII et Philippes le Bel roy de France* (Paris: S. et G. Cramoisy, 1655).

Dupuy, Pierre, *Histoire de la condamnation des Templiers* (Bruxelles: F. Foppens, 1713).

Dürrholder, Gottfried, *Die Kreuzzugspolitik unter* Papst Johann XXII *(1316–1334)* (Strasbourg: J. H. E. Heitz, 1913).

Duval, Michel, 'La dévolution des biens du Temple aux Hospitaliers en Bretagne', in: *Actes du 97e Congrès national des Sociétés Savantes (Nantes, 1972). Assistance et assistés jusqu'au XVIe siècle* (Paris 1979), pp. 287–298.

Edbury, Peter W., *The Kingdom of Cyprus and the Crusaders, 1191–1374* (Cambridge: Cambridge University Press, 1991).

Elm, Kaspar, 'Der Templerprozeß (1307–1312)', in: *Macht und Recht. Große Prozesse in der Geschichte*, ed. A. Demandt (München: C. H. Beck, 1990), pp. 81–102.

Favier, Jean, *Un conseiller de Philippe le Bel: Enguerran de Marigny* (Paris: PUF, 1963), reed. in: Favier, Jean, *Un roi de marbre. Philippe le Bel, Enguerrand de Marigny* (Paris: Fayard, 2005), pp. 509–874.

Favier, Jean, *Philippe le Bel* (Paris: Fayard, 1978).

Favier, Jean, *Les papes d'Avignon* (Paris: Fayard, 2006).

Favreau, Robert, 'L'enquête pontificale de 1373 sur l'ordre de l'Hôpital dans le grand prieuré d'Aquitaine', *Bibliothèque de l'École des chartes*, 164 (2006), pp. 447–538.

Félibien, Michel, *Histoire de la ville de Paris*, vol. 1–5 (Paris: G. Desprez, 1725).

Finot, Jules, *Les sires de Faucogney, vicomtes de Vesoul: notices et documents* (Paris: H. Chamion, 1886).

Forey, Alan J., 'The Military Orders in the Crusading Proposals of the Late-Thirteenth and Early-Fourteenth Centuries', *Viator*, 38 (1980), pp. 317–345.

Forey, Alan, *The Military Orders. From the Twelfth to Early Fourteenth Centuries* (Toronto and Buffalo: Macmillan, 1992).

Forey, Alan, *The Fall of the Templars in the Crown of Aragon* (Aldershot: Ashgate, 2001).

Forey, Alan, J., 'Ex-Templars in England', *Journal of Ecclesiastical History*, 53 (2002), no. 1, pp. 18–37.

Forey, Alan, 'Templars after the Trial. Further Evidence', *Revue Mabillon*, 23 (2012), pp. 89–110.

Forey, Alan, 'Otto of Grandson and the Holy Land, Cyprus and Armenia', *Crusades*, 16 (2017), pp. 79–93.

Forey, Alan, 'Fugitives during the Templar Trial', in: *The Templars. The Rise, Fall, and Legacy of a Military Religious Order*, ed. J. Burgtorf, S. Lotan, E. Mallorquí-Ruscalleda (London–New York: Routledge, 2021), pp. 188–208.

Fossier, Robert, 'Les Hospitaliers et les Templiers au nord de la Seine et en Bourgogne (XIIe–XIVe siècles)', in: *Les ordres militaires: La vie rurale et le peuplement en Europe occidentale (XIIe–XVIIIe siècles)*, ed. C. Higounet (Toulouse: Presses universitaires du Midi, 1986), pp. 13–36.

Frale, Barbara, *L'ultima battaglia dei Templari. Dal codice ombra d'obedienza militare alla construzione del processo per eresia* (Rome: Viella, 2001).

Gaulejac, Bernard de, *La liquidation des biens de l'ordre du Temple dans le Sud-Ouest de la France*, 1925 (unpublished thesis, ADHG, BH wms 731).

Gavrilovitch, Michel, *Étude sur le traité de Paris de 1259 entre Louis IX, roi de France & Henri III, roi d'Angleterre* (Paris: E. Bouillon, 1899).

Geslin de Bourgogne, Jules Henri, *Anciens évêchés de Bretagne*, vol. 6, *Bretagne féodale et militaire* (Saint-Brieuc: F. Guyon, 1879).

Gilmour-Bryson, Anne, '*Vox in excelso* Deconstructed: Exactly What Did Clement V Say?', in: *On the Margins of Crusading. The Military Orders, the Papacy and the Christian World*, ed. H. Nicholson (Farnham: Ashgate, 2011), pp. 75–88.

Glénisson, Jean, 'L'enquête pontificale de 1373 sur les possessions des Hospitaliers de Saint-Jean de Jérusalem', *Bibliothèque de l'École des chartes*, 129 (1971), pp. 83–111.

Goineaud-Bérard, André, *Templiers et Hospitaliers en Perigord* (Bordeaux: Pilote, 2002).

Goñi, Carlos Barquero, 'La Orden del Hospital y la recepción de los bienes templarios en la Península Ibérica', *Hispania Sacra*, 51 (1999), no. 104, pp. 531–556.

Guérard, Louis, 'La succession de Clément V et le procès de Bertrand de Got, vicomte de Lomagne (1318–1321)', *Revue de Gascogne*, 32 (1891), pp. 5–20.

Guéry, Charles, *La Commanderie de Saint-Etienne-de-Renneville (Eure) fondée par Richard d'Harcourt* (Évreux: l'Eure, 1896).

Guillemain, Bernard, *Les recettes et les dépenses de la Chambre apostolique pour la quatrième année du pontificat de Clément V (1308–1309): introitus et exitus 75* (Rome: École française de Rome, 1978).

Hamilton, Jeffrey S., 'Apocalypse Not: Edward II and the Suppression of the Templars', *Medieval Perspectives*, 12 (1997), pp. 90–100.

Hamilton, Jeffrey S., 'King Edward II of England and the Templars', in: *The Debate on the Trial of the Templars (1307–1314)*, ed. J. Burgtorf, P. F. Crawford, H. J. Nicholson (Farnham: Ashgate, 2010), pp. 215–224.

Heidelberger, Franz, *Kreuzzugsversuche um die Wende des 13. Jahrhuderts* (Berlin: W. Rothschild, 1911).

Higounet-Nadal, Arlette, 'L'inventaire des biens de la commanderie des templiers de Sainte-Eulalie du Larzac en 1308', *Annales du Midi*, 68 (1956), pp. 255–262.

Hillgarth, Joclyn N., *Ramon Lull and Lullism in Fourteenth-Century France* (Oxford: Oxford Univeristy Press, 1971).

Histoire de Carcassonne (2nd ed.), ed. J. Guilaine, D. Fabre (Toulouse: Privat, 1990).

Hooghe, Filip, 'The Trial of the Templars in the County of Flanders (1307–1312)', in: *The Debate on the Trial of the Templars (1307–1314)*, ed. J. Burgtorf, P. F. Crawford, H. J. Nicholson (Farnham: Ashgate, 2010), pp. 285–299.

Housley, Norman, 'Pope Clement V and the Crusades of 1309–10', *Journal of Medieval History*, 8 (1982), pp. 29–43.

Housley, Norman, *The Avignon Papacy and the Crusades, 1305–1378* (Oxford 1986).

Jefferson, Michael J., 'Edward II and the Templar Lands in Lincolnshire', in: *L'économie templière en Occident. Patrimoines, commerce, finances: Actes du colloque international, Troyes, abbaye de Clairvaux, 24-26 octobre 2012*, ed. A. Baudin, G. Brunel, N. Dohrmann (Langres: D. Guéniot, 2013), pp. 295–321.

Jefferson, Michael J., *The Templar Estates in Lincolnshire, 1185–1565: Agriculture and Economy* (Woodbridge: The Boydell Press, 2020).

Johnson, Charles, 'The Homage for Guienne in 1304', *English Historical Review*, 23 (1908), pp. 728–729.

Josserand, Philippe, 'Les Templiers en Bretagne au Moyen Âge: mythes et réalités', *Annales de Bretagne et des Pays de l'Ouest,* 119 (2012), no. 4, pp. 7–33.

Josserand, Philippe, 'Les Templers en France: histoire et héritage', *Revue Historique*, 316 (2014), no. 1, pp. 179–214.

Kedar, Benjamin Z., Schein, Sylvia, 'Un projet de "passage particulier" proposé par l'ordre de l'Hôpital, 1306–1307', *Bibliothèque de l'Ecole des chartes*, 137 (1979), pp. 211–226.

Kreiser, Johannes, 'Wirtschafts- und Finanzgebaren nordfranzösischer Templer-Häuser am Beispiel der Komturei Payns (Champagne)', in: *Erwerbspolitik und Wirtschaftsweise mittelalterlicher Orden und Klöster*, ed. K. Elm (Berlin: Duncker und Humblot, 1992), pp. 115–123.

Lalou, Elisabeth, 'Les négotiations diplomatiques avec l'Angleterre sous le règne de Philippe le Bel', in: *La « France anglaise » au Moyen-Âge: Colloque des historiens médiévistes français et britanniques. Actes du IIIe congrès national des sociétés savantes* (Poitiers 1986). *Section d'histoire médiévale et de philologie*, vol. 1 (Paris: CTHS, 1988), pp. 325–355.

Lambin, Jean-Jacques, 'Les Templiers d'Ypres', *Messager des sciences et des arts de la Belgique*, 2[illegible] (1934), pp. 189–199.

Langlois, Charles – Victor, 'Le procès des Templiers', *Revue des Deux Mondes*, 61 (1891), pp. 382–421.

Langlois, Charles – Victor, 'L'affaire des Templiers', *Journal des Savants*, 6 (1908), pp. 417–435.

La Torre, Ignacio de, *Los Templarios y el Origen de la Banca* (Madrid: Dilema, 2004).

La Torre, Ignacio de, 'The Monetary Fluctuations in Philip IV's Kingdom of France and Their Rlevance to the Arrest of the Templars', in: *The Debate on the Trial of the Templars (1307–1314)*, ed. J. Burgtorf, P. F. Crawford, H. J. Nicholson (Farnham: Ashgate, 2010), pp. 57–68.

La Torre, Ignacio de, 'The Templars' Banking Activities and Their Potential Connections to the Order's Demise', in: *The Templars. The Rise, Fall, and Legacy of a Military Religious Order*, ed. J. Burgtorf, S. Lotan, E. Mallorquí-Ruscalleda (London–New York: Routledge, 2021), pp. 179–187.

Lavenia, Vincenzo, 'Confisca dei beni', in: *Dizionario storico dell'Inquisizione*, ed. A. Prosperi, V. Lavenia, J. Tedeschi, vol. 1 (Pisa: Edizioni della Normale. 2010), pp. 375–376.

Lavocat, Louis-Léon-Lucien, *Procès des frères et de l'ordre du Temple d'après des pièces inédites publiées par J. Michelet et des documents imprimés anciens et nouveaux* (Paris: E. Plon, 1888).

Lea, Henry C., 'Confiscation for Heresy in the Middle Ages', *The English Historical Review*, 2 (1887), no. 6, pp. 236–259.

Lea, Henry C., *A History of the Inquisition in the Middle Ages*, vol. 1–3 (New York: Macmillan, 1887–1901).

Lecler, Joseph, *Histoire des conciles oecuméniques*, ed. G. Dumeige, vol. 8, *Vienne* (Paris: Éditions de l'Orante, 1964).

Legras, Anne-Marie, Lemaître, Jean-Loup, 'La pratique liturgique des Templiers et des Hospitaliers de Saint-Jean de Jérusalem', in: *L'écrit dans la société médiévale. Textes en hommage à Lucie Fossier*, ed. C. Bourlet, A. Dufour (Paris: CNRS, 1991), pp. 77–137.

Léonard, Emile, *Introduction au cartulaire manuscrit du Temple (1150–1317)* (Paris: E. Champion, 1930).

Leys, Agnes M., 'The Forfeiture of the Lands of the Templars in England', in: *Oxford Essays in Medieval History Presented to Herbert Edward Salter*, ed. F. M. Powicke (Oxford: Oxford University Press, 1934), pp. 155–163.

Lizerand, Georges, *Clément V et Philippe le Bel* (Paris: Hachtte, 1910).

Lunt, William E., *Financial Relations of the Papacy with England to 1327* (Cambridge: Cambridge University Press, 1939).

Luttrell, Anthony, 'The Hospitallers in Cyprus after 1291', in: A. Luttrell, *The Hospitallers in Cyprus, Rhodes, Greece and the West, 1291–1440. Collected Studies* (London: Variorum Reprints, 1978), pp. 161–171.

Luttrell, Anthony, 'The Hospitallers of Rhodes: Perspectives, Problems, Possibilities', in: *Die geistlichen Ritterorden Europas*, ed. J. Fleckenstein, M. Hellmann (Sigmaringen: J. Thorbecke, 1980), pp. 243–266.

Luttrell, Anthony, 'Papauté et Hôpital: l'enquéte e 1373', in: *L'Enquête pontificale de 1373 sur l'Ordre des Hospitaliers de Saint-Jean de Jérusalem*, ed. A. M. Legras, vol. 1, *L'enquête dans le prieuré de France* (Paris: CNRS, 1987), pp. 3–42.

Luttrell, Anthony, 'Gli Ospitalieri e l'eredità dei Templari, 1305–1378', in: *I Templari. Mito e storia*, ed. G. Minucci, F. Sardi (Siena: Viti-Riccucci, 1989), pp. 67–86, repr. A. Luttrell, *The Hospitallers of Rhodes and Their Mediterranean World* (Aldershot: Ashgate, 1992), no. III.

Luttrell, Anthony, 'The Hospitallers and the Papacy, 1305–1314', in: *Forschungen zur Reichs, Papst- und Landesgeschichte: Peter Herde zum 65. Geburtstag*, ed. K. Borchardt, E. Bünz, vol. 2 (Stuttgart: A. Hiersemann, 1998), pp. 595–622, repr. A. Luttrell, *Studies on the Hospitallers after 1306* (Aldershot: Ashgate, 2007), no. V.

Luttrell, Anthony, 'The Hospitallers and Their Florentine Bankers, 1306–1346', in: *Karissime Gotifride: Historical Essays Presented to Professor Godfrey Wettinger*, ed. P. Xuereb (Malta: Malta University Press, 1999), pp. 17–24, repr. A. Luttrell, *Studies on the Hospitallers after 1306* (Aldershot: Ashgate, 2007), no. VI.

Luttrell, Anthony, 'Observations on the Fall of the Temple', in: *Élites et ordres militaires au Moyen Âge: Rencontre autour d'Alain Demurger*, ed. P. Josserand, L. F. Oliveira, D. Carraz (Madrid: Casa de Velázquez, 2015), pp. 365–372.

Mannier, Eugène, *Ordre de Malte. Les commanderies du Grand – Prieuré de France d'après les documents inédits conservés aux Archives nationalse à Paris* (Paris: A. Aubry, 1872).

Mansuet Jeune, Claude, *Histoire critique et apologétique de l'Ordre des chevaliers du Temple de Jérusalem, dits Templiers*, vol. 1–2 (Paris: Guillot, 1789).

Menache, Sophia, 'Contemporary Attitudes Concerning the Templars' Affair: Propaganda's Fiasco?', *Journal of Medieval History*, 8 (1982), no. 2, pp. 135–147.

Menache, Sophia, 'La naissance d'une nouvelle source d'authorité: l'Université de Paris', *Revue Historique*, 268 (1982), pp. 305–327.

Menache, Sophia, 'A Propaganda Campaign in the Reign of Philip the Fair, 1302–1303', *French History*, 4 (1990), pp. 427–454.

Menache, Sophia, 'The Templar Order: A Failed Ideal?', *The Catholic Historical Review*, 79 (1993), pp. 1–21.

Menache, Sophia, *Clement V* (Cambridge: Cambridge University Press, 1998).

Menache, Sophia, 'The Hospitallers during Clement V's Pontificate: The Spoiled Sons of the Papacy?', in: *The Military Orders*, vol. 2, *Welfare and Warfare*, ed. H. Nicholson (Aldershot: Ashgate, 1998), pp. 153–162.

Menache, Sophia, 'When Ideology Met Reality: Clement V and the Crusade', in: *La Papauté et les Croisades/The Papacy and the Crusades*, ed. M. Balard (Franham: Ashgate, 2011), pp. 105–116.

Mercuri, Lorenzo, *L'Enclos du Temple: topografia e forme di un'assenza della Parigi medieval* (Rome: RES AEDIFICATORIA MEDII AEVI EUROPAE, 2025).

Métais, Charles, *Les Templiers en Eure-et-Loir, histoire et cartulaire* (Chartres: Lafolye, 1902).

Miguet, Michel, *Templiers et Hospitaliers en Normandie* (Paris: Comité des travaux historiques et scientifiques, 1995).

Miguet, Michel, *Templiers et Hospitaliers de Bure: histoire et rayonnement d'une commanderie bourguignonne* (Langres: D. Guéniot, 2012).

Mollat, Guillaume, 'Dispersion définitive des Templiers après leur suppression', *Comptes rendus des séances de l'Académie des Inscriptions et Belles-Lettres*, 96 (1952), no. 3, pp. 376–380.

Morice, Pierre-Hyacinthe, *Mémoires pour servir de preuves à l'histoire ecclésiastique et civile de Bretagne*, vol. 1–3 (Paris: C. Osmont, 1742–1746).

Müller, Ewald, *Das Konzil von Vienne 1311–1312. Seine Quellen und seine Geschichte* (Münster: Aschendorff, 1934).

Nicholson, Helen J., *The Knights Templar on Trial. The Trial of the Templars in the British Isles 1308–1311* (Stroud: The History Press, 2009).

Nicholson, Helen J., 'Review of Alain Demurger, Le peuple templier, 1307–1312…', *Speculum*, 97 (2022), no. 1, pp. 168–170.

Nicholson, Helen J., Slavin, P., 'The Real Da Vinci Code': The Accounts of Templars' Estates in England and Wales during the Suppression of the Order', in: *Templars, their Sources and Their Competitors, 1119–1314*, ed. K. Borchardt (Farnham: Ashgate, 2016), pp. 233–246.

Niepce, Léopold, *Le Grand-prieuré d'Auvergne: ordre des hospitaliers de Saint-Jean de Jérusalem* (Lyon 1883).

Paravicini Bagliani, Agostino, *Boniface VIII. Un pape hérétique?* (Paris: Payot & Rivages, 2003).

Partner, Peter D., '*Camera Papae*: Problems of Papal Finance in the Later Middle Ages', *The Journal of Ecclesiastical History*, 4 (1953), no. 1, pp. 55–68.

Perkins, Clarence, 'The Wealth of the Knights Templars in England and the Disposition of It after Their Dissolution', *The American Historical Review*, 15 (1910), no. 2, pp. 252–263.

Pernoud, Régine, *Les Templiers* (11th ed.) (Paris: Que sais-je ?, 2018).

Perrichet, Lucien, *La Grande chancellerie de France des origines à 1328* (Paris: L. Larose et L. Tenin, 1912).

Pétel, Auguste, *Les Hospitaliers de Saint-Jean de Jérusalem, seigneurs de Sancey, aujourd'hui Saint-Julien (Aube)* (Troyes: P. Bage, 1903).

Pétel, Auguste, *La Commanderie de Payns et ses dépendances à Savières, à Saint-Mesmin, à Messon, et au Pavillon* (Paris: H. Champion, 1905).

Pétel, Auguste, 'Templiers et Hospitaliers dans le diocèse de Troyes. Comptes de régie de la commanderie de Payns, 1307–1309', *Mémoires de la Société académique d'agriculture, sciences et arts du département de l'Aube*, 71 (1907), pp. 283–372.

Pétel, Auguste, 'Templiers et Hospitaliers dans le diocèse de Troyes. Le Temple de Bonlieu et l'Hôpital d'Orient', *Mémoires de la Société académique d'agriculture, sciences et arts du département de l'Aube*, 73 (1909), pp. 257–358; 74 (1910), pp. 11–350.

Petit, Ernest, *Histoire des ducs de Bourgogne de la race capétienne, avec des documents inédits et des pièces justificatives*, vol. 1–9 (Dijon: Darantière, 1885–1905).

Petit, Joseph, *Charles de Valois (1270–1325)* (Paris: A. Picard, 1900).

Phillips, Simon, 'The Hospitallers' Acquisition of the Templar Lands in England', in: *The Debate on the Trial of the Templars (1307–1314)*, ed. J. Burgtorf, P. F. Crawford, H. J. Nicholson (Farnham: Ashgate, 2010), pp. 237–246.

Picot, Jean, 'L'inventaire des biens de la commanderie du Temple de Monferrand en Basse Auvergne (vers 1308)', *Bibliothèque de l'École des chartes*, 174 (2018–2019), pp. 107–157.

Piquet, Jules, *Des banquiers au Moyen Âge: les Templiers. Étude de leurs opérations financières* (Paris: Hachette, 1939).

Porro, Clive, 'Reassessing the Dissolution of the Templars: King Denis and Theirs Suppression in Portugal', in: *The Debate on the Trial of the Templars (1307–1314)*, ed. J. Burgtorf, P. F. Crawford, H. J. Nicholson (Farnham: Ashgate, 2010), pp. 171–182.

Prutz, Hans, *Entwicklung und Untergang des Tempelherrenordens: mit Benutzung bisher ungedruckter Materialien* (Berlin: G. Grote, 1888).

Raybaud, Jean, *Histoire des grands prieurs et du prieuré de Saint-Gilles*, ed. N. César, vol. 1–3 (Nîmes: Clavel et Chastanier, 1904–1906).

Rayniers, Alain, 'Le procès des templiers dans l'espace belge actuel au début du XIVe siècle (1307–1312)', *Le Moyen Age*, 129 (2023), no. 3, pp. 757–791.

Redoutey, Jean-Pierre, 'Philippe le Bel et la Frenche-Comté', in: *Provinces et États dans la France de l'Est: Le rattachement de la Franche-Comté à la France. Espaces régionaux et espaces nationaux. Colloque de Besançon, 3 et 4 oct. 1977*, ed. R. Fiéter, F. Lassus (Paris: Belles Lettres,1979), pp. 207–231.

Renouard, Yves, 'Les papes et le conflit franco – anglais en Aquitaine de 1259 à 1337', *Mélanges d'archéologie et d'histoire*, 51 (1934), no. 1, pp. 258–292.

Renouard, Yves, 'Édouard II et Clément V d'après les Rôles gascons', *Annales du Midi*, 67 (1955), pp. 119–141.

Richard, Jean, *Les ducs de Bourgogne et la formation du Duché du XI au XIV siècle* (Dijon: Bernigaud & Privat, 1954).

Riley-Smith, Jonathan, *The Knights Hospitaller in the Levant, c. 1070–1309* (Basingstoke: Palgrave Macmillan, 2012).

Roger, Jean-Marc, 'Les maisons des Ordres du Temple et de l'Hôpital dans le bailliage de Chaumont au début du XIVe siècle, d'après l'enquête de 1333', *Cahiers Haut-Marnais* 167 (1986), pp. 49–54.

Roger, Jean-Marc, 'La prise de possession par l'Hôpital des maisons du Temple en Poitou et en Bretagne (mai 1313)', *Revue historique du Centre-Ouest*, 7 (2008), pp. 215–243.

Roger, Jean-Marc, 'Antonio Pessagno', in: *Prier et combattre: Dictionnaire européen des ordres militaires au Moyen Âge*, ed. N. Bériou, P. Josserand (Paris: Fayard, 2009), p. 98.

Roger, Jean-Marc, 'La réforme de l'Hôpital par Jean XXII: Le démembrement des prieurés de Saint-Gilles et de France (21 juillet 1317)', in: *On the Margins of Crusading: The*

Military Orders, the Papacy and the Christian World, ed. H. Nicholson (Farnham: Ashgate, 2011), pp. 101–138.

Roger, Jean-Marc, 'Les biens de l'Hôpital au bailliage de Troyes en 1333: la prisée de 1333, la déclaration de Coulours de 1338', *Mémoires de la Société académique du Département de l'Aube*, 135 (2011), pp. 243–298.

Roger, Jean-Marc, 'L'inventaire de la maison du Temple de Bret (15 mai 1313)', *Revue historique du Centre-Ouest*, 10 (2011), pp. 363–367.

Roger, Jean-Marc, 'La prisée des biens de l'Hôpital au bailliage de Chaumont en 1333', *Mémoires de la Société académique du Département de l'Aube*, 136 (2012), pp. 349–432.

Roger, Jean-Marc, 'La dévolution à l'Hôpital des biens du Temple dans les bailliages de Troyes et de Chaumont', *Bulletin de la Société nationale des Antiquaires de France*, 2012 (2018), pp. 242–254.

Salavert y Roca, Vincente, *Cerdeña y la expansión mediterránea de la corona de Aragón 1297–1314*, vol. 1–2 (Madrid: Consejo Superior de Investigaciones Científicas, Escuela de Estudios Medievales, 1956).

Samaran, Charles, Mollat, Guillaume, *La Fiscalité pontificale en France au XIVe siècle: période d'Avignon et grand schisme d'Occident* (Paris: A. Fontemoing, 1905).

Sans i Travé, Joseph Maria, *El procés dels Templers catalans. Entre el turment i la glòria* (Lleida: Pagès, 1991).

Sans i Travé, Josep Maria, *La fi dels templers Catalans* (Lleida: Pagès, 2008).

Satora, Magdalena, 'Mowa Wilhelma de Plaisians o sprawie templariuszy jako przykład francuskiej propagandy politycznej początku XIV wieku', in: *Odkrywcy, principesi, rozbójnicy*, ed. B. Śliwiński (Malbork: Muzeum Zamkowe, 2007), pp. 217–232.

Satora, Magdalena, *Społeczny odbiór procesu i upadku zakonu templariuszy we Francji w pierwszej połowie XIV w.* (Malbork: Muzeum Zamkowe, 2008).

Satora, Magdalena, *Sprawa templariuszy w dyplomacji zachodnioeuropejskiej 1307–1312* (Poznań: Wydawnictwo Poznańskie, 2011).

Satora, Magdalena, 'The Role of the Cardinals in the Templars' Affair 1307–1308', *Ordines Militares. Colloquia Torunensia Historica. Yearbook for the Study of the Military Orders*, 16 (2011), pp. 93–103.

Satora, Magdalena, 'Dyplomaci Filipa IV Pięknego (1285–1314) – mechanizmy wyboru', in: *Między misją a profesją. Ewolucja roli dyplomaty w stosunkach międzynarodowych na przestrzeni wieków*, ed. R. Simiński, A. Szczepańska-Dudziak (Szczecin: Wydawnictwo Naukowe Uniwersytetu Szczecińskiego, 2016), pp. 19–34.

Satora, Magdalena, 'Filip Piękny i majątki templariuszy – uwagi o działaniach francuskiego aparatu państwowego w sprawie zakonu (1307–1314)', *Saeculum Christianum*, 32 (2025), no. 2, pp. 20–32.

Schein, Sylvia, 'Philip IV and the Crusade: a Reconsideration', in: *Crusade and Settlement. Papers read at the First Conference of the Society for the Study of Crusades and the Latin East and presented to R.C. Smail*, ed. P. W. Edbury (Cardiff: University College Cardiff Press, 1985), pp. 121–126.

Schein, Sylvia, *Fideles Crucis. The Papacy, the West and the Recovery of the Holy Land 1274–1314* (Oxford: Oxford University Press, 1991).

Schenk, Jochen, 'The Documentary Evidence for Templar Religion', in: *The Templars and Their Sources*, ed. K. Borchardt, K. Döring, P. Josserand, H. Nicholson (London–New York: Routledge, 2017), pp. 199–211.

Schmidt, Charles, 'Les commanderies et les hôspitaux dans l'Yonne', in: *Inventaire sommaire des archives départementales postérieures à 1790. Yonne, Archives hospitalières: série H, suppl.*, vol. 4, ed. F. Molard (Auxerre: A. Gallot, 1897), pp. V–CLIV.

Schmidt, Hans – Günter, *Administrative Korrespondenz der französischen Könige um 1300. Edition des »Formelbuches« BNF ms. lat. 4763. Verwaltung – Gerichtsbarkeit – Kanzlei* (Göttingen: K. Hess, 1997).

Schottmüller, Konrad, *Der Untergang der Templer – Ordens*, vol. 1–2 (Berlin: Mittler, 1887).

Schwarzfuchs, Simon, 'The Expulsion of the Jews form France, 1306', *Jewish Quarterly Review*, 75 (1967), pp. 482–489.

Slavin, Philip, 'The Fate of the Former Templar Estates in England, 1308–1330', *Crusades*, 14 (2015), pp. 209–235.

Soutou, André, *La commanderie de Sainte-Eulalie de Larzac* (Nîmes: C. Lacour, 1999).

Starnawska, Maria, 'The Commanderies ot the Templars in the Polish Lands and Their History after the End of the Order', in: *The Debate on the Trial of the Templars (1307–1314)*, ed. J. Burgtorf, P. F. Crawford, H. J. Nicholson (Farnham: Ashgate, 2010), pp. 301–314.

Strayer, Joseph R., 'Italian Bankers and Philip the Fair', *Explorations in Economic History*, 7 (1969), no. 1–2, pp. 113–121.

Strayer, Joseph R., *The Reign of Philip the Fair* (Princeton: Princeton University Press, 1980).

Suau, Bernadette, 'La maison du Temple à Toulouse: un site méconnu', *Mémoires de société archéologique du Midi de la France*, 70 (2010), pp. 203–237.

Tanon, Louis, *Histoire des tribunaux de l'inquisition en France* (Paris: L. Larose et Forcel, 1893).

Theiner, August, *Annales Ecclesiastici*, vol. 23, *1286–1312* (Bar-le-Duc: Guerin, 1871).

Théry-Astruc, Julien, 'The Flight of the Master of Lombardy (13 February 1308) and Clement V's Strategy in the Templar Affair: A Slap in the Pope's Face', *Rivista di Storia della Chiesa in Italia*, 70 (2016), no. 1, pp. 35–44.

Thier, Ludger, *Kreuzzugsbemühungen unter Papst Clemens V (1305–1314)* (Werl: D. Coelde, 1973).

Timbal, Pierre, 'La confiscatiòn dans le droit français des XIIIe et XIVe siècles', *Revue historique du droit français et étranger*, 21 (1943), pp. 44–79.

Toomaspoeg, Kristjan, 'Le patrimoine des grands ordres militaires en Sicile, 1145–1492', *Mélanges de l'École française de Rome. Moyen-Age,* 113 (2001), no. 1, pp. 313–341.

Trudon des Ormes, Amédée, *Étude sur les possessions de l'Ordre du Temple en Picardie* (Amiens: Yvert et Tellier, 1892).

Tyerman, Christopher J., 'Sed Nihil Fecit? The Last Capetians and the Recovery of the Holy Land', in: *War and Government in the Middle Ages,* ed. J. Gillingham, J. C. Holt (Cambridge: Cambridge Univeristy Press, 1984), pp. 170–181.

Vaivre, Jean-Bernard de, *La commanderie d'Épailly et sa chapelle templière durant la période médiévale* (Paris: Boccard, 2005).

Vann, Theresa M., 'The Assimilation of Templar Properties by the Order of the Hospital', in: *The Debate on the Trial of the Templars (1307–1314)*, ed. J. Burgtorf, P. F. Crawford, H. J. Nicholson (Farnham: Ashgate, 2010), pp. 339–346.

Vertot, René Aubert de, *Histoire des Chevaliers hospitaliers de S. Jean de Jérusalem, appellez depuis les Chevaliers de Rhodes, et aujourd'hui les Chevaliers de Malte*, vol. 1–4 (Paris: Rollin, 1726).

Vidal, Henri, 'Les conciles méridionaux aux XIIIe et XIVe sièces', *Cahiers de Fanjeaux*, 29 (1994), pp. 147–180.

Vilar Bonet, Maria, *Els Béns del Temple a la Corona d'Aragó en suprimir – se l'orde (1300–1319)* (Barcelona: Fundació Noguera, 2000).

Vinas, Robert, 'Le destin des templiers du Roussillon, 1276–1330', *Cahiers de Fanjeaux*, 41 (2006), pp. 187–210.

Warnkönig, Leopold August, Gheldolf, Albert Eugene Marie, *Histoire de la Flandre et de ses institutions civiles et politiques, jusqu'à l'année 1305*, vol. 1–5 (Bruxelles: M. Hayez, 1835–1864).

Wenck, Karl, 'Aus den Tagen der Zusammenkunft Papst Klemens' V und König Philipps des Schönen zu Lyon, November 1305 bis Januar 1306', *Zeitschrift für Kirchengeschichte*, 27 (1906), pp. 189–202.

Wetzel, Lilian, *Le Concile de Vienne (1311–1312) et l'abolition de l'Ordre du Temple* (Paris: Dervy, 1993).

Wilmart, Mickaël, 'Salariés, journaliers et artisans au service d'une exploitation agricole templière. La commanderie de Payns au début du XIVe siècle', in: *L'économie templière en Occident. Patrimoines, commerce, finances. Actes du colloque international (Troyes – abbaye de Clairvaux, 24–26 octobre 2012)* ed. A. Baudin, G. Brunel, N. Dohrmann (Langres: D. Guéniot, 2013), pp. 273–293.

Index

Names in the source language are written in small capitals.
Names whose identification is uncertain are written with a question mark.
Page numbers followed by n. denote endnotes.

The following abbreviations are used:
ap–administrator of the Templar property
archbp–archbishop
archdioc–archdiocese
B–bailiwick
b–bailiff
bp–bishop
c–commander
ct–count
d–deputy
dioc–diocese
H–Hospitaller brother
k–king
l–lord
n–notary
pd–place of detention of the Templars
s–sergeant
S–seneschalship
sen–seneschal
T–Templar brother
t–Templar commandery, house, or other property
te–tenant of the Templar property
visc–viscount
w–wife

For Product Safety Concerns and Information please contact our EU representative GPSR@taylorandfrancis.com Taylor & Francis Verlag GmbH, Kaufingerstraße 24, 80331 München, Germany

Batch number: 10449958

Printed by Printforce, the Netherlands